Italian Prisons in the Age of Positivism, 1861–1914

History of Crime, Deviance and Punishment

Series Editor:
Anne-Marie Kilday, Professor of Criminal History, Oxford Brookes University, UK

Editorial Board:
Neil Davie, University of Lyon II, France
Johannes Dillinger, University of Maine, Germany
Wilbur Miller, State University of New York, USA
Marianna Muravyeva, University of Helsinki, Finland
David Nash, Oxford Brookes University, UK
Judith Rowbotham, Nottingham Trent University, UK

Academic interest in the history of crime and punishment has never been greater and the *History of Crime, Deviance and Punishment* series provides a home for the wealth of new research being produced. Individual volumes within the series cover topics related to the history of crime and punishment, from the later medieval to modern period and in both Europe and North America, and seek to demonstrate the importance of this subject in furthering understanding of the way in which various societies and cultures operate. When taken together, the works in the series will show the evolution of the nature of illegality and attitudes towards its perpetration over time and will offer their readers a rounded and coherent history of crime and punishment through the centuries. The series' broad chronological and geographical coverage encourages comparative historical analysis of crime history between countries and cultures.

Published:
Policing the Factory, Barry Godfrey
Crime and Poverty in 19th-Century England, Adrian Ager
Print Culture, Crime and Justice in Eighteenth-Century London, Richard Ward
Rehabilitation and Probation in England and Wales, 1900–1950, Raymond Gard
The Policing of Belfast 1870–1914, Mark Radford
Crime, Regulation and Control during the Blitz, Peter Adey, David J. Cox and Barry Godfrey

Forthcoming:
Deviance, Disorder and Music in Modern Britain and America, Cliff Williamson (2019)
Fair and Unfair Trials in the British Isles, 1800–1940, eds. David Nash and Anne-Marie Kilday (2019)

Italian Prisons in the Age of Positivism, 1861–1914

Mary Gibson

BLOOMSBURY ACADEMIC
LONDON • NEW YORK • OXFORD • NEW DELHI • SYDNEY

BLOOMSBURY ACADEMIC
Bloomsbury Publishing Plc
50 Bedford Square, London, WC1B 3DP, UK
1385 Broadway, New York, NY 10018, USA
29 Earlsfort Terrace, Dublin 2, Ireland

BLOOMSBURY, BLOOMSBURY ACADEMIC and the Diana logo are trademarks of
Bloomsbury Publishing Plc

First published in Great Britain 2019
This paperback edition published in 2021

Copyright © Mary Gibson, 2019

Mary Gibson has asserted her right under the Copyright, Designs and Patents Act, 1988, to be identified as Author of this work.

For legal purposes the Acknowledgments on p. ix constitute an extension of this copyright page.

Cover image: Illustration of Apostolic Hospice in San Michele a Ripa, Rome, Italy.
(© colaimages / Alamy Stock Photo)

All rights reserved. No part of this publication may be reproduced or transmitted in any form or by any means, electronic or mechanical, including photocopying, recording, or any information storage or retrieval system, without prior permission in writing from the publishers.

Bloomsbury Publishing Plc does not have any control over, or responsibility for, any third-party websites referred to or in this book. All internet addresses given in this book were correct at the time of going to press. The author and publisher regret any inconvenience caused if addresses have changed or sites have ceased to exist, but can accept no responsibility for any such changes.

A catalogue record for this book is available from the British Library.

A catalog record for this book is available from the Library of Congress.

ISBN: HB: 978-1-3500-5532-2
PB: 978-1-3501-9609-4
ePDF: 978-1-3500-5533-9
eBook: 978-1-3500-5534-6

Series: History of Crime, Deviance and Punishment

Typeset by Newgen KnowledgeWorks Pvt. Ltd., Chennai, India

To find out more about our authors and books visit www.bloomsbury.com and sign up for our newsletters.

For Jim with love

Contents

Acknowledgments ix
Illustrations xi
Graphs xiii
Abbreviations xv

Introduction 1

1. Punishment before Italian Unification 15
2. The Failed Revolution in Punishment 41
3. Prison Consolidation and Reform 67
4. Women and the Convent Prison 97
5. Men: From Chains to the Penitentiary 131
6. Juvenile Reformatories between State and Charity 163
7. Prisons on the Margins: Police Camps and Criminal Insane Asylums 197
8. Laboratories of Criminal Anthropology 225

Conclusion 239

Notes 243
Bibliography 293
Index 307

Acknowledgments

This book began as a microhistory of a girls' reformatory and expanded into a history of women's penitentiaries before taking its definitive form as an analysis of prisons for all Italian citizens between unification and World War I. To support this widening scope of research, I received a number of invaluable grants: the Rome Prize from the American Academy, a Senior Fellowship from the International Research Center for Cultural Studies (IFK) in Vienna, a Fulbright Senior Research Award, a National Endowment for the Humanities Research Fellowship, and grants from the American Philosophical Society and the Trinity College Barbieri Center. In New York City, I have also benefitted from a residential fellowship at the Advanced Research Collaborative at the Graduate Center of the City University of New York and travel awards from my university union, the Professional Staff Congress. Finally, a Schoff Fund Award, from the Columbia University Seminars Office, has partially defrayed publication expenses of this book. I am extremely grateful to each of these organizations, without whose support I could never have completed such a complex project.

I am also deeply indebted to the many archives and libraries where I searched for the often elusive documentary sources on prison history. My special thanks go to Assunta Borzzachiello, Antonio Parente, and Loredana Mari at the Department of Penitentiary Administration (DAP); Marina Pieretti at the Historical Archives of the City of Rome (ASR); Maria Chiara Di Filippo and Monica Sperabene of the Historical Archives of the Province of Rome; Domenico Rocciolo of the Vicar's Archives in Rome; and the staffs of the Central State Archives, the Historical Archives of the Chamber of Deputies, the Capitoline Archives, the library of the juvenile reformatory at Casal del Marmo, and the Archive of the Association Ronconi-Pennesi. Only with such tremendous assistance was I able to locate and piece together the many disparate sources on the origins of prisons in Rome and Italy as a whole.

Over the years, many colleagues have facilitated my research. For introducing me to research repositories or new sources, I am grateful to Angela Groppi, Giulia Barrera, Silvano Montaldo, Francesco Sidoti, Daniela Rossini, Rosanna de Longis, Falk Bretschneider, Chiara Lucrezia Monticelli, Gabriella de Strobel Picotti, and Diego Pasquale. The book has been improved immeasurably by the generosity of Steven C. Hughes and Richard Bach Jensen, who read the entire manuscript, and David Rothman, Guido Neppi Modona, James Whitman, Guy Geltner, and Sara MacDougall, who commented on individual chapters. Their critiques encouraged me to strengthen and clarify the interpretative arguments. Completion of the book was also facilitated by collaboration with Veronika Horwath, Diana Moore, Sultana Banulescu, and Davide

Colasanto, my wonderful research assistants from the CUNY Graduate Center. Laura Vann prepared the map and Hannah Aizenman the graphs. Finally, I want to give my heartfelt thanks to James K. Cohen who, in addition to having been immersed, if not imprisoned, in my topic for many years, patiently read and expertly edited the entire manuscript.

Illustrations

0.1	An "Imaginary Prison" by Piranesi	2
1.1	Restored interior of San Michele Reformatory for boys	29
2.1	Anti-Papal cartoon in which prisoners of the Inquisition are freed by "Rome"	46
2.2	Prisoners condemned to hard labor on city streets	59
3.1	Uniforms of prison guards next to an insignia of merit	92
4.1	Villa Altieri before conversion to a women's prison	105
4.2	Women and their work at the penitentiary of Perugia	119
5.1	The monastery at Tre Fontane	143
5.2	Classroom in a men's prison with "School is a Prize" written on the blackboard	156
6.1	Boys exercising at the reformatory of San Michele	182
6.2	Inmates of a girls' reformatory	192
7.1	Group of men exiled to a penal colony	207
7.2	A postcard of the criminal insane asylum at Montelupo Fiorentino	218
8.1	A cephalometer, an instrument for measuring the head	230
8.2	The water jug of the prisoner Cavaglià with a picture prefiguring his suicide	234

Map

1.1	Map of Roman prisons, 1650–1914	26

Graphs

2.1	Reasons for release from jail, 1871–1914	53
2.2	Background of New Prison guards, 1873–83	63
3.1	Total number of prisoners in Italy, 1871–1914	89
4.1	Average number of inmates by gender, 1863–1914	116
4.2	Family status of penitentiary inmates, 1910–14	117
5.1	Men in penitentiaries and *bagni*, 1868–85	153
5.2	Birthplace of inmates by region, 1866–80	154
6.1	Age of children in Roman reformatories, 1904–14	177
6.2	Inmates in public and private reformatories by gender, 1871–1914	185
7.1	Length of sentence for inmates in penal colonies, 1900–11	205
7.2	Annual deaths in criminal insane asylums, 1900–14	220

Abbreviations

Archives

AC: Archivio Capitolino (Capitoline Archive)
ACS: Archivio Centrale dello Stato (Central State Archive)
AR: Associazione Ronconi-Pennesi (Ronconi-Pennesi Archive)
ASR: Archivio di Stato di Roma (State Archive of Rome)
AV: Archivio Vicariato (Vicar's Archive)
CM: Istituto penale per minorenni di Casal del Marmo (Library of the Penal Institution for Minors at Casal del Marmo)
CD, Arch: Camera dei Deputati, Archivio Storico (Historical Archive of the Chamber of Deputies)
DAP: Biblioteca Storica dell'Amministrazione Penitenziaria (Historical Library of the Prison Administration)

Archival Series

DGAC: Direzione Generale Affari di Culto (Divison of Religious Affairs)
DGC: Direzione Generale delle Carceri (Divison of Prisons)
DGPS: Direzione Generale della Pubblica Sicurezza (Divison of Public Security Police)
Ist. PP: Istituti di Prevenzione e di Pena (Institutions of Prevention and Punishment)
M. GG: Ministero di Grazia e Giustizia (Minister of Grace and Justice)
M. Int.: Ministero dell'Interno (Minister of the Interior)
M. Lav.: Ministero dei Lavori Pubblici (Minister of Public Works)
SSP: Scuola Superiore di Polizia (Advanced School of Policing)

Statistical Publications

Ann. Stat: Annuario Statistico (Statistical Annual)
Congrès pen.: Actes du Congrès Penitentiaire de Rome (Proceedings of the Penitentiary Congress in Rome)
Prosp. Stat.: Prospetti Statistici (Statistical Tables)
Rel. DG: Relazione del Direttore Generale (Director General's Report)
Somm. Stat: Sommario di statistiche storiche italiane (Summary of Italian Historical Statistics)
Stat. Carc.: Statistica delle Carceri (Prison Statistics)
Stat. Dec.: Statistica Decennale delle Carceri (A Decade of Prison Statistics)

Stat. Rif.: Statistica dei Riformatori (Reformatory Statistics)

Journals

AAC: *Archivio di antropologia criminale, psichiatria e medicina legale* (Archives of Criminal Anthropology, Psychiatry, and Legal Medicine)
RDC: *Rivista delle Discipline Carcerarie* (Journal of Prison Sciences)

Introduction

Prisons hold a privileged place in Italy's history and culture. In the eighteenth century, Giovanni Battista Piranesi created a series of memorable prints that instantly evoke claustrophobia and horror (Illustration 0.1). Calling them "imagined prisons," his series of scenes are dominated by guard towers, cages, barred windows, stairs that lead nowhere, and pulleys resembling instruments of torture. Set in multilevel rooms with vaulted ceilings, these images recall ancient Roman ruins, medieval castles, or Hell itself.

It is possible that, despite their fantastic quality, Piranesi was commenting obliquely on his own historical period. Enlightenment thinkers of his time believed that Europe was constricted by the twin control of absolute monarchy and intolerant religions. Later, Italian patriots decried the subjugation of a large part of the peninsula to foreign dynasties from Austria and Spain as well as the temporal monarchy of the Pope. For many liberal proponents of unification, the prisoner in chains represented Italy itself, especially since castle towers and palace dungeons were concrete spaces in which political opponents were confined, sometimes for years, by rulers of the various pre-unitary kingdoms on the Italian peninsula. Thus, after unification and the establishment of a parliamentary state in 1861, shame about traditional modes of punishment propelled a strong movement for penal reform.

A long culture of prison writing in Italy has also sustained the symbolic conflation of penal confinement with oppression. Some authors of prison memoirs were not political protestors, such as Giacomo Casanova, who was confined in the Piombi prison in eighteenth-century Venice on vague charges of religious offenses.[1] Published posthumously, his *History of My Life* described the horrible conditions of incarceration in a hot and rat-infested attic cell from which he ingeniously escaped. But the majority of prison autobiographies and letters have been written by political dissenters during the last two centuries, which have been marked by the dramatic transition from the monarchies of the old regime to the post-unification periods of liberal, fascist, and finally republican governance. Among the most well known are Silvio Pellico's memoir of his confinement for anti-Austrian activities during the Risorgimento; Anna Kuliscioff and Filippo Turati's correspondence while being jailed in 1898 for participating in the *fatti di maggio*, a working-class demonstration that was brutally suppressed by the military; and *Letters from Prison* by the communist intellectual Antonio Gramsci

Illustration 0.1 An "Imaginary Prison" by Piranesi

following his arrest by fascist police. While these texts are in no way homogenous, they demonstrate that a long tradition of prison writing has characterized Italian society under a multiplicity of political regimes.

Despite the prominence of confinement as a symbol of captivity and repression, little is known about the history of Italian prisons and the experience of the mostly poor and illiterate inmates who populated these institutions. Unlike political prisoners, who were often middle class and capable of leaving written testimony, most incarcerated women and men have left few traces of their captivity. This book explores alternate sources in order to give those people a voice. It also introduces Italy into the international debate about the origins of the prison as the dominant form of punishment in the modern world. That debate was initially framed by the publication, in 1975, of Michel Foucault's brilliant book, *Discipline and Punish: The Birth of the Prison*.[2] Subsequent controversy has focused on the timing and causes of the radical transition from corporal punishment, including torture, hard labor, and death, to confinement in the modern penitentiary.

While initially focused narrowly on Northern Europe and America, prison historiography has expanded to encompass the establishment of the penitentiary in Latin America, Africa, and Asia. Most recently, transnational studies have begun to trace global networks of punishment by examining the relationship between prisons and colonial transportation, forced labor, and slavery.[3] What once appeared to be a simple and relatively rapid process—from a past era of punishing the body to the modern practice of rehabilitative confinement—is now understood to be more complex and less unidirectional. The understudied factors of gender, age, and race complicate the Foucauldian analysis and suggest alternate periodizations and varying motives for the adoption of enclosure as a strategy of punishment. Prison structures and purposes have also varied widely as the original north European and American penitentiary models were reinterpreted and redeployed across the globe.

Within this flourishing body of new research, Italy offers an important and instructive vantage point, where stimulus for the abolition of corporal punishment derived successively from three indigenous sources: the Catholic Church, Enlightenment philosophy, and positivist criminology. First, as the center of Catholicism, the Italian peninsula harbored a long tradition of punishing clergy through enclosure and repentance rather than corporal punishment. In Rome, the papacy expanded this practice by erecting "convent" prisons for women and children in the early decades of the eighteenth century. These early penal institutions adopted the widespread Catholic model of simultaneously disciplining and protecting marginal groups through prayer and work in a monastic setting. Second, Cesare Beccaria's influential book of 1764, *On Crimes and Punishments*, laid out the major Enlightenment arguments against torture and capital punishment that are still employed today.[4] While this Milanese economist and *philosophe* did not specifically address prisons, he enunciated fundamental Enlightenment principles, such as the proportionality of punishment to the crime and equality before the law, which became the hallmark of legal reform in Europe and the Americas during the age of revolutions. Beccaria's ideas, however, sparked little immediate change in Italy, which was dominated by old-regime monarchs and the Catholic Church. In 1861, however, unification ushered in a secular, parliamentary state and fostered a third inspiration for prison reform, the new field of positivist criminology. Through his companion volumes, *Criminal Man* (1876) and *Criminal Woman* (1893), Cesare Lombroso challenged Enlightenment universalism by classifying criminals into those exhibiting atavistic biological traits ("born criminals") and those whose behavior was shaped by an impoverished environment ("occasional criminals").[5] Thus, Italy inspired the nineteenth-century movement to establish criminology as a new field of research, purportedly based on the scientific method, which preached the individualization of punishment according to gender, age, race, and physical traits.

This book focuses on the era between Italian unification and World War I, when the new Italian state developed a hybrid prison system based primarily on positivist principles, which also incorporated characteristics from its Catholic and Enlightenment past. The term "positivism" is used here in two ways. At a general level, the positivist age refers to the period of the late nineteenth and early twentieth centuries when science, rather than religion or metaphysics, became the hegemonic model of knowledge. Also labeled as the age of imperialism, scientific racism, international socialism, or American progressivism in reference to other dominant currents, positivism seems most emblematic for Italy because of its particular importance across scholarly disciplines and political thought as a counterweight to the religious tradition of the pre-unitary states. In the words of Eugenio Garin, positivism became a "lay faith" of Italian academia in the early decades after unification.[6] In a more narrow sense, positivism refers to the school of criminology that was founded by Lombroso and therefore particularly associated with Italy. While liberal Italy's network of prisons had important roots in earlier eras, its political, administrative, and scientific architects were deeply influenced by Lombroso's popular and admired theories. Thus, Italy's philosophy of prison reform, whatever its imperfections in execution, sought to incorporate empirical knowledge from the fields of criminology, medicine, psychiatry, and statistics.

Drawing on the Italian experience, this book advances three main perspectives. First, the age of positivism, which I label the "second wave" of prison reform, deserves as much scholarly attention as the Foucauldian "first wave" has received. While the "birth of the prison" during the age of revolutions was restricted to Northern Europe and America, the second wave constituted a global phenomenon that reached Africa, Asia, and Latin America. Italy provides an important case study for exploring the second wave because of its sharp political transition across the peninsula, between 1861 and 1871, to parliamentary rule. Introduction of the modern penitentiary was central to Italy's project of constructing a new liberal state and secular national identity. Second, gender and age must be incorporated as significant factors in the history of punishment. Even though the earlier convent prisons had been established principally for women, prison reform became masculinized after unification. As part of its nationalizing project, the Italian state focused its attention and resources on transforming penal institutions for men and boys into crucibles of secular citizenship, while, concurrently, women and girls remained under the charge of the same religious orders that had managed prisons for the previous monarchies of the peninsula. Thus the new Italian state deprived women of full citizenship in terms of not only "positive" rights (to vote, own property) but also the "negative" rights to equality in penal law and to a secular and rehabilitative form of punishment. Finally, this study reconstructs the history of specific Roman prisons and explores their architecture, spatial placement, and relationship to the city's urban fabric and cultural identity. In this way, Italian prisons are analyzed not just as abstract ideological entities but also as material institutions interrelated to the society around them and as important sites of historical memory

Prison Historiography

Any attempt to construct a chronology of Italian prisons must take into account the rich historiography about changing modes of punishment throughout the world. Current debates about periodization date to the 1970s, when David Rothman, Michel Foucault, and Michael Ignatieff produced provocative accounts of the "birth of the prison" in the United States, France, and England respectively.[7] Quickly labeled the "revisionist school," these historians argued that the era between 1760 and 1840 constituted a radical turning point when corporal punishment was replaced by imprisonment. Instead of mutilating the body through torture, branding, and death, nation states began to alter their penal codes in favor of sentences of nonviolent incarceration.[8]

Revisionist historians trace the theoretical underpinnings of the new penitentiary to two main sources, the Enlightenment and religion. In critiquing the old regime,

Enlightenment thinkers championed reason and humanitarianism as weapons for denouncing the inequities of feudal legal codes, the violence of corporal punishment, and the unsanitary conditions of traditional jails. Many eighteenth-century *philosophes* expressed repugnance for the infliction of bodily pain and taught that progress depended on the elimination of torture. Believing that criminals, like all human beings, were rational and endowed with free choice, they trusted that rehabilitation would be possible through deprivation of freedom, moral introspection, and work. This emphasis on the influence of the environment explains the lively debates during these years about prison architecture, which was held to be central to the remolding of character. Religion provided a second cultural inspiration for the new penitentiary and its promise of moral reform. In the writings of revisionist historians, the impact of religion is most clear in Protestant countries such as Britain, with its evangelical revival in the early nineteenth century, and the United States, where the early system of complete cellular confinement was engineered by Quakers. In both cases, Protestant reformers believed that the isolation, silence, and moral introspection characteristic of the new penitentiary would have the additional benefit of promoting the religious conversion of inmates.

That the birth of the prison correlated with other significant historical changes—including the Enlightenment, the demographic revolution, the industrial revolution, and the fall of absolute monarchy—was central to the revisionist interpretation. For David Rothman, population growth and increased mobility in the early American Republic caused anxiety about the breakdown of social ties, especially within the family. In response, reformers promoted a series of institutions, such as prisons, asylums, almshouses, and orphanages, to rehabilitate seemingly deviant individuals. Foucault focuses more directly on the political challenge to absolute monarchy by a rising bourgeoisie that demanded parliamentary rights for itself accompanied by a series of "normalizing" institutions to discipline the poor. In England, Ignatieff emphasizes the class nature of prison reform, seen as an answer to the social unrest and perceived crime waves generated by the concentration of factories and industrial workers in burgeoning cities. Despite these national differences, all three historians document a common project of widespread prison construction during the "age of revolutions" in Europe and North America.

Rothman, Foucault, and Ignatieff are suspicious of the self-proclaimed humanitarian intentions of liberal reformers, which had been generally accepted by the few historians and sociologists who addressed the history of punishment before the 1970s. In contrast, the revisionists interpreted the new penitentiaries in a more sinister light, as institutions that subjected the lower classes to intrusive, secretive, and dehumanizing regulation of both the mind and the body. Inmates underwent demeaning rituals upon entrance to prison that stripped them of their identity, followed by the severance of contact with outside society, and the prohibition of communication except with wardens and chaplains (even contact with guards was minimized and highly regulated). Employing, in the words of Foucault, a "micro-physics of power," the state required all inmates to follow a uniform daily schedule in a fashion borrowed from the army or the factory.[9] Whether in their cells, the workshop, or recreation yard, tasks had to be carried out with the same mechanical gestures and sometimes in lockstep. For revisionists, the main purpose of the new penitentiary was the exercise of power rather than humanitarian reform or even the reduction of crime.

While the powerful analysis of the revisionist school has long defined the contours of prison history, it has been challenged from several perspectives. First, Pieter Spierenburg has demonstrated that, as early as the seventeenth century, new "prison workhouses" in Holland and northern Germany carried out the primary aim of the modern penitentiary, that is, the reform of inmates through labor.[10] Therefore, according to Spierenburg, the transition between corporal punishment and incarceration occurred slowly, over several centuries, rather than constituting a sharp break as posited by Foucault. Spierenburg uses Norbert Elias's theory of the "civilizing process" to explain the gradual change in European sensibilities toward a rejection of punishments that inflicted pain and suffering on the body. Several English historians have made arguments consistent with those of Spierenburg, by characterizing the early modern bridewell, or house of correction, as an example of "the prison before the prison."[11] Dating to the sixteenth century, bridewells employed both religion and work to punish and reform their inmates.[12] By pushing back by several centuries the initial employment of incarceration as punishment, such proponents of what I term the "proto-prison" emphasize the importance of Protestantism, the civilization of sensitivities, and changing definitions of poverty as the primary cultural forces shaping the earliest penitentiaries.

Women's historians have formulated a second critique of the revisionist analysis by pointing out its exclusive focus on male penal institutions. Did "the birth" of the female penitentiary occur simultaneously with that of men under the same ideological framework? Until now, the relatively scant historiography on gender and punishment has offered a variety of answers. In early modern Amsterdam, according to Spierenburg, prison workhouses were established for both sexes, although types of work were different for men and women. Patricia O'Brien has instead identified the early nineteenth century as the period of general French prison reform, although the introduction of nuns as prison matrons ensured that religious, rather than secular, precepts predominated in female institutions.[13] Religious orders, dedicated to "reparation" of sexual honor, were also brought into many women's prisons in Latin America during the second half of the nineteenth century.[14] Concurrently, female "reformatories" were established in Britain, with a psychological approach to female reform, and in the United States, where they adopted a familial organization.[15] In contrast to the Catholic model, Anglo-American nations employed secular women, who were well-educated and sometimes feminist, as directors. Because of such regional disparities in terms of chronology, types of personnel, and underlying religious approaches, no overarching theory of female punishment has yet emerged aside from a general recognition that early prison reform was gendered.

A third challenge to the revisionist school, although not always framed as such, has come from the outpouring of research on the expansive prison-building programs of the late nineteenth and early twentieth centuries outside of Northern Europe and America.[16] One group of studies documents the spread of the penitentiary to peripheral nations in Southern and Eastern Europe; to newly independent states in Latin America; and to Asian countries such as China and Japan. By adapting and reinterpreting the

Foucauldian model in various ways, these new prisons became transnational symbols of each nation's modernity and progress. A second body of scholarship explores colonial punishment of both European convicts transported from the metropole or of indigenous subjects in Africa, Asia, or the Caribbean. Types of incarceration varied widely, as some imperial powers erected buildings that architecturally resembled modern penitentiaries, and others simply confined prisoners in traditional outdoor penal colonies. Despite their superficial differences, colonial institutions of punishment almost single-mindedly pursued profit from forced labor while submitting inmates to harsh living conditions. Rehabilitation, the goal of prison reform in the metropole, was held to be unnecessary, and even ineffective, for colonial subjects defined as inferior by contemporaneous theories of "racial science." In short, the transnational expansion of incarceration during the age of positivism numerically surpassed the ideologically important, but more limited, project of prison building a century earlier.

While scholarship on Italian prison history is not extensive, several important studies build upon these various bodies of historiography. In *The Prison and the Factory*, Dario Melossi and Massimo Pavarini made a pioneering theoretical contribution to the 1970s' revisionist debate by comparing the role of these two institutions in creating a disciplined industrial workforce.[17] Guy Geltner has enriched the literature on the "proto-prison" by arguing that institutions of punishment resembling the Foucauldian model were established as early as the medieval era in Florence, Bologna, and Venice.[18] Anna Capelli has addressed the first wave of prison reform, during which many lawyers and scientists vigorously supported the abolition of corporal punishment but achieved few practical results.[19] Gender history has been slighted with the exception of Simona Trombetta's reconstruction of a significant but forgotten instance of female prison reform in early nineteenth-century Piedmont.[20] Guido Neppi Modona's pathbreaking article of 1973, "The Prison and Civil Society," remains the best analysis of Italian prison policy during the positivist era, while Roberto Giulianelli has more specifically analyzed patterns of convict labor.[21] The fascist era between the world wars remains relatively unexplored except for the police camps that interned political opponents and other "asocial" individuals, as defined by the dictatorship.[22] Christian De Vito has offered a rare account of prison developments during the postwar Italian Republic with particular emphasis on their entanglement with politics. Well-grounded in archival research, these disparate studies provide a foundation for rethinking the periodization of Italian prison history. This book takes on that challenge, addressing periodization, gender, and everyday prison conditions for inmates at both the local and national levels.

Layers of Italian Prison Reform

In Rome, and Italy in general, the birth of the prison occurred in three stages between the late seventeenth and the early twentieth centuries. The first stage, built on Catholic legal tradition, becomes visible only if the historical lens is widened to include penal institutions for women and children. After the "legal revolution" of the Middle Ages and the consolidation of Canon law, the Church employed enclosure in monasteries or jails as punishment for clergy and other groups under its jurisdiction. Therefore, ecclesiastical courts imposed prayers, pilgrimages, and imprisonment to induce repentance. As James Whitman has argued, the Church prefigured modern criminal law by developing "doctrines of mitigation through culpability analysis" based on individual intent or state of mind.[23] While in practice religious authorities routinely turned over offenders convicted of serious crimes to the state for execution, they were forbidden themselves from shedding blood and thus inflicting corporal punishment. Outside of Church courts, punishment by internment was rarely employed and then only for debtors. Jails were widespread but held suspects awaiting trial or held for ransom rather than convicted criminals.

The architectural and organizational model of the monastery also points to the importance of the Catholic tradition for the development of the modern penitentiary. Long before the early nineteenth-century debates about the virtues of solitary confinement for inmate rehabilitation, monasteries had practiced cellular separation for spiritual contemplation and moral reform. The typical Carthusian charterhouse, for example, with its individual living quarters connected to small private gardens, prefigured the early nineteenth-century "Pennsylvania" system of complete separation of prisoners. Except for attendance at mass, Carthusian monks spent their days and nights alone in their cells. Other religious orders, such as the Benedictines, worked together during the day but slept separately at night as would be true of the later "Auburn" model.[24] In both cases, monasteries followed a rigid schedule, marked by the church bell, which required prayer, silence, and often work. Nineteenth- and early twentieth-century prisons followed similar routines, disciplined by minutely detailed regulations.

In Italy, the monastic model was most influential for shaping the punishment of women and children. In the early eighteenth century, innovative prisons were established at San Michele in Rome for the purpose of rehabilitating both groups through religious devotion and work. These "convent" prisons, modeled on other early modern philanthropic institutions—such as foundling homes, orphanages, refuges for unmarried women, and old-age homes—employed enclosure and isolation from the outside world as a strategy for both punishing and protecting groups considered weak and impressionable. Like the large network of Roman charities, they were meant to demonstrate the benevolence of the Counter-Reformation Church in the face of the Protestant challenge. Rather than disappearing with the Enlightenment, these convent prisons assumed a long life as relatively unchanging penal institutions for women and girls until the 1970s. Staffed by nuns and focused on religious conversion, female penitentiaries and reformatories retained a Catholic stamp even after the unification of Italy as a secular state. Thus, the Catholic stage of "proto-prison" reform, while involving the establishment of a relatively small number of convent prisons during the Counter-Reformation, constituted a significant but often unrecognized historical underpinning for the later modern penitentiary.

The second influence on Italy's prison system was Enlightenment thought. The Italian peninsula, however, which was divided among old regime monarchies, did not offer fertile soil for penal change during the late eighteenth and early nineteenth centuries. Beccaria's book was championed by liberals and supporters of the Risorgimento, the movement for Italian unification, but circulation was initially hampered by local censorship and its placement on the Index of Forbidden Books by the Catholic Church. Nevertheless, the enlightened despot, Pieter Leopold of Tuscany, promulgated a strikingly progressive criminal code in 1786, which integrated many of Beccaria's reforms including the abolition of the death penalty. In 1795, the Bourbon king of Naples built a panopticon prison on the island of Santo Stefano, one of the few penal institutions in the world to copy the model put forth by Jeremy Bentham. Cited by Foucault as an exemplary embodiment of the first wave of prison reform, the panopticon was imagined as a circular prison with several stories of individual cells and a central tower from which the guards could control inmates by their "gaze."[25] After the Napoleonic interlude, lawyers of the "classical school," the liberal current inspired by Beccarian principles, resumed debates about the need for penal reform. Yet, the era between 1760 and 1840 saw little change in prison practice across the Italian peninsula.

The relative immobility of the old regime states naturally placed prison reform high on the Risorgimento agenda. From the perspective of early patriots, the absence of proportionality in punishments and the perpetuation of torture and the death penalty symbolized the backwardness and barbarity of the pre-unitary monarchs. Furthermore, large numbers of nationalists, who supported unification through propaganda or armed insurrection, were themselves incarcerated in dark and dirty jails, where they were held in chains and sometimes subjected to forced labor. Foreign liberals, whether volunteers in the Risorgimento cause, journalists, or government officials, were also liable to incarceration by Italian rulers bent on repressing popular dissent. Through the writings of both Italian and foreign political prisoners, Italian prisons gained such a dreadful reputation that they attracted an inspection visit by the British prime minister, William Gladstone. From both personal experience and a sense of shameful backwardness, Risorgimento leaders called for prison reform immediately after victory.

Introduction of parliamentary liberalism, however, did not bring immediate change in policies of punishment. Few new prisons were built or even remodeled during the first three decades after unification. Unable to agree on broad penal principles, legislators simply adopted the criminal code of Piedmont, whose king was now titular head of the peninsula. Advocacy of liberal ideas was strong among many veterans of the wars of independence, but controversy over the abolition of forced labor and capital punishment became stumbling blocks in debates that stretched over decades. It was left to the new Division of Prisons, within the Ministry of the Interior, to begin the complex process of knitting together the disparate penal institutions inherited from the pre-unitary states. In Italy, therefore, the triumph of liberalism over absolute monarchy was necessary but not sufficient to usher in the modern penitentiary.

Only during the late nineteenth and early twentieth centuries, or the second wave of prison reform, did Italy's system of punishment bring significant change for certain inmate groups. Men were major beneficiaries of the new criminal code of 1889, which abolished the *bagni*, or hard labor camps, with their practice of chaining prisoners both night and day. Under the subsequent Ordinance of 1891, men's penitentiaries adopted the Irish system, under which punishment was individualized and good behavior brought promotion to less restrictive institutions and possibly parole. While budget limitations prevented the complete overhaul of all prison buildings, progress was made on replacing large dormitories with separate sleeping cells and expanding professional workshops in new and remodeled institutions. Equally radical innovations occurred in state reformatories for boys where, after 1904, prison guards were replaced by teachers, and, as a result, access to education and professional training expanded dramatically. Reformatory directors diversified the experience of the interned boys by expanding physical education and organizing excursions to the surrounding cities and countryside. Although prison administrators exaggerated in labeling the new reformatories as schools, they differed markedly from the old "houses of custody" inherited from the previous regimes.

Positivism as a specific criminological approach was instrumental in shaping the Italian prison system. Most notably, Lombroso and his fellow psychiatrists successfully lobbied the national prison administration to establish criminal insane asylums for mentally-ill prisoners. Consonant with the biological and psychological bent of criminal anthropology, they argued for specialized institutions, under the direction of medical personnel, to both treat and restrain insane inmates, whether convicted or acquitted. Jails and penitentiaries became centers of positivist research carried out by resident physicians and prominent criminologists from the outside. A prison physician himself, Lombroso became a model for his colleagues across Italy by conducting physical and psychological examinations on inmates and collecting artifacts of prisoner culture, such as graffiti, sculptures, and tattoos. Subjected to anthropological measurements and psychological interviews, Italian inmates provided the voluminous and supposedly scientific data that filled the treatises of criminal anthropologists.

Despite the dominant role of positivist thought and practice during the consolidation of Italy's prison system at the turn of the twentieth century, the earlier reform philosophies did not entirely disappear. On the eve of World War I, women and girls were still interned in dilapidated convent prisons organized around religious principles, untouched by positivist tenets of prison reform such as individualization of punishment, cellular architecture, and professional training. As in the early modern period, the majority of girls' reformatories remained private and subject to little state oversight. Certain Enlightenment precepts also survived into the positivist period, as new short-term jails and long-term penitentiaries continued to be architecturally designed according to the Philadelphia and Auburn models, respectively. Positivist administrators implemented humanitarian features that had first been advocated by eighteenth-century reformers, such as fresh air, light, sanitation, and sufficient diets. Finally, the importance of work in post-unification prisons tied all three stages of reform ideology together whether it served the ends of discipline, rehabilitation, or financial gain to the governing authorities.

In sum, the birth of the prison in Italy occurred in overlapping layers that reached back to the Catholic Reformation, was nurtured during the era of liberal revolutions, and came to fruition during the age of positivism. The process was cumulative rather than linear, with no conclusive turning point. The Ordinance of 1891 represented the most important reform because it unified and standardized, at least on paper, the entire system of jails, penitentiaries, and reformatories. In practice, however, confinement was highly gendered with modern positivist principles, such as individualization of punishment, bestowed only on adult men. Similarly, boys in public reformatories became primary subjects of new strategies of child protection, while women and girls were left in a religious sphere that was inconsistent with the secular principles of the Italian constitution and law codes. Such disparities in punishment, in correlation with severe inequalities in civil and political rights, deprived women and girls of full citizenship in liberal Italy.

National and Local Perspectives

Within this national context, Rome provides a fascinating laboratory for analyzing the transformation of punishment in Italy from violence against the body of the offender to enclosed rehabilitation. As the capital of the Papal States and then of secular Italy, the city experienced a particularly dramatic transition to parliamentary rule involving sharp conflict between Church and state. Rome additionally offers the advantage, absent from most other cities, of having harbored a rich array of penal institutions for women, men, girls, and boys that facilitates comparisons by gender and age. Through micro-histories of specific prisons within this matrix—such as San Michele, Regina Coeli, and the Mantellate—this book will describe their architecture, social profiles of their inmates, conditions of everyday life, and place in historical memory. To measure their typicality, the analyses of local prisons are then compared with the national network.

The Roman perspective reveals that prisons were not "total institutions" but instead interconnected in many ways to the outside world.[26] Most obviously, a variety of personnel—wardens, clerks, doctors, chaplains, teachers, nuns, guards, and contractors—passed through prison walls, sometimes daily, to transfer knowledge and goods. After promulgation of the Ordinance of 1891, members of surveillance and visiting committees also had legal access to inmates. Certain types of punishment, such as hard labor or agricultural work, required prisoners themselves to leave institutional confines; others, such as juvenile correction, promoted educational trips to the outside. Criminal anthropologists, as well as jurists and defense lawyers, were permitted into prisons to conduct research or meet with prisoners. As a result of their investigations, positivist criminologists transferred knowledge about prisoners to the public through illustrated writings and new "scientific" museums filled with objects, ranging from criminals' skulls to inmate art.

Furthermore, Roman prisons were swept up in larger historical developments that shaped their internal organization and character. National, regional, and sometimes idiosyncratic forces framed local prison life. The long history of the convent prison, the most famous of which was San Michele, influenced post-unification penal institutions for women and girls. Rome's wealth of Catholic charities encouraged the proliferation of prisoner aid societies. Its economic profile, which heavily relied on the construction and printing trades, caused conflict between industrial workers and the prison administration over the employment of convict labor in those sectors. In the rural Agro Romano to the south of Rome, the centuries-old problem of malaria became a catalyst for establishing a penal colony to combat it. The efforts of feminists drew attention to the plight of women prisoners and brought real, if limited, reforms to the local jail. Rather than unchanging black boxes, prisons shaped and were shaped by the political, social, economic, and cultural currents of the epoch.

With its abundance of prisons, Rome also offers the opportunity for mapping the relationship between space and punishment. From the sixteenth through the mid-twentieth centuries, Roman prisons tended to cluster along the Tiber River, mostly on the right bank, in Trastevere. Several local factors determined the location of this "penal zone." Historically, Trastevere had been thick with public and private charities for the poor, such as hospitals, conservatories, and workhouses, because of its working-class population. The river banks, while central in terms of transportation, were also associated with groups that were considered marginal and possibly polluting, such as the Jews in the ghetto across from Trastevere. After unification, an additional factor made Trastevere attractive for prison building: the availability of monasteries eligible for appropriation by the new state. Concurrently, the few penal institutions in less densely populated areas of Rome had become nuisances in the eyes of the middle classes and were closed. Thus, in a pattern very different from the era after World War II, Rome's network of prisons became more concentrated rather than dispersed to the periphery.

During the positivist era, prisons were integral to Rome's urban fabric and cultural identity. Located in buildings from diverse epochs of its history—ancient Roman baths, medieval monasteries, early modern workhouses, and aristocratic villas—they evoked memories of Rome's layered past through the recycling of public and private spaces. That a significant percentage of the *popolani*, or popular classes, spent part of their lives incarcerated assured a circulation of prison subculture through prison walls. Facilitated by the location of penal institutions in central zones of the city, family members and friends visited, brought food, sent letters, and even shouted news to prisoners from the outside. Prisons also entered popular culture through songs, or *stornelli* in local dialect, that are still remembered today. One song laments the loneliness of life in the women's jail of the Mantellate, where the day was marked by the mournful ringing of a church bell. Another asserts that a man cannot consider himself a real Roman or *trasteverino*, that is, an inhabitant of Trastevere, if he has not climbed the steps of the men's jail of Regina Coeli. Thus a local perspective provides an important lens for viewing the self-fashioning of Rome as the capital city of Italy.

A Note on Sources and Terminology

This book employs a wealth of "evidence," produced by prison administrators and criminal anthropologists, to analyze not only the development of state policy but also the experience of inmates themselves. It thus seeks to reconstruct the theory and practice of prison reform from both "above" (state and professional elites) and "below" (inmates). Such a methodology is tricky because the major documentary sources for this study—administrative reports and official correspondence located in public archives, parliamentary debates, professional journals, and books by criminal anthropologists—were mostly produced "from above" and consequently shaped by political, institutional, and intellectual imperatives. Nonetheless, imaginative use of official documents can provide a useful method for illuminating daily life in penitentiaries, where the vast majority of Italian prisoners were illiterate and left few personal records behind. In addition, criminal anthropologists—and most notably Lombroso—collected songs, poems, slang, graffiti, art, tattoos, and other examples of a vibrant and creative prisoner subculture.

Among the many official sources, prison statistics are central to investigating a world characterized by invisibility and silence. Quantitative sources have been almost completely neglected by Italian historians, perhaps because of the inherent difficulties in working with the confusing sets of overlapping and sometimes incomplete statistics published by the state beginning in 1862.[27] Yearly volumes of prison statistics offer extremely detailed information, including data on individual prisons, but ceased publication between the mid-1880s and mid-1890s. To fill this gap, annual compendiums of administrative statistics provide tables on some but not all of the same variables. Over the half century of this study, categories were frequently dropped, added, or changed. Despite these difficulties, these two series of statistical volumes offer a wealth of information about the different types of Italian jails, penitentiaries, hard labor camps, reformatories, criminal insane asylums, and police camps in terms of the quantity of institutions, cells, personnel, and prisoners. Data on birthplace, age, marital status, education, and profession offer a social profile of inmates, almost invariably broken down by gender and therefore offering a rich source on women convicts. To make up for the paucity of writings by prisoners themselves, statistics allow a glimpse into everyday life in terms of the numbers who attended school, read library books, sent letters, received visitors, revolted against prison rules, and were subjected to differing degrees of punishment. It can only be hoped that, in the future, funding can be found for a professional *equipe* of historians to study, standardize, and publish this statistical data in an accessible form that can serve as the basis for further studies in Italian prison history.

Finally, several key terms, which recur throughout this study, must be understood within the context of their time. "Prison reform," for example, refers to theoretical philosophies and practical goals that were considered progressive and desirable in specific eras and which changed over time. During the nineteenth and twentieth centuries, Italians looked toward Northern Europe and America, the International Penitentiary Congresses, and positivist criminology for models of prison reform. Similarly, "modern" refers to the perspective of nineteenth- and twentieth-century statesmen, criminologists, lawyers, and doctors who typically championed a linear notion of progress based on the values of liberalism, nationalism, and scientific inquiry. In neither case does the use of these words imply a positive or uncritical evaluation on my part of past penal projects.

1

Punishment before Italian Unification

In the early eighteenth century, Rome joined a small but significant group of early modern European cities that began to employ confinement as a mode of punishment. At San Michele on the Tiber River, the papal government instituted a prison for boys (1703) and a second for women (1735), which employed a new penal strategy of rehabilitation through prayer and work. Unlike the traditional jails for pretrial detention, which were crowded, unhealthy, and run for private profit, San Michele provided separate cells, food, and employment under a patronage of lay and religious notables. In its innovative architecture and philosophy of punishment through reform rather than bodily mutilation, San Michele demonstrates Italy's centrality to the era of the "proto-prison," which preceded the birth of the Foucauldian penitentiary. While proto-prisons were not numerous in Europe, they demonstrate that experiments in incarceration arose before the Enlightenment and drew on alternative, often religious, ideologies.

Unlike the better-studied prison workhouses of Northern Europe and bridewells of England, the prison at San Michele can usefully be labeled a "convent prison," because it rested on Catholic tradition in terms of its rationale, form, and purpose. Canon law was unique in medieval Europe in prescribing incarceration as punishment for not only clerics but also certain groups of laity. Early prison sentences were served in monasteries, which became the architectural and organizational model for a wide spectrum of institutions of enclosure that dotted the medieval world and multiplied during the early modern period. Such institutions, usually administered by a combination of religious and secular authorities, included foundling homes, orphanages, refuges for women, homes for the aged, and hospitals. Not surprisingly, early prisons drew on this Catholic tradition of interning "marginal" persons—usually women and children who lacked the support of a family—for protection, discipline, and moral reform.

Prisoners were also early objects of pity for certain confraternities, lay brotherhoods that had received papal approval for specific works of charity. To display their religiosity and pursue rewards in the afterlife, confraternities in many Italian cities supplied food, clothing, and solace to prisoners or accompanied them to the gallows. Because of this mixture of religious and lay participation in early initiatives to address the plight of prisoners, it would be wrong to see the earliest Italian penitentiaries as a simple or inevitable consequence of Church doctrines and policies. In fact, the even earlier prisons identified by Geltner in several northern Italian communes were administered solely by municipal rather than religious authorities. But Catholicism, understood as a complex tradition of institutions and mentalities that permeated medieval and early modern Italian society, created a legal and cultural framework for experimentation with enclosure for the purpose of punishment far in anticipation of the Enlightenment and age of revolutions.

After the publication in 1764 of Beccaria's famous call for radical penal reform, Italy participated in the international enthusiasm for replacing corporal punishment with incarceration. In place of religious piety, this Foucauldian "first wave" of prison reform in Italy took its inspiration from Beccaria's call for punishment that was mild, equal for all social ranks, and proportionate to the crime. Such universal principles redirected the focus of penal reform from women to men, who were being conferred citizenship throughout Europe and the United States by the wave of revolutions between 1776 and 1848. Although Tuscany heeded Beccaria's call by abolishing the death penalty, few other penal experiments occurred on a peninsula dominated absolute monarchs and a papacy firmly opposed to Enlightenment ideals. After the Napoleonic interlude, a group of distinguished reformers began to advocate for the Focauldian penitentiary as an answer to both the inhumanity and ineffectiveness of traditional types of punishment. Yet on the eve of unification, despite lively debates among jurists and scientists, only a few states had erected penal institutions based on Enlightenment principles.

Early Modern Rome

The development of the early modern convent prison can be understood only within Rome's unique judicial framework and the wider network of Italian charities, whose disciplinary functions often blurred with penal sanctions. From the sixteenth to the early nineteenth centuries, Roman institutions of punishment were embedded in a larger governmental and judicial system that determined their purpose and even their location within the city. Because the Pope held both temporal power in central Italy and spiritual power over the Catholic world, the political structure of his kingdom was particularly complicated. As Fiorella Bartoccini has observed, "the government of the Church and the government of the State should have been separate at the executive level but in reality appeared to be connected by an inextricable group of reciprocal ties" because both were presided over by ecclesiastical administrators only loosely bound by a hodgepodge of laws.[1] Although the popes ruled their territories as absolute monarchs, they nevertheless had to take into consideration the will of the cardinals, to whom they owed their election and who dominated the departments of state administration called congregations. In addition, the great houses of the secular nobility jostled for influence over the affairs of the city, which by glorious tradition was in principle the prerogative of the Senate.[2] The authority of the Senate, however, was undercut by the Governor of Rome, a cleric subordinate to the Vatican who managed the city administration.

This pattern of overlapping and often conflicting jurisdictions was replicated in the legal system characterized by a proliferation of courts. Under the aegis of the Church were the courts of the Auditor Camerae and the Governor, which handled civil and criminal offenses respectively. Clergy were under the jurisdiction of the tribunal of the Vicar of Rome, who served as the disciplinary arm of the Pope. The Senate administered justice in the Capitoline Court, which heard mostly civil disputes between local residents. Over the centuries, the popes increasingly encroached on the power of the Capitoline Court, the symbol of secular power within the city, but were not able to abolish it until 1848.[3] Aristocratic families had patents from the city to arrest and try certain types of petty criminals, such as thieves and prostitutes, in their own private tribunals, a legacy of the medieval prerogative of powerful families to imprison their enemies in castle dungeons. Specialization was slow to develop during the early modern period so that each court in practice handled a wide variety of cases. The Auditor Camerae and Capitoline tribunals, for example, began to hear criminal as well as civil cases, and the Vicar's court tried not only clergy but also lay people charged with morals crimes such as rape, adultery, and incest.[4] Many complaints could be taken to more than one of these tribunals, and cases were sometimes tried multiple times.[5] Only the Inquisition, which oversaw the prosecution of heresy and related crimes such as witchcraft, was autonomous and stood outside of this confusing web of municipal justice. As an arm of the Congregation of the Holy Office, it answered directly to the Vatican.

The courts of Rome applied a jumble of laws that emanated not only from the Pope but also from the Congregations, the Governor, and the Senate, all of which had legislative powers. Not until 1832 did the Papal States issue a unified criminal code. However, most tribunals applied some mixture of Canon, Roman, and customary law that relied on the inquisitorial method and offered a wide range of penalties. According to Irene Fosi, the Roman justice system was characterized by "a striking disproportionality between guilt and punishment"; the excessive brutality of the latter thus functioned as "a collective purification, a warning, and a lesson in blood."[6] The most severe punishment was the death sentence, which took a variety of grisly forms: simple hanging and beheading; execution accompanied by torture, such as being stretched on the rack; or, at worst, being drowned in a leather bag or burned at the stake.[7] Executions took place in public squares as a theatrical warning to the crowd of spectators not to contemplate similar crimes, political rebellions, religious transgressions, or moral violations. A frequent site of executions was the Piazza in front of Castel Sant'Angelo, because of its symbolic location in front of the papal stronghold and its proximity to several municipal prisons. The tradition of displaying the heads of executed criminals on the posts of the adjacent bridge was meant to reinforce awe of the sovereign. Other squares that witnessed executions were those of the Campidoglio, St. Maria Cosmedin, Campo dei Fiori, and Piazza Navona. The bodies of brigands were displayed outside the city gates, to the horror of many tourists, with placards attesting to their names and crimes.[8] Thus papal Rome was dotted with a series of "penal signs" that reminded residents that crime would bring bodily pain and horrific degradation.[9]

Less spectacular but more common than execution was the punishment of hard labor (*lavoro forzato*) in the form of galley slavery. From the sixteenth until the early nineteenth century, the Papal States patrolled its western shores with a flotilla of ships stationed at the coast city of Civitavecchia.[10] The need for manpower clearly fueled the widespread practice of sentencing male convicts to the galleys, who joined two other groups at the oars—prisoners of war and unemployed men.[11] All were chained to benches lining both sides of the vessel on which they worked, ate, and slept. Sentences to the galleys, levied for property crimes (mostly theft and cattle-rustling) as well as violence (especially homicide), could run from three years to life. Most Roman jails had a special holding cell for convicts awaiting transfer to the galleys, a process centralized by the eighteenth century in the New Prison.[12] The transport of galley prisoners, in their striped uniforms and chains, from Rome to Civitavecchia constituted a public spectacle during the sixteenth and seventeenth centuries, another "penal sign," or reminder of the papal power of retribution, in the urban landscape. By the mid-eighteenth century, however, these parades of prisoners began to incite such public disorder that Pope Benedict XIV ordered their transfer to take place at night. Publicity continued to be assured by the posting of printed lists on the doors of the various criminal courts and in the major piazzas, like Campo dei Fiori, with the names, birthplaces, crimes, and length of sentence for each convict.[13]

As sail and eventually steam replaced rowers as the main source of naval power, convicts were kept on land to work in dockyards and, by the early nineteenth century, in other types of hard labor. The Criminal Code of 1832 reaffirmed the centrality of two types of hard labor: "*galera*," a designation recalling the old punishment of galley rowing, for those sentenced from ten years to life, and "public works" for those with shorter sentences.[14] Interchangeably dubbed "*galeotti*" (galley slaves) or "*forzati*" (forced laborers), prisoners in these two categories continued to wear distinctive striped uniforms, had their head and beards shaved, and wore legchains. Many continued to be transferred to Civitavecchia, where they lived and labored in government shipyards. Others remained in Rome, where they were employed a variety of public works such as construction and road maintenance. *Forzati* were also employed in early excavations of the archeological ruins, such as the Roman forum and Ostia Antica, which were becoming a passion of scholars at the turn of the nineteenth century.[15] Convicts built the large Verano cemetery on the outskirts of Rome, consecrated in 1834 by Pope Gregory XVI in order to discourage burials in churches, a traditional practice that was increasingly understood to be unhygienic and a threat to the urban population. When St. Paul outside the Walls, one of the four papal basilicas and a prime destination for pilgrims, burnt to the ground in 1823, it was rebuilt by prison labor. George Head, a foreign visitor to Rome, encountered the *forzati* at St. Paul's and found them willing to discuss their crimes forthrightly. Convicted mostly of assault and homicide, they were employed in polishing granite columns in a slow, and according to Head, "slothful" manner.[16] For those criminals who escaped execution and the galleys, penalties included exile, land confiscation, mutilation, and fines.

Although sentences of imprisonment were rare during the sixteenth and seventeenth centuries, medieval precedence could be found in both theory and practice. As the Church became increasingly critical of corporal punishment during the Middle Ages, canon law began to recommend incarceration in bishops' palaces or monasteries as punishment for both secular and regular clergy. Confinement for the purpose of expiation and prayer was consistent with the official purpose of ecclesiastical justice, which was repentance rather than retribution. Geltner has pointed out that, as early as the sixth century, lay persons could also be subjected to this procedure of *detrusio,* or penal cloistering. "Harness[ing] punishment to personal salvation through monitored confinement," secular judges applied *detrusio* sparingly but regularly in place of exile, which promised no moral correction, or corporal punishment, which seemed too severe.[17] In the thirteenth century, the practice of *detrusio* was appropriated by the medieval Inquisition, which began to build its own prisons for lay heretics who had been sentenced to repentance rather than death. In 1624, Pope Urban VIII established a special prison in the town of Corneto for Roman clergy, many of whom would have previously undergone corporal punishment alongside laymen. It must be emphasized that this gradual acceptance of incarceration as punishment did not preclude the Church from continuing to use torture as a method of extracting confessions before trial or from turning over heretics to secular authorities for death by burning, hanging, or the guillotine. Yet the medieval practice of *detrusio,* as applied by a variety of ecclesiastical and secular courts, constitutes an important precedent for the later convent prisons in early modern Rome.[18]

Roman Charity

The finely articulated system of charity is as important as the judicial context for explaining the birth of the convent prison in early modern Italy. The network of jails and early prisons that characterized Papal Rome was embedded in a much denser web of enclosed spaces that included monasteries and convents, hospitals, foundling homes and orphanages, refuges for women, hospices for the aged, and even an insane asylum. In addition to institutionalization, philanthropy took the form of subsidies for food and medical care as well as dowries for poor girls and licenses to beg for the deserving poor or those unable to work. As Angela Groppi has argued, the rich array of Roman charities arose not only from the Christian imperative to help the poor and needy but also from the Counter-Reformation campaign against Protestantism. In response to Protestant attempts to paint Rome as a new Babylon, beset by vice and corruption, the popes of the late sixteenth and seventeenth centuries increasingly defended their legitimacy by making the city a showplace of Christian charity.[19] The establishment of both the New Prison, an innovative jail dedicated to mild punishment, and the penitentiaries for boys and women at San Michele, with their mission of reform rather than revenge, fit neatly into this papal project.

Prisons lay on one end of a spectrum of Roman institutions of enclosure that ran from protective to repressive. Foundling homes and hospitals were located at the far end of the spectrum characterized by protection; orphanages, refuges for women, and homes for the aged—with their strict rules and requirements to work—near the middle; and jails and prisons at the end of extreme repression. This strategy of institutionalization was considered most appropriate for groups that could not be self-supporting. Despite the conventional stereotype of premodern society as one centered on self-sufficient families, in fact large numbers of Romans fell outside of traditional patterns and instead spent part or, in the case of certain categories of women, all of their lives in these institutions. As early as the middle ages, foundling homes and orphanages were established throughout Italy to discourage infanticide and take care of abandoned children. The sixteenth and seventeenth centuries witnessed the creation of a massive number of specialized female institutions such as conservatories for young girls whose families could not provide moral and economic support; refuges for unmarried women (*zitelle*); asylums for "unhappily married women" (*malmaritate*), a category that included both victims of domestic violence and wives expelled from their homes by their husbands; and reformatories for prostitutes. Intended to save the honor and sexual purity of women by removing them from the temptations and dangers of city streets, these institutions were modeled on the convent. Yet internees were not expected to take the veil and, in the case of young girls, were provided dowries to facilitate marriage. Adult men were expected to work and therefore were rarely candidates for enclosure. Only if sick or aged were they eligible for admission to the hospitals and old-age institutes of the city. While this rich array of charity institutions were all inspired by a spirit of Christian charity, they were not exclusively under control of the Church. Members of noble families often founded, funded, and administered favorite philanthropies; visiting committees were composed of prominent aristocratic men and women; and working-class Romans served as domestic staff. Thus the Catholic model of enclosure, adopted by the first Roman prisons from the world of charity, represented a hybrid of religious and lay patronage and management.

In addition to institutions of enclosure, a second branch of Roman charity—the confraternity—shaped the world of early modern punishment. Made up of laymen with the official approval of the Church, confraternities dedicated themselves to pious causes including the assistance of prisoners. Dating back to the thirteenth century, Roman confraternities proliferated during the Renaissance and Counter-Reformation.[20] Founded in 1490, the Confraternity of S. Giovanni Decollato was dedicated to assisting inmates facing the death penalty.[21] On the night before an execution, the members of the confraternity would process, two by two, to the prison wearing sackcloth to emphasize the necessity of repentance. Passing the night with the condemned prisoner, they would comfort him and urge him to confess and receive communion. The ritual continued the following morning, when members of the confraternity accompanied the prisoner to the scaffold to offer sympathy and religious counsel. Those who confessed were privileged to have their ashes buried in the confraternity's church; those who refused had their unconsecrated ashes scattered in the wind. Subsidies were also provided to the needy widows and children of men who had repented before execution.

Two confraternities founded in the sixteenth century, S. Girolamo della Carità and the Pietà dei Carcerati, paid room and board for destitute or foreign (non-Roman) prisoners whose families could not provide meals. According to their contract of 1615 with the state, S. Girolamo della Carità, for example, promised to supply inmates awaiting trial in the Tor di Nona jail with "good bread and wine, both of which must be uncontaminated ... in this manner: half in the morning and half in the evening."[22] Confraternities sometimes paid the creditors of prisoners confined for debt and held the privilege of freeing several prisoners a year, usually on religious holidays. Both confraternities also sent confessors to the jails to instruct and comfort inmates. Because of its growing expertise and adroit political maneuvering, S. Girolamo was awarded administrative control over the Tor di Nona jail in 1568 and subsequently the New Prison when it opened in 1658.[23]

Inmates also received protection from the Committee for Prison Inspection (*Tribunale della Visita alle Carceri*), a mixed body of religious and lay notables appointed by the Pope. Its secretary, who carried the title of "attorney for the poor" (*avvocato* or *procuratore dei poveri*), was a member of S. Girolamo della Carità and took special care to identify prisoners who were confined illegally. The tradition of prison visitation was originally a practice of the popes themselves but was handed over to a committee in the sixteenth century because of the growing number of inmates. On Thursdays, the Inspection Committee visited each jail, tested the quality of food and wine, and listened to complaints by inmates. Its power was more than nominal for members could order the release of both debtors and minor criminals if deemed to be held unjustly. At Christmas and Easter, special "benevolent inspections" (*visita graziosa*) practically emptied the jails of all but the most violent convicts.[24]

Prisoners could appeal directly to the Pope or the Governor of Rome about problems with corrupt guards, the quality of food, or mistreatment by fellow prisoners.[25] One such letter from "the poor inmates" of Tor di Nona, accused the administration of removing the box that they had affixed to the grate of their window to collect alms.[26] This entreaty is evidence of the widespread custom of begging through prison windows, a right of the poor condoned by prison wardens happy to turn the destitute into paying customers for food and other prison necessities. It is not clear how often these letters to the popes brought results, although the state did issue periodic statutes intended to prevent contractors from overcharging for food and lodging, overcrowding cells, or denying medical care to sick inmates. Papal visits to jails were infrequent, but the tradition continued into the nineteenth century. On July 26, 1824, Pope Leo XII had lunch with prisoners at the New Prison, part of his campaign to emphasize the charity of the Church and re-sacralize the image of Rome after the defilement of Napoleonic rule.[27]

The vast network of philanthropic institutions and confraternities in early modern Rome created a cultural humus that was conducive to experimentation with imprisonment as a new type of punishment. Their growing numbers during the Counter-Reformation attested to the dual aim of Catholic charity: to assist the needy and to demonstrate the benevolence of the wealthy patron. Such good works were thought to redound to the spiritual benefit of philanthropic individuals and confraternities, including those concerned with prisoners. The popes themselves directed attention to inmates as worthy of objects of Christian charity through their tradition of visiting jails. Thus the inspiration for the first modern penitentiaries in Rome lay in a Catholic culture shared by clergy and laypersons that held prisoners to be deserving of assistance and the convent model effective for bringing about their reform. The implementation of the convent model came slowly, gradually modifying the practices of several of Rome's traditional jails and finally replacing them in the late seventeenth century with the New Prison.

Roman Jails

In the sixteenth and early seventeenth centuries, Rome hosted six municipal jails: the Capitoline, with its substation across the river at the Ripa port; the Borgo and Castel Sant'Angelo near the Vatican; and the Savelli and Tor di Nona near Via Giulia. Rather than serving as institutions of punishment, these jails held suspects awaiting trial, debtors, and vagrants or prostitutes arrested as public nuisances by the *birri*, the sometimes draconian and highly unpopular papal police.[28] Jails were often attached to specific courts, such as the Capitoline and Savelli. Thus as the number of tribunals proliferated in early modern Rome, so did jails. During 1620, one of the few years for which we have statistics, the Capitoline and Borgo prisons each admitted over 1,000 individuals and the Tor di Nona and Savelli prisons 3,000.[29] Many were debtors while others were awaiting trial or punishment, such as death, foreign exile, or transfer to the galleys. While periods of incarceration were generally short, these numbers demonstrate that a significant proportion of Rome's population, which numbered about 120,000, passed through its jails each year.[30]

Perhaps the oldest jail was the Capitoline, heir of the Mamertine prison that had been built in classical times on the side of Capitoline Hill.[31] Also called the Tulliano jail, referring to its position over a cistern (*Tullianum*) into which the dead bodies of prisoners were dumped, the Mamertine prison reportedly had held a succession of famous captives including the north African king Giugurta, the Gallic leader Vercingetorix, and, most famously, saints Peter and Paul.[32] Composed of an upper chamber that held suspects awaiting trial and a lower dungeon for those already convicted and awaiting execution, the ruins of the Mamertine prison have been visited by countless tourists and pilgrims over the centuries. Nathaniel Hawthorne, who lived in Rome from 1858–9, wrote that the lower dungeon "looks just as bad as it is; round, only seven paces across, yet so obscure that our tapers could not illuminate it from side to side—the stones of which it is constructed being as black as night."[33]

Although the Mamertine fell into disuse during the fifth century, its legacy was revived in the twelfth century under the name of the Capitoline or Campidoglio prison. Located first in the old Roman Registry Office (*Tabularium*) on the side of Capitoline Hill overlooking the forum, it was later moved to the Senatorial Palace.[34] The Capitoline prison held suspects undergoing investigation by the Senatorial Court, which represented municipal power in Rome and had the right to try local residents in both civil and criminal matters. It also tried suspects transferred from the Ripa jail, a temporary lockup at the major river port across the Tiber. The Senatorial Court leased out the right to manage its prison to the Alberini family in 1519, a privilege that afforded substantial profits and remained in the family until the male line died out in 1679. After that date, the popes asserted their power over the choice of administrators of the Capitoline prison as part of their campaign to subdue the autonomy of the municipal government. Innocent XI decided to award the patent to a religious body, the Hospital of SS. Salvatore ad Sancta Sanctorum, rather than to another aristocratic family.[35]

On the right bank of the river, near the Vatican, were located two other institutions housing small numbers of prisoners. The first, the Borgo, handled only those crimes committed in the neighborhood of the same name near the St. Peters Basilica. Between 1550 and 1667, the Borgo boasted its own governor and court because of its privileged status near the papal palace but afterwards was absorbed into the jurisdiction of the Governor of Rome.[36] Nearby was the imposing Castel Sant'Angelo, a fortress built on the tomb of the Roman emperor Hadrian and forming part of the defensive system of the Aurelian walls.[37] By the tenth century, Castel Sant'Angelo began to confine prisoners of war and subsequently "elite" prisoners, such as Benvenuto Cellini and Giordano Bruno.[38] By the nineteenth century it also housed political opponents of the papal regime, thus likening it to the Bastille in Paris. Despite the prestige of its prisoners, Castel Sant'Angelo was not luxurious. In his *Italian Notebooks*, Hawthorne described several prison vaults, located on the upper floors of the fortress, "as damp and subterranean as if they were fifty feet under the earth" with the worst being "an inscrutable pit" where prisoners had sometimes been buried alive.[39]

While the jail of Castel Sant'Angelo still stands as a museum, most inmates during the sixteenth and early seventeenth centuries were held in two other institutions that have vanished from historical memory. These were the Savelli and the Tor di Nona jails. The former was managed privately for over two centuries by the powerful aristocratic Savelli family. Appointed as Marshals of the Roman Curia in the mid-fifteenth century, the princes Savelli held a patent giving them the right to try and imprison debtors, petty criminals, and particularly prostitutes.[40] The family commanded its own private force of *birri* to arrest suspects, demonstrating that policing as well as judicial powers were not yet centralized under state control. The Savelli prison was located on the Via di Monserrato, which runs between the Tiber River and Campo dei Fiori, and is today marked by a plaque commemorating one of its most famous prisoners, Beatrice Cenci. Characterized by unhealthy conditions, mixing of the sexes in adjoining cells, and corrupt administration, the Savelli prison was "among the worst" in early seventeenth-century Rome.[41]

Until the mid-seventeenth century, the Tor di Nona jail, popularly called "the Pope's prison" (*la presone dello papa*), was the largest and most important in Rome. It served three courts—that of the Governor, the Vicar, and the Auditor Camerae. Thus the Tor di Nona held a mixture of inmates charged with both criminal and civil offenses as did the Capitoline and Savelli prisons. Under direct papal control by 1408, the administration of the Tor di Nona prison was contracted out to the Capodiferro and subsequently the Bongiovanni families until 1556, after which the patent was awarded to the Confraternity of San Girolamo della Carità.[42] The confraternity promised to curb corruption and provide more humane conditions for inmates than had been the case under private familial control. For a time the Tor di Nona indeed represented an improvement over the Savelli in that it provided separate dormitories for men, women, and children and established an infirmary for sick inmates. Yet its gloomy cells became increasingly overcrowded during the following decades, causing the separation of different groups of inmates to break down by the seventeenth century.

Despite their mission to hide suspects behind walls, both to prevent flight and extract information, early modern Roman jails were themselves visible landmarks in the urban topography. Except for the Inquisition's court, which dispensed global rather than local justice, they clustered in the heart of medieval Rome near the Tiber River, a pattern that persisted until after World War II. On the left side of the Tiber, where the majority of Romans have always lived, was the Capitoline prison on the hill of the same name; the Savelli prison in Via Monserrato near Campo dei Fiori; and the Tor di Nona at the end of Via Giulia. All three were within easy walking distance from each other within the older neighborhoods characterized by narrow streets, outdoor markets, and artisanal workshops. Castel Sant'Angelo, as well as the smaller jails of the Borgo and Ripa, were located on the less-populated right bank of the Tiber but nevertheless near two important hubs of activity, the Vatican in the case of the first two and the river port of Ripa Grande in the case of the last. Because the Tor di Nona faced Castel Sant'Angelo across the Tiber, historian Michele Di Sivo has called this area, with its adjoining bridge, "the focal point of Roman prison geography" in the sixteenth century.[43] The massing of penal institutions in the oldest districts of Rome was unsurprising in light of the small size of the built city, which took up less than one-third of the land within the Aurelian walls.[44]

Occupying familiar and often distinctive buildings, Roman jails were well-known to local inhabitants and woven into urban life. Rather than being total institutions entirely cut off from the outside world, they were shaped by the municipal environment and in turn constituted important landmarks in the Roman imagination. As symbols of the legal system and more generally of papal power, they dominated certain neighborhoods and impinged on the lives of residents across the city, many of whom were interned involuntarily as inmates or served as wardens, guards, contractors, priests, doctors, or other prison staff. Families visited daily to bring food to interned relatives, and grated windows allowed conversations with friends and begging for alms. Residents and visitors to Rome periodically glimpsed prisoners outside the walls of their institutions when being transported to the galleys, performing hard labor at construction projects, or undergoing corporal punishment or execution in public squares. Such public appearances could even take on a festive atmosphere, as when the inmates of the Tor di Nona prison were paraded down Via Giulia to the New Prison at its opening in 1658.

Whether large or small, Roman jails shared some common characteristics that clearly differentiated them from the modern penitentiary. First, incarceration was predominantly an instrument to confine prisoners before trial. The majority of inmates were being held for interrogation and may have been subjected to torture, which was regulated by written law and considered legitimate to secure confession and to encourage suspects to name accomplices. In an age that lacked forensic science, confession was prized as the "Queen of Proofs" and considered more trustworthy than the testimony of family, friends, and neighbors. In addition to those awaiting trial, several other smaller groups shared the premises of each jail: debtors who did not have the money to pay their creditors; convicted criminals awaiting execution or transfer to the galleys; and petty criminals and prostitutes arrested by police and interned as public nuisances. Periods of incarceration tended to be short and neither work nor reform was expected of inmates.

Second, early modern Roman jails mixed various types of prisoners in shared or adjoining cells. Thus different legal categories—suspects, debtors, convicted criminals awaiting trial, and vagabonds—shared lodgings. Most prisons had no separate quarters for women and children, although ecclesiastical personnel and Jews were kept more strictly apart. Differentiation in living conditions was instead linked to social class, with wealthier inmates paying for better rooms and the most impoverished consigned to basement cells, the "*bassi*." Money could buy better accommodations in both the "*segrete*," the small cells for prisoners who had not yet given testimony, and in the "*larghe*," the large cells for those awaiting sentencing, punishment, or payment of their debts. But even the *segrete* held more than one prisoner, so that early modern Roman jails in no way resembled the later cellular model. Housed in buildings built for other purposes, they were haphazard and disorganized architecturally.[45] With form rarely following function, inmates suffered from insufficient air, extremely hot and cold temperatures, and even flooding in the case of the Tor di Nona, whose ground floor was below river level.

While major reform did not occur until the establishment of the New Prison, the popes began as early as 1556 to introduce an innovative vision of penal internment that allied charity with punishment. By replacing private management of the Tor di Nona with the Confraternity of San Girolamo, the popes showed a preoccupation with the lot of prisoners. This transfer of jurisdiction to a body that was semireligious was not completely disinterested, as papal policy strove over the centuries to marginalize the political power of the secular aristocracy. Confraternities, although staffed by lay people, were chartered by the popes and promised to be more obedient to the Vatican than the great Roman nobles. In turn, the Confraternity of S. Girolamo eagerly sought the jail contract not merely out of Christian charity but also to enrich its coffers. Profits came from the fees paid by prisoners for bedding, food, and the privilege to occupy dry, airy, and less-crowded cells. Nevertheless, a trend toward humanitarian reform through the fusion of punishment and charity was visible during the sixteenth century, one that continued with the designation in 1679 of the Hospital of SS. Salvatore as warden of the Capitoline jail in place of the aristocratic Alberini family. This impulse to ease the plight of prisoners and, ultimately, to establish the convent model as a uniquely Italian form of punishment culminated in the New Prison and San Michele.

The New Prison

As a first step of reform, Pope Innocent X centralized punishment by initiating the construction of one large jail—opened in 1658 and aptly called the New Prison—to replace those of the Tor di Nona, Savelli, Ripa, and Borgo.[46] Of the preexisting jails, only those at Capitoline Hill and Castel Sant'Angelo continued to function autonomously. The New Prison was built in Via Giulia, a prestigious street whose layout as a straight line from the Tiber River toward Capitoline Hill marked it clearly as a product of the Renaissance. Because Via Giulia cut through the same medieval quarter that had held the Savelli and Tor di Nona jails, the New Prison did not shift the penal geography of Rome. Many historians have interpreted the placement of the New Prison—halfway between the Vatican and Capitoline Hill—as symbolizing the role of mediation that the Pope wished to play between the religious and political spheres[47] (Map 1.1). More likely, the New Prison represented a visible sign of the steady encroachment of papal power over the powerful noble families that had traditionally dominated the Roman

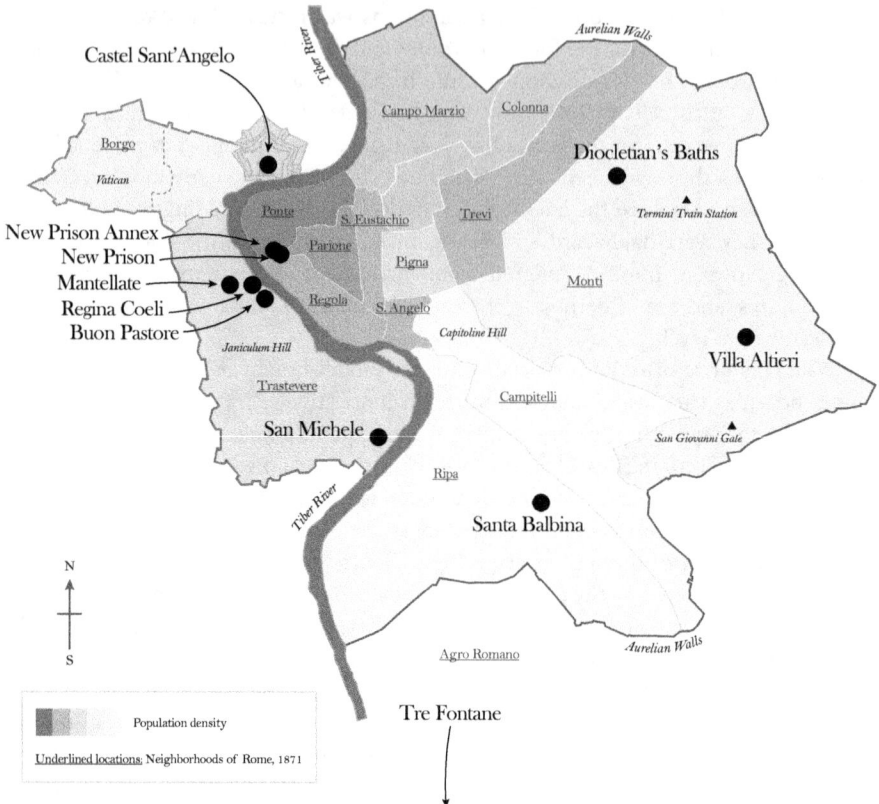

Map 1.1 Map of Roman prisons, 1650–1914

justice system. The choice of Via Giulia—with its grand palaces, wealth of churches, and bustling shops—shows the will of Pope Innocent X to publicize rather than hide his new institution of confinement. Urban residents would have quickly integrated the New Prison into their mental and symbolic map of Rome.

The opening of the New Prison was spurred by advocacy of the cleric Gianbattista Scanaroli, who for several decades had drawn attention to the appalling living conditions of the burgeoning inmate population of Rome. A bishop who served as the "attorney for the poor"—and therefore secretary of the Committee for Prison Inspection—for fifty-five years, Scanaroli knew the jails of Rome from the inside. In his role as attorney for the poor, he routinely interviewed prisoners about their legal problems and complaints of ill-treatment. His work as the official voice of Rome's inmates culminated in a detailed account of conditions in the six jails of early seventeenth-century Rome, including statistical information about their prisoners. Published in 1655 and a valuable source for historians, Scanaroli's book has been compared to the more famous muckraking account of European jails published a century later by John Howard, an English pioneer of prison reform.[48] Critical of the Roman jails of his day,

Scanaroli opposed torture and advocated reform rather than retribution as the aim of punishment, with a special emphasis on education for juvenile offenders. Such views received the approval of Pope Innocent X who, like his immediate predecessors, took a special interest in the work of the Committee for Prison Inspection and its commitment to protecting the rights of inmates.[49]

Several historians have pronounced the New Prison to have represented "the avant-garde" of seventeenth-century prison design.[50] In his nineteenth-century survey of Roman prisons, Cardinal Carlo-Luigi Morichini hailed it as "an everlasting testimony that the Roman popes were among the first to consider humane treatment for unfortunate prisoners."[51] While his writings were biased in favor of the Vatican, Morichini was correct in characterizing the New Prison as ahead of its time in comparison to the jails in Rome and most of Europe. Unlike traditional jails, it was located in an entirely new building designed to incorporate the principles of "justice and clemency," as proclaimed on a plaque over its door.[52] Several motives lay behind the decision of Pope Innocent X to furnish Rome with a new penal institution. As the urban historian Wolfgang Braunfels has pointed out, seventeenth-century Rome "could do nothing but build monument after monument to that successful Counterreformation it had striven for."[53] Part of an ambitious program, the New Prison bolstered the reputation of Catholicism as the true religion and of the popes as benefactors of the poor in contrast to Protestant charges of luxury and corruption. Concurrently, the papal government managed to strip the Savelli family of its judicial prerogatives and further concentrate power in its own hands.[54]

To emphasize papal grandeur and power, the New Prison, designed by the architect Antonio del Grande, had an impressive facade and sweeping internal staircase.[55] Rising five floors, it offered enough space to separate different categories of prisoners as well as the administrative offices from the cells. The first and third floors, reserved mostly for staff, included a records office, examination room (for newly admitted inmates), guardroom, kitchen, and rooms for the chaplain. That religion was central to the mission of the New Prison as was clear from the incorporation of four chapels within the building. Most of the *larghe*, or large dormitories, were on the first floor with eighteen *segrete*, or smaller cells, on the fourth and fifth floors. In both the large and small cells, the inmates were separated by sex and age and, unlike the Tor di Nona, by seriousness of their crime. The building, shaped like a trapezoid, also contained two internal courtyards where residents of the large cells could get fresh air and which contained wells assuring an abundance of fresh water. Two hospital wards treated sick patients with attached kitchens for preparing healthy food. Although capable of holding 600 men and 100 women, the New Prison was rarely full in its early years. Even a century after its founding, Howard, who was touring penal institutions on the continent, pronounced the New Prison to be among the best in Europe.[56]

Yet in many ways the New Prison resembled its predecessors more than the model modern penitentiary. Rather than separate cells, inmates lived in groups even in the *segrete*, each of which held up to ten beds. Classification defied later understandings of equality under the law. More lavish rooms were available to the rich because prisoners continued to pay for accommodations. Religious discrimination—with Jews occupying separate cells from the majority of Christians—correlated with papal policy outside prison walls where Jews had been confined to a ghetto since 1555. In sharp contrast to later punitive philosophies based on the moral and economic value of labor, prisoners were not required to work. Instead, prisoners in the *larghe* lived in leisure and had a certain freedom of movement within the institution, being permitted to walk in the courtyards, eat in the *osteria* or restaurant on the first floor, or talk to family and friends through the grated windows.[57] The fact that most inmates were awaiting trial or serving sentences for debt partly explains this permissiveness. This seeming lack of discipline did not, however, prove that mildness of treatment prevailed. Inmates in the *segrete*, even though only suspects of crime, remained locked in the darkest and most stuffy rooms; the poor still relied on charity to pay for their food and straw mattresses in the "*bassi*" or the most lowly rooms, and misbehavior could be punished by legchains. Most ominously, the New Prison featured a room for torture on the first floor, signaling that Roman courts still relied on corporal pain to extract confessions during interrogations. In short, rather than revolutionary, the New Prison represented an evolutionary step toward the establishment of the convent prison.

San Michele

While the New Prison was innovative for its time, San Michele was indeed revolutionary and deserves to be recognized as the birthplace of the modern Italian penitentiary. The name San Michele originally designated two distinct penal institutions—a boy's reformatory and a separate women's prison—that were annexed in the early eighteenth century to the larger charity complex founded by Pope Innocent XII in 1693 at the river port of Ripa Grande.[58] Dedicated to Saint Michael, this almshouse was the centerpiece of a larger effort to reduce the number of vagabonds and beggars on city streets. As in other European countries, papal authorities sought to distinguish the deserving poor from the lazy, who were thought to prefer begging to work. For the deserving poor, material support was offered in the form of monetary subsidies for married couples and shelter in refuges for single individuals lacking familial support. Intended to centralize institutions of confinement directly under papal control, San Michele opened specialized sections for orphaned boys (1693), for the aged (1715), and for single girls (*zitelle*) (1794). Illegal beggars were forcibly brought to San Michele by police in its early years but popular opposition to such a coercive policy soon made admission to the refuge voluntary. Each group was rigidly separated in the workshops, dining room, and even the central Church, but all were united in their work for the wool factory located at the center of the complex.[59] Because of its large and concentrated workforce, San Michele represented one of the largest economic enterprises in Rome and a profitable source of income for the papal government.

In 1703, Pope Clement XI opened a new wing that was designed as a house of correction for minors serving criminal sentences. Soon dubbed by Romans "S. Michele for bad boys" in contrast to the nearby orphanage, or "S. Michele for good boys," the house of correction incorporated most of the characteristics of the modern penitentiary.[60] Like the New Prison, San Michele was designed specifically as a penal institution, in this case by the prominent architect Carlo Fontana. Although the outside was not grand, the interior was strikingly modern with three tiers of individual cells along each side of a long hall lined with balconies. Windows in both the interior and exterior walls allowed air and light into each of the sixty cells, which were equipped with latrines. From one end of the long hall, a single guard could see all the cells, while a chapel at the other end was visible to all inmates. The boys' house of correction, therefore, corresponded to the ideal architecture later proposed by reformers at the turn of the nineteenth century, which included strict separation of inmates; ventilation and light for a healthy atmosphere; and control by the gaze of the guards (Illustration 1.1).

With its cellular structure, San Michele clearly adopted a monastic model that included prayer, work, and complete silence. During the day, the boys left their cells to gather in the long hall where they participated in the same industry as the "good boys," that is in textile production. Work was considered part of an agenda of reform, an innovative approach to punishment outlined in the regulation of 1703 for the house of correction.[61] This decree began by recalling the failure of the New Prison, despite its special section for children, to bring about moral reform. Instead, inmates in San Michele "would be taught the principles of Christian Life, and learn the Rules of Ethical Living."[62] In return, the boys would receive food, clothes, oil for lamps, and other necessities of life in contrast to the other prisons of Rome, where inmates paid for their upkeep. That reform was clearly the aim of Clement XI is clear from the inscription of the wall proclaiming that "it is insufficient to restrain the wicked by punishment unless you render them virtuous by corrective discipline."[63] This pledge of

Illustration 1.1 Restored interior of San Michele Reformatory for boys

rehabilitation was more ambitious than that on the plaque adorning the New Prison, which simply promised just and mild treatment, although the practice of chaining the boys to their benches while working looked to the past rather than the future. Contravention of the rules, including that of silence, could be punished by whipping at a trestle located opposite the altar.

The House of Correction also differed from the New Prison in the legal status of its inmates, most of whom had already been convicted by a court and sentenced to prison as punishment. Corporal punishment, common for adult men, was now deemed inappropriate for youth, who were considered malleable enough to be reformed and too young for the infliction of pain. San Michele also confined a second category of boys, who were defined in papal documents as "naughty boys and adolescents (*discoli*) who are disobedient to their parents and to others under whose guardianship and care they live, and whose bad morals show a dreadful inclination to Vice."[64] At the request of parents, who were required to pay a daily fee, such youth were interned "to correct and reform them" alongside the boys serving penal sentences. This mixture of criminal and noncriminal minors in the same institution points to the ambiguous nature of the House of Correction, which combined legal and charitable functions.

In 1735, a second prison was opened in San Michele, in this case for women, by Pope Clement XII.[65] Also designed by a well-known architect, Ferdinando Fuga, the women's prison was located next to the boy's reformatory and for the most part imitated its cellular plan. The main differences lay in the slightly larger size of the cells, which were arranged along only one wall rather than two. In several key aspects, the women's prison resembled that for boys and thus can also be considered a modern penitentiary. Established because of reports of immoral contact between the sexes in the New Prison, San Michele was the first Roman penal institution devoted uniquely to women. While the New Prison continued to hold female suspects awaiting trial, San Michele was instead an institution of punishment where women served sentences handed out by the courts of the Governor and the Vicar. Many inmates at San Michele were prostitutes or women punished by the Vicar's court for illicit sexual behavior. That sexual immorality was considered intrinsic to female crime was clear from the plaque erected over the door of the women's prison, in which Pope Clement XII promised "to restrain the licentiousness and punish the crimes of women."[66] Although these words, still visible today from the piazza of Porta Portese, had a harsher ring than the dedication to the boys' reformatory, women nevertheless enjoyed far more comfortable conditions than did adult male convicts. Like the other categories of poor in San Michele, female prisoners participated in the production of wool and learned skills that would be valuable after release. At night, they occupied private cells with windows for light and air. Finally, the dedication of an entire institution to women offered them protection from sexual molestation by male inmates and guards.

Like earlier Roman jails, San Michele was on the Tiber River, a feature of the city that has long remained central to its penal geography. The Castel Sant'Angelo, Ripa, and Tor di Nona jails bordered the river while the Capitoline, Borgo, and Savelli jails, as well as the New Prison, were located only a few blocks from the water. The Tiber, which cut the city in two, was not particularly beautiful but instead had "the hue of a mud-puddle" in the words of Hawthorne.[67] The "yellow Tiber," as it was often characterized, played a central role in an urban economy of Papal Rome where goods were transported mainly by water.[68] The old Ripa jail had been located next to the Ripa Grande, the largest river port of Rome, which handled commercial traffic with Fiumicino and Civitavecchia on the sea.[69] Renovated in the late seventeenth century, the port received a new customs house and piazza as well as the nucleus of the workhouse of San Michele.[70] As only two bridges linked the right and left banks, ferry landings dotted the shore in between large blocks of buildings whose backs hung out over the river. Floating mills, bathing platforms, and archeological fragments crowded the Tiber, increasing the severity of periodic flooding.[71]

San Michele's position on the river, and particularly near the port, facilitated the import of raw materials for its wool factory and the export of the finished product, mainly military uniforms. Some historians have suggested that the river, yellowed by mud and waste, symbolized impurity and its banks a polluted and liminal space appropriate for the confinement of disreputable groups. On the right bank, the Tiber hosted several institutions of charity, including not only the workhouse at San Michele but also the Hospital of Santo Spirito and the Asylum of S. Maria della Pietà, all of which served the poor. On the left bank was the Jewish ghetto, where a growing population was forced to live in a small and chaotic neighborhood that measured little more than two acres.[72] Like the poor, sick, insane, and Jews, prisoners constituted a marginal group that might not have been welcome in the Renaissance neighborhoods around the Piazza di Spagna and Porta del Popolo favored by foreign travelers and artists as well as many noble and bourgeois families. On the other hand, the working classes considered, in the words of Bartoccini, the Tiber to be a "friend" with whom they had "a very close relationship, not only for transportation and work."[73] In that sense, the prisons of papal Rome were integrated closely into the medieval neighborhoods along the river from which many of their inmates came and to which they would return.

Papal Prisons on the Eve of Unification

By the early nineteenth century, the New Prison and San Michele had lost the reforming impulse that had given them birth and had degenerated into the unsavory institutions deplored by political prisoners in their letters and memoirs. Due to the loss of Counter-Reformation humanitarian zeal and alarmed by the challenge of the Enlightenment and liberal nationalism, the popes became more likely to treat prisoners, particularly political dissenters, with intimidation rather than benevolence. In a pattern significantly different from the Foucauldian model, penal law and modes of punishment in Rome underwent little change during the Enlightenment and age of revolutions. Despite the extraordinary establishment of San Michele a century earlier, the popes, who condemned liberalism and nationalism, took no role in the new wave of penal reform that swept England, France, and the United States. The introduction of the Napoleonic Criminal Code of 1810 by the French promised radical legal change but was quickly reversed after the papal restoration of 1814, which looked backward toward the old regime. As the number of arrests increased during the nineteenth century, partially as a result of the escalating repression of liberal opponents of papal rule, Rome became the locus of a chaotic system of penal institutions, a series of bloody executions, and an expanding contingent of forced laborers dispersed throughout the city. On the eve of unification, a jumble of penal institutions dotted the Roman landscape, none of which any longer met the standards of a modern penitentiary.

It was perhaps inevitable that Rome would fall behind Northern Europe and the United States since legal reform during the age of revolutions was inspired largely by the Enlightenment principles of Beccaria. In his famous treatise, *On Crimes and Punishments*, he argued that penal sentences should be only severe enough to deter potential criminals from breaking the law and should never include the barbaric practices of torture, bodily mutilation, or death.[74] Trials should be short and fair, with judges simply applying a public and clearly written criminal code without regard to social class or personal favor. Such a rational system would dissuade an increasingly educated populace from choosing to break the law—or in more philosophical terms violate the social contract—because it no longer represented the arbitrary whim of an absolute monarch but the will of the people. Beccaria's book was eagerly read throughout Europe and the American colonies, where revolutionaries, reformers, and even "enlightened despots" such as Catherine the Great drew on its principles when rewriting criminal codes to make punishment more humane.

The Vatican, however, placed Beccaria's treatise on the Index of Forbidden Books only two years after its publication, because it preached the secularization of justice under lay authorities and the restriction of ecclesiastical jurisdiction to infractions internal to the Church. Such teachings were an anathema to the popes, whose authority was built uneasily on a fusion between church and state and, as absolute monarchs, feared the Enlightenment doctrine of popular sovereignty. They were subsequently alarmed by the demand by Italian liberals and radicals for national unification, a cause that began immediately after the restoration in 1814 and gained force during the following decades with its waves of local revolutions.[75] Thus the last decades of papal rule were characterized more by stagnation than reform in criminal law and by the exacerbation of punishment.

The New Prison and San Michele remained in operation until the death knell of the Papal States, but lost their former spirit of reform and reverted to the chaotic state of those early modern jails that they had replaced over a century earlier. As Elvira Grantaliano has demonstrated, the substantial increase in the inmate population of the New Prison by the early nineteenth century led to the collapse of a system that had separated prisoners and provided them with relatively spacious and airy cells. Instead, violence increased among inmates and between prisoners and guards, while papal authorities exercised little oversight over contractors who routinely failed to supply the New Prison with adequate quantities of food, clothing, and other necessities.[76] Similarly, San Michele lost its original function when the boys were moved to an annex of the New Prison in 1827. The unadorned facade of the new annex, compared to the gracious design of the adjoining New Prison, symbolized the steep decline in papal interest in prison reform.[77] Women also lost their prison at San Michele and underwent a peripatetic journey from one institution to another. Sent first to a new prison at Diocletian's Baths in 1826, they were returned to San Michele in 1830 and definitely transferred back to the Baths in 1850. This frenetic circulation of children and women among institutions demonstrates the absence of any comprehensive planning or dynamic vision for the prison system as a whole.

However, the last forty years of the Papal States finally saw a modest wave of legal reform. The new Criminal Code, issued by Pope Gregory XVI in 1832, continued to rely mainly on sentences of execution, exile, and hard labor for men. Yet, the list of possible punishments now included "detention or reclusion," thus codifying the papal practice of sentencing women and children to confinement and extending it to men convicted of minor crimes.[78] To incarcerate these male prisoners, a penitentiary section was added in 1834 to the hard labor camp at Diocletian's Baths. Thus, the 1830s marks the beginning of a long transition in male punishment in Rome from forced labor in chains to reclusion, one that would extend into the early twentieth century.

Initially, however, conditions for men sentenced to hard labor and reclusion were not clearly differentiated. The "Disciplinary Regulation for the Houses of Punishment" of 1830, the first unified prison legislation for Rome, lumped the two groups together except in rates of pay.[79] The law's preamble promised to lay out "a system of uniform discipline" for the purpose of "reforming and improving the morals of those who are confined, encouraging them more through emulation than fear of chastisement to lead a quiet and industrious life."[80] While the tone of these words was soothing and mild, the law itself consisted for the most part of lists of disciplinary restrictions on inmates: requirements to attend religious services and say prayers (Arts. 5–13); rules for workshops (Arts. 14–16, 43–47); punishments for insubordination (Arts. 19–29, 54–79); and the rigid schedule of daily activities (Arts. 25–38, 42). Other articles charged the prison director and guards with keeping close surveillance over inmates and recording their conduct in a variety of registers. At the end of the regulation, Article 95 resumed the tone of the preamble, counseling directors to use "severity and love" in reprimanding those who had broken the rules and to promise that good behavior might warrant a recommendation for a "Papal Pardon." In many ways the Regulation of 1830 seemed to emulate the goals of the modern penitentiary—humanity, discipline, and work—and to constitute a serious attempt to centralize and standardize the management of Roman prisons. Yet this initiative had severe limits for it permitted the use of chains (*catene al posto*) in all Roman prisons. Furthermore, it exempted the forced labor camp at Civitavecchia, in which the majority of Roman men served their sentences, from implementing the law and thus left its traditional practices intact.

Only after 1846, with the accession of Pope Pius IX, was there any attempt to systematize the Roman justice system. The courts of the Governor, Auditor Camerae, and Capitoline were abolished and their cases divided between new Criminal and Civil courts.[81] Only the Vicar's court, governed by Canon law and with continuing jurisdiction over both clergy and laity, remained independent. In the following year, the reorganization of the papal government into modern ministries abolished the post of Governor completely, creating a Ministry of the Interior to oversee police and prisons. Yet this rationalization came too late to have any significant impact on the chaotic state of Rome's penal institutions before the Papal States disappeared into modern Italy.

Whatever modest modernization occurred during the last decades of papal rule was overshadowed in international public opinion by reports of political persecution and the increasingly oppressive and inhumane conditions in local prisons. Rome became notorious as the scene of a series of grisly and public executions of liberal and republican opponents of papal rule.[82] In 1825, for example, two members of the Carbonaria, Angelo Targhini and Leonida Montanari, were beheaded by guillotine in Piazza del Popolo. According to the memoirs of Mastro Titta, who served as the infamous papal executioner for over fifty years, the enormous crowd filling the piazza turned the execution into a massive spectacle.[83] Such exhibitions of papal repression angered Risorgimento patriots and inflamed the international press. The establishment of San Michele lay far in the past and only Italian unification would make Rome again a center of debate about prison reform.

Reform across the Italian Peninsula

Across the Italian peninsula, the first wave of Enlightenment prison reform inspired debate and some scattered experiments. As the Roman enthusiasm for penal innovation declined throughout the late eighteenth and early nineteenth centuries, other pre-unitary states took up the cause by beginning to discuss and implement Beccarian principles. Despite the vast excitement surrounding the publication of *On Crimes and Punishment* in 1764, only a few moments of penal reform occurred in Italy during the late eighteenth century. Nonetheless, these Enlightenment experiments were significant because they began to curtail corporal punishment and extend the new strategy of incarceration from women and children to adult men. While these initiatives brought little practical change to the lives of most prisoners, who continued to be sentenced primarily to forced labor, they mark an era of transition in which the convent prison was beginning to be reconceived for male prisoners. Architectural innovation characterized several new institutions and signaled the impact of new Enlightenment approaches to punishment.

The first moment of reform took place in Milan, where the Austrian empress, Maria Theresa, authorized the construction of a House of Correction for boys, modeled on the innovative Maison de Force in Ghent, another outpost of the Habsburg Empire. Completed in 1766, this innovative institution, designed in the shape of a "T" by architect Francesco Croce, contained 120 individual cells to provide the nocturnal separation of inmates who, as in San Michele, worked in common to produce textiles during the day. However, the introduction of adult prisoners, not envisioned in the original plan, soon led to overcrowding and the addition of large dormitories.[84] Nevertheless, the Milanese House of Correction, as Dario Melossi and Massimo Paverini have pointed out, represented "a crucial transition in the history of the Italian prison" because it employed adult male convicts—rather than simply the young or the poor—in industrial labor.[85]

Tuscany boasted the second and more influential reform of the Enlightenment era, the promulgation of an extremely progressive Criminal Code. Issued by Duke Pieter Leopold in 1786, this code offered extensive protection for the rights of defendants and, most extraordinarily, abolished the death penalty and other severe corporal punishments such as mutilation and branding. It stopped short, however, of establishing a system of modern penitentiaries and instead retained more traditional methods of punishment including exile, whippings, and public shaming in the stocks. Hard labor became a primary punishment for men, often carrying life sentences in order to provide a substitute for the death penalty. To increase its effectiveness as a deterrent to crime, hard labor continued to be humiliating and painful. Convicts had to wear signs indicating their crime, and recidivists, as well as those sentenced to more than five years, leg chains. Those condemned for life worked in bare feet and a double chain.[86] Thus despite its international fame as one of the most enlightened examples of penal reform, the Tuscan code failed to establish a modern system of penitentiaries to complement its abolition of the death penalty.

The third important eighteenth-century reform came in the Kingdom of the Two Sicilies, where, in Antonio Parente's words, a "rare example in the entire world of a panopticon prison" was inaugurated on the island of Santo Stefano, off the coast north of Naples, in 1795.[87] Designed by the engineer Francesco Carpi, this building was shaped like a horseshoe with three floors of cells visible from a central guard tower. This design allowed the categorization of prisoners (by floor), the use of the tower for both surveillance of inmates and religious services, and lodging for personnel in quarters built across the opening of the horseshoe. Despite its surprising architectural modernity, Santo Stefano became overcrowded within five years; each cell, originally projected to hold three to four persons, now housed up to ten. Increasingly devoted to incarcerating political opponents of the monarchy, during the restoration period Santo Stefano became a symbol of Bourbon repression and backwardness through the writings of famous Risorgimento inmates such as Luigi Settembrini. Yet, as one of the few prisons in the world ever built according to Jeremy Bentham's famous panopticon plan, Santo Stefano shows the remarkable penetration of international debates about prison architecture to the European periphery.

With the Napoleonic invasions and French occupation of most of the peninsula, Italian law changed dramatically. While the importation of the French Criminal Code of 1810 did not entirely incorporate Beccarian philosophy, it nevertheless significantly expanded the number of crimes that incurred sentences of internment in modern penitentiaries rather than corporal punishment. Because of the short and stormy period of Napoleonic domination, however, few new prisons were erected to implement this new legislation.[88] After the restoration in 1815, the Italian rulers without exception sought to return to the legal structure of the old regime although traces of the French influence remained and would constitute the basis for the subsequent crusade for penal reform.

This crusade, which took place mostly in northern Italy, gathered steam only in the 1830s at a time when a surge of prison construction, inspired by Enlightenment principles, was almost complete in Northern Europe and the United States. Inspired by this international movement to abolish corporal punishment, Italy produced some articulate voices whose sophisticated proposals formed the basis for several modern penitentiaries before unification and subsequently for the grand policy debates that quickly followed the establishment of the new nation. The most vigorous and effective critics of the wretched state of their local carceral institutions were Carlo Ilarione Petitti di Roreto of Piedmont and Carlo Peri of Tuscany, both of whom held key government positions and thus were instrumental in formulating practical policy. Less effective in promoting reform but as prolific in his writings was Filippo Volpicella of Naples, who lived long enough to be nominated to an early committee to investigate conditions in Italy's prisons immediately after unification.[89]

Drawing on his experience as an inspector of institutions of charity and punishment for the Piedmontese monarchy, Pettiti di Roreto outlined his recommendations in an 1837 treatise, *An Essay on the Good Governance of Almshouses, Institutions of Charity and Prisons*. He deplored that "in former times, and still today ... different types of prisons are united into one building and have the drawback of inflicting, according to their flawed rules, premature torment on those who do not deserve punishment and should have been freed," that is, suspects in preventive detention.[90] An admirer of the French penal reformer Charles Lucas, he endorsed the general European agenda of separating different types of prisoners (by gender, age, and legal status); providing healthy but spartan living conditions with adequate medical care; offering religious, moral, and general education; and requiring work which he considered "one of the most efficacious means for assuring their reform."[91] A proponent of the Auburn system, he gradually came to accept the Pennsylvania model of strict cellular confinement specifically for inmates awaiting trial or serving short sentences. In this way, those who were possibly innocent or simply guilty of mild misdemeanors would avoid contact with more vicious peers. For Pettiti, moral reform was the major purpose of incarceration and was to be encouraged by frequent visits by chaplains from Catholic religious orders and silent self-examination by inmates of their own consciences. Prisoners were also to have frequent contact with the director, "a person of proven good sense, both shrewd and benevolent," willing "to take care of them like a family."[92] His two-tier model, in which the Pennsylvania system would be applied to jails and the Auburn to long-term penitentiaries, had significant influence on Piedmontese and subsequently Italian legislation.

In Tuscany, Peri similarly criticized prisons of the past although his prescription for reform lay in a thorough application of the Philadelphia system to both jails and penitentiaries. After becoming a prison inspector in 1842, he sought to ameliorate Tuscan penal institutions, which he found in "a state of vileness and squalor."[93] To his horror, "prisoners had continuous and unlimited contact with the Public because the windows had been constructed to make them accessible to passersby."[94] Instead, he promoted the "cellular confinement and complete isolation of convicted criminals mitigated by frequent visits [from administrators] to instill moral reform and certain comforts depending on the severity of their sentences."[95] In his book, *Notes on Prison Reform in Tuscany*, he proudly argued that the new prison law of 1845 had begun to implement his recommendations to centralize the "multiform and incoherent" prison administration, to separate suspects from inmates with long sentences, and to implement the Philadelphia model.[96]

The third reformer, Volpicella, served as advisor to the Kingdom of the Two Sicilies, which issued perhaps the most modern penal code of the restoration states of the peninsula. Its capital, Naples, was the largest city in Italy and a European cultural center during the Enlightenment, boasting an impressive group of intellectuals with a bent toward social science. Like Pettiti, Vopicella was an admirer of Lucas and demonstrated a similarly broad knowledge of international developments in his pioneering work published in 1840, *On Prisons and the Improvement of their Organization*. Although proud that Howard, during his tour of Italy in the 1770s, had judged the prisons of Naples among the best, Volpicella complained that fifty years later "the defect of our prisons lies principally in their ancient, squalid, and cramped buildings which make improvements difficult."[97] Inmates lacked hygienic quarters, including baths, as well as decent food and clothing. Like Petitti and Peri, he was particularly concerned about establishing special institutions for suspects awaiting trial, many of whom might be innocent and therefore merited particularly humane treatment, as well as for women and children. For those already convicted of crime, "prisons should solely aim to reform, by treating the soul no less than the body."[98] To this end, he recommended that work be organized according to the Auburn model and be free of chains, which "cannot be reconciled with penitential education."[99] He also opposed whippings, instead recommending lighter penalties to maintain discipline such as warnings or confinement in punishment cells with a diet of only bread and water.

Petitti, Peri, and Volpicella were representative of a larger group of intellectuals across the Italian peninsula who were in correspondence with prison reformers throughout Europe and engaged in an international discourse inspired by Enlightenment ideals. Through their detailed and erudite books, educated Italians learned about penal reform in both a historical and comparative context; moreover, through their practical work as royal advisors and inspectors, they directly shaped new legislation. That the question of prison reform had gained high visibility by the 1840s is clear from its prominence on the agenda of several early congresses of Italian scientists.[100] Historians of the Risorgimento have emphasized the importance of these congresses in demonstrating how a process of cultural unification helped to lay the groundwork for later political unity. As part of their innovative initiative to work together across the boundaries of the pre-unification states, these scientists debated many prominent issues of the day including hygiene and particularly the health of prisoners.

Although proponents of both the Auburn and Philadelphia models used the congresses of Italian scientists as a platform to advance their cause, no final vote was ever taken to ratify one of them as more fitting for Italy. Petitti's argument that perpetual enclosure of long-term inmates in individual cells could harm their physical and mental health was opposed by supporters of the Philadelphia school, who contended that such problems could be prevented by regular conversations with staff and outdoor exercise in segregated yards. Prestige for the latter argument was boosted by the support of Carlo Cattaneo, a political theorist and Risorgimento patriot renowned throughout Italy. Despite the failure of the delegates to come to a consensus, the debates nevertheless introduced professionals outside of the field of law to the issue of prison reform and aroused interest among physicians, who would become essential figures in the new penitentiaries.

Recognition of the sorry state of Italian prisons and ferment of ideas about models for change inspired what Anna Capelli has dubbed the "age of reforms" during the two decades preceding unification.[101] Modernization of prison legislation, however, characterized only a few states and, even there, was not always implemented in everyday practice. Piedmont and Tuscany made the most progress in renovating their prisons, while the Kingdom of the Two Sicilies implemented innovative but short-lived experiments in prison architecture. Lagging far behind were the provinces of Lombardy-Venice, now directly ruled by an Austrian Empire that had lost all progressive tendencies in its role as the guarantor of the conservative restoration after the Napoleonic interlude. Stagnation in penal thought also characterized the Papal States, thus likening them more to Lombardy-Venice than to Piedmont and Tuscany, with their belated but real attempts at reform, and even the Kingdom of the Two Sicilies.

The Kingdom of Piedmont, under the influence of Petitti, began to implement the Auburn system in the 1840s. Before that, Piedmont had made certain strides in modernizing its institutions of punishment, especially those for women. Giulia Falletti di Barolo, an admirer of the British reformer, Elizabeth Fry, became a tireless proponent of improvements for female inmates, whom she believed deserved moral education in buildings separate from male prisons. In 1821, she was handed private control over the female jail of Le Forzate, an unparalleled power, as Trombetta has argued, for a woman in the early nineteenth century.[102] In 1834, the prison at Pallanza was dedicated entirely to women serving sentences of over two years and, in 1845, the first institution renovated on the Auburn plan was opened for youth at "La Generala." New facilities for men, modeled on the same "silent system," opened in Alessandria and Oneglia in the 1840s. Control over institutions of punishment was centralized and regularized with the establishment of a General Inspector of Prisons in 1849 and a General Board of Prisons in 1851. A shift in direction came in 1857, however, when Prime Minister Camillo Cavour convinced parliament that all jails should be converted to the Philadelphia system of total isolation. Thus on the eve of unification, Piedmont possessed a mixed system that was transferred to the new nation after its monarch, Victor Emmanuel II, was crowned the king of Italy in 1861.

In Tuscany, Peri, Cattaneo, and other proponents of the Philadelphia system propelled a radical restructuring and simplification of the scale of punishment. A new criminal code was adopted in 1853, which required that all sentences of incarceration be carried out in modern penitentiaries. Hard labor and internal exile were abolished. The code also gave official approval to the trend over the previous decades to convert Tuscan jails and prisons to the Philadelphia system. In the 1830s, after the closing of the ancient Florentine prison of Le Stinche, men began serving their sentences at Volterra, women at San Gimignano (later transferred to Lucca), and children at Le Murate, a convent in the capital converted to a house of correction. While all three institutions initially had individual cells for separation only at night, they were reconfigured according to the Philadelphia system after 1849.[103] Dubbed the "system of good company," the Philadelphia model was preferred by Tuscans as a tool of reeducation that was thought severe enough to replace the death penalty and forced labor as a mode of deterrence.[104]

One of the only states in Europe to apply the Philadelphia system so thoroughly, Tuscany pulled back on the eve of unification by decreasing the number of years that each category of prisoner would serve in the confines of a small cell. This partial reversal of policy came in response to an investigation by the physician Carlo Morelli of the long-term penitentiary of Volterra, which provided him with "a real natural laboratory" of a large number of inmates—almost half of those in Tuscany—living in conditions of complete isolation.[105] His devastating report of the multiple physical and psychological maladies as well as high rates of death among the prisoners of Volterra did not completely convince "Philadelphians" such as Peri, but embarrassed the government of the Grand Duke to the point that it devoted one of its last acts in 1860 to softening the ideological purity of its prison organization. This modified Philadelphia model would remain intact until 1889, when Tuscany finally gave up its criminal code and was belatedly absorbed into the national penal system.

Very promising penal experiments also marked the Kingdom of the Two Sicilies, although fears provoked by the rise of Italian nationalism ultimately undercut and destroyed them. In Palermo, the establishment of the Ucciardone prison in 1840 crowned the quest by the monarchy for a "penitentiary utopia," in the words of Giovanni Tessitore.[106] Earlier stages of legal reform had included the promulgation a progressive criminal code as well as the construction in 1821 of a radial jail in Avellino. The Ucciardone boasted a similarly modern architectural style associated with the international campaign to bring health and humanity to punishment.[107] The Bourbon monarchs may have developed this reforming tendency from their close contact with the English who, during the Napoleonic wars, sent troops and advisors to Sicily to protect the king who had fled Naples.[108] These good intentions were reinforced by Volpicella, who, as advisor to Ferdinand II, wrote a sweeping set of progressive "Instructions" for all prisons, which required the classification of inmates; the provision of work and education to bring moral reform; and hygienic, spacious, and comfortable living quarters.[109] But reality did not match the theory of Bourbon prison reform, and, within a few years, conditions in the Ucciardone had deteriorated badly. In 1851, Gladstone hammered the nail in the coffin of Bourbon pretensions to prison reform with his letters denouncing the wretched conditions of political prisoners throughout the realm.

On the eve of unification, only a handful of prisons on the Italian peninsula—mostly in Piedmont and Tuscany—approached the Enlightenment model characterized by cellular confinement (at least at night), work, and rehabilitation. Although law codes in all pre-unitary states had been moderately reformed, most men continued to be sentenced to the death penalty or hard labor, punishments associated with the old-regime principle of retribution through pain. Women and children served their sentences in insalubrious institutions that little resembled the ideal penitentiary as envisioned by reformers such as Pettiti, Peri, and Volpicella. Unlike the nations of Northern Europe, no radical change had occurred in actual Italian practices of punishment during the age of revolutions.

2

The Failed Revolution in Punishment

For Italian patriots of the Risorgimento, the dark, filthy, and tyrannical prisons of the pre-unification states of the peninsula symbolized the larger evils of an outdated political system that they sought to overthrow. They depicted Italian prisons, which were located in dungeons, towers, forts, and convents, as places of torture where inmates lived in dank, dark, and insect-infected cells and were forbidden from reading or writing. Their denunciations of the intolerable conditions of prison life derived not only from abstract principles but also from personal experience, because many had themselves endured incarceration for their political opposition to the absolutist regimes that controlled most of the Italian peninsula. These included the Austrian Hapsburgs, who dominated northern Lombardy and Venice, and indirectly Tuscany; a branch of the Spanish Bourbons, who ruled all of southern Italy, called the Kingdom of the Two Sicilies; and the Pope, who served as the secular monarch of the Papal States, a large swath of central Italy reaching from the Tyrrhenian to the Adriatic sea. Through letters and memoirs, the laments of political prisoners reached a wider European audience that often reacted with shock and sympathy. Britain and France became havens for Italian liberal exiles, whose tales of the barbarity of their previous political confinement contributed to escalating moral and financial support for the liberation of Italians from oppressors reviled as both feudal and foreign. For Italian patriots and their international supporters, the figure of the prisoner in chains came to epitomize the more general repression of civil and political rights throughout the peninsula.

The writings of political prisoners offered detailed and harrowing portraits of prison life that did not spare any region of Italy. One of the earliest and certainly the most famous memoir of political captivity was *My Prisons*, published in 1832 by a northerner, Silvio Pellico. Arrested in Milan for membership in the Carbonaria, a secret political sect opposed to Austrian rule, Pellico served his sentence in a series of prisons including the historic Piombi of the Doge's Palace in Venice and the infamous Spielberg on a mountaintop in the Hapsburg Empire. As Charles Klopp has pointed out, Pellico's widely-read book became a touchstone for future political prisoners not only during the Risorgimento but also into the twentieth century.[1] *My Prisons* was read throughout Italy and Europe as an indictment of foreign rule and a manifesto for Italian independence.[2] This political interpretation derived partially from Pellico's laments about the terrible conditions of prison life, particularly at Spielberg where he experienced grinding hunger, wore legchains, and was permitted outside his cell only twice a week—under the supervision of armed guards—for fresh air.[3] Although the fetters were eventually removed and recreational hours increased after he and other political prisoners fell severely ill, Pellico continued to suffer such extreme isolation from family, friends, and even fellow prisoners that he was frequently brought to tears and periodically to thoughts of suicide.[4] Comparing the Spielberg prison to "a real tomb," he popularized a metaphor that was often employed by later nineteenth-century prison critics, whether they were inmates or members of parliament.[5]

Life in the Mantuan prison of Mainolda was equally harrowing for one anonymous member of the "martyrs of Belfiore," who was subsequently executed by the Austrians for his Mazzinian sympathies. His story was recounted by Leone Carpi in a collection of biographical sketches of Risorgimento heroes. Upon admittance to the prison, the "martyr" was put in shackles after being required to undress *"until nude."*[6] His underground cell, so humid that the floor was muddy, was furnished with only two large pans, one for water and one to serve as a toilet, and a "crude sack filled with straw and a coarse woolen blanket" for a bed. Lunch consisted of "a horrible black broth with some even blacker noodles" in which "filthy worms floated" and dinner of only two small pieces of bread that made him nauseous.[7] To eat the soup, he was given "an old wooden spoon scraped by tooth-marks that were possibly produced by the rage of some murderer who was the last guest of this horrendous prison."[8] For the nine months leading to his execution, he was kept in isolation and allowed neither books nor news of his family.

While political prisoners in the Austrian lands of northern Italy bemoaned their loneliness, those in the southern Kingdom of the Two Sicilies lived amidst a larger group of "common" prisoners, or those jailed for nonpolitical crimes. In a few cases such as that of patriot Luigi Settembrini, the possibility of communicating with fellow inmates betokened larger freedoms. Incarcerated on the island of Santo Stefano, Settembrini and his fellow political prisoners were left unshackled and permitted to buy food from the outside as well as to read and write.[9] More typical of southern prisons, however, was the experience of Duke Sigismondo Castromediano, whose memoirs constitute an indictment of how political prisoners were "unjustly oppressed and persecuted by the anger and cruelty of the Bourbons."[10] Although a moderate reformer rather than a revolutionary, Castromediano nevertheless was interned in a series of increasingly harsh penal institutions characterized by bad air, humidity, insects, atrocious food, disease, and—for most of his sentence—iron fetters. Castromediano described his legchain, weighing 10 kilograms, as "a perfidious snake ... to which you remain subjected for days, months, and years, and from which you cannot be free for a second; a snake so tenaciously relentless that it crushes the intellect and annihilates life when it bites and squeezes with its teeth and coils."[11] He was fettered not simply to his bed, as Pellico had been, but to a fellow prisoner with whom he had to share every moment and every movement. This torment became so central to his memory of his imprisonment that after his eventual escape and subsequent return to Naples upon the completion of Italian unification, Castromediano bought his own chain and took it back as a keepsake to his castle in Caballino, near Lecce.

The practice of shackling prisoners together also typified the hard labor camps of Montefusco and Montesarchio, to which Castromediano was subsequently transferred. In his memoir, he castigates King Ferdinand for instituting "special" penal camps—one of which was in a cave and the other on a mountaintop—that were "more abominable and harsh than regular prisons and to which only a few, possibly the most hated, prisoners were assigned."[12] Contact between inmates and the outside, including immediate family members, was restricted by "dictates that are draconian and more than draconian."[13] Communication took the form of censored letters or visits in which the inmate and his relatives were separated by a double grate and monitored by police. Letter writing was allowed only during certain hours in a heavily guarded room since prisoners were forbidden "any type of book, paper, pen, ink, or other writing instrument" in their cells.[14]

Carpi recounts a similarly appalling story of the voyage of an anonymous political prisoner through a network of the same Bourbon institutions of punishment. After being convicted, he and his fellow inmates were chained together by the wrists and paraded through the streets of Naples to the dockyard, where they were forced to strip, don the clothing of galley prisoners, and then be re-chained at the ankles in strings of sixteen. According to our anonymous author, "Ferdinand II and his wife cynically watched this brutal spectacle from the terrace of the Royal Palace"; he was then shipped to the hard labor camp of Nisida and later those of Ischia, Montefusco, and Montesarchio.[15] When rumors of the horrible conditions of prisons in the Kingdom of the Two Sicilies spread throughout Europe, Carpi's anonymous inmate experienced the attempts of the English to intervene in support of political prisoners. William Gladstone, during a visit to Nisida in 1851, declared himself "profoundly moved to see us treated like the most uncouth wrongdoers."[16] In his famous "Letters" condemning the Bourbon judicial system, Gladstone subsequently gave a detailed description of the humiliating and painful system of chains imposed on prisoners:

> Each man wears a strong leather girth round him above the hips. To this are secured the upper ends of two chains. One chain of four long and heavy links descends to a kind of double ring fixed round the ankle. The second chain consists of eight links, each of the same weight and length with the four, and this unites the two prisoners together, so that they can stand about six feet apart. Neither of these chains is ever undone day or night.[17]

Published widely throughout Europe and the United States, Gladstone's letters aroused international outrage at the barbarity of punishment in the Italian South.

The prisons of the Papal States in central Italy rivaled those of the Bourbons in their sinister reputation. Even foreigners were mistreated according to the French journalist Jean-Baptiste Paya, who was arrested at the port of Civitavecchia and stripped of his passport. In his account of the experience, published in 1865 under the title *The Dungeons of the Pope*, he complained that Roman prisons were run by "papal police and soldiers" rather than "a director, employees, and civilian guards as in France."[18] Locked into a tiny, dark, and airless cell in the prison of San Michele, he had to pay for a mattress with sheets and eat with his hands "like a wild beast" since forks and knives were forbidden.[19] To prevent communication among inmates, the windows of the small cells were covered with wooden boards, making them intolerably dark and stuffy. Having already served a ten-year sentence in a French prison, Paya was not naive about the rigors of incarceration. Yet he concluded that "in total, all the physical suffering of those ten years were nothing compared to that of one night passed in San Michele in Rome."[20]

The experience of Anna Grassetti Zanardi, a Mazzinian arrested for subversive activity, confirmed that prison conditions were equally dispiriting in other parts of the Papal States. In the Fortress of Ferrara, where she was incarcerated in 1851 for thirty months awaiting trial, she lived in complete isolation in a *segreta*, a small isolation cell for dangerous suspects. Her only companion was an enormous mouse, dubbed Maddalena by other inmates, which gave birth to a batch of "microscopic little mice" that scurried over her chest during the night.[21] Although fortunate to have a stove for heat, she almost suffocated from smoke when the guard tried to asphyxiate her—according to Grassetti Zanardi—by refusing to unlock her cell. After a month of daily interrogations, she was moved to even more horrible quarters, a punishment cell (*segreto di castigo*) next to the stables "from which emanated a terrible smell of manure and which was full of scorpions and other disgusting insects."[22]

These testimonies of political prisoners, which constitute only a small sample of a much larger body of similar literature, offer an invaluable glimpse into the conditions of incarceration during the last decades of the Risorgimento. Because the overwhelming majority of criminals, who were convicted for common or nonpolitical offenses, were illiterate under the pre-unitary monarchies, little other first-person evidence exists to illuminate the realities of prison interiors, which were closed and invisible to the public. Political prisoners were not representative of the larger body of inmates because of their small numbers, high social class, and advanced education. Yet they shared prisons, and sometimes the same cells or chains, with common criminals, and thus their writings bear witness to the reportedly deplorable conditions for all inmates. So embarrassing was this portrait of barbaric punishment that unification brought immediate calls for prison reform.

Unification and the "Masculinization" of the Prison

On September 20, 1870, Italian troops opened a breach in the walls of Rome near Porta Pia and, after a short battle, deposed Pope Pius IX as its secular ruler. Retreating to his palace next to St. Peter's Basilica, the Pope proclaimed himself a "prisoner of the Vatican," a telling image for a ruler who had confined so many of his political opponents to the harsh conditions of Castel Sant'Angelo and San Michele. Although he immediately launched an international appeal for the restoration of papal sovereignty, the effort proved unsuccessful, partially because the political factions supporting Italian unification were unanimously agreed that the new nation was hitherto incomplete without Rome as the capital. The capture of Rome was the last step in a series of wars of independence that had begun in 1859 when the Kingdom of Piedmont waged a successful campaign against the Austrians who controlled most of northern

Italy. The liberated regions—which included the papal province of the Romagna—voted immediately to annex themselves to Piedmont. In the meantime, the republican nationalist, Giuseppe Garibaldi, organized a successful expedition to Sicily where he and his "Thousand" volunteers conquered the Kingdom of the Two Sicilies, which he then handed over to his sometime rival, King Victor Emmanuel II of Piedmont. After the official declaration of the new Italian state in 1861, unification was completed by the acquisition of Venice in 1866 and finally Rome.

With the "breach of Porta Pia," Rome underwent a sudden change in status from the capital of a theocratic monarchy to that of a modern parliamentary state. Although Italy had not become a republic as envisioned by Garibaldi and Giuseppe Mazzini, the constitutional monarchy under the Piedmontese royal house possessed the hallmarks of nineteenth-century liberalism: a constitution (the *Statuto*), an elected Chamber of Deputies (although the right to vote was initially limited to a small elite of men), and an administrative structure based on merit rather than birth or, as previously for Rome, ecclesiastical rank. Such a sharp transition to secular sovereignty had significant implications for the Roman legal system including its prisons. Most immediately, it brought the closing of the Vicar's court, which had enforced religious law and disciplined public morals, as well as the hated political prisons at Castel Sant'Angelo and San Michele. More difficult was the task of integrating the remaining Roman institutions of punishment into the national system, which had been managed from the two temporary capitals of the kingdom, Turin (1861–6) and Florence (1866–71). Because conditions varied across the peninsula, the new Italian state faced the bewildering task of consolidating a hodgepodge of penal institutions into a uniform system that would become the pride, rather than the shame, of the new nation.

Urgency to consolidate a new network of punishment stemmed not only from national embarrassment but also from a fear of political instability and even the possible collapse of the newly unified nation. For decades, Italians throughout the peninsula had felt engulfed by threats from paupers, brigands, bandits, and, after 1848, urban workers. As John Davis has argued, the failure of the pre-unitary monarchs to guarantee order was an important factor in attracting members of the ruling classes into the nationalist movement.[23] Such anxieties clearly characterized Bologna, the second largest city of the Papal States, where elites formed a Civic Guard that, in the words of Steven Hughes, became "a rallying point of reform and eventually revolution."[24] In response to rising crime and the ineptitude of papal police, even moderate elites began to look to the Kingdom of Piedmont, the only constitutional monarchy on the peninsula, to lead the wars of unification and subsequently to reform the criminal justice system (Illustration 2.1). That moderates joined republicans in supporting the Risorgimento explains the disagreements within the subsequent national parliament over penal reform and the proper balance between liberty and order. A belief that Italy was prone to lawlessness—and particularly violence—also outlived the promulgation of the new constitution in 1861 and became a negative trope in public discourse.[25] Even as crime rates declined after unification, the conviction that delinquent tendencies somehow defined the Italian character continued to haunt debates in parliament, pronouncements of criminologists, and ultimately the shape of penal legislation.

Illustration 2.1 Anti-Papal cartoon in which prisoners of the Inquisition are freed by "Rome"

With the specter of crime haunting a new and fragile nation, the gendered valence of prisons changed markedly after unification. In the early modern period, women and children had been singled out as the most appropriate subjects for institutionalization. Considered weak and legally inferior, both groups were already the main clients of charitable institutions such as refuges and conservatories that employed enclosure on a monastic model. When applied to the "proto-prisons" at San Michele, this charitable model retained the objective of protection even while emphasizing discipline. In contrast, the proponents of liberal prison reform focused their policies principally on adult men as potential fomenters of social disorder. The nation-state sought new ways to tame the perceived violence of men and harness their energies into productive labor. Sites of production as well as repression, prisons—like schools and the army—were to mold the male worker into the new, disciplined, Italian citizen. As in the rest of Europe, popular sovereignty, despite its pretensions to universality, conferred full civil rights, and potentially the right to vote, on a gendered basis. Thus in the mid-nineteenth century, Italian prison reform became masculinized, with debate and innovation devoted to constructing a new system of male punishment. Women's institutions were left to stagnate, and interest in juvenile reformatories—and significantly only in those for boys—revived only at the turn of the twentieth century.

Thus the history of Italian prisons is less one of Whiggish progress than of a series of distinct moments when a conjuncture of historical forces made incarceration attractive as a means of punishment. In the early modern period, a Catholic culture of charity formed the ideological foundation for the establishment of convent prisons to solve what was perceived as a major social problem, the sexual deviancy of women. Enclosure provided a space for them to regain their honor, that is, the moral purity thought to be consonant with their female natures and their role in society. Within the project of nineteenth-century nation building, men had become the object of resocialization that emphasized a curbing of violent instincts and retraining as productive laborers. Because corporal punishment was now perceived as incapable of attaining these goals, reformers reenvisioned the prison as a laboratory of citizenship. Such a shift is consonant with the more general ethos of the Risorgimento which, according to the analysis of Alberto Banti, thrived on stories of male heroism, honor, and valor.[26] Attributing Italy's supposed backwardness and moral decline to effeminacy, patriots of all stripes focused on the regeneration of men as necessary to win the wars of independence and construct a modern state. In this narrative, women remained in the shadows as passive figures whose only value lay in their ability—as mothers, sisters, and wives—to excite the military spirit of their male relatives.

That the architecture of the ideal male penitentiary closely resembled the earlier convent prison demonstrates a certain continuity between these two moments of prison reform. A cultural heritage that associated monasticism with moral reform and purification led Italian prison advocates to accept willingly the notion that enclosure could change souls. In fact, many overestimated the potential benefits of the Philadelphia model, which was more popular in Italy than in many other European nations. As the writings of Italy's eminent Director General of Prisons Beltrani Scalia made clear, the historical memory of San Michele and other early institutions had not been lost and was indeed a source of pride.[27] Yet, in his tremendous effort to modernize Italy's penal institutions for men, he allowed women's prisons to continue the decline that had begun under papal rule. Instead, men now became the beneficiaries of a new penitentiary ideal borrowed from Northern Europe and America rather than from Italy's past.

Notwithstanding the early and vigorous debates about prison reform, parliament failed to bring substantive legal change—or even integration—to Italy's penal system during the first three decades after unification. Rather than approving a new criminal code or unitary prison legislation, it simply reconfirmed existing law. Although "Piedmontization"—or the extension of Piedmontese legislation to the rest of Italy— was not unusual after 1861, penal law constituted a particularly complicated issue. Because Tuscany refused to give up its previous criminal code, Italy became a nation of two penal systems in which scales and modes of punishment, including imprisonment, differed according to region.[28] Thus, rather than a turning point, Italian unification marked a "failed revolution" in punishment, a phrase borrowed from Antonio Gramsci's larger condemnation of the Risorgimento. He accused middle-class patriots of allying with the traditional aristocracy to protect their privileges rather than implementing a bourgeois revolution that would have injected the Italian political system with liberal values and laid the groundwork for the rise of a vigorous working class. While the general validity of Gramsci's characterization of the Risorgimento has been long debated by historians, it aptly captures the lost opportunity for a radical reform of punishment. Not until 1889 did parliament pass a new criminal code and finally, two years later, a unified regulation for all penal institutions. Italy thus provides a counterexample to the argument that the birth of the modern penitentiary was inevitably linked to the transition from absolutist to parliamentary government. The radical political change across the peninsula occasioned by unification found few immediate echoes in penal law. In the absence of parliamentary legislation, the Ministry of the Interior in Rome scrambled to bring some homogeneity to prison management by creating a new professional class of administrators as well as a working-class corps of guards. Thus, despite failures of legal reform, the national prison bureaucracy participated actively in state building by creating a centralized bureaucracy that reached into every province of Italy and sought to inculcate all of its personnel with loyalty to the new state.

Criminal Law

With unification, the *Statuto* of the Kingdom of Piedmont became the constitution of the new parliamentary state. Issued during the revolutionary era of 1848, the *Statuto* was moderately liberal in its proclamation of equality before the law, protection of personal and property rights, establishment of fairly broad freedom of the press and right to assembly, and secularization of the state. It also introduced a parliament with strong legislative powers made up of an appointed Senate and an elected Chamber of Deputies. During the first few decades after unification, only about 2 percent of the population was eligible to vote because of restrictions based on property, education, and gender. Nevertheless, the bourgeoisie rather than the aristocracy dominated the Chamber of Deputies, and members of both houses were overwhelmingly patriotic supporters of the Risorgimento. United in their determination to equip Italy with new law codes consonant with the principles of the *Statuto*, parliament quickly passed a new civil code, commercial code, and Codes of Civil and Criminal Procedure in 1865 to replace the disparate judicial traditions of the pre-unitary states with national homogeneity. Surprisingly, however, the Italian parliament failed to agree on a new criminal code and thus left the new nation with a patchwork of penal legislation inherited from the past. Piedmont's Criminal Code of 1859, relabeled the Sardinian-Italian criminal code after unification, became operative in most northern and central regions of the peninsula and, with some modifications, in the former Kingdom of the Two Sicilies.[29] Tuscany, however, refused to give up its own penal code, which it considered progressive in its abolition of the death penalty and hard labor and therefore superior to that of Piedmont. Because of strong disagreements between proponents of the two codes as well as political instability that sharpened anxieties about the proper balance between liberty and order, parliament did not approve a unitary Italian code until 1889. This absence of national legislation defining a uniform scale of punishments left prison reformers in confusion during the first three decades after unification. The number and type of penal institutions would ultimately depend on whether legislators retained the death penalty and forced labor or instead replaced them with detention and rehabilitation in modern penitentiaries.

The slow pace of penal reform cannot be blamed on an immature or inadequate legal culture. As Mario Sbriccoli has demonstrated, Italian jurists, proud of their Beccarian tradition, were at the forefront of European criminal jurisprudence during the early nineteenth century. Dedicated to liberal reform and engaged in political debates, the majority strove for "punishment that was at the same time public, rational, certain, secular, and civil."[30] In the decades preceding unification, criminal law became independent of civil law in both the universities and the courts, gaining prestige from its centrality to a larger political project of restraining the overweening and often arbitrary power of the monarchical states over individuals, their families, and their property. An illustrious example of this lively and learned legal culture was Gian Domenico Romagnosi, a Risorgimento patriot who was arrested several times during the early decades of the nineteenth century and finally forbidden from teaching by the Austrians. After unification, younger jurists, such as Francesco Carrara, Enrico Pessina, and Luigi Lucchini, participated vigorously in the prolonged but intellectually rich debates about the drafting of a new criminal code. Because they came from the differing legal traditions that marked the peninsula, these jurists did not initially consider themselves a unified group, although they have been subsequently labeled the "classical school" of criminology. Despite doctrinal disagreements, they supported a common patriotic project of political unification and penal reform.

These liberal penologists, however, had only limited success in influencing the Sardinian-Italian Code of 1859, promulgated on the eve of unification to buttress Piedmont's reputation as a modern state worthy of leading the final wars of unification. Transitional in nature, this code reflected the relatively conservative character of Piedmontese rule. Despite his energetic project to build a modern state and economy during the 1850s, the Piedmontese prime minister Camillo di Cavour feared social disorder and opposition from the republican Left. In criminal legislation, his obsession with perpetuating control over the lower classes and political radicals translated into a penal system still predicated more on retribution than reeducation of the delinquent. Typical of the hybrid nature of the code of 1859 was its complex and confusing list of punishments, which only partially met the demands of liberal jurists for proportionality, rationality, and humanity. On the one hand, penalties were clearly ranked in the Beccarian spirit according to the severity of the crime, and corporal mutilation was abolished. The centerpiece of the code was an elaborate system of modern incarceration divided into four categories: reclusion, relegation, correctional prison, and custody. For most crimes, judges could choose among a clearly defined range of punishments and had the discretion to take into account attenuating circumstances or reduce sentences for accomplices. Conversely, recidivism and "aggravating" circumstances, such as the use of a weapon to commit robbery, could elicit a more severe punishment according to a scale that was outlined minutely in the legislation (Arts. 81–6). This more nuanced scale of punishment represented a mark of modernity compared to the unrelenting rigidity of the codes of the old-regime states. In accordance with the liberal legal doctrine that assigned guilt only to the individual, the Sardinian code also prohibited the extension of minor punishments, such as fines and exclusion from public office, to families of the convicted.

On the other hand, remnants of the past continued to characterize the judicial system. Although internment had, for the most part, replaced corporal punishment, the distinctions among the four overlapping subcategories remained confusing. These subcategories were defined not solely by the length of sentence but also by older notions of degradation that, as James Whitman has argued, pervaded early modern

European systems of justice.[31] For example, serious crime could bring either reclusion or relegation depending on the quality of the crime and class of the criminal.[32] What distinguished one from the other was the degree of shame associated with specific types of offenses and offenders. Reclusion was considered more degrading and therefore imposed on "common" criminals, those who committed violent and property crimes for personal gain. Relegation instead was reserved for authors of political crimes and crimes of passion, who were thought to have acted from a sense of honor or ideology rather than malice.[33] Similarly, those who committed lesser crimes received either "criminal" or "correctional" sentences of incarceration, the first being more degrading but not necessarily longer than the second. This multiplicity of detentive punishments, not clearly differentiated by length of sentence, marked the 1859 criminal code as less than modern.

Even more retrograde, in the eyes of liberal jurists, was the retention in the Sardinian-Italian code of both the death penalty and forced labor. According to Articles 23 and 24, both sentences carried the taint of "infamy" and were to be publicized in broadsheets posted in the cities of the presiding court, the scene of the crime, and the residence of the prisoner.[34] Absent from Tuscan law, the death penalty and forced labor represented the most important stumbling blocks in the parliamentary negotiations over a unified criminal code for Italy.[35] Having abolished the death penalty, Tuscany boasted perhaps the strongest opposition to capital punishment in Europe, a movement not limited to the political and professional elites.[36] Yet the Piedmontese, and later the Italian state, were loath to give up the death penalty without first identifying an equally intimidating punishment for particularly heinous crimes such as treason, brigandage, and homicide. The Tuscan solution of life sentences served in solitary confinement was opposed by many jurists across the peninsula who judged the Philadelphia system too harsh, too costly, or not sufficiently intimidating to prevent crime by the supposedly idle, ignorant, and vicious poor. Forced labor was defended on the less principled grounds that it offered a punishment that terrorized and degraded the perpetrators of the most egregious felonies, who were not thought to deserve the comforts of the modern penitentiary. Chained to each other during the day and to their beds at night, forced laborers were constantly reminded of their disgrace in being sentenced to a corporal punishment with its roots in galley slavery.

The Code of Criminal Procedure, although newly promulgated after unification, was too restrictive of individual rights to please many liberal jurists. As Luigi Lacchè has written, this code was characterized by both "light and dark," that is, signs of progress and of reaction.[37] One sign of "light" was the equalization of procedures in cases involving major and minor offenses.[38] These two categories of offense, originally derived from the Napoleonic code, came to be treated similarly by the courts. Yet, the code was marked by "dark" characteristics, such as the subjection of vagabonds, beggars, and other members of the so-called dangerous classes to preventive incarceration for even minor crimes. An additional indication of the class nature of the code, the concession of "provisional liberty," or release before trial, could be denied to "suspicious persons," most of whom were from the popular classes. Thus judges enjoyed the power to treat differently "gentlemen," whose rights were respected, and "scoundrels," whose poverty alone invited more repressive treatment.

As a result, most suspects remained in jail for long periods, sometimes for months or even years, because of the slowness of the Italian legal process. This paradoxical situation of jailing suspects for long periods or, in the words of Lacchè, of "punishment without delinquency," undercut the liberal principle that suspects were innocent until proven guilty.[39] Furthermore, because pretrial detention was not generally deducted from the period of punishment, even those eventually found guilty suffered injustice under the legal process instituted in 1865. These abuses of preventive custody became a topic of lively debate among liberal jurists, who began to call for a radical revision of the Code of Criminal Procedure immediately after its passage. This campaign, however, was overshadowed by the ongoing struggle to pass a new criminal code, the absence of which delayed the formulation of national prison policy for decades. A new Code of Criminal Procedure was not passed until 1913.

Varieties of Prisons

While theoretical wrangling dragged on about revision of the criminal code, the new Italian state was faced with the material fact that it had inherited a large and tangled web of penal institutions filled with suspected and convicted criminals. Unification brought the immediate release of political prisoners, the most famous of whom were now national heroes and moved quickly into government posts. However, the large majority of inmates were common criminals from the lower classes who continued to languish within the same prison walls. Aware of the dramatic political developments during the wars of unification, many inmates hoped that the fall of absolutism across the peninsula would signal a new era of justice and equality that would translate into release or at least improved living conditions.[40] However, little immediate change occurred despite the revival of debate in parliament over the sad state of Italian prisons and the need for reform. Widespread brigandage in the South, the apparent expansion of criminal syndicates, such as the mafia and camorra, and continued political opposition to the monarchical solution to unification, by republicans and Catholics, raised fears among moderates about abolishing the most severe punishments.

A statistical snapshot of the prison system in 1871 offers a general profile of the inmate population and of the heterogeneity of the institutions in which they were held. This year provides a useful statistical baseline because it marks the completion of Italian unification with the declaration of Rome as the capital.[41] In 1871, prisoners numbered 76,066 out of a total population of 26,801,000 or a rate of 28.4 per 10,000 Italians.[42] Women and girls constituted only 5 percent of all inmates, making incarceration an overwhelmingly male phenomenon. As fewer than 5 percent of the total were assigned to youth reformatories, the inmate population was for the most part over twenty-one years of age.[43]

Rates of imprisonment varied geographically as the new nation had incorporated a variety of diverse regions stretching from the more industrialized North to the predominantly rural South. In 1871, 18 percent of all inmates came from the northern regions of Piedmont, Lombardy, and Venice; 22 percent from the central regions of Parma, Modena, Tuscany, and Lazio; and 59 percent from the provinces south of

Rome and the islands of Sicily and Sardinia.[44] This regional imbalance reinforced the stereotype—perpetuated by the Piedmontese, positivist criminologists, and even many southern intellectuals—that the South was backwards and prone to violent crime. Although further research is needed to explain this geographical divergence in rates of offending, it is clear that jail more frequently constituted a stage in life for southerners than for other Italians.

In 1871, Italian inmates were spread among 353 penal institutions that corresponded roughly with the scale of punishment. For the new state, devising uniform categories for the patchwork of existing prisons was difficult, because the pre-unification monarchies had often employed different terminology for similar types of institutions, and even those with the same names could diverge drastically in their architectural structure and internal organization. The most fundamental distinction was between jails, intended for suspects awaiting trial or serving very short sentences, and institutions for long-term punishment. Jails (*carceri giudiziarie* or judicial prisons), which totaled 252 in 1871, were by far the most numerous institutions of incarceration.[45] Each was located in a capital city of a larger district called a *circondario*, which also served as the seat of a lower-level "correctional court" that tried minor crimes.[46] Because judges were loath to approve provisional liberty before trial, the majority of suspects were held for months or even years in preventive detention.[47] The large number who were interned without having been yet found guilty—almost twenty-eight thousand individuals or 37 percent of the entire incarcerated population in 1871—remained a persistent and illiberal feature of the Italian justice system for decades to come (Graph 2.1). High rates of preventive detention fueled criticism of the Code of Criminal Procedure as too repressive and of the court system as unpardonably slow. Clearly the mass incarceration of individuals who had not yet gone to trial violated the Beccarian principle of the presumption of innocence. There were also material consequences for the families of suspects, most of whom came from the popular classes and suffered loss of income when a member—often the husband and father—was confined for long periods.

Most of the remaining jail inmates were serving short sentences that, according to the criminal code, were not to exceed six months. Yet, because of the absence of sufficient space in penitentiaries and reformatories, many convicted adults and children spent long periods in jail awaiting transfer to the appropriate long-term institutions. This deprived them of work, education, and other programs that were mandated for convicted criminals and available only in penitentiaries. Jails also held small numbers of prisoners in police custody, awaiting transfer or execution, or held for debt. This jumble of inmates made separation difficult according to legal status, age, or length of sentence.

While jails were at least systematized under one designation and spread uniformly across the peninsula, institutions of punishment (*case di pena*) carried a bewildering number of names and were clustered in the northern and central provinces. In addition to the twenty-four hard labor camps, official statistics enumerated the remaining thirty-seven institutions of punishment under a welter of designations: "life-sentence prisons, prisons of reclusion, prisons of correction, prisons of relegation, agricultural prison colonies, prisons for the chronically ill, and women's prisons."[48] All but the last were reserved for men. The forced labor camps remained under the management of the

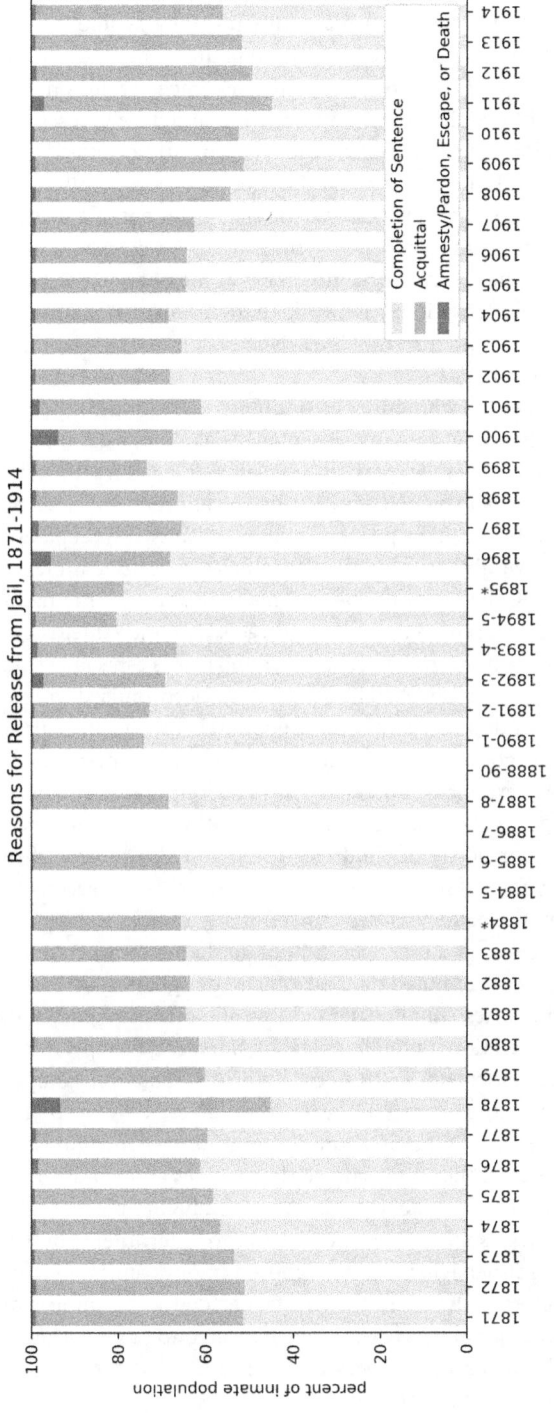

Graph 2.1 Reasons for release from jail, 1871–1914 (with gaps; * indicate irregular six-month periods). Source: Ann. Stat.

Ministry of the Navy until 1866, a reminder that this punishment had replaced galley slavery. Interning 60 percent of all male inmates, they symbolized the premodern character of the Italian prison system.[49] The remaining male institutions, organized according to the level of punishment (life sentence, reclusion, correction, and relegation), were little differentiated in practice and rarely resembled the model penitentiaries of Northern Europe. Instead, they mostly occupied old buildings ill-adapted to the application of new penal theories based on isolation and reform. The only true innovation for male prisons was the establishment of a new corps of guards, who received special training and were promised to be markedly more professional than the often brutal and corrupt prison keepers of the old regime. The reorganization of prison guards into a national network with uniform qualifications and duties signaled a small step toward inserting the prison system into the larger project of post-unification state-building.

Women were provided with only one undifferentiated type of penitentiary despite their exposure to the same diversity of sentences as men. That only 5 percent of all inmates in 1871 were women partially explains the failure to provide the same specialization of treatment which was, in theory, afforded to men. But the absence of any attempt to apply modern penal principles—such as the separation of different types of prisoners within individual institutions—reflects a more general neglect of female inmates. Rather than establish a new secular administration for women's prisons, the Italian state renewed written contracts with the same religious orders that had managed these institutions before unification. This is especially surprising in light of the anticlerical views of most Italian patriots, who promised to wrest power over education, charity, and family law from the Church. Yet, women prisoners seem to have been largely forgotten. The paucity of women's penitentiaries, which numbered only six after the annexation of Rome, necessitated long transfers across the peninsula for women serving sentences of more than six months.

Like women, the majority of children were under the control of religious orders since, in 1871, only four of Italy's juvenile reformatories were directly managed by the state.[50] In addition, the paucity of beds forced many minors to languish in local jails. Thus uniform principles and practices did not guide the incarceration, and promised reform, of children. As connoted by their official designation as "houses of custody," even public reformatories simply detained juvenile offenders rather than seeking to replicate the new educational model typical of Northern European institutions. Both public and private reformatories hosted a hybrid population composed of minors convicted of crime, young beggars and vagabonds arrested by the police, and children interned by their parents. Although the three groups were supposed to be held in separate quarters, in fact they often shared dormitories and workrooms. In 1871, girls made up 14 percent of reformatory inmates, a much higher percent than the 5 percent of women in adult prisons.[51] Girls were liable to internment, by both police and parents, for sexual misbehavior that was ignored in boys and not technically a crime. Reformatory directors, rather than the courts, decided when minors merited release. Thus children, and especially girls who were expected to strive for moral purification, were institutionalized for longer periods than adults, whose sentences were more strictly regulated by the criminal code.

Finally, Italy's web of prisons included penal colonies for persons suspected of being politically subversive or dangerous to society. Located on islands off the southern coast, these penal camps were intended to remove "suspicious" persons from the mainland and force them to develop better habits through work. Because police rather than the courts issued orders of internal exile (*domicilio coatto*), the practice raised strong objections from liberals as infringing on civil rights. Indeed the arbitrary nature of internal exile has led the historian Richard Bach Jensen to dub it Italy's "peculiar institution" that, like American slavery, was an embarrassing anomaly in a liberal society.[52] Because escape was difficult, the *coatti*, as internal exiles were called, were free to wander the island in search of work while remaining under the surveillance of prison officials. That the penal colonies held an ambiguous status within the prison system is clear from their absence from official statistics before 1876. In 1871, penal colonies may have held between three thousand and four thousand inmates as they did in the later part of the decade.[53] Unlike the forced labor camps, that were transferred rather quickly from the Ministry of the Navy to the Interior, the island penal colonies remained under a mixed jurisdiction through two world wars only to be finally abolished with the establishment of the Italian Republic.

The problem of bringing uniformity to this wide network of penal institutions was compounded by the wretched physical state of most of the buildings. In a book titled *Prisons and Prisoners in the Kingdom of Italy*, Federico Bellazzi, a member of the Chamber of Deputies, provided a detailed census that categorized existing prisons by their modernity in terms of both hygiene and architectural adaptability to a cellular plan for the separation of inmates. According to Bellazzi, the new nation had inherited a horrible legacy from the old regime states, with "ancient prisons in towers and guardhouses, at the level of ditches and marshes or even of the sea, not ventilated and often not able to be ventilated, low, dark, sepulchral, meant to be instruments of torture and vendetta rather than of legal punishment."[54] He blamed the new Italian government for failing to make improvements, writing that "our prisons are a real disgrace to Italy, a civilized nation that in the early eighteenth century initiated the penitentiary reform that has been continued by other nations."[55] By recalling the early establishment of San Michele, and Italy's past as a pioneer of rehabilitation through enclosure, Bellazzi tried to shame the government into taking action. Out of 123 jails, he rated only 18 in "good condition" and another 18 "in tolerable condition" and easily convertible to a cellular structure. The rest he found alternately "unhealthy," "badly ventilated," "humid," "insecure," or "generally in sad condition."[56] He pronounced only two of the thirty-five long-term penitentiaries as modern, that is, constructed purposely for rehabilitation through cellular isolation and work, while the others were lodged in castles, forts, and convents that could not be adapted to promote reform.[57] The twenty-four hard labor camps, which were located in former naval yards, forts, barracks, and leper hospitals, were in even worse physical condition.[58] In response to Bellazzi and other parliamentary critics, the government cited a paucity of public funds. But even the Minister of the Interior, Antonio Starabba Marchese di Rudini, admitted that "the state of the buildings are generally defective; most lack security [to prevent escapes] and many are unhealthy."[59] Such an admission by di Rudini, typical of many others by government officials, surely revived traumatic memories for the many parliamentarians who had been imprisoned during the Risorgimento. Yet a broad project of reform was slow to take shape.

Parliamentary Response

The legal disorganization and physical degradation of the nation's penal system incited grave concern within the two legislative houses but resulted in few practical remedies. Initially, the opportunity for debate was circumscribed by quick adoption, by government decree, of the Piedmontese laws on penal institutions. While this maneuver was perhaps necessary to provide immediate guidelines for prison administrators, it reinforced the fragmented nature of the penal network. Following the Piedmontese model, five separate regulations were issued: one in 1860 for hard labor camps; one in 1861 for jails; and three in 1862 for penitentiaries, prisons of relegation, and government reformatories.[60] Although legislation regulating the island penal colonies was not promulgated until 1871, the practice of internal exile was already in practice during the 1860s.[61] Uniformity was further undermined by Tuscany's partial exemption from national prison laws because of the requirements of its separate criminal code. Thus Italy's first prison regulations mainly replicated the past rather than looking to the future. They provided neither a coherent vision of penal reform nor equality of treatment for inmates. State administrators blamed the delays in prison reform on the absence of a new criminal code and the budgetary problems after unification. Yet a wide-ranging parliamentary debate might have produced more adequate legislation and provided a path for further reform.

Having lost their opportunity to write the earliest initial prison regulations, legislators called on the government to institute a special commission to investigate the state of the prison system. In response, Prime Minister Bettino Ricasoli appointed a mixed group of senators, deputies, and administrators that included Giuseppe Boschi, the Director General of Prisons, and Peri, the noted penal reformer from Tuscany.[62] He charged the commission with studying several questions including whether "the punishment of hard labor, as now practiced in the camps, is compatible with civilization today."[63] If the hard labor camps were to be preserved, should they be transferred from the naval to the prison administration and amalgamated with the other institutions of internment? Should the entire prison system be reorganized under the Philadelphia, Auburn, or a mixed model? The final report was to form the basis for a legislative proposal to be debated by parliament.

The commission prepared a careful and exhaustive report in response to Ricasoli's questions although opinions were not always unanimous. The commission's underlying principle of reform was to "restore the repressive and intimidating force of punishment while at the same time offering an opportunity and the means for encouraging the moral regeneration of convicted criminals."[64] Specific recommendations leaned toward the latter of these two, often conflicting, goals. First, the commission voted to abolish the current hard labor camps along with the required leg chains. Inmates would be transferred to new penitentiaries under the supervision of the Ministry of the Interior. Second, in line with the philosophy of Peri, the commission ruled that all prisoners be held in solitary confinement with the obligation to work.[65] Only a few small categories of inmates would be exempted from this Philadelphia model: minors, the aged (over seventy), the sick, the mentally insane, and those convicted of minor misdemeanors punished merely with short "custodial" sentences. One member of the commission, Deputy Giovanni Minghelli Vaini, issued a minority opinion arguing for the superiority of the Auburn system on both moral and financial grounds. Lively debate also ensued about the suitability of northern models of prison architecture for women and southerners. Would women, who were considered delicate and social, and southerners, with their excitable and loquacious characters, be able to adapt to solitary confinement? While the final vote dictated equal treatment and thus the application of the Philadelphia system to all healthy adults, the question of the suitability of Northern European and American models—with their emphasis on isolation and silence—to the Italian character continued to be raised in future decades. On March 29, 1863, the government published the commission's report accompanied by proposed legislation based on its recommendations. However, uprisings in the South deflected parliamentary attention to political affairs and, as a result, the commission's report was never discussed nor was new prison legislation approved.

The only major legislative step occurred the following year when the Minister of the Interior, Ubaldino Peruzzi, proposed the adoption of the Pennsylvania model for all future construction or remodeling of Italian short-term jails. Under governmental pressure, the law passed without wider deliberation about prison policy, which had been requested by several deputies, most notably Bellazzi.[66] Although evoked frequently in parliamentary debates, this law of 1864 had little practical effect because funding was approved for only a few new cellular jails—in Palermo, Cagliari, Sassari, and Turin—during the 1860s.[67] In the following years, no further legislative action was taken to modify the prison system, although the many iterations of the proposed criminal code periodically continued to draw attention to Italy's unreformed system of penal institutions. For example, a commission of 1865 again recommended the abolition of the hard labor camps as part of its proposed revision of the scale of crime and punishment. But no immediate legislative action resulted.

The issue of prison reform remained, however, the subject of lively parliamentary debates in response to the government's proposed yearly budget for the Ministry of the Interior, which incorporated funding for prisons. While this forum was not conducive to the development of integrated projects of reform, it did reveal which issues were of most concern to the legislators. During the debates, the Minister of the Interior was present to answer questions and, more often, rebut criticism of the state's penal policy. In emotional speeches, members of parliament often employed the trope of shame to express their embarrassment at Italy's inability to overcome its feudal legacy of decrepit prisons. For Deputy Guglielmo Tocci, the prison system constituted a "pernicious source of depravity which, like a net, encircles and crosses the whole body of Italy from one end to the other."[68] How could "the fatherland of Beccaria" not find the financial resources to remedy this scandalous situation? Deputy Antonio Arrivabene was especially sensitive to foreign opinion, expressing embarrassment that a recent international congress in London of penitentiary experts had noted "the wretched state of Italian prisons." In light of the history of previous denunciations of Bourbon penal policies by Gladstone and other British statesmen, European interest understandably focused on the southern prisons, which Arrivabene characterized as, more than a decade after unification, still "filthy and stinking pits."[69] For many legislators, comparisons with the Italian past as well as the European present marked Italy as antiquated in its prison policies and more generally in the absence of justice afforded its citizens.

Several other problems evoked the most scrutiny in parliament aside from the terrible physical state of most prisons: legal abuses in jails, the appropriateness of hard labor as an extreme punishment, and the organization of prison work. Jails represented an especially burdensome penal institution for the state budget because of the large number of suspects who had to be housed and fed while awaiting trial. In addition to expense, however, members of parliament denounced the injustice of preventive detention for violating the rights of individuals not yet convicted by the courts. Citing prison statistics for 1871, Deputy Pietro Lacava lamented that twenty-eight thousand inmates or 61 percent of the jail population was awaiting trial and that "it was not rare for some of them to be released years later after being exonerated and found innocent!"[70] Deputy Salvatore Parpaglia compared the poor record of Italy, where most suspects languished in jail for over half a year, to France where preventive detention averaged only three months. He argued that such long periods in jail were "harmful to civil liberty and to public morality because a good citizen, if left for a long time in contact with bad ones, can also become bad."[71] During discussions in 1876 about possible modifications of the Code of Criminal Procedure, Senator Raffaele Conforti declared preventive detention to constitute "the greatest misfortune that can befall a citizen" because it severed relations with his family, interrupted his employment, and ruined his reputation. In response to conservatives who feared for public order, he insisted that the spirit of the proposed law "was not generosity for the guilty but justice for the innocent."[72]

Jails were also criticized for holding large numbers of long-term convicts who by law should have been transferred to hard labor camps, penitentiaries, or reformatories. Deputy Michele Coppino suggested that certain jails be assigned to hold only convicted prisoners in order to avoid "dangerous contact between those who may be pronounced innocent and those who have already been judged criminal."[73] According to Bellazzi, Italy needed eight more long-term institutions of punishment to hold all the prisoners being illegally detained in local jails.[74] Focusing attention on the mixture of minors with adults, he expressed "a sense of profound distress" that 245 children were serving their sentences in jails rather than youth reformatories.[75] He offered the specific example of the jail at Ancona, where eight boys from the ages of 12 to 16 occupied "a large dark room on the first floor" where they languished "without any type of work, without being watched, in tattered clothes, [and] barefoot."[76] Several of the boys had already been convicted while others were awaiting trial.

A second major concern of parliament focused on the hard labor camps, which many members considered a barbaric relic of the past. Calling them "a disgrace to a civilized nation," Bellazzi denounced their organization into large dormitories holding "fifty, eighty, one hundred, and sometimes one hundred and fifty really villainous men."[77] Such overcrowding, so contrary to the modern ideal of the cellular prison, encouraged moral contamination and the spread of disease. Deputy Martino

Speciale was particularly critical of "the horrible punishments" meted out in the hard labor camps, which he considered "an anachronism in our present civilization"[78] (Illustration 2.2). Small acts of subordination could bring severe—and completely legal—corporal penalties such as caning. Despite the passage of the hard labor camps from the jurisdiction of the Ministry of the Navy to the Interior in 1866, the government did not promulgate a new regulatory law abolishing caning until 1878.[79] Yet even after that, the forced labor camps, with their chains, continued to elicit "a certain feeling of shame" among many in parliament until their final abolition with the Criminal Code of 1889.[80]

A third issue much discussed in parliament was that of the organization of prison work. Deputy Coppino voiced the sentiments of many when he declared that "nothing is better than work for redeeming so many souls corrupted by crime and vice."[81] While

Illustration 2.2 Prisoners condemned to hard labor on city streets. Courtesy of the Bibliothèque nationale de France

his conviction that most criminals had not lost all notion of morality and could be reformed was not shared by all deputies on the right, there was agreement about the disciplinary value of work. Legislators also expected profits from convict labor to provide the necessary funds for building new cellular jails and renovating older penitentiaries. Yet, too many inmates, according to Deputy Carlo Italo Panattoni, passed their time in "squalor and idleness" rather than rehabilitating labor.[82] His solution was the establishment of agricultural and industrial colonies where convicts with good behavior could be sent to reclaim untilled land or develop new types of manufacture that would benefit the national budget. While agricultural colonies were popular with many of his colleagues, industrial prison work caused more controversy because prisoners received considerably lower wages than free workers. As in Northern Europe and America, politicians from the Left, who were particularly sensitive to the interests of the working classes, demanded that prison labor not compete with external markets.

It would be inaccurate to represent parliament as unified in its philosophy of punishment or irrevocably opposed to governmental policies. Certain issues, such as the legality of preventive detention and proper organization of convict labor, found members of the liberal Right and liberal Left on different sides of the issue. Conservatives tended to value public order over inmates' civil liberties, and the profitability of prison workshops over the rights of free workers.[83] It would also be incorrect to characterize the relation between the legislative and executive branches as always one of opposition. For example, both Parliament and the Ministry of the Interior wanted to curtail prison escapes, which elicited both embarrassment and alarm.[84] Members of legislative budget commissions could prove even more frugal than the government in their recommendations to reduce proposed expenditures.[85] Nevertheless, the voices heard during parliamentary debates tended to criticize the repressive nature of the prison system and call for reform.

Yet during the early decades after unification, the power of parliamentary critics, mostly from the democratic and liberal Left, was weak and unable to bring significant change in punishment. Early prime ministers, drawn from the ranks of the liberal Right, prized public order and fiscal restraint over building institutions whose beneficiaries were mostly the poor. The horrors of Italy's penal institutions were quickly forgotten by these middle-class statesmen who were no longer threatened by incarceration for their political activities and instead had become obsessed with preserving stability. Only in later decades, when power shifted to the left, would social legislation, such as prison reform, become a focus of government policy.

Constructing a New Administration

In the absence of a new criminal code or unified penal legislation, power over prison policy fell by default to the national Division of Prisons (*Direzione Generale delle Carceri*), established in 1861. Although some legislators recommended that the prison administration be housed within the Ministry of Justice, it remained within the Ministry of the Interior as it had been under the Piedmontese. Placement within the Ministry of the Interior, alongside the Division of Police, signaled that the primary role of prisons was to guarantee social order rather than individual rights. The director general presided over his own offices of inspection, finance, statistics, and engineering, functions that other divisions had to cede to their superiors.[86] That the directors general for the first half-century after unification were all experts in prison affairs only added to the prestige and power of this semi-autonomous fiefdom. As Giovanna Tosatti has pointed out, the prison administration had more continuity and autonomy during the period preceding fascism than any other branch of the Ministry of the Interior.[87] In the absence of a new criminal code, the first director general, Giuseppe Boschi, began to impose a unified administrative network over the disparate institutions under his control. To centralize oversight, he appointed two national inspectors and began to publish statistics on both the inmates and administrators in all penal institutions. As these statistics reveal, Boschi and his successors used their power to create a hierarchical bureaucracy that stretched down to the local level and sought to bring uniformity to the management of jails, penitentiaries, reformatories and, after 1866, to hard labor camps. Thus in the realm of punishment, state building began with practical administration rather than a new penal philosophy.

The national administration in Rome was personified at the local level by the prison warden, who was responsible for internal security, programs of reform, health, and the finances of his institution. In larger prisons, wardens were assisted by deputies; an office staff of accountants and secretaries; and part-time professional personnel such as chaplains, doctors, and teachers. Penitentiaries, reformatories, and larger jails for women and girls were managed by nuns, who were nominally under the supervision of the male warden of a nearby institution. According to law, wardens had sweeping powers over their administrative staff, prison guards, and inmates. But with this power came a series of detailed responsibilities enumerated in the general regulations for each type of penal institution. For example, the Regulation of 1862 for penitentiaries offered minute instructions on how to both keep order and implement the limited rights of inmates. To ensure security, the warden himself was required to read inmates' mail; oversee the cleanliness of their bodies, clothes, and cells; make periodic surprise inspections of the premises to assure that the inmates were in their proper places and that guards were carrying out their duties; punish indiscipline among inmates and guards; maintain proper conduct among the office staff; and manage contractors.[88] In the interest of inmates, the warden had to organize the workshops, school, and infirmary; supervise visits and letters from family members; and maintain the quality and quantity of food as prescribed by exhaustive tables attached to the law. In addition, twenty-two registers were required to document these various duties.

Despite their apparent authority within their institutions, wardens were nevertheless strictly subordinate to their superiors. As Neppi Modona has argued, wardens seemed to lack autonomy in decision-making as attested by the hundreds of letters they sent yearly to the director general asking for clarification of prison regulations. Furthermore, they had to ask permission from Rome to leave the prison premises for even one day. A culture of rigid hierarchy made them wary of judging even insignificant matters in a manner that might anger the central prison administration. After 1877, wardens of jails became subject as well to regional prefects, whose approval was needed to set internal rules for individual jails, hire administrative and security personnel, make agreements with contractors, and operate schools for inmates.[89] Constituting the administrative and political arm of the central state, prefects were powerful and sometimes intimidating overlords of local officials within their district. Thus wardens of penitentiaries and jails occupied an important but sometimes ambiguous position between the central state and their individual institutions.

Not every penal institution, particularly jails, had a resident warden. In 1871 only 31 out of 252 jails had an onsite director while deputies or chief guards managed day-to-day affairs in smaller institutions.[90] Long-term penitentiaries as well as hard labor camps were more likely to have a residential director.[91] The yearly salaries of wardens were relatively high, ranging from 3,000 to 5,000 lire.[92] Clerical staff—secretaries and accountants—were paid much less, although they were middle-class graduates of high schools or technical institutes. Well-educated in a nation characterized by widespread illiteracy, clerks were eligible for promotion to the positions of assistant warden and eventually warden.[93] In 1871, penal institutions employed a total of 211 office workers with jails again being notably understaffed.[94] This pattern of promotion allowed mobility within the white-collar bureaucracy and assured that wardens had experience in prison affairs rather than being simply general civil servants as was common in most other ministries.[95]

Small administrative staffs, typical of all but the largest urban prisons, were supplemented by a host of part-time personnel. Most important, in terms of their professional qualifications and their salaries, were the chaplain and the doctor, who were paid up to 1,800 lire per year. In 1871, the number of prison chaplains employed in the forced labor camps, penitentiaries, and jails was 279, while the number of prison doctors was 362.[96] The central role of the chaplain was consistent with the classical wave of prison reform, which emphasized the importance of religion in encouraging inmates to reflect on their crimes and seek spiritual redemption. Given lodgings in the prison, chaplains held mass and confession on Sundays, offered lessons in moral education, visited the sick in the infirmary, and checked on the condition of inmates, particularly those in solitary confinement.[97] Doctors, who were also key figures in the Enlightenment model of the ideal penitentiary, were responsible for physical hygiene as a context for spiritual cleansing. Charged with oversight of the health of both staff and inmates, the doctor examined the sick twice daily in the infirmary or their cells and oversaw the cleanliness of the prison as well as the quality of the food. Part-time personnel also included elementary school teachers, who were paid very little in the early years, but later became central to the improvement of the youth reformatories and, as a consequence, better remunerated.[98] Master artisans were employed by prisons with large workshops.

The lowest-paid administrative employees were the nuns who managed the women's penitentiaries and the larger women's jails. Receiving salaries of only 200–600 lire per year, nuns worked full-time under the nominal supervision of the male director of a nearby male penal institution. That the nuns were considered marginal to the civil service system erected for male employees is clear from both their low pay and the carelessness with which they were classified in official documents. Sometimes grouped with other adjunct administrators such as chaplains, doctors, and teachers, at other times they were categorized as more lowly guards. Such confusion resulted partly from the wide number of responsibilities they exercised, which included overall supervision as well as everyday security. It also reflected the state's inexperience in employing women and refusal to integrate them into the regular civil service. While their literacy and experience in social work were attributes of the administrative ranks, their subordinate status as women made them an anomaly. Usually referred to as "sisters of charity," the nuns in Italian prisons were affiliated with new and often foreign religious orders that were dedicated to a nineteenth-century model that emphasized the importance of social work rather than monastic reclusion. Despite its more general conflict with the Catholic Church over control of education and charity, the Italian state increased its employment of nuns in female penal institutions after unification, with their numbers rising from 61 in 1871 to 143 in 1912.[99] These totals did not include the even larger number of religious personnel who managed private reformatories for children.

The largest category of personnel was composed of male prison guards, who were organized along military lines. The highest ranks earned no more than the lowest-paid members of the administrative staff and their subordinates considerably less. In 1871, for example, commanders' salaries ranged between 900 and 1,200 lire while that of regular guards was only 560–750 lire.[100] The disparity in pay between the civil servants in the offices and the militarized security personnel in each prison signaled a clear demarcation of class. Unlike administrators who were bourgeois and held at least high school diplomas, guards were drawn from the popular classes and simply expected to have basic competence in reading, writing, and arithmetic.[101] Preference went to men with significant military experience (Graph 2.2).

Guards were required to be young, unmarried and live in a barrack, with only a few hours of free time every day. Subjected to surveillance by both their commanders and administrative personnel, they were liable to a wide array of punishments for breaking any of the numerous rules. The most severe infractions, such as desertion or violent

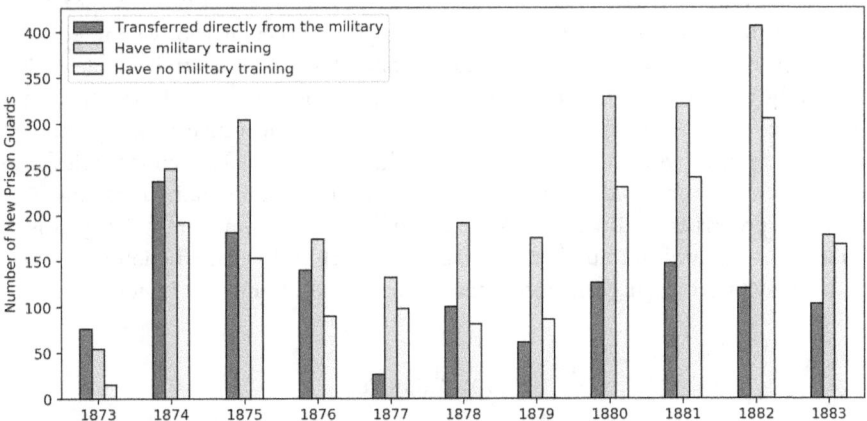

Graph 2.2 Background of New Prison guards, 1873–83. Source: Rel. DG.

insubordination, were tried in military tribunals. Organized like the public security police, prison guards were mainly responsible for order inside the prison while army personnel patrolled outside the walls.

Such severe subordination was partly counterbalanced by professional opportunities not available to the private jailors in the old regime states. Salaries, while low, were at least guaranteed by law, and promotion through the ranks from guard to chief guard to commander was possible after long and meritorious service. Obligated to serve for a term of six years after enrollment, guards held a secure job in an impoverished nation with high unemployment.[102] During a three-month trial period, all guards underwent training in a special school and were required to pass an exit examination. Established in Rome in 1873, the school offered "theoretical and practical instruction" that included elementary education, familiarization with prison legislation; the use of weapons; and the everyday duties within the prison.[103] At the end of their courses, they were examined in each subject before being assigned to a particular institution. While the training was rudimentary, the school demonstrated the commitment of the Italian state to professionalize its prison service. It was one of the few new initiatives that the prison administration managed to complete during the complicated and underfunded period of transition from the old regime to the new.

The female counterparts to male guards had neither the advantages of men's salaries nor their training. Often wives of male guards, female guardians performed mostly domestic chores under the direction of nuns or, in jails too small to support a religious order, the male warden. Female guardians received very low wages, little job security, and no training. Employed mainly to make sure that male personnel did not enter the living quarters of female inmates, female guards never constituted an object of interest or debate within the prison administration or parliament. Their lowly and marginal status attested to a general disregard for professionalizing or incorporating female personnel into the project of nation building.

Centralized in the capital, the prison administration stretched its tentacles throughout the peninsula to create two new public professions: middle-class prison administrator and working-class prison guard. They represented two new groups of civil servants who were to work for the public good rather than private interest, as had often been the case in the pre-unitary states. Subject to centralized legislation regulating the content and conditions of work, prison personnel began to gain a national consciousness which was reinforced in the administrative ranks by frequent transfers from province to province. Across the peninsula, jails, penitentiaries, and hard labor camps employed approximately 338 full-time administrative personnel; 641 part-time professionals (doctors, chaplains, and teachers); 61 nuns; and 4,300 guards.[104] Thus, a not insignificant number of Italians took part in the construction of the new prison system, which, in turn, encouraged their identification with the new state.

Conclusion

The "failed revolution" in the Italian system of punishment after unification showed that the introduction of liberal, parliamentary government was not a sufficient catalyst for prison reform. Many reasons explain the delay in approving new penal legislation by the new state during its first three decades. First, the complexity of integrating the populations of multiple states, which differed widely in wealth, education, and historical traditions, meant that political stability took precedence over other issues. This was especially true in the 1860s, when the government was preoccupied with the acquisition of Venice and Rome as well as the suppression of secessionist uprisings in the South. Second, budget problems were real despite the exaggerated use of financial excuses by successive interior ministers for the failure to institute a large project of prison building. Largely a rural country, Italy was plagued by poverty, and therefore its tax base was weak, particularly in the middle and southern provinces. Third, the liberal Right dominated every government until 1876, and its priorities of fiscal conservatism and social order did not fit well with progressive ideas of prison reform. As Risorgimento patriots who wanted their new nation to copy what was considered the modern policies of Northern Europe, members of the liberal Right were embarrassed by the failure to pass a new criminal code and the worst excesses, such as the hard labor camps, of the prison system. However, they were loath to renounce the repressive tools believed necessary to counter the supposed enemies of the new state, which included southern secessionists (often denigrated as bandits), republicans still loyal to the ideas of Mazzini and Garibaldi, and Catholics eager to restore papal power.

The delay in prison reform, however, cannot be attributed simply to partisan politics because even the early governments of the liberal Left, after coming to power in 1876, implemented little change. The failure to implement the "first wave" of prison reform, already in place in Northern Europe and America by the 1840s, illustrates a general disregard, if not contempt, for lower-class inmates by the governments of both the Right and the Left during the first three decades of unification. Even though many members of both wings of the liberal movement had endured harsh imprisonment for their opposition to the old regime, few identified with the poor convicts who crowded Italian prisons and jails. That the only real progress in using the prison system to "make Italians"—in the famous phrase attributed to the Risorgimento patriot, Massimo D'Azeglio—occurred within the nascent prison administration foreshadowed the general pattern to follow. Rather than parliament, the increasingly powerful directors general would mold the reform movement of the 1890s and the early twentieth century.

3

Prison Consolidation and Reform

In 1891, Italy finally promulgated a comprehensive law for homogenizing and reforming its network of jails, penitentiaries, and youth reformatories. This date places Italy squarely into the second wave of prison reform, which swept the globe in the late nineteenth and early twentieth centuries. Nations that had launched the first wave of reform a century earlier—France, England, and the United States—revised their earlier penal legislation in response to rising rates of recidivism and the beginnings of a movement for prisoners' rights, catalyzed by liberal and socialist movements. Simultaneously, nations in Latin America, Asia, and Africa, as well as those on the European periphery such as Italy, were establishing and expanding their networks of penitentiaries to replace older modes of punishment. What tied these disparate initiatives together was an appeal to the sciences, including biology, psychiatry, sociology, pedagogy, and statistics, for new explanations of the etiology of crime and recommendations for appropriate modes of punishment. Positivist criminology, with claims to empirical methodology, responded with a general prescription to individualize punishment based on prisoners' physical and psychological traits. Such an approach benefitted certain inmates but provided a convenient, pseudoscientific rationale for severe mistreatment of groups deemed biologically inferior according to contemporary gender and racial theories. Italy's experience encapsulates the complex dynamics of this second wave of prison reform.

Why was the Italian prison ordinance passed only in 1891, a full thirty years after the transition from absolute to parliamentary monarchy? The answer to this question lies in a conjuncture of overlapping factors that include a changing political climate, a new attention by the state to social legislation, and the lively debates about punishment engendered by the rise of the positivist school of criminology. In terms of national politics, 1876 marked the "parliamentary revolution" when the liberal Left replaced the liberal Right, which had ruled since unification. Although both parties, as their names suggest, had supported a parliamentary solution to unification, many members of the liberal Left were, or had been, republicans critical of the decision to create a monarchical state under the House of Savoy. Heavily influenced by Mazzinian ideals of democracy and brotherhood, the liberal Left took seriously the problems of the working classes, who experienced little improvement in their economic or social position during the early decades after unification. For the majority of Italians, wages were low, taxes heavy, medical care often unavailable, and education rudimentary. The expansion of male suffrage in 1882 broadened the electorate to include larger portions of the middle and lower middle classes although not yet the poor. Finally, the establishment of the Italian Socialist Party (PSI) in 1892 gave voice to organized industrial and agricultural workers, who had been forming cooperatives and mutual assistance societies during the preceding decade. This new configuration of power, which kept successive governments almost uninterruptedly in the hands of the liberal Left until World War I, created a positive context for the revival of prison reform.

However, the shift in power after 1876 was not enough to secure a unified prison law. It was only during the first governments of Francesco Crispi, from 1887 to 1891, that the state began to turn its attention to social legislation.[1] Formerly a fierce supporter of Garibaldi and a participant in the campaign of "The Thousand" to conquer the South, Crispi switched his loyalties to the monarchy soon after unification. He, nevertheless, remained determined to address the "Social Question," or the inequality between the rich and poor. A sponsor of the reform bill of 1882, which brought the vote to a widening circle of men, he became prime minister with the intent of constructing a national social policy for Italy. While not ignoring internal politics and foreign affairs, Crispi brought his formidable personality and energies to bear on issues that had been ignored during the first three decades of unification and which promised to benefit not only the bourgeoisie but also the working classes. In 1888, he democratized local government by supporting a law that substituted elected for appointed mayors and relaxed the qualifications for exercising the "administrative" vote for this office.[2] In the same year, his government introduced the first national law on public health, which equipped all municipalities with a government doctor responsible for medical assistance to the poor.[3] This legislation complemented a reform bill on prostitution that restricted arbitrary police powers and closed the *sifilicomi*, the lock hospitals for prostitutes that resembled prisons.[4] Furthermore, in response to increasing rates of emigration, Crispi sponsored a bill to impose certain state regulations on the rapacious middlemen who took advantage of poor peasants buying passage to the Americas.[5] In 1890, the state formally recognized its duty to assist the poor more broadly by tightening controls over charities that were often run by the Church in a manner that, according to many in parliament, was corrupt and inconsistent with the secular value of religious toleration.[6]

The Prison Ordinance of 1891 formed an integral part of this astonishing bundle of social legislation pushed through parliament by Crispi and his ministers. While historians have rightly critiqued the bank scandals and repression of political dissent that marked Crispi's subsequent period as head of government in the 1890s, less attention has been paid to his social legislation, which addressed a series of issues that had been debated in parliament for decades and were already subject of state intervention in other European nations. Though less than perfect, this series of "Crispi" laws embodied the fundamental spirit of late nineteenth-century liberalism that aimed for both the expansion of civil and political rights as well as the establishment of a modern welfare state. The passage of unified legislation for all penal institutions signaled Italy's commitment to the international consensus that, at least in rhetoric, condemned corporal punishment and promoted rehabilitation of convicted criminals.

The Ordinance of 1891 fit into a second wave of prison reforms that went beyond the Pennsylvania and Auburn models of uniform penitentiaries to include differentiated penal institutions for specific types of prisoners (juvenile, insane, sick, and alcoholic) and alternatives to incarceration such as parole and probation.

The increasing popularity of the positivist school of criminology, whose origins can be traced to the publication of Lombroso's *Criminal Man* in 1876, reinforced political awareness of the "social question."[7] Established by Lombroso and his two disciples, Enrico Ferri and Raffaele Garofalo, the positivist school was composed of a large and diverse group of professionals that included doctors, lawyers, psychiatrists, and sociologists. Focusing on the criminal rather than the crime, positivists promised to bring scientific methods to the measurement and classification of individuals who broke the law. Rejecting Beccaria's belief in free will, they argued that human behavior, including crime, was determined by biological, psychological, and social factors. Even if criminals were not responsible for their illegal actions, however, the state had the right to punish in the name of "social defense."

Positivists both exaggerated the need for social defense against criminals and called for new approaches to their rehabilitation. Underlying such seemingly antithetical goals was the firm belief that lawbreakers could be scientifically classified as "born criminals," who were biologically disposed to violate legal norms, or "occasional criminals" who simply broke the law because of poverty or other environmental factors. To categorize criminals, Lombroso and other criminal anthropologists examined their bodies and psyches for irregularities, or "anomalies," which purportedly marked born criminals as atavistic and therefore irredeemable. Members of each category—as well as of smaller ones composed of insane, alcoholic, or political criminals—deserved separate types of punishment depending on their biological and psychological potential for reform. Such individualization of punishment led positivists to call for specialized institutions such as prisons for incorrigibles, who were to be locked away from society for life; penal institutions for the treatment of the chronically ill or alcoholic; and criminal insane asylums, to offer psychiatric treatment to mentally-ill prisoners. That most positivist criminologists, including Lombroso, became members of the Socialist Party demonstrates that their theoretical approach, though potentially illiberal in its fixation on biological determinism, was conceived as an instrument of social progress and amelioration. Increasingly prominent as professors, directors of mental asylums, attorneys, and members of parliament, Lombroso and his followers reignited debate over punishment and offered a plethora of practical solutions, many of which were ultimately accepted even by classical jurists who continued to oppose the underlying positivist belief in biological and psychological determinism.[8]

This chapter follows the careers of two long-serving directors general of the national prison administration, both of whom energetically employed their considerable expertise to consolidate and reform Italy's institutions of punishment. The first, Beltrani Scalia, founded the *Journal of Prison Sciences* as a forum on criminal justice in the new state; raised Italy's visibility in the International Penitentiary Association by hosting its 1885 conference in Rome; established the first criminal insane asylums; and, as a capstone to his career, drafted the Prison Ordinance of 1891. His successor, Alessandro Doria, encouraged the passage and implementation of Italy's first probation legislation;

ameliorated conditions in male prisons including the final abolition of chains; and reorganized boys' reformatories along educational lines. Such substantial initiatives defy the common belief that Italian prisons remained backward, immobile, and uniformly dismal for the fifty years after unification. While some remained "tombs of the living," in Pellico's memorable phrase, others underwent significant change and amelioration. On the eve of World War I, the number of prisoners, like the crime rate, had fallen significantly, and conditions had improved for men and boys although female institutions experienced little change.

Martino Beltrani Scalia

As the architect of Italy's prison system, the towering figure of Martino Beltrani Scalia brought prestige to his nation within the international movement for penal reform. Director general for most of the period between 1879 and 1898, he began to shape Italy's prison system even earlier as a young and ambitious prison inspector and continued after the turn of the twentieth century as member of the Senate.[9] After a series of investigative trips throughout Europe, Beltrani Scalia wrote a number of comparative studies that brought him recognition and important roles in the International Penitentiary Association. His prime achievement was the passage of the Prison Ordinance of 1891, a massive piece of legislation that finally unified the regulations for Italian jails, penitentiaries, and reformatories. Not hesitant to wield his considerable power within the Ministry of the Interior, he carried out many of his projects without the consent of parliament and sometimes in direct contradiction to its wishes.

Born in 1828 in Palermo and raised with revolutionary ideals, Beltrani Scalia fought on the barricades against Bourbon rule in 1848 and against Napoleon's coup d'état in Paris three years later. He was briefly imprisoned in the Vicaria prison in 1860, but was soon liberated by Garibaldi's campaign as it swept through Sicily on its way to topple the Bourbons in Naples. Within two years he entered the administration of the new Italian state and moderated his democratic views to include acceptance of the Piedmontese monarchy. Trained in law, he joined the prison administration in 1864 and remained there for the rest of his bureaucratic career.[10] Unlike many of his colleagues in high ministerial positions, Beltrani Scalia did not have a parliamentary career until nominated to the Senate in 1898. He did not, therefore, exemplify the "osmosis" between the political and administrative spheres that Guido Melis has identified as a defining trait of the Italian state during the early decades after Italian unification.[11] Yet Beltrani Scalia shared with other statesmen of his generation a passionate patriotism and dedication to nation building rooted in his active participation in the Risorgimento. Many years later, in 1891, he evoked this historical memory when he promised further reform so that Italy's prisons would not fall back "to the level of the Bourbons."[12] Guided by a pragmatic liberalism, the evolution of his penal philosophy uneasily combined the humanitarian dedication to individual rights typical of his youth with a fierce defense of the prerogatives of his administration and thus of state power.

Journal of Prison Sciences

This tension between liberty and order characterized the ambitious projects that put Beltrani Scalia's stamp on Italy's prison administration even after his death in 1909. The first of these grand initiatives was the founding in 1871 of a new government periodical, the *Journal of Prison Sciences* (hereafter *RDC*) while he was a prison inspector. The *RDC* replaced the *Effemeride Carceraria*, an earlier organ of the Ministry of the Interior, which had been established in 1865 to convey policy from the center to the many penal institutions across the peninsula. Seeking a wider audience outside of the prison administration, the *RDC* invited articles on a variety of subjects such as penal law, criminology, and punishment from specialists in parliament, universities, and other administrations. Its hybrid nature was signaled by its organization into two distinct parts.[13] The official part, the *Bulletin*, constituted an appendix to each volume and reprinted recent laws and decrees directly related to prison management. Its purpose was to inform personnel—administrators, doctors, chaplains, and guards—of new rules and regulations to which they were subject or which they had to implement. The much longer section of the *RDC* was nonofficial in that it hosted voices from both inside and outside the structures of the state. Some rubrics were strictly informative, such as reprints of parliamentary discussions and penal statistics. Others featured articles of opinion by leading jurists and criminologists, sometimes arranged in the format of a debate between opposing views. These theoretical essays were supplemented by clinical analyses of individual delinquents by criminal anthropologists or psychiatrists seeking to explain and categorize "deviant" behavior, often in positivist terms. Such contributions were not subject to censorship by state authorities although at times the editor added a footnote objecting to certain lines of argument. This coexistence of "objective" and "subjective" articles typified the spirit of a journal that thrived on variety rather than unity.

With the *RDC* as his mouthpiece, Beltrani Scalia was not shy about taking clear and sometimes controversial positions on issues that were being debated in legal and criminological journals, in parliament, or even by his superiors in the Ministry of the Interior. His views were showcased prominently in prefaces to certain issues titled "programs" or "letters to readers." In 1871, Beltrani Scalia boldly announced the purpose of the *RDC* to collect and organize of all the "factors of crime ... based on the study of the offender (*l'uomo colpevole*) ... which relate to the methods of punishing and reforming that offender."[14] In contrast to the *Effemeride Carceraria*, he promised that the *RDC* would employ approaches from other disciplines—most importantly psychiatry—to investigate the biological and mental characteristics of "criminal man." The interdisciplinary nature of the journal was conveyed by its subtitle that associated the "prison sciences" with "anthropology, criminal law, and statistics, etc."[15] It was also confirmed by the long list of "contributors" on the *RDC*'s masthead who, while professing to agree with most of its "program," nevertheless came from a variety of academic fields.[16] In addition to encouraging wide-ranging debate among the contributors, Beltrani Scalia reserved the right to criticize his own government for, among many other matters, the slow pace of penal reform, the multiplication of contradictory reports put out by the series of commissions appointed to write a new criminal code, and even the veracity of the statistics published by the state.[17] Proclaiming that "in Italy, it is possible to reconcile liberty of opinion with the duties of public office," he delighted in his dual role as powerful administrator and government gadfly.[18]

In his quest to modernize the Italian prison system, Beltrani Scalia sided, for the most part, with the positivist school by declaring, in the first issue of the *RDC*, that penal reform must be based on the study of the offender. He repeatedly pronounced himself in favor of practical rather than theoretical solutions to penal problems, a stance that recalls Lombroso's rejection of the abstract philosophies of the classical school.[19] Consonant with its identity as a pioneer of positivism, the *RDC* published excerpts of the first edition of *Criminal Man* even before its publication in 1876. Praising its author as a "distinguished psychiatrist," it counted among its contributors not only Lombroso but also other members of the positivist school such as Ferri, Garofalo, Giuseppe Sergi, Lorenzo Tenchini, and Antonio Marro.[20] For thirty years, Lombroso published a large number of articles in the *RDC*, many of which were clinical diagnoses of individual criminals. Beltrani Scalia considered Lombroso's method to be an appropriate model for prison directors and physicians, encouraging them to test his theories—such as the claim that left-handedness was a sign of atavism—on the inmates in their institutions.[21] In 1891, after twenty years of publication, the *RDC* continued to boast about its role as "the cradle of criminal anthropology . . . searching for truth guided solely by the incontrovertible facts."[22]

International Penitentiary Association

Beltrani Scalia's second major initiative, the insertion of Italy into international debates on prison reform, began early in his career. In 1867, while still a prison inspector, he published a long and well-documented historical survey entitled *On the Governance and Reform of Prisons in Italy*.[23] Beginning with ancient Rome and ending with Italian unification, this book argued that prisons were not a new invention but instead had always been employed as a method of punishment. Citing San Michele, he claimed that Italy had taken a pioneering role in humanizing incarceration but lamented that the peninsula had fallen behind in recent decades. While centered on Italy, he made ample reference to developments in other parts of Europe and showed a close acquaintance with the writings of foreign penal experts. This book established Beltrani Scalia's international reputation and won him an invitation to tour the prisons of England and Ireland under the tutelage of the prominent Irish reformer, Crofton. His exploratory trips to study diverse prison systems resulted in a prodigious outpouring of works in comparative penology, which included *The Prison System of England and Ireland* (1874), *The Present State of Prison Reform in Europe and America* (1874), *International Prison Statistics* (1875), and articles in the *RDC* on prisons in Austria, the United States, and Switzerland.[24]

To showcase Italy's past achievements and current commitment to prison reform, Beltrani Scalia took an active role in the International Penitentiary Commission. Elected secretary of the Commission at its first meeting in London in 1872, he became its president in 1880.[25] The most public role of the Commission was to organize congresses, which were held roughly every five years and which addressed both philosophical questions about the right to punish and more practical matters such as the organization of prison labor.[26] Such congresses were typical of the nineteenth-century impulse to address scientific, medical, legal, and other social "problems" through the collection of data and international debate. Beltrani Scalia became a major proponent of the rigorous systemization of penal statistics in both Italy and across international borders. Italy sent increasingly large delegations to international congresses composed of representatives of both the positivist and classical schools. That a wide array of specialists was eager to present papers and engage in cross-cultural discussions with foreign colleagues demonstrates that prison reform remained a central focus of anxiety and debate in Italy.

As a result of Beltrani Scalia's persistence in elevating Italy's international profile, the third International Penitentiary Congress was held in Rome in 1885. Whereas the first two conferences, in London and Stockholm, had been partially funded by private means, the one in Rome was supported by the Italian state.[27] Indeed, the Italian parliament approved a special appropriation for the congress so that, in the words of Senator Augusto Pierantoni, "we can introduce ourselves to the civilized world as a country that cannot yet be proud of past achievements but which has set a path for implementing prison reform."[28] Despite the seeming modesty of these words, Pierantoni reminded his parliamentary colleagues that Italy's history of pioneering prison reformers, such as Petitti di Roreto, Cattaneo, and Volpicella, made Rome a worthy seat for the international gathering.[29] That the president of the planning committee was Leopoldo Torlonia, the mayor of Rome, signaled the desire to showcase one of the newest capitals of Europe.

The opening ceremony, which featured a welcoming speech (in French) by Prime Minister Agostino Depretis and a telegram from the king, confirmed the official status of the event. Held in the new National Fine Arts Exhibition Building, inaugurated only two years earlier, the ceremony purposely drew attention to one of the prominent architectural landmarks of the new Italy.[30] Although its facade was classical, the Exhibiton Building boasted a transparent ceiling of glass and iron similar to the modern arcades being built throughout Europe. According to the official transcript of the proceedings, this "glass room" was thronged on opening night by a large crowd that included "materialists and believers, luminaries of classical penology and practitioners of anthropological studies, ministers and statesmen, philanthropic women, priests, administrators, [and] members of the press."[31] The size of the positivist faction was boosted by the decision to hold a Congress of Criminal Anthropology contemporaneously in Rome, many of whose members—such as Lombroso, Ferri, Garofalo, Marro, and Augusto Tamburini—attended both conferences.[32] But the prominence of the classical penologist Pessina in the planning for the Rome congress also confirmed the wide enthusiasm for prison reform across ideological lines. While women and priests were in a minority, their presence at the conference demonstrated that humanitarian concern for prisoners could bring two groups of political outsiders into discussion over public policy. The opening ceremonies were covered extensively by journalists, several of whom had been invited to serve on the planning committee. This explicit involvement of the press showed the increasing recognition of the importance of public opinion, particularly after the enlargement of the male franchise in 1882.

Accompanying the congress were several side events intended not only to demonstrate the cross-cultural nature of the "prison sciences" but also to highlight the successes, albeit limited, of Italian penal reform. The first was an international exhibition of the products of prison labor. To encourage neighboring European nations to participate in this display of agricultural, artisanal, and industrial objects made by inmates, the Italian government funded a trip by Senator Tancredi Canonico and Deputy Francesco De Renzis to inspect foreign prisons and request the cooperation of their directors.[33] As a result, the exhibit included fashionable garments from France, wrought ironwork from Belgium, pine furniture from Norway, local textiles from Switzerland and Germany, and agricultural products from Hungary.[34] Seventy-three penal institutions from Italy sent products of the labor of male, female, and juvenile prisoners.[35] According to an article by De Renzis in the leading literary magazine, *Nuova Antologia*, the public flocked to this display, praised the quality of the merchandise, and "not long after its opening bought everything ... that was for sale."[36] Conference organizers were clearly successful in drawing popular attention to not only the centrality of work for the rehabilitation of prisoners but also the potentially high quality of their products.

The second exhibition featured a historical survey of prison cells that began with "an exact reproduction of a dark cell" from the medieval Venetian Pozzi jail and ended with "a comfortable little bedroom" of the contemporary Freiburg penitentiary that featured heat, fresh air, a modern mattress, a cupboard, and a toilet. The Italian entries included early experimental institutions that anticipated modern penal principles, such as San Michele, and a few contemporary prisons, mostly from Tuscany and Piedmont, that rivaled their best European counterparts. Marveling at this revolution in the treatment of prisoners, De Renzis invoked the memory of both Beccaria and Pellico whom he surmised must feel "a quiver of joy in their graves."[37] According to Adophe De Foresta, a senator and prominent participant in prison debates, these architectural models constituted "the real *key* to the exhibition, and both foreigners and Italians were astonished to see all the types of cellular systems employed in Europe and America reproduced and juxtaposed in such a clear and precise manner."[38]

In addition to the exhibition, the organizing committee arranged for the delegates to visit several "agricultural colonies," including the Tre Fontane near Rome and Castiadas in Sardinia. Held to represent the newest trend in punishment, agricultural colonies were praised for replacing internment in dark and dank cells with healthy outdoor work—like land reclamation—that would benefit Italy's economy. According to De Foresta, the foreign delegates "were very satisfied with their excursion and never tired of praising the excellent conditions of our colonies and their useful results."[39] The Rome congress thus put Italy back on the map of penal tourism, which drew prison officials and reformers across borders to inspect model facilities. Having once attracted visitors and praise for eighteenth-century establishments such as San Michele in Rome and the Reformatory for Boys in Milan, Italy was now making a bid to regain its place as a showcase of penal institutions.

After 1885, Italy remained active in the International Penitentiary Congresses to which it sent large delegations that continued to include members of both the classical and positivist schools.[40] They were often joined by Lydia Poët, one of the few female representatives at the early congresses. Famed as the first woman in the new nation to receive a degree in law, she had nevertheless been barred from public practice by national legislation restricting women's right to participate in the professions. Beltrani Scalia took a major role in the fourth and fifth congresses, in St. Petersburg and Paris, respectively, but was prevented by ill health from traveling to Brussels and Budapest for the sixth and seventh congresses. In recognition of his contributions to the movement for international prison reform, he was named honorary president of these final two meetings before his death in 1909.

Criminal Insane Asylums

Beltrani Scalia's third major initiative before the passage of the Prison Ordinance of 1891 was to establish Italy's first criminal insane asylums (*manicomi criminali*). Mentally ill criminals constituted a major problem for penal reformers. In prison they received no medical treatment but could pose a threat to other patients if transferred to a civil mental hospital. The positivist answer was the criminal insane asylum, a new institution that would combine the security of a prison with the therapy of a medical facility. Opponents of the idea, many of whom came from the classical school, warned of the potential threat to individual liberties of an institution that, unlike the prison, had the discretion to hold inmates indefinitely until deemed cured. They were most concerned about two groups, which most proponents of the criminal insane asylum wished to intern alongside convicted prisoners: suspects who became insane during preventive detention in jails and defendants absolved of crime for reasons of insanity. From the liberal perspective, the state did not have the right to incarcerate any individual unless pronounced guilty by a court of breaking the law.

Beltrani Scalia had two strong allies in the positivist school and in the emerging psychiatric profession, many of whose members overlapped. Most prominent was Lombroso, who had initiated a campaign in favor of the criminal insane asylum as early as 1865 that continued throughout the five editions of *Criminal Man*.[41] In his writings and public lectures, many reprinted in the *RDC*, Lombroso chided Italy for falling behind England and other European countries that had already established these modern and practical institutions. In his opinion, only the criminal insane asylum could "bring to an end that eternal conflict between justice and public security" evoked by the figure of the insane criminal.[42] Beltrani Scalia also published a series of articles by the prominent psychiatrist Tamburini, who argued for the crucial role of "experienced specialists" in diagnosing criminals during court proceedings and treating them in special asylums. Psychiatrists alone had the expertise to draw the line between "perversity and illness" because "the same degenerative traits" marked both criminals and the insane.[43] Claiming wide support for his position within the psychiatric community, Tamburini called on the Director General of Prisons for the immediate establishment of criminal insane asylums.

In the absence of a general law on mental institutions, the prison administration took advantage of the muddled situation and heeded his call. In a demonstration of the power of the central bureaucracy to bypass parliament, the Ministry of the Interior established criminal insane asylums in Aversa (1876), Montelupo Fiorentino (1886), and Reggio Emilia (1897).[44] Such a daring initiative would have been unlikely without the forceful and obstinate support of Beltrani Scalia and the *RDC*, which offered intellectual cover for a policy of questionable legality. By 1904, when parliament finally gave its approval to the criminal insane asylum, the already existing institutions held a total of 727 patients.[45] That these patients were considered prisoners is clear from their inclusion in government statistics on penal institutions. Under the tutelage of Beltrani Scalia, a new type of penal institution had been born.

Ordinance of 1891

The "Ordinance on Prison and Reformatories" of 1891 represented the capstone of Beltrani Scalia's career. It finally standardized the rules for all types of penal institutions and integrated them into one mammoth piece of legislation. Running to 891 articles, the ordinance was modeled on the much shorter Penitentiary Law of 1862.[46] Both were composed of three sections: the organization and duties of personnel, the discipline and moral reform of inmates, and the financial administration of prison work, procurements, and other budgetary matters. The largest section, comprising about 40 percent of each law, laid out painstakingly detailed procedures for controlling the lives of inmates, embodying what Foucault has termed the "micro-physics of power."[47] That such "discipline of the minute" was written into national law demonstrates both Beltrani Scalia's mania for systemization and distrust of the judgment of his prison directors.[48] The section on financial accounting also demonstrated a creeping bureaucratization as it almost tripled in length between 1862 and 1891.[49] With an appendix of 319 registers to be filled out for each prison, the ordinance required administrators and office staff to devote much of their attention to keeping accounts. The section on personnel actually shrank by 1891 but this can be explained by the proliferation over the years of separate legislation devoted to both the administrative and militarized employees of the public jails, prisons, and reformatories.

The long-awaited passage in 1889 of a new criminal code—called the Zanardelli Code after the Minister of Justice—determined the timing and scope of the Ordinance of 1891. Before 1889, the Italian penal system was bifurcated between the old Sardinian-Italian code, applied throughout most of the peninsula, and the Tuscan code applicable only in that region. The Zanardelli Code not only defined a national scale of crimes and punishments but also signaled the definitive transition from corporal punishment to internment. A testament to the liberal principles of classical jurisprudence, Italy distinguished itself internationally by abolishing the death penalty. Two other punishments were also dropped from the new criminal code: hard labor in chains and relegation.[50] Hard labor was tainted by its association with the cruelty of the galleys while relegation seemed a relic of a feudal past marked by aristocratic privilege. By reducing the poor convict to a type of slavery, in the case of the former, or providing better treatment for "gentlemen," in the case of the latter, these two punishments conflicted with the dominant liberal principle of equality before the law.[51] The resulting list of penalties nevertheless remained complex, as incarceration carried three designations: reclusion for the most serious crimes; detention for milder offenses, and arrest for simple misdemeanors. In general, however, the Zanardelli

Code laid the legal basis for a simplified, two-tiered prison system divided between local jails for preventive detention (and short sentences) and national penitentiaries for long-term punishment. Like Northern Europe and the United States, Italy now defined punishment primarily in terms of confinement for periods of time proportional to the crime. In the words of Sbriccoli, the Zanardelli Code stood out as a "monument to liberalism" in a nation still marked by class hierarchy and limited political equality.[52]

The prison ordinance, however, was a more hybrid document. Formulated during the reigning years of positivist criminology, it built on the classical foundation of the Zanardelli Code but also incorporated a newer paradigm, that of the "individualization" of punishment. If criminals lacked free will, as positivists claimed, then penalties had to be tailored to the specific combination of physical, psychological, and sociological forces that had determined their deviant behavior. Therefore, Beltrani Scalia used his administrative power to move toward a more Lombrosian practice of punishment. By adding a third category of institutions, those for "special punishments," the Ordinance contradicted the principles of simplification and uniformity espoused in the Zanardelli Code. Typical of the second wave of prison reform, it drew its inspiration from the post-Darwinian "medical model," which equated crime to disease and recommended diagnosis and treatment by scientific specialists such as criminal anthropologists and psychiatrists.

Rather than relying on the Philadelphia or Auburn models—the hallmarks of the earlier wave of prison reform—Beltrani Scalia chose the more recent "Irish model" as the centerpiece of his Ordinance. By the late nineteenth century, rising rates of recidivism had dampened enthusiasm for systems that subjected all inmates to a single approach, such as those prescribed by the Philadelphia or the Auburn models. Such uniformity, typical of Enlightenment rationalism, had proven ineffective. Furthermore, increasing evidence indicated that the Philadelphia system, which subjected prisoners to long periods of isolation, was leading to high rates of mental illness. Early in his career Beltrani Scalia had become a champion of a newer "mixed" system that required prisoners to serve the first period of their confinement in complete cellular segregation; the second in nocturnal separation but congregate work; and the third in "intermediary" or low-security institutions with expanded privileges. Graduation from one stage to the next depended on the accumulation of merits, or "marks," earned for good behavior while demerits could return a prisoner to isolation. Invented in the 1840s by Alexander Maconochie, the warden of the English penal colony of Norfolk Island, the mark system replaced fixed sentences by offering early release to inmates who accumulated credits for commendable conduct and hard work. In the 1850s, Crofton elaborated the mark system into a three-tier model that underpinned Italy's Ordinance of 1891. By choosing the Irish system, Beltrani Scalia demonstrated his wide knowledge of international developments and an ambition to adopt the most up-to-date penal philosophy. Thus, to some extent, Italy skipped over the earlier, classical wave of prison reform, characterized by the duel between the Philadelphia and Auburn models, and constructed its first national penitentiary system on the principles that advocated the individualization of punishment as the answer to recidivism.

Beltrani Scalia's conversion to the Irish system dated back to his early writings; in 1868, he dedicated *On the Administration and Reform of Italian Prisons* to Crofton, and in 1879, elaborated on the many virtues of the Irish system in *Penitentiary Reform in Italy*. Believing man to be "eminently sociable," Beltrani Scalia denounced long periods of cellular isolation as simply punitive and debilitating.[53] At best, the Philadelphia system would turn the inmate into a "Trappist monk" when the true aim of rehabilitation should be the "soldier under fire," who possessed the self-mastery to resist evil.[54] Through his metaphor, Beltrani Scalia projected a vision of Italian masculinity that resembled more the citizen soldier than the passive churchman. To accomplish such transformation, the Irish system relied on the "sentiment of hope" that was intrinsic to human nature and would encourage good behavior and hard work for the promise of better living conditions and early release.[55] In response to critics who feared that prisoners would only make a pretense of rehabilitation, he pointed out that dissembling was much easier in cellular isolation. For administrators, "it was indispensable to know the character of a convict," and only the progressive system allowed them to observe how each prisoner responded to the three stages of increasing freedom.[56]

With its emphasis on the individualization of punishment, the Irish system was consistent with the tenets of the positivist school and had already received the endorsement of Lombroso. In general, Lombroso was less than enthusiastic about penitentiaries, which he labeled "schools of crime," as a rehabilitative tool for occasional criminals. He was therefore at odds with Beltrani Scalia, who argued that prison constituted an integral part of western civilization and represented the most advanced type of punishment.[57] But Lombroso also believed that serious offenders must be cordoned off from society and, in that case, preferred the progressive to the cellular model. As he wrote in *Criminal Man*, the Philadelphia system simply "prevents criminals from getting worse but does not in itself improve them."[58] The Irish system, on the other hand, held out the promise of rehabilitation by appealing to inmates' vanity in the rewarding of merits. It constituted "a superb way of making coarse minds appreciate virtue," especially if it held out the possibility of parole, a policy that Lombroso admired in other nations and had long sought to bring to Italy.[59] Because "liberty is the prisoner's dream and constant preoccupation," Lombroso and his positivist colleagues advocated flexibility in sentencing for all but the most atavistic criminals.[60] Thus despite his minor disagreements with Beltrani Scalia about the universal effectiveness of internment, he was more satisfied with the Ordinance of 1891 than with the Zanardelli Criminal Code, which had almost completely ignored the teachings of criminal anthropology.

To implement the merit system, the Ordinance of 1891 required that each city with a prison establish three types of committees to provide oversight. Composed primarily of judicial personnel and community members, these committees were meant to expand protections for prisoners who had been previously subjected solely to discipline by internal administrators and possessed only limited rights of appeal to outside authorities. First, each penitentiary was required to have an oversight committee composed of the district attorney and the president of the local aid society for released prisoners as well as the prison warden.[61] Required to meet at least twice each year, the oversight committee decided which prisoners, based on their accumulation of merits, were worthy of transfer to one of the "intermediate" institutions that formed the last stage of the progressive system. It also reviewed requests for parole, although the final decision was made by higher officials in the Ministry of Justice. While the new oversight committees rewarded inmates for improvement, they had no jurisdiction over punishment for bad behavior, which was left to the discretion of wardens, or in the most serious cases, to internal committees.

Second, in addition to the oversight councils, the ordinance established visiting committees to bring outside observers into the closed space of the penitentiary.[62] Previously, inspections had been carried out by internal personnel, such as Beltrani Scalia during his early career. The visiting committees instead resuscitated the role of early modern confraternities in their mission to certify that prisoners were receiving the services promised by law. Each commission was composed of the local mayor, district attorney or magistrate, and a priest, as well as two ordinary residents of the city. Because women were eligible to inspect female institutions, the visiting committees offered a rare opportunity for female participation in prison oversight. During its visit, the commission was allowed access to the cells, infirmary, workshops, schools, and kitchen in order to assess the cleanliness of the facilities and the quality of food, bedding, and clothing provided to inmates. It listened to complaints of prisoners, including those in punishment cells, interviewed inmates about to be released, and oversaw examinations in reformatory schools.

Prisoner aid societies for released prisoners were a third organization that brought private individuals into the prison. Like the visiting committees, the aid societies had their roots in early modern confraternities and were often managed by a mixed group of religious and lay persons. Few in number during the early decades after unification, the ordinance sought to regularize and expand services for the reinsertion of inmates into society.[63] Concern was greatest for "youth who were orphaned or whose families lacked the means to take care of them or were the cause of their moral corruption."[64] Aid societies assisted children after their release by housing them in their own dormitories, placing them with "honest families," or finding them jobs.[65] Upon request, adults could also receive advice, financial help, and employment guidance from aid societies. Members of the aid societies were granted free access to penitentiaries and reformatories to begin preparing inmates for release up to six months in advance. Although aid societies were private, they were eligible for state subsidies upon presentation of their statutes and proof of their activities.

While these three committees had the potential to reduce abuse of prisoners by introducing external oversight, the Ordinance of 1891 was not otherwise particularly humanitarian. Instead it retained most of the disciplinary measures typical of earlier legislation. Everyday life was regulated by the ringing of a bell and talking was forbidden, even during the hour of recreation, for all but a few privileged groups in the special institutions.[66] Convicted inmates were referred to not by name but by number, which was sewn onto their striped uniforms in a color corresponding to their group of merit.[67] Bands of these same colors—black for those sentenced to life, green for reclusion, red for detention—also marked men's caps and shirts and women's bonnets.[68] In a signal of their subordination, prisoners were required to use the honorific pronoun "lei" with both administrators and guards while they themselves were addressed with the more informal "voi."[69] Admonished to always display "a respectful demeanor" toward their superiors, prisoners were hemmed in by elaborate restrictions on their right to receive visitors or letters.[70] The Ordinance listed forty-two types of bad behavior, including "neglect of cleanliness" and "absence of attention in school," which could subject inmates to a minutely graded scale of punishment.[71] The most severe penalties required restraint by chains or, in a new twist of the law, a straitjacket.[72]

As exemplified by the long list of bad behaviors, the Foucauldian discipline of the minute reached an absurdity in the Ordinance of 1891. While the section on punishments was somewhat counterbalanced by another allowing prisoners certain perquisites for good behavior, Beltrani Scalia's obsession with categorization made the law unwieldy and almost impossible to implement.[73] Sections devoted to punishment and rewards, to wages for work, to the right to receive visitors and letters, and to items permitted to be purchased at the commissary were subdivided by type of institution and classification of prisoners according to sex, age, and frequency of recidivism. Such a bureaucratic nightmare presented problems to even the most sympathetic administrators, who were required to spend more time taking care of paperwork than the prisoners themselves. Some aspects of the Ordinance—such as establishment of special prisons for alcoholic inmates—were never implemented, and others were simply too elaborate to be enforced in older, un-renovated institutions. Such weaknesses opened the new law to widespread criticism and, under his successor, partial revision. Yet Beltrani Scalia's wider campaigns to spark informed debate about punishment within the new nation and to raise Italy's profile within the international community of prison reformers laid the groundwork for more concrete innovations after the turn of the twentieth century.

Alessandro Doria

A second formidable administrator, Alessandro Doria, held the post of Director General of Prisons for most of the "Giolittian era," the fifteen years preceding World War I that were dominated by Prime Minister Giovanni Giolitti. Less well-known than Beltrani Scalia and not as colorful a personality, Doria nevertheless gained admiration for his ability to impose change on the large and unwieldy network of penal institutions. When he became director general in 1902, Doria already possessed deep knowledge of the workings of the national prison system in which he had spent his entire career. Beginning as a low-level clerk in 1870, he had been promoted to the rank of accountant, assistant warden, and warden at the local level before becoming a regional director, inspector general, and finally director general in 1902. This background of career mobility within one administration was unusual in other state bureaucracies but typical of high prison officials who, like Doria and Beltrani Scalia before him, spent a lifetime acquiring specialized expertise. According to Epaminonda Querci-Seriacopi, a later director general, Doria displayed "a youthful enthusiasm and steadfast credo" which brought to the prison administration "a breath of new life and a stimulus for quick and tireless action."[74] Like Giolitti, Doria genuinely sought social reform but within moderate limits and without ideological passion.[75]

After the retirement of Beltrani Scalia, Doria had taken over the editorship of the *RDC* and continued to oversee its production during and even after his term as director general. Proud to follow in the footsteps of his mentor, Doria boasted that the *RDC* still followed "its traditional direction of unbiased eclecticism and of accepting contributions from both theorists and practitioners of any school in a field that is vast and still invites exploration."[76] While the journal did in fact air opinions of both classical and positivist criminologists, it continued to favor the latter. Like his predecessor, Doria emphasized the importance of employing "experimental methods" to study "criminal man in relation to the typical stages of his formation and the evolution of his moral structure."[77] In the positivist tradition that sought the etiology of crime in the biological and psychological makeup of the individual, he emphasized the importance of "criminal clinics" for illustrating the "live and real manifestations" of deviancy.[78] In place of the portraits of criminals by Lombroso, who was now approaching the end of his life, Doria began to publish the transcripts of lessons held by Lombroso's student, Salvatore Ottolenghi. Director of the new School of Scientific Policing in Rome, Ottolenghi sought to identify criminal types by measuring and diagnosing prison inmates in front of classes of guards, police officers, or students at the University of Rome.[79] By emphasizing the practical rather than theoretical contributions of positivism, Doria refashioned the *RDC* to serve less as a combatant in the wars between criminological schools and more as an educational tool for prison administrators.[80]

In terms of policy, Doria continued many of Beltrani Scalia's crusades although with less flamboyancy. These included the passage of legislation in 1904 authorizing the expansion of agricultural colonies for men; the legalization of the existing criminal insane asylums; and the establishment of special institutions for prisoners with tuberculosis and other chronic illnesses. All these measures showed his allegiance to the principle that individualized punishment should be carried out in multiple types of penal institutions. Like Beltrani Scalia and most positivist criminologists, Doria also argued for the abolition of the island penal colonies of *domicilio coatto*, which he considered to be repressive and ineffective. Yet he was no more successful than his predecessor at convincing the state to abolish this police instrument of internal exile.

Despite his frequent praise for Beltrani Scalia, Doria was not blind to the many shortcomings in the Ordinance of 1891 and was a major force behind a series of laws to modify some of its more repressive or convoluted aspects. The most important milestones of his tenure were the approval of probation; the softening of discipline for male inmates, including the final abolition of leg chains; and the pedagogical transformation of boys' reformatories.

Parole and Probation

Parole and probation formed part of a cluster of measures developed in the last half of the nineteenth century to serve as an alternative to the penitentiary. After the first wave of prison building, enthusiasm for Enlightenment ideals of rehabilitation through incarceration slowly cooled in Northern Europe and America. Because of continuing or even increasing rates of recidivism, nations began to search for alternatives to the uniform treatment of inmates under the Pennsylvania and Auburn models. On the one hand, the punishment of recidivists became harsher in the form of longer sentences, more rigid prison rules, or even deportation to overseas penal colonies, such as French Guinea. On the other hand, minor criminals were offered alternatives, such as parole and probation, which would keep them out of closed institutions now thought to promote corruption rather than reform. Lombroso, who held only tepid faith in the reformative potential of prisons, was wildly enthusiastic about these noncustodial measures, publicly praising their reputed success in other nations and lamenting their absence in Italy. Dubbed "penal substitutes" by Ferri, alternatives to prison were promoted by positivists for occasional criminals, thought to be free of biological anomalies and moral depravity, in order to keep them out of contact with incorrigible inmates. While Beltrani Scalia and Doria had much greater confidence in the beneficial effects of incarceration than Lombroso and Ferri, they shared the general conviction of late nineteenth-century criminologists that only the individualization of punishment would effectively decrease crime.

Supporters differentiated the new penal substitutes sharply from the traditional royal prerogatives of pardon and amnesty. Based on a legal tradition stretching back to the Middle Ages, pardon and amnesty allowed monarchs to demonstrate their benevolence by reprieving court sentences of chosen inmates. Both the Sardinian-Italian and Zanardelli codes continued to recognize this executive power by authorizing the king to abolish or commute sentences of either specific individuals or of entire classes of prisoners.[81] Often proclaimed in conjunction with religious holidays or celebrations of royal marriages or births, group pardons lightened the punishment of a large number of prisoners by commuting their sentences. Both classical and positivist jurists tended to deplore this royal power for distorting the rule of law.[82] For the heirs of Beccaria, the practice of pardon decreased the certainty of punishment and violated the sacred axiom that punishment should fit the crime. They feared that the hope of pardon would encourage lawbreaking. For positivists, disparity of sentences for the same crime posed no theoretical problem because punishment was to be tailored to each individual criminal. However, pardons and amnesties did not satisfy their objective of social defense because grounds for pardon appeared arbitrary rather than scientific. Although parliament never abolished the practice of pardon and amnesties, in recognition of both the historical prerogatives of the king and the necessity of retaining a practical method of reducing overcrowding in Italy's jails and penitentiaries, it eventually approved both parole and probation.[83]

A subject of debate since unification, parole, or early release, was one of the few positivist measures to be incorporated into the Zanardelli Code and was in its experimental phase when Doria took office as director general. As early as 1862, the first commission for penal reform had advocated parole, and the Chamber of Deputies revived the issue in 1875 by calling for new legislation. In response, the Ministers of Justice and the Interior introduced a draft law that aroused intense discussion in 1876 and 1877 but never received approval of both legislative chambers.[84] As finally elaborated in the Zanardelli Code, parole was reserved for inmates who had served three-fourths of their sentences and "had behaved in a manner that demonstrated rehabilitation."[85] This general rule was, however, ringed by exceptions that restricted its scope: neither individuals convicted of organized crime, kidnapping, extortion, and homicide nor recidivists in aggravated theft were eligible for parole. Once released, prisoners had to carry a special identity card (*libretto*) with their photograph, notation of their crime, dates of parole, and the legal restrictions on their activities.[86] Intended to assure future employers that parolees had undergone rehabilitation, these "passports" also ironically marked them as members of the dangerous classes.[87] Unlike pardons and amnesty, parole was revocable if liberated prisoners committed another crime or simply breached prescribed rules of conduct.[88] Those who violated parole were returned to prison, demoted to a lower "stage" in the Irish system, and never again qualified for early release.

Proponents of parole tended to align with the positivist school as well as with the parliamentary Left. Arguments for parole were both practical and theoretical. By releasing prisoners before the end of their sentences, the government expected "an economic advantage" that would ease the underfunding of the penal system.[89] More importantly, supporters emphasized the "great moral advantage" of parole, which would offer to inmates "the means by which to redeem themselves through work and good behavior, and prepare their return to free society" by a gradual transition under state supervision.[90] As Deputy Pietro Antonio Fossa pointed out, parole constituted "the last stage of the progressive penitentiary system" that, on the Irish model, began with cellular confinement and advanced to work in common and then transfer to a low-security intermediate institution.[91] The final period of parole, according to Deputy Pasquale Antonibon, would reduce recidivism because ex-inmates, with the assistance of aid societies, would no longer be shunned but instead welcomed by employers and neighbors.[92] By adopting parole, Italy would join the vanguard of modern nations that—like England, Ireland, and many of the American states—had implemented similar polices with good results. The International Penitentiary Congresses, to which the Italian state always sent a large delegation, had also voted in favor of early release for rehabilitated prisoners.[93]

Opponents of parole came mostly from the liberal right and included many, although not all, members of the classical school. For the jurist Carrara, the "certainty of punishment" constituted "an axiom" that protected both individual defendants and society from arbitrary manipulation by the state.[94] Born in the era of absolute monarchy, classical penology sought to curb the executive branch—in this case prison directors—from wielding overweening and arbitrary power over the judiciary. In addition to this theoretical objection, he also questioned the practical problems of judging whether inmates were truly rehabilitated and concluded that parole would be successful only "if the Oversight Committee was composed of angels delegated by God."[95] Yet other representatives of the classical school, such as Pessina, found parole to be perfectly compatible with the Beccarian principle that reform should be the object of punishment and therefore sided with the positivist camp on this issue.

The most vociferous parliamentary critics of parole attacked not the theory of early release but its implementation. Deputy Calcedonio Inghilleri declared that "those liberated today will become the wrongdoers of tomorrow" because the Irish system itself was still not fully functional.[96] Still lacking an adequate number of isolation cells for the first stage of incarceration, of intermediate prisons for the final stage, and of aid societies for released prisoners, Italy was not yet ready to institute parole. Di Rudinì, now a member of parliament, expressed similar reservations despite looking forward to "the triumph in Italy" of the Irish system, "which is vouched for by science and accepted by the most civilized nations."[97] By legalizing parole, parliament would be handing power to the executive branch to release arbitrarily large numbers of prisoners who had not undergone the requisite "period of intimidation" during the early stage of cellular isolation or the later experience of work during the last stage.[98] Proponents countered that parole did not constitute "a right of prisoner" that the state was obligated to grant.[99] They also compared parole favorably to pardon: the latter had the drawback of being "absolute and unconditional" while the former would hold "the sword of Damocles" over the head of the liberated prisoner while he endured "proofs and counterproofs" of his rehabilitation.[100] By 1889, such arguments had gained enough support, even from members of the classical school, to assure the incorporation of parole into the Zanardelli Code.

Upon becoming director general, Doria continued the tradition of Beltrani Scalia by arguing for a second type of penal substitute, probation, or conditional release, as a complement to parole. Passed in 1904, the new probation law allowed judges to suspend the punishment of individuals sentenced to no more than six months of incarceration. Recidivists of serious crimes were excluded.[101] For women, children under eighteen years, and the elderly over seventy, eligibility extended to sentences up to one year.[102] After "a stern warning" by the judge, criminals granted probation were to be set free but subject to arrest, and the completion of the original sentence, if they committed another crime.[103] Those who broke no laws had their conviction erased.[104]

Arguments against probation resembled previous warnings about the hazards of parole but were less persuasive even among classical jurists. Opponents again worried that probation violated the principle of certain punishment and therefore promised to decrease the deterrent effect of the penal code and promote the release of possibly dangerous convicted criminals. Supporters of the law, including Minister of Justice Mario Ronchetti, countered with familiar arguments that probation, after being tested successfully in America and northern Europe, was championed by the International Penitentiary Association.[105] From a practical point of view, probation would lighten the prison budget by decreasing the number of inmates who had to be housed and fed by the state. In theoretical terms, probation, according to Ronchetti, had two aims: "on the one hand, to remove convicted persons from contact with institutions of punishment; and, on the other, to promote and favor their rehabilitation."[106] His arguments prevailed, drawing votes from proponents of both the classical and positivist schools.

Despite the similarity of their underlying philosophy and goals, parole and probation differed greatly in their frequency of application during the two decades before World War I. Parole was granted sparingly. During its first years, between 1891 and 1897, the rate of parolees never exceeded 1 percent of all released prisoners.[107] In a report to di Rudinì, who was now prime minister, Beltrani Scalia pronounced "this percentage really small" and recommended a "wider application of parole."[108] Despite his assurance that the majority of parolees, most notably women, were behaving well, the rate of early release rose only slowly after the turn of the century.[109] In contrast, probation was accepted immediately and granted more liberally by state authorities. According to a parliamentary report by Carlo De Negri, the director of the statistical bureau, the percent of all convicted criminals receiving probation rose from 19 to 26 during the years 1905–7.[110] The rate was even higher for those individuals eligible for probation, that is, those with short sentences and no record of recidivism. Of this smaller group, suspended sentences were granted to almost one-third by 1907.[111] In De Negri's opinion, the effects of the law were moderately positive: it had led to a decrease in the number of appeals in the lower courts and slowed, although did not reverse, rates of recidivism. He was "happy to declare ... that the policy of probation has been received favorably by the Italian judiciary" in contrast to other alternatives to prison.[112]

Several factors explain the widespread support for probation and its quick integration into legal procedures. Unlike parole, it was reserved for convicts with light sentences, who promised to be amenable to reform. Second, judges entirely controlled the process of probation while prison administrators, who were generally less respected and trusted by classical jurists and liberal members of parliament, played a major role in the selection of candidates for probation. Third, advocates such as Lucchini envisioned probation as a policy meant primarily to benefit juvenile offenders who were increasingly becoming an object of both anxiety and pity among specialists in law, criminology, sociology, and pedagogy. Both classicists and positivists were willing to bend their ideological principles in the case of children. Held to be more malleable than adults, juvenile delinquents seemed the appropriate group for experimentation with flexible alternatives to prison. Despite their differing rates of application, however, parole and pardon both contributed to bringing Italian policy into line with international developments in punishment.

Reforming Male Penitentiaries

During his tenure, Doria also instituted a series of important measures for male prisoners, which promised to lighten discipline and expand benefits. Doria was too young to have participated in the Risorgimento, yet he continued to envision prison reform as part of the larger project of building a modern Italian state that would redeem the abuses of the old regime. In 1903, not long after assuming his role as director general, he contrasted the "ancient prison system inspired by the concept of social vendetta" to the "new civilization" of punishment whose aim was "the moral improvement of inmates, their correction and their rehabilitation."[113] In 1907, he claimed that the public was finally devoting attention to the issue of prisons after a long period of "distrust inherited from the barbarism of the old regimes."[114] While this last judgment failed to take into account the class conflict and increasing political polarization of his era, it is nonetheless true that Doria sought to bring Italian prisons up to international standards.[115] Among these was the recognition of education as "less a privilege for the convict than a duty of the state"; the prohibition of transferring prisoners with short sentences far from their families; an increase in pay for prison work; and more frequent visits by national inspectors to hear inmate complaints and oversee living conditions.[116] In a tribute to Doria, Ferri singled out these achievements among the many prison initiatives that had won the approval of Giolitti as part of his program of moderate democratization.[117]

Most dramatic of Doria's reforms was the final abolition of chains for male prisoners sentenced to hard labor.[118] While the Zanardelli Code had eliminated this category of punishment for newly convicted criminals, large numbers of inmates remained in Italian prisons, sometimes for life, serving sentences of hard labor meted out before 1889. As a transitional measure, the penal code abolished the practice of chaining these prisoners in pairs though it continued to require lighter shackles on their left leg.[119] In 1902, Doria sought and received Giolitti's support for erasing, in his words, one of those "ancient practices" that was incompatible with the Ordinance of 1891.[120] Although this "humanitarian benefit" affected only a minority of prisoners, it carried heavy symbolic weight. Chains evoked the historical memory of the plight of imprisoned Risorgimento patriots. As an "intolerable vestige of ancient, inhumane, and cruel barbarism," in the words of Querci-Seriacopi, they also represented Italy's failure to modernize its prison system immediately after unification.[121]

A year later, the government issued a second decree to further reduce physical restraints on inmates, in this case the use of straitjackets and fetters as modes of internal punishment for breaching prison rules.[122] In his report to the prime minister, Doria presented this reform as a logical extension of the abolition of chains for hard laborers and a further sign that Italy had overcome the vindictive justice of the pre-unification states. Realism rather than idealism, however, explained the timing of the decree. The immediate impetus came from the death of a straitjacketed prisoner several months earlier, in the "D'Angelo case," which had caused public outcry and led to the appointment of a government commission.[123] After finding the Ordinance of 1891 "excessively strict and burdensome," the Commission, which included Doria, recommended modifications that would "decrease, as much as possible, the intensity and the length of punishments" meted out within penitentiaries.[124] The resulting decree of 1903, in addition to abolishing straitjackets and chains, eased penalties moderately for men and more markedly for women and children. Ill and pregnant inmates became exempt from the most serious chastisements, including long periods of cellular confinement and diets of bread and water.

Although Doria promised to eliminate "every instrument of bodily coercion and physical torture" from the prison experience, the 1903 decree retained the use of "security belts" to restrain violent inmates who exhibited "momentary psychological exaltation" or "deliberate attempts at open rebellion."[125] While smaller than straitjackets, security belts nevertheless constituted a type of physical restraint. The use of a security belt had to be approved, on a case by case basis, by the prison physician while the imposition of cellular isolation on women and children also became a medical decision. Many legal experts, such as Ferri, applauded Doria for enhancing the authority of prison doctors over decisions regarding prison discipline.[126] Yet their power continued to be circumscribed by the elaborate scale of punishment controlled principally by the warden.

Juvenile Reformatories

In 1904, Doria began the most fundamental reform of his tenure as director general, the overhaul of penal institutions for minors. He could rely on support from Giolitti as well as many in parliament, such as Deputy Pilade Mazza who warned in 1902 that "an innumerable army of abandoned adolescents are growing up in the poisoned atmosphere of the streets and tomorrow will become the advanced contingent of a phalanx of habitual criminals."[127] Mazza's use of the label "habitual criminal" echoed criminal anthropology, which taught that bad environment could turn even normal children into occasional criminals and finally into such severe recidivists that they would be unable to break the habit of crime.[128] Yet at the turn of the twentieth century, children evoked not only fear but also sympathy. A host of professionals—criminologists, lawyers, doctors, sociologists, and pioneers in the new field of pedagogy—began to draw public attention to the plight of children who were neglected, abandoned, or even abused by their families. These "childsavers," as Anthony Platt has called their American counterparts, called for state intervention to rescue helpless but potentially delinquent children.[129] In the context of this early international movement for children's rights, juvenile reformatories became, as they had in the early modern period, a focus of public attention.

Doria took advantage of this new climate of opinion to implement an idea that had been discussed for several decades: the conversion of reformatories from prisons into schools. In 1877, the first prime minister of the Left liberals, Giovanni Nicotera, had taken a small step toward this goal by promulgating legislation to bolster the role of education and training in houses of custody.[130] Yet, as denoted by their names, these institutions continued to emphasize simple detention rather than reform and were staffed mostly by the same type of personnel assigned to other prisons. Doria went much further by beginning to detach reformatories from the prison system. According to a law passed in 1904, primary school teachers were to replace prison guards in all government reformatories; their main duty, in addition to maintaining order, was to train children in skills that would turn them into useful citizens.[131] A second law of 1907 promised future courses in criminal law, pedagogy, and "the elementary principles of anthropology" for the purpose of further specializing the training of reformatory instructors.[132] This incorporation of positivism into teacher training was one small sign of the larger influence of Lombrosian theory on the prison administration. In the same year, a new regulation for the internal management of reformatories completed their administrative separation from adult prisons.[133]

Doria's reorganization of youth reformatories constituted the most radical innovation in Italy's prison system during the fifty years after Italian unification and received international recognition for privileging the reform of children over their punishment. Yet, his packet of legislation was not as sweeping as he boasted in several ways. First, girls were excluded in practice because they were interned in reformatories managed by religious orders rather than the state. Second, public reformatories had the capacity to admit only about half of the male juvenile population; the rest remained, like girls, in private reformatories. Third, only two groups of male youth—those interned by their parents and those arrested as vagabonds—were eligible for admission to the new reformatories. Minors convicted of more serious crimes were considered sources of moral contamination and therefore excluded.[134] While it seems curious that the group most in need of reform, convicted adolescents, were left in the traditional houses of custody, Doria's legislation was consistent with the positivist warning that children who continued to display deviant behavior after puberty were either born or habitual criminals.

Finally, the absence of space in the new government reformatories further circumscribed the impact of the reforms. In 1909, Alessandro Stoppato complained that nine thousand minors remained in adult penitentiaries and therefore in contact with "assassins, thieves, pimps, swindlers, and similar filth."[135] On the eve of World War I, another member of parliament, Camillo Peano, estimated that over two thousand youth still remained in regular prisons.[136] Such limitations on the practical implementation of the reformatory philosophy were a reminder of the ambiguous status of even the most exemplary juvenile institutions, which remained under the jurisdiction of the Division of Prisons. Although staffed by teachers and offering a wide choice of educational and professional training, even the best children's institutions employed the principles of enclosure and discipline typical of the adult penitentiary. Therefore children, while enjoying improved conditions, remained in the web of incarceration.

In 1912, Doria left his post as director general after being nominated, as had Beltrani Scalia before him, to the Council of State. He continued to be involved in prison affairs, however, by editing the *RDC* until his death in 1925. Before departing, he prepared the draft of a new prison ordinance to replace that of 1891, but with the advent of the colonial campaign against Libya and then World War I, it was never approved.[137] Doria's retirement ended an era when directors general came up through the ranks and therefore possessed a specialized knowledge of penal law and practice; instead, their successors most often came from the post of prefect.[138] Nevertheless, the era of Beltrani Scalia/Doria defined many of the characteristics that persisted into the interwar period of fascism. The central administration would continue to shape prison policy with only short periods of legislative interventions such as the appointment of an investigative parliamentary commission in the immediate years after World War I.[139] By 1926, the fascist dictatorship, which reintroduced the death penalty, had eliminated any pretense of democratic debate about appropriate methods of punishment. Beltrani Scalia and Doria, both liberal in political outlook, would have deplored many fascist penal policies but their preference for bypassing the legislature and imposing change by executive decree left a legacy that was congenial to a fascist regime unwilling to tolerate public debate about institutions of punishment.

Prisons on the Eve of War

In 1914, the year before Italy entered World War I, the general outlines of Italy's penal system exhibited both continuities and change from the baseline year of 1871. The total number of inmates had decreased dramatically from 76,066 to 41,755.[140] This 45 percent drop paralleled the uneven but clear decline in crime rates over the period,

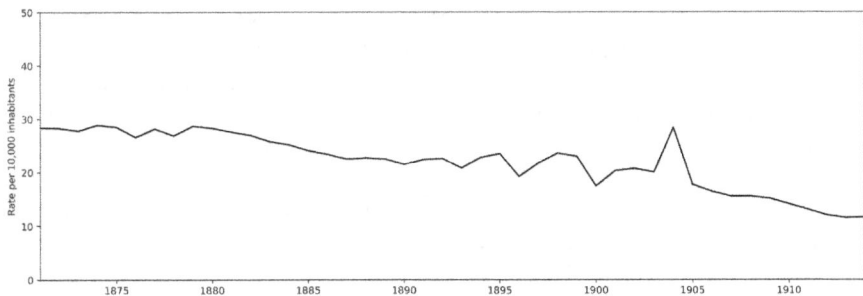

Graph 3.1 Total number of prisoners in Italy, 1871–1914. Source: Ann. Stat.

especially in homicide and other felonies.[141] The establishment of parole in 1889 and probation in 1904 also lowered the rates of incarceration by freeing minor criminals on good behavior. This striking decrease in rates of incarceration between 1871 and 1914—from 28 to 12 per 10,000 inhabitants—did not significantly shift the ratio of men to women or adults to youth in penal institutions[142] (Graph 3.1).

While women remained a distinct minority of the inmate population, their share increased from 5 to 9 percent after the turn of the twentieth century and then fell back to 8 percent on the eve of the war.[143] In reformatories, the number of interned children rose sharply in the 1870s, peaked in 1900, and then slowly decreased.[144] A majority of adult prisoners continued to come from the South, a fact that fueled continuing stereotypes of northern moral superiority.[145] In 1914, rates of incarceration for inhabitants of the southern provinces were more than double those for the North.[146]

With the passage of the Zanardelli Code of 1889 and the Ordinance of 1891, the classification of penal institutions underwent change. The hard labor camps were officially closed although their buildings were usually converted to penitentiaries with special sections in which the remaining *forzati* completed their sentences of hard labor.[147] After 1904, reformatories replaced most of the old houses of custody for minors. Three criminal insane asylums were opened for inmates who showed severe signs of mental illness. While Doria had established a penal institution for chronically ill and tubercular inmates, he could not get approval from Giolitti for special prisons for alcoholics.[148] Despite the concerted opposition of most classical and positivist criminologists, the island penal colonies continued to function although with ever fewer inmates.

While holding the majority of all prisoners, jails followed the general pattern of decline, with numbers falling from 46,377 in 1871 to 24,974 in 1914.[149] Yet, on the eve of the war, jails still held about half of Italy's inmates. Within the jail population, the percentage awaiting trial—about 60 percent—remained constant, fueling continued complaints about high rates of preventive detention. Because of declining numbers of inmates and consolidation of institutions after unification, the total number of jails throughout the peninsula dropped from 252 to 173.[150]

In contrast to jails, the number of penitentiaries rose from 39 in 1871 to 68 in 1914.[151] The closure of the forced labor camps and transfer of their inmates to penitentiaries accounts for part of this growth.[152] During the same period, encouraged by the positivist directive to individualize punishment, specialized types of male penitentiaries—such as agricultural colonies and criminal insane asylums—proliferated. Inversely, the number of penitentiaries for women fell from a maximum of seven in the 1890s to three on the eve of the war.[153] Government reformatories for boys increased from four in 1871 to nine in 1914, while the sole public institution for girls at Perugia closed in 1909. The number of private reformatories—eleven for boys and twenty-one for girls—remained roughly the same as fifty years earlier.[154] Finally, eight island colonies held a decreasing number of individuals sentenced to police exile.[155] As this distribution of penal institutions demonstrates, legal and prison reform did not reduce the complexity of the system. Instead of a simplification of punishments, as propounded by the classical school, Italy followed the positivist path of establishing individualized prisons based on distinctions in gender, age, legal categories, and health.

The fifty years after unification saw modest improvement in the physical state of penal institutions, although prison officials, members of parliament, and journalists continued to voice complaints. Progress was slow before the passage of the Ordinance of 1891, with only a handful of new jails—in Milan, Cagliari, and Rome—being built according to the cellular plan. In recognition of the deplorable conditions in both jails and prisons, the state established a special office of civil engineers in 1888 within the Division of Prisons. In the opinion of Querci-Seriacopi, the seven engineers employed by this office were "extremely able technicians who were specialized in the construction and architecture of prisons."[156] Yet they lacked the necessary financial resources to make rapid progress in either remodeling the old buildings inherited from the pre-unification states or completing new ones.

Conditions continued to be especially bad in prisons located in the southern provinces. In 1896-7, Jessie White Mario—a former supporter of Garibaldi, a feminist, and an investigative reporter—visited a number of facilities mostly, although not exclusively, in Sicily. She criticized the jail in Caltanissetta for its "foul smell, overcrowding, and absence of the most elementary rules of hygiene," and found the jail at Agrigento to be little better.[157] In contrast to these Sicilian prisons, the jail in Venice exhibited "order, cleanliness, [and] good food," although suspects and convicts lived in close proximity in violation of the Ordinance of 1891.[158] The government continued to cite tight budgets as the excuse for the slow pace of prison building and renovation. In 1898, at a meeting of the High Council of Prisons, a committee of experts on penal policy, Prime Minister di Rudinì admitted that "if we have excellent and good [jails], we also have many that are still wretched" such as those in Caltanissetta and Naples.[159]

More progress was made under the stewardship of Doria. In 1904, he announced that, despite severe budget limitations, several projects were in progress including new jails in Brescia, Catania, Monza, and Gerace Marina; a penitentiary in Portolongone; and two reformatories in Bologna and San Lazzaro Parmense. Under study, but still not begun, was a new cellular jail for Naples. Yet, he admitted that conditions at several jails continued to be "worthy of tears."[160] During the rest of his tenure, which can be characterized as the most active period of prison construction before World War I, Doria continued to add new jails and reformatories to the national network.

Nevertheless, even after the war an internal ministry report admitted that "the reform of prison architecture ... [was] ... far from being complete."[161]

In addition to focusing on the physical state of prisons throughout the peninsula, Doria sought to improve the numbers and pay of their staff. Proclaiming himself tied to local prison administrators by "bonds of indestructible solidarity," he worried that they often felt "neglected and consequently dispirited and exhausted."[162] Yet for the most part, improvements were modest. In 1914, the number of penitentiary wardens was no larger than in 1871, although Doria had managed to restore their numbers after a decline in the 1890s.[163] In contrast, the lower administrative ranks—vice-wardens, accountants, and secretaries—more than doubled, probably as a result of the mammoth amount of paperwork required by the Ordinance of 1891. Jails fared better with the number of wardens increasing from thirty-one to forty-six between 1871 and 1891; because the number of jails had sharply decreased, the percentage of jails with resident directors actually jumped from twelve to twenty-seven. Salaries increased slowly and only marginally over the entire period; for example, directors received yearly remuneration of only 4,000–6,000 lire in 1914 compared to 3,000–5,000 lire thirty years earlier.

Guards, whose working lives had been marked by long hours, low wages, and abject subordination to their superiors, fared better. Understaffing became less of a problem as their numbers rose by about 25 percent between 1871 and 1914.[164] The improvement in the ratio of guards per institution was even more dramatic in the context of the decreasing number of jails and the substitution of teachers in juvenile reformatories. For all ranks, pay roughly doubled in the same period.[165] Guards still earned less than clerical workers but the gap between their annual salaries closed significantly.

In 1907, a new regulatory law attenuated other restrictions that humiliated prison guards and differentiated them from most other working-class occupations. Required to live on the prison grounds, seek permission to marry, and submit unquestioningly to discipline from superiors, the prison guard resembled more the domestic servant than the factory worker who, by the turn of the twentieth century, was free to join unions and participate in strikes.[166] Although strict rules continued to govern the behavior of this militarized force, Doria marginally improved working conditions. For example, new recruits had to sign on for only five years rather than the eight required by the earlier regulation of 1873; guards were allowed to leave their barracks daily for up to four hours instead of two; they were eligible for a much wider range of honorary and financial rewards for good work; and some of the lighter punishments for bad conduct were replaced by fines (Illustration 3.1). Perhaps most importantly, at least in symbolic value, was the liberalization of permission to marry. Under the 1873 law, new recruits had to be single and could request permission to marry only if they possessed property worth several times their yearly salary. That meant that wives had to bring a substantial dowry to the marriage, which was impossible for most working-class women. In addition, guards had to certify the "good moral character" of their prospective brides.[167] Guards resented these restrictions, and some evaded them by contracting religious marriages that were not recognized by the state.[168] After decades of complaints, in 1907 the prison administration decreased the dowry requirement to a small sum.[169]

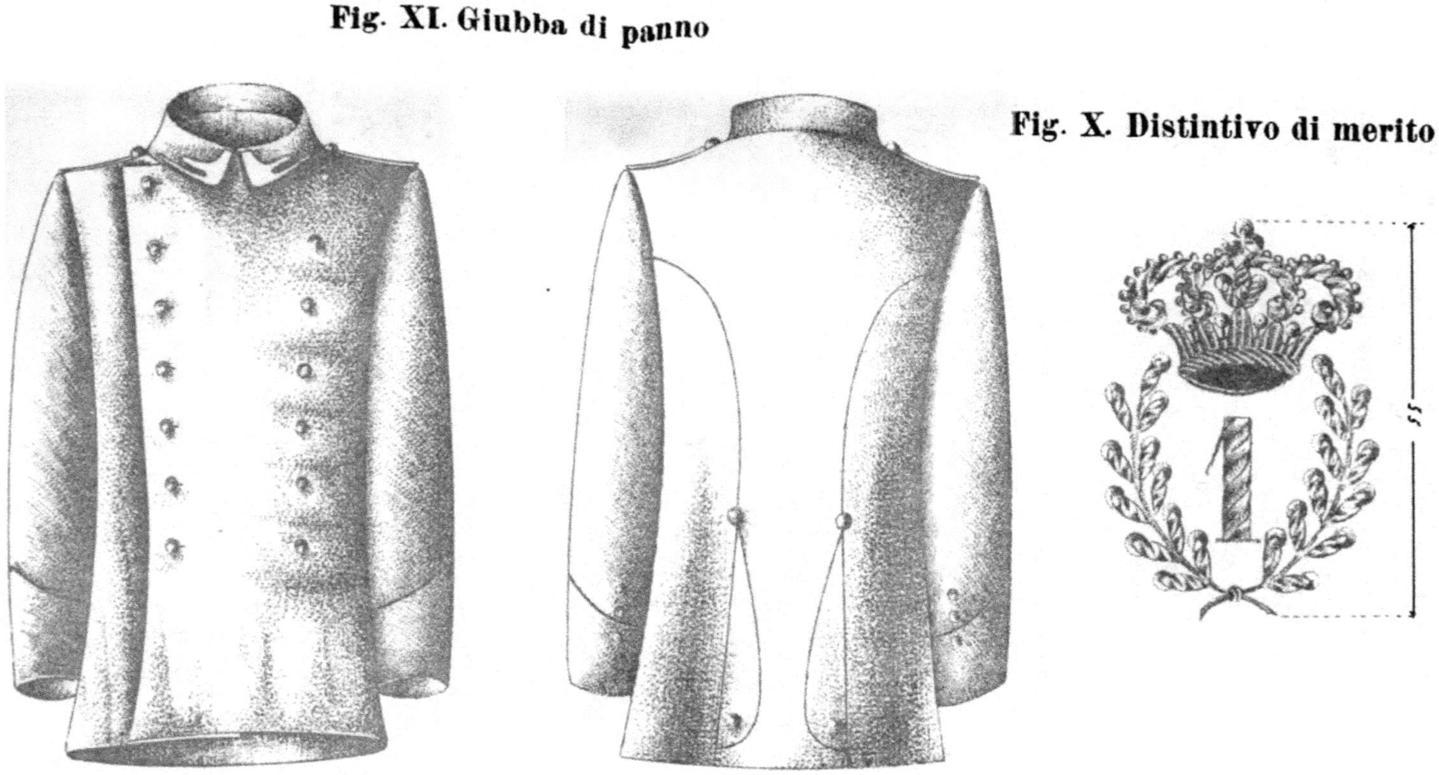

Fig. X. Distintivo di merito

Fig. XI. Giubba di panno

Illustration 3.1 Uniforms of prison guards next to an insignia of merit

The concessions to guards after the turn of the twentieth century derived less from humanitarian than practical reasons. Both Beltrani Scalia and Doria faced the difficulty of finding sufficient applicants for the post of prison guard, which, like that of police, was generally viewed with disdain by the Italian public. Even with high unemployment and poverty within the working classes, the lower-level ranks of the military staff in prisons were rarely filled. Because of bad working conditions, resignations were frequent. By the 1890s, prison guards began to agitate for reform with the encouragement of sympathetic voices such as that of Professor Andrea Marinelli. In a pamphlet dedicated to Prime Minister Luigi Pelloux, he argued that low wages, understaffing, and restrictions on marriage made the lot of the Italian prison guard worse than those in other European nations. Rather than a "pariah," the prison guard deserved "*a bit more of that liberty for which you honorably fought at Porta Pia*," referring to the battle for Rome in 1870.[170] That guards were beginning to protest the terms of their service is clear not only from newspaper reports but also from Doria's vehement but defensive insistence that only a few malcontents were causing trouble.[171] In 1914, Doria's successor complained that "quite a few guards (the worst elements without doubt)" continued to contact the press with "deplorable gossip" about supposedly bad working conditions.[172] Undoubtedly, the founding of the Italian Socialist Party in 1892 and the growing union movement within private industry created a climate that encouraged guards to reject the docile subordination expected by their superiors.

Nuns and prison matrons did not share the modest but real advancements of their male counterparts. As inexpensive alternatives to male personnel—who had guaranteed pay scales, pensions, and mechanisms for promotion—they received much lower salaries that were not standardized but "determined on a case by case basis by the Minister" in Rome.[173] The only concession to female guardians was their right to room and board at the prison and to be supplied with an apron as a uniform. The regulation of 1907, like that of 1873, explicitly sought matrons among wives of prison guards, who were to possess "a healthy physical constitution, good morals, and no criminal record."[174] Although prison matrons had the same duties and were subject to identical punishments as men, they lacked any job security or possibility for advancement. The absence of improvement in pay or conditions for female personnel in both jails and prisons mirrored the abysmal state of women prisoners, who were treated as second-class citizens even at the height of national penal reform during the Giolittian era.

Conclusion

In 1910, the jurist Ugo Conti happily reported that

> crime in Italy today resembles that in other modern states that call themselves civilized. In quantity and quality (and the decrease is most evident in the penitentiaries), we now stand equidistant between the most advanced nations and those that remain back where we were a few years ago ... Italian prisons are functioning well and the reformatories even better.[175]

Published in the Bolognese newspaper, the *Resto del Carlino*, this evaluation delighted Doria who reprinted it in the *RDC*. Although exaggerated, Conti's words held much truth. Rates of crime, and particularly violent offenses, had fallen dramatically since the turn of the twentieth century. Prison building, stalled after unification, accelerated after Doria became director general; male prisoners benefitted the most from the new and renovated buildings that replaced the hard labor camps abolished by the penal code of 1889. Stripped of their chains, an increasing proportion of men enjoyed individual sleeping cells, an expanded range of vocational training, the possibility of transfer to intermediary institutions, and finally parole. Prison reform also advantaged boys in public reformatories, which were dramatically recast as educational institutions offering instruction in crafts, music, and gymnastics. In both cases, the Ordinance of 1891 had formalized tutelage by citizens outside the prison bureaucracy through the committees charged with oversight, visiting, and prisoners' aid. Admittedly, the application of these reforms was markedly uneven across the peninsula and many male prisoners, especially in the South, continued to endure wretched living conditions. Nevertheless, Beltrani Scalia and Doria had initiated a process that placed rehabilitation at the core of public penal institutions for men and boys, although institutions for women and girls had been for the most part forgotten in public debate and policy.

Because of the timing of the Ordinance of 1891, Italy's prison system was molded more by the positivist school than by the Enlightenment values that had inspired an earlier wave of reform in France, England, and the United States. Although one of the hallmarks of the classical stage of prison building, the Pennsylvania model, was retained for jails, the newer Irish system, with its progressive stages, became the hallmark of Italy's male penitentiaries. To individualize punishment, as called for by Lombroso and his school, the state established a web of differentiated institutions: juvenile reformatories, criminal insane asylums, prisons for the chronically ill, and agricultural colonies. The newly established policies of parole and probation offered alternatives to prison for "occasional" criminals, who were perceived to have been motivated by environmental factors, in contrast to "born" criminals, who were relegated to special high-security institutions. Positivist criminologists—who frequently served as prison doctors, prosecutors, defense attorneys, and expert witnesses—were key agents in assessing the degree of "dangerousness" posed by individual inmates, which then determined their progress in the merit system and eligibility for parole and probation. Thus, the path to modernity for the Italian prison administration lay not in a replicating the earlier classical stage of prison reform on the Pennsylvania or Auburn model but in adopting the tenets of its own acclaimed positivist school as a blueprint for its new system.

Despite its unique characteristics, such as the particularly strong role of positivist criminology, Italian prison legislation echoed the wider global movement for penal reform during the late nineteenth and early twentieth centuries. Nations in Northern Europe and America, which had already replaced corporal punishment with incarceration during the first wave of prison reform, were now revising their approaches, in different ways, to incorporate the new principle of individualized punishment. In the United States, progressive elites softened the rigid uniformity of the classical prison by adopting probation, parole, indeterminate sentences, and the juvenile court.[176] The British took a more punitive approach by developing a mark system based on "hard labor, hard board, and hard fare" meant to combat recidivism.[177] The French Republic combined liberal measures—such as parole, pardon, and expansion of education in youth reformatories—with deportation to Guiana and New Caledonia for serious crimes.[178] Strategies also varied among regions in the non-western world, which were erecting prison systems for the first time. A symbol of modernity, the penitentiary was prized among independent nations in Asia and Latin America, which adapted and reinterpreted positivist principles to their own exigencies.[179] New prisons in the colonial world, while brutal rather than rehabilitative, were touted as instruments of the "civilizing mission" exercised by the metropole.[180] On the margins of Europe, Italy—like Spain, Portugal, and Russia—shared aspects of the western legal tradition but consolidated its prison systems only during this second wave of reform.[181] As will be discussed in the next three chapters, the "birth of the prison" in Italy held different consequences for women, men, and children.

4

Women and the Convent Prison

Women constituted only a footnote to the energetic and expansive project of prison building and reform during the positivist era. The deafening silence about the treatment of female inmates appears curious within the longer historical context stretching back to the convent prison of San Michele. Even though women had benefitted much earlier than men from the replacement of corporal punishment with enclosure, they became invisible during the second wave of prison reform. Neither Beltrani Scalia nor Doria implemented measures to individualize punishment in female institutions, reorganize them according to the Irish system, or expand secular education and professional training. In the voluminous nineteenth-century literature on prison reform—which included parliamentary debates, legal tracts, criminological studies, and professional journals—women were rarely mentioned. Instead, prison reform became masculinized as the state reenvisioned the penitentiary as an institutional incubator for male citizenship.

Even after the Italian armies defeated the Pope and annexed Rome to the new state, the punishment of women remained in the religious sphere. Despite the anti-clericalist bent of the new parliamentary government, it routinely renewed contracts with the various orders of nuns who had been given control of all female penitentiaries by the pre-unitary monarchs. In Rome, nuns accompanied the transfer of female inmates to the penitentiary at Villa Altieri, a former aristocratic country house, in 1871 and to the jail of the Mantellate, a former convent, in 1884. Although newly converted into penal institutions, neither Villa Altieri nor the Mantellate was renovated according to the architectural and philosophical principles laid out in the prison regulations of 1862 and 1891. Less innovative than the original women's prison at San Michele, they were characterized by large dormitories rather than the individual sleeping cells of the earlier institution. The hegemonic role of religion in the routines of everyday prison life, with its narrow emphasis on sexual purification, clearly marked women as second-class citizens in a new nation otherwise dedicated to secular and liberal values. Only after the turn of the twentieth century did feminist critics draw attention to the neglect of women prisoners, but the outbreak of war interrupted their projects of reform.

For the purpose of providing a detailed comparison of prisons for different inmate groups, the organization of this chapter on women will be replicated in the subsequent discussion of men and children. Each will begin with a synopsis of the legal framework of civil, criminal, and prison legislation that shaped and constrained philosophies of punishment according to gender and age. The major demographic, spatial, and architectural changes undergone by Rome immediately after unification that impinged on the placement and nature of local prisons will then be explored. It was within this dynamic geography that, in the case of women, the new Italian state established the Villa Altieri penitentiary and Mantellate jail, both of which had particular architectural histories, types of inmates, and conditions of everyday life. These two institutions will then be compared to female prisons in other areas of the peninsula utilizing national statistics. Each chapter will conclude with an analysis of a central issue distinguishing debates about punishment of each particular group, which, in the case of women, was the role of nuns as prison personnel.

Women in Criminal and Prison Legislation

The conditions of women's imprisonment after unification, at both the local and national level, can be evaluated only within the context of civil, criminal, and prison law. The Zanardelli Criminal Code of 1889, like the Sardinian-Italian code before it, made little reference to gender and therefore seemed to prescribe equal treatment for women and men. In terms of legal accountability, it contained no general principle that held women either more or less responsible than men for their criminal behavior. Making little reference to gender, it implicitly affirmed that the two sexes were equally able to distinguish right from wrong and to choose whether to break the law. This apparent equality before the law was consistent with the best tradition of the classical school, which taught that all persons possessed free will and therefore should be subject to identical standards of evidence and degrees of punishment.

The gender-blind nature of the criminal codes was surprising in light of the markedly inferior position of women in civil and family law. The Civil Code of 1865—commonly referred to as the Pisanelli Code—subordinated wives to their husbands. At marriage, a woman had to adopt her husband's name and reside where he chose.[1] Although wives had the right to own property, they needed their husbands' permission, according to the doctrine of *autorizzazione maritale*, to work or to carry out financial transactions such as opening bank accounts, taking out mortgages, or bequeathing gifts.[2] Another traditional doctrine, that of *patria podestà*, gave men the exclusive right to make decisions about minor children, while women became the legal head of the household only in the absence of their husbands through separation, desertion, emigration, or prolonged imprisonment.[3] Divorce was not legal, and the grounds for separation favored husbands.[4] Single women, in an improvement from their status under the old regime, exercised more legal autonomy than married women. Under papal law, for example, even adult daughters had been forbidden from managing their own property without the consent of their fathers.[5] Yet, despite their legal emancipation from paternal authority under the Pisanelli Code, single women were nevertheless bound by general prohibitions against women serving as witnesses to civil acts, being admitted as lawyers to the bar, holding high administrative positions such as judge, and, of course, voting or holding political office. During the first fifty years after unification, only the restriction on women's right to witness civil acts was reformed because of its obvious absurdity in light of women's right to testify in criminal court.[6]

A few traces of this gender disparity could also be found in the Zanardelli Code. In the case of adultery, the punishment was equivalent for the two sexes, but husbands enjoyed much broader legal grounds for bringing charges. Men could have their wives arrested for even short or clandestine affairs, while wives had to prove that their husbands "maintained a concubine in the family house or elsewhere in a notorious manner."[7] While these measures pertaining to adultery were discriminatory, the sections of the penal code on infanticide and abortion offered the possibility of reduced sentences to both women and men.[8] A female defendant could invoke the attenuating circumstance of "honor" if her child was illegitimate or the offspring of an adulterous affair. If a male accomplice had acted to protect his own honor or that of his "wife, mother, offspring, adopted daughter, or sister," he could also plead for light punishment in such cases.[9]

The other exceptions to the principle of sexual equality before the criminal law concerned punishment. In the case of *contravvenzioni*, or misdemeanors, women who were sentenced to less than a month of jail and not recidivists might be allowed by the judge to serve their sentence at home.[10] In all other cases of incarceration, the law simply stated that women would be sent to "special institutions."[11] According to a detailed commentary on the Zanardelli Code by Pessina, a respected leader of the Classical School, this article was purposely worded in a vague manner in order "to avoid special measures for women in the list of punishments."[12] While this rather candid remark illustrates the commitment of legislators to produce a model code dedicated to equality before the law, it also pointed to the existence of an escape clause. By relegating the definition of the "special institutions" to administrative ordinance, the Zanardelli Code could preserve a type of surface purity while permitting the state to perpetuate a system of gendered punishment in practice. Although the abolition of capital punishment and hard labor in the Zanardelli Code promised a convergence in punishment for women and men, the perpetuation of special institutions for women undercut the seemingly universal prescriptions of the criminal code.

The inconsistencies between the civil and criminal codes about women's legal capacity derived partially from the enduring strength of the principle of *infirmitas sexus*, which held women to be inferior in body and mind and therefore incapable of distinguishing right from wrong. As Marina Graziosi has argued, jurists continued to cite this ancient principle of Roman and canon law to justify discrimination against women in both civil and criminal matters.[13] Kept alive by important early modern jurists such as Prospero Farinacci, the concept of *infirmitas sexus* or gender weakness took on a new life with the development of positivist theories about female biological, psychological, and mental inferiority. The strength of this prejudice, sometimes at an unconscious level, may explain the near silence about the implications of the clause permitting "special institutions" for women among both classical and positivist jurists. Despite the support of many liberals for gender equality in the penal code, few questioned the relegation of women to institutions untouched by the modern ideas of prison reform. Equal in court, women were forgotten once they entered the administrative world of punishment.

What differentiated most markedly women's prisons from those of men was the presence of nuns as both directors and security staff. Unlike male institutions, which were managed by middle-class bureaucrats and a professional corps of secular guards, female penitentiaries and the larger jails employed a religious staff that jealously protected its autonomy. Although nominally subjected to the oversight of the national government, which provided a subsidy for the room and board of each inmate, women's prisons underwent little change after unification. Disinterest in female reform is clear from the cursory attention given to women's institutions in the text of the Prison Regulation of 1862 and the supposedly reform-minded Ordinance of 1891. In the Prison Regulation of 1862, only fourteen of the 558 articles concerned the role of the nuns, who were allowed to live according to the rules of their order.[14] They functioned under the supervision of their mother superior who, although theoretically subordinate to the director of a nearby male prison, had the authority to negotiate the contract of her order with the Italian state and to supervise the daily management of her institution. The sisters under her control had no right to contact state administrators without her consent. Only one article directly addressed the supervision of female inmates. While it exhorted the nuns to reform the women under their care, it lacked any specific guidelines about philosophy or methods of punishment beyond a warning to avoid "useless discussions, especially about what is taking place outside the institution."[15] Written in a period when unification was not yet complete, these words may have constituted a warning against rallying female prisoners in support of the Church against the expanding secular state.

In the longer Ordinance of 1891 that constituted the crowning achievement of Beltrani Scalia's career, the number of articles pertaining to the administration of female prisons shrank to thirteen.[16] Most of these simply echoed the 1862 Regulation, for example, confirming that the state would draw up "special conventions" with each order of nuns.[17] The mother superior retained her role as the liaison between the religious order and the state; while the sisters owed strict obedience to her, she in turn was required to send regular reports to the prison administration. In contrast to the 1862 Regulation, the duties of the sisters were patterned somewhat more on those of the guards. To maintain discipline, the nuns—like the guards—were advised to treat the inmates "always with a just but firm humanity and to never converse with them about any matters that are not required by your job."[18] They were explicitly given the right to punish refractory prisoners by locking them in isolation cells. Despite the apparent equivalence with men in terms of duties, the nuns received no guaranteed benefits except free lodging in the prison and permission to leave each day for two hours. The many silences in the regulatory codes of 1862 and 1891 about women's institutions contrasted sharply with the careful and sometimes overly complex project for modernizing male prisons.

Roma Capitale

In 1871, less than five months after Italian troops breeched its walls, Rome was declared capital of the Kingdom of Italy. Formerly under absolute control of the papal authorities, the international capital of Catholicism now underwent a process of secularization.

Although the Pope continued to occupy and rule the small area of the Vatican, many church properties were confiscated and turned into government ministries or other symbols of the new liberal state. The Quirinale, the former summer papal palace, became the residence of King Victor Emmanuel II, while Montecitorio, a former law court and police station under the papacy, was converted into the Chamber of Deputies. After losing their function as political prisons, Castel Sant'Angelo became an army barracks while San Michele was demoted to a police lockup. The left bank of the Tiber, dominated by the newly secularized municipal council on the Capitoline Hill, became completely identified with the new order and open to immediate reconfiguration as a part of a modern city. The parliamentary government was more hesitant to intervene immediately on the right bank dominated by the shadow of the Vatican, which had declared itself intent on retaking the city. Nevertheless, the entire urban space quickly became the site of monuments to the new Italy that sought to replace or overlay the traditional religious character of Rome.[19]

Despite the deliberate and studied steps to furnish Rome with symbols of the new nation-state, much of the marked geographic and architectural transformation was, at best, unplanned and, at worst, the result of unbridled speculation. The largest force for change was demographic as immigration to the new capital soared. Not as sleepy and immobile as described by many visitors, papal Rome had experienced slow but steady growth since the end of the Napoleonic wars. Yet its population was only 244,484 in 1871, far less than London, Paris, and even Naples. By 1914, however, the number of inhabitants had more than doubled.[20] Although a drop in infant mortality accounted for a small part of this growth, most resulted from immigration. For centuries, papal Rome had attracted a diverse group of outsiders from other Italian and foreign states including churchmen, bankers, artists, tourists, merchants, and specialized artisans. It is striking, for example, that in 1843 only 43 percent of marriages involved two native Romans while the rest involved at least one immigrant spouse.[21] After unification, the influx of new residents, mostly from other regions of the peninsula, increased for two reasons. First, the transfer of the capital to Rome involved a huge apparatus of ministries, houses of parliament, and high courts. Previously dominated by clerics and a wealthy aristocracy, the city now acquired a new bourgeois class of state administrators, which was joined by large numbers of lawyers, journalists, and other professionals whose livelihood was related to national politics. The ranks of the lower middle classes also expanded as droves of clerks, secretaries, and accountants relocated to staff the vast government bureaucracy.

A second wave of immigration involved poorer workers who were drawn to Rome by the explosion of new construction jobs. By the 1880s, a "building fever" took over the city as new complexes of government buildings and entire neighborhoods were built from scratch. Unlike the administrators and office workers, who were predominantly northern by birth and had accompanied the transfer of their offices from Piedmont and Florence, lower-class immigrants came mostly from the central and southern provinces. Unlike Milan and Turin, Rome did not become an industrial center but remained largely an administrative hub with a large tertiary sector. In fact the early government of the liberal right, fearing the social unrest of London and Paris, made a deliberate decision to discourage the establishment of large factories in the capital. Nevertheless, the economic boom in building as well as other modern industries—such as printing, which became the backbone of a press newly freed from censorship—drew large numbers of peasants and workers to the new capital.

To provide housing for the influx of public administrators and office workers, the city expanded outside its original fourteen districts, which clustered on lowlands near the river. As early as 1871, the census commission predicted the imminent creation of at least one new district tentatively named "Esquilino," referring to an incipient new neighborhood that ran from Piazza Venezia to the new train station.[22] Replacing Porta del Popolo, the north gate of Rome and the traditional entrance for visiting dignitaries and pilgrims, the train station now welcomed travelers in a rural area within the Aurelian walls near the ruins of Diocletian's Baths, with its prison for women and men. With the construction of a new thoroughfare linking the station to the older city center, urbanization came quickly to the Esquiline. Given the patriotic denomination of Via Nazionale (Street of the Nation), this new avenue ran close to the Quirinal Palace, once the summer residence of the popes but soon to be surrounded by blocks of new housing for middle- and lower-middle-class immigrants. During the next few decades, several important buildings reinforced the identification of Via Nazionale with the new secular state: the National Fine Arts Exhibition Building (1883), site of the International Penitentiary Congress in 1885; the Banca d'Italia (Palazzo Koch, 1892); and the Eliseo Theater (1900). The first urban plans, issued in 1873 and 1883, confirmed the importance of the Esquiline neighborhood for both the symbolic and practical reconfiguration of the new capital.

Little planning went into housing for poor immigrants, who initially crowded into the older working-class neighborhoods of Monti and Trastevere near the river. In these districts, population density was even higher than the over-twenty residents per building typical of the city as a whole.[23] By the twentieth century, the lower classes had spilled over into the less populated areas of San Lorenzo and Testaccio. Not until 1909, however, when the progressive mayor Ernesto Nathan initiated a public housing project in Testaccio, did the communal government offer the same residential planning as it did for the middle classes.

Within this rapidly changing urban environment, the prison administration encountered both opportunities and problems for modernizing punishment. Relatively rural areas within city walls offered space for the construction of new penal institutions, although they would be far from the courts in the central city. The state could also take advantage of empty monasteries, which had been confiscated from the Church, or aristocratic villas put up for sale by the declining aristocracy. However, prisons were not wanted in new and prestigious neighborhoods, such as the Esquiline hill, where they reminded middle-class residents and tourists alike of the poverty and crime that continued to tarnish the new capital. At the local level, then, spatial constraints became an important factor in decisions about the locations of new prisons for women,

Women's Prisons in Rome

Throughout the eighteenth and into the early decades of the nineteenth century, the same two penal institutions continued to intern Roman women: the New Prison for suspects and convicts with short sentences and San Michele for long-term prisoners. Yet this stability was shaken during the last decades of papal rule, when different groups of prisoners—not only women but also men and children—began to circulate among old and new penal institutions. One reason for the flurry of transfers was overcrowding and the consequent degradation of living conditions, which led papal officials to shift inmates back and forth in an attempt to match their numbers with the size of different institutions. A second factor was the promulgation of the Criminal Code of 1832, which decreed for the first time that adult men who had committed minor crimes were eligible for the punishment of incarceration similar to that for women and children. Finally, the increasingly violent nature of the political opposition to papal rule, most notably the Revolution of 1848 that instituted a short-lived republican government in Rome, provoked equally violent repression by police and courts. Thus room had to be found for the growing number of political prisoners who were languishing in cells or awaiting capital punishment. While neither directly affected by the new criminal code nor arrested in large numbers for political conspiracy, women did experience the pressures of overcrowding. And as a small and neglected group, their fate was at the mercy of the growing numbers of male prisoners whose need for housing took precedence. Thus the tradition of carceral innovation for women, symbolized by San Michele, began to fade by the 1820s.

In an attempt to arrest this decline, the papal government replaced the secular staff of women's prisons with nuns during the last decades of its rule. Several motives explain this curious incursion of religion into state institutions during an era of widespread secularization. First, the introduction of nuns was consistent with the general nature of the convent prison, which emphasized the value of enclosure for reforming the morals of criminal women. While San Michele had employed a secular staff, its organization and principles nevertheless echoed those of the many conservatories that, during the early modern period, offered refuge to "endangered" girls, such as orphans and beggars, or sought to redeem "fallen" women who were already prostitutes. In 1870, Rome still hosted fifteen conservatories to protect and restore female honor, many of which were located near San Michele along the Tiber in the Trastevere neighborhood.[24] Whether administered by lay or by religious boards, these conservatories followed a monastic model of removing women from the outside world and introducing them to a life of work and penance.

Second, nuns provided the type of female workforce needed to fulfill the requirement, central to Enlightenment prison reform, of strict separation between women and men. In the late eighteenth and early nineteenth centuries, female religious orders dedicated to philanthropic activities began to appear first in northern and afterward in southern Catholic territories. These "sisters of charity," as they were called, represented a sharp change from the model of cloistered life imposed on convents during the Counter-Reformation. During this earlier period, nuns led mostly a contemplative life, forsaking trips outside their monastery and communicating with their few permissible visitors through a grated door (*parlatorio*) that prevented the interlocutors from touching or even seeing each other clearly.[25] In contrast, the new charitable orders traveled extensively to provide services to the secular world such as teaching, nursing, or administering orphanages, conservatories, reformatories, and women's prisons.[26] Subjected to fewer regulations than traditionally cloistered orders, the new "sisters of charity" required neither a dowry nor submission to a life-long vow of poverty for admittance. A larger variety of women outside of the aristocratic class, therefore, joined the sisters of charity and carried out evangelical activities similar to those of male missionaries. Such philanthropic work was particularly suited to enclosed institutions such as women's prisons, where nuns could live according to the rules of their order, yet were permitted to interact with the secular world. The mother superior, free from the control of male churchmen, became a commanding figure in the new charitable orders. Thus, during the restoration following the defeat of Napoleon, conservative monarchies found a staff for women's prisons in the sisters of charity. While not trained in any professional sense, they were thought to embody a religious vocation and dedication to the poor that naturally prepared them to take on a mission of moral reform.

For the most part, the nuns employed in Italian women's prisons had their roots in Northern Europe, where the movement into charity work had its origins. The predominant orders that established branches in Italy were the sisters of St. Vincent de Paul, St. Joseph of the Apparition, and the Good Shepherd from France as well as the sisters of Providence of the Immaculate Conception of Belgium.[27] During the fifty years after unification, the state continued to leave these same nuns in place, simply renewing old contracts from the pre-unitary states. That oversight was lax is clear from the absence of any contract at all with the nuns managing the jails of Bologna, Naples, and Udine as late as 1891, when the new Ordinance went into effect.[28] This type of continuity typified the Roman penal institutions for women at Villa Altieri and the Mantellate monastery, both of which were managed by foreign religious orders.

Villa Altieri

In 1871, the year that Rome became the national capital, the Italian state opened a new women's penitentiary at Villa Altieri. For almost twenty-five years, Villa Altieri offered a more settled life for long-term female prisoners, who had been transferred several times between San Michele and Diocletian's Baths during the last decades of papal rule. Unlike those earlier institutions, which had incarcerated both sexes, Villa Altieri was dedicated solely to women. One of only six penitentiaries for women on the peninsula, Villa Altieri drew its inmates not only from Rome but also neighboring provinces, particularly those to the south and as far away as western Sicily.

Like the prison at Diocletian's Baths, Villa Altieri was located in the "green ring" of Rome between the central city and the Aurelian Walls. A zone of many aristocratic summer houses, this ring was designated as "green" because of the elaborate gardens and large parks that surrounded these elegant buildings. Before constructing a villa in the 1600s, the ancient aristocratic Altieri family had acquired extensive holdings near the papal basilica of San Giovanni and the Church of Santa Croce in Gerusalemme. Devoted to fields and vineyards, the Altieri lands became more accessible after Popes Gregory XIV and Sixtus V built new roads in the late sixteenth century to encourage foreign pilgrims to visit outlying churches; several of these routes bordered on the Altieri lands and still define the urban landscape of that modern neighborhood on the

Esquiline hill. Yet the area remained rural for several more centuries and Villa Altieri, like other Roman villas, took up only a small part of the Altieri holdings while the remainder was devoted to traditional farming.[29]

The residential building itself was begun in the 1660s under the oversight of architect Giovanni Antonio De Rossi.[30] In a typical pattern of Roman aristocrats, the Altieri family already possessed a winter palace in central Rome, also designed by De Rossi, which was located near the Church of the Gesù, the seat of the Jesuit order.[31] The exact date of construction of the summer villa is unknown but coincided with a period of particular family glory signaled by the ascension of Emilio Altieri to the rank of Cardinal and finally that of Pope, taking the name of Clement X (1670–6). Consonant with the artistic taste of the era, Villa Altieri was designed as a "house of delights" (*casino di delizie*) for the prominent family and their guests. Baroque in style, it was endowed with typical seventeenth-century features such as a horseshoe-style staircase ascending to the second floor (the *piano nobile* or public reception rooms); a fountain with jumping tritons and dolphins; a "secret" walled garden; and an elaborate labyrinth of circular box hedges[32] (Illustration 4.1). Known for its extensive collection of art and antiquities, as well as its enormous grounds dotted by statues and fountains, Villa Altieri was featured in the earliest guidebooks to Rome as a noteworthy stop on the eighteenth-century grand tour.

During the final years of the Papal States, the neighborhood around the villa began to change. The Esquiline Hill became the projected site for the first railway lines in Rome, which would link the city with outlying towns. In 1858, the Altieri family sold their villa to the General Society of Railroads, a corporation that planned to lay tracks across its lands. Yet Villa Altieri was initially left intact because the new station at Termini, near Diocletian's Baths, required a reorientation of routes.[33] A year later, however, it passed into the hands of Monsignor Frédéric-François-Xavier de Mérode,

Illustration 4.1 Villa Altieri before conversion to a women's prison

an enterprising papal official who was quickly buying up large tracts of land in the green belt of Rome in anticipation of urban expansion.[34] A colorful character, de Mérode was born into the Belgian aristocracy and began his career as a soldier. He came to Rome in 1847 to study for the priesthood where, after ordination, he enjoyed a rapid rise under the patronage of Pope Pius IX. Best known as the papal Minister of Arms during the early wars of unification, he also served for many years as "secret chamberlain" in charge of distributing alms to the poor and overseeing prisoners.[35] In this capacity, he convinced the Pope to bring the Sisters of Providence from Namur Belgium to take over the administration of the women's section of Diocletian's Baths. He also began to use Villa Altieri as a refuge for poor women and children. After unification, De Mérode, not adverse to cooperation with the secular state for a profit, leased Villa Altieri to the new prison administration.

Information about the physical transformation of Villa Altieri into a prison is sparse. Most of the surrounding lands were sold off as new neighborhoods were established on the Esquiline to house the expanding Roman population. The fate of the art and antiquities that furnished the palace itself is unknown. While the double circular staircase and much of the exterior decoration remained, the building underwent a major modification with the addition of a third floor. Deplored by architectural historians, this additional floor destroyed the original architectural lines of the building and replaced an elegant tower that offered beautiful views of the surrounding Roman hills.[36] But this utilitarian reconfiguration of the villa allowed for addition space for inmate dormitories, living quarters for the nuns, isolation cells for punishment, workshops, a kitchen, and an infirmary.[37] To prevent escape, a high wall was erected around the secret garden behind the villa where inmates spent their short periods of recreation. For the same purpose, a small building was added in front for the male guards who were prohibited from entering the female space of the prison.[38]

Inmate dossiers, admission forms (*matricole*), and published government statistics offer glimpses into the experience of female inmates in Villa Altieri. Although each of these sources is fragmentary, they offer useful albeit indirect tools for reconstructing the lives of women who themselves have left no written record. Full inmate dossiers are available only for women admitted between 1871 and 1876 and include those transferred from Diocletian's Baths as well as for new convicts.[39] Including notations by the nuns, these dossiers offer the richest documentation of inmates' lives. A second source—admission registers—has survived for not only this early period but also the last years of institution, between 1889 and 1895. Despite the gap, this distribution allows comparison of certain variables over time. Third, published prison statistics, issued yearly by the state, although less detailed, track information by individual institution. In sum, these three types of documentation, although incomplete, offer an important perspective into certain key conditions at Villa Altieri and other Roman institutions of punishment.

Over its life as a penitentiary, Villa Altieri maintained a steady population of inmates. After sixty-six women were transferred from Diocletian's Baths in 1871, their numbers rose quickly to 130–140 on the average until the institution closed in 1897.[40] Most women were admitted directly from local jails where they had been held, sometimes for many months, while awaiting trial. Over the almost three decades of

Villa Altieri's life as a penitentiary, the largest category of convictions shifted from property to violent crimes, with the latter constituting almost 50 percent of those admitted during its final years.[41] Property crimes were often trifling, such as domestic theft by servants or lodgers. Margherita Poccetti, for example, was accused by her employer, Cav. Giustiano Bonci, of having pilfered clothes and extracted money from his wallet.[42] Another inmate, Barbera Marchini, was convicted of stealing from her landlord after showing up in court "suddenly dressed in clothes ornamented by gold and silver jewelry whereas previously she was unadorned and ragged."[43] In some cases, women conspired together, for instance, Leonilda Corradetti and Maria Pucci from the small town of Castignano in the Marche burglarized the house of a local widow by entering "a hole in the wall" and stealing wine, oil, flour, salt, and linens.[44] Other crimes were thought to have been instigated by men although the sentences could still be long. For example, Illuminata Sparvoli, a servant from Viterbo who probably acted on behalf of her lover, was sentenced to ten years for "repeated thefts of money, linens, and other objects" from her aristocratic employer.[45] That a large proportion of Villa Altieri's inmates had been convicted of theft is not surprising given their extreme poverty and types of work—such as domestic service or even fortune-telling—that lent themselves to pilfering and fraud.[46]

More unexpected was the high rate of sentences for violent crime among Villa Altieri inmates. Although murder and assault were relatively rare among women in other parts of nineteenth-century Europe, frequent cases of infanticide partially explain the unique pattern in Italy, where information about birth control was scarce among the predominantly rural population. For example, Rosa Massi was convicted for "voluntarily taking the life of her illegitimate child and throwing it into a remote and inaccessible place, where it died pitiably from asphyxiation."[47] However, her sentence was reduced from the fifteen to two years, mainly because the jury found her to be driven by "an almost irresistible force" that attenuated her responsibility.[48] Rosa Di Battista received a similarly light sentence of two years for "taking the life of her living and healthy infant ... and throwing it into a latrine, where it drowned."[49] Such relative impunity for infanticide, and for the fewer cases of abortion, was officially written into the Italian Criminal Code, which reduced the sentences of women seeking to salvage their "honor" by concealing their illicit pregnancies.[50]

While infanticide and abortion were considered female crimes, women sometimes committed other types of violence more typical of men and carried longer sentences. Anger was often turned again family members, such as in the case of Maria Grazia Noce, who "wounded her own husband with a knife" and received a sentence of six years.[51] Another inmate, Genovessa Bocci, was serving only four years, even though she killed her brother with "a knife stab on his left side that pierced his heart."[52] Attenuating circumstances included her "fit of anger in response to serious provocation," an emotional state that was considered temporary and out of her control.[53] Much longer sentences were meted out for brigandage or participation in criminal organizations such as the mafia or camorra. Such women were convicted of violent crime even though some of them, such as Angiola Giorgi, only gave shelter to male collaborators.[54]

Admittance to Villa Altieri was a new experience for the large majority of its inmates and therefore must have provided a special shock. Only 10 to 15 percent female prisoners were recidivists and thus had experienced conditions of incarceration in the past. Rather than habituated to a life behind bars, the majority had been born in rural areas and continued to reside in these same small towns as adults.[55] Not uniformly young, most inmates were in their thirties and some remained in prison until fifty or sixty years of age.[56] At least two-thirds of female inmates were married or widowed, demonstrating integration into family and community life; even many single women indicated that they were living with their parents when arrested.[57] The majority of married inmates, and also many widows, had children as part of their domestic households.[58] The strength of family ties is clear from the frequent inquiries by inmates about their relatives that were forwarded by the nuns to their home towns. The mayor of Rieti, for example, assured Domenica Olivieri that her daughter was "in good health" while officials in Roccagorga confirmed that the parents of Maria Grazia Noce were well enough to meet her at the train station upon her release.[59]

Over the life of Villa Altieri, the residential patterns of female prisoners changed dramatically and distances became much longer. Before unification, most prisoners convicted in Papal courts came from central Italy. With few railroads, transportation was difficult even from villages close to Rome, and therefore visits were probably rare because family members were unlikely to have the financial means to travel to the capital. By the 1890s, 78 percent of new inmates came from the South and thus from regions even further away from the capital not only geographically but also in terms of culture and dialect.[60] In addition, widespread illiteracy, which minimized even the exchange of letters, contributed to prisoners' isolation from family and friends.

Upon admission, female inmates were fortunate to encounter a physical environment at Villa Altieri that was not as dismal as that of most other prisons on the Italian peninsula. Having been until recently an aristocratic palace, the building was surely more comfortable than the subterranean dungeons of many male prisoners. As the number of inmates rarely exceeded the 140 beds included in official plans, overcrowding was not a problem.[61] However, the configuration of space was modeled neither on the Philadelphia nor the Auburn plans, both of which prescribed separation at night. Instead, women prisoners slept in nine large dormitories, each containing fifteen to sixteen beds, arranged over the three floors of the Villa.[62] Thus the Italian state did not take advantage of the opening of Villa Altieri to reconfigure its new space according to international guidelines and modernize the conditions of female punishment.

Despite the relatively benign physical surroundings at Villa Altieri, inmates rarely found a path to a better life, as promised by prison reformers. Education was scarce and work afforded little variety. Although 80 to 90 percent of women prisoners were illiterate at admission, less than half attended school and few made progress in reading, writing, or counting. Education, a vital part of nineteenth-century philosophy of rehabilitation, did not seem to be encouraged by the nuns, who noted on the dossiers of many inmates that they did not attend school.[63] Few women took advantage of the prison library, which in any case never held more than seventeen books during the years when these numbers were recorded.[64] Despite championing education as a necessary tool for forming new citizens, the national state failed to enforce this policy at Villa Altieri.

Training in skills commensurate with the newly industrializing economy was similarly absent for female prisoners. Such skills would have benefitted a group who identified themselves, upon admission, as mostly destitute (*nullatenente*) or, at best, poor.[65] About half had worked in agriculture before arrest while the second largest profession was domestic service.[66] Neither promised steady income nor economic advancement, especially in the south where few peasants owned their own land. Before arrest, only a minority of women had held potentially more lucrative jobs in manufacturing, garment-making, or shopkeeping, but even these were located in poor rural areas that were not very profitable. Rarely did the economic prospects for convicted women improve during their time in prisons. Once transferred to long-term penitentiaries, all female inmates were expected to work; in fact, the percent of women at Villa Altieri with employment rose from 83 percent in the 1870s to 99 percent in the 1882.[67] But types of occupation changed little, however, with knitting, sewing, and embroidery dominating.[68] Organized by the Sisters of Providence, who served as contractors and therefore reaped the profits, some of this work—such as embroidery and lace-making—required specialized skills.[69] Other tasks, such as sewing, knitting, laundering, and cleaning, simply replicated housework.[70] In any case, these types of labor did not prepare women to take an active place in the modernizing economy of the new state.

The evidence is mixed as to whether the disciplinary atmosphere of Villa Altieri approached the extreme repressiveness of the Foucauldian paradigm. Clearly the Sisters of Providence, who served as both administrators and guards, sought to fashion their charges according to a normative model of womanhood that emphasized religiosity, sexual purity, submission, and industry. The average day was taken up mainly with work punctuated by prayers and religious readings; male priests regularly visited the prison to hold mass and hear confessions. Inmates were subjected to myriad rules that forbade a wide range of behaviors from talking among themselves to mutiny. According to official statistics kept by the nuns, violation of these rules was not particularly frequent; the number of inmates punished each year for breaking the rules dropped from roughly 70 percent in the 1870s to 40 percent in the 1890s, with most accused of only one offense. But these figures must be handled with caution because the mother superior herself recorded the number of offenses and prescribed the punishments without strict oversight from the state.[71] Individual inmate dossiers, for example, attest to frequent instances of disrespect, threats, or even rebellion by inmates. Maria Grazia Noce was consigned to an isolation cell for "making a racket in the dormitory and talking back with arrogance to a Nun"; Elisa De Barrè for threatening a nun "while armed with rocks"; and Maddalena Benigni for refusing to attend Mass on Pentecost.[72] Solitary confinement, usually accompanied by a reduced diet of bread and water, was the most severe punishment among those allowed by prison law.

Despite the high rate of convictions for violent crimes, women's sentences were not particularly long, usually five years or less.[73] At least a third of all inmates received amnesties or pardons that shortened further their actual prison terms. While the state sometimes decreed mass amnesties in honor of royal marriages or other festive occasions, it queried the nuns in cases of individual pardons. The mother superior, for example, confirmed to the Ministry of Justice that Genovessa Bocci had "maintained good behavior" during her four months at Villa Altieri and that the conduct of Caterina Napoleoni had been "praiseworthy" in that she was "industrious, resigned, and repentant."[74] Because some amnesties simply shortened rather than erased existing sentences, inmates might profit from this procedure several times. Except for inmates who died, were transferred to other institutions, or granted parole, the remaining women completed the periods of internment set by the courts.[75] All women left with a small fund saved from their pay but otherwise received little assistance from either the state or private charity.[76]

In 1897, the state closed Villa Altieri because, according to the ministerial decree, the "decreasingly number of female inmates no longer necessitated so many women's penitentiaries."[77] The remaining inmates were transferred to the other six long-term prisons across the peninsula. Although the decree signaled an intention to turn Villa Altieri into a juvenile reformatory, it instead became a private girls' school run by the Sisters of Dorothy (*Suore Dorotee*). Only in the 1930s did it cease to be a women's institution, when the state made Villa Altieri the seat of a public school. Over the course of the twentieth century, the gardens were sold off so that the building now occupies only a small plot of land surrounded by busy thoroughfares and urban construction. In 2012, after a major renovation, it was inaugurated by President Giorgio Napoletano as the seat of the Provincial Archives of Rome.

Mantellate Jail

As did all provincial capitals in Italy, Rome remained the locus of a jail for women awaiting trial and those serving short sentences even after the closure of the Villa Altieri penitentiary. Until 1854, this institution was the New Prison, which had been founded in 1658 on Via Giulia as a progressive and model institution. In the last edition of his admiring census of papal charity institutions, published on the eve of unification, Cardinal Morichini continued to describe the New Prison as bright and airy with plenty of water from both aqueducts and a cistern.[78] This positive characterization, however, is contradicted by archival documents, which indicate a deteriorating institution marked by overcrowding, lack of cleanliness, inadequate food, and abusive guards.[79] The architectural plan of the New Prison, which had seemed so innovative in the seventeenth century, was no longer in accord with nineteenth-century ideals of prison reform. Instead, approximately sixty women were clustered into three large dormitories on the first floor and four smaller cells on the second.[80] While they had their own chapel and infirmary, they were not provided with the individual cells required for all new jails by the 1864 Law.

Because of overcrowding and deterioration in the New Prison, a small number of inmates had been transferred in 1854 across the river to a conservatory that dated back to the seventeenth century. Like Villa Altieri, this conservatory had recently come under the control of a foreign order of nuns, in this case the Buon Pastore or Good Shepherd. At the request of the papal government, this French order widened the scope of the institution by adding a prison wing for women arrested by police.[81] This pattern of housing different legal categories of marginal women—orphans, prostitutes, and convicts—in one institution was typical of the early modern era and is reminiscent of the eighteenth-century convent prison of San Michele, in which women prisoners had shared a larger charity complex with refuges for orphaned children, unmarried women, and aged adults.

After unification, the prison administration sought to repair this anomaly by building an autonomous women's jail, which would function according to the more modern philosophy of separating criminals from the sick and the poor. Located only a few blocks from the Buon Pastore, the new jail occupied the site of the Mantellate convent after it was confiscated by the Italian state. The religious complex had been erected by Pope Clement IX in 1669 for a Salesian order of nuns, the Sisters of the Visitation, who remained there for over a century.[82] Bought in 1793 by a silk merchant, Vincenzo Masturzi di Sorrento, the building was reconsecrated as a convent several years later for a new order founded by his daughter. Formally denominated the "Servants of Maria," these nuns were informally known as the "Mantellate" after the long black hoods, or "*mantelle*," that formed part of their habit.[83] Taking over this moniker, the new women's jail was officially designated "the Mantellate."

The opening of the Mantellate jail followed a complicated and lengthy process of property transfer from Church to state after unification. In 1865, the Italian parliament passed legislation that allowed the government to expropriate monasteries and convents "in the name of public utility or for governmental use" unless they were devoted to social purposes such as education or charity.[84] After annexing the city of Rome, the state designated the Mantellate—as well as the adjacent convent of Regina Coeli that was concurrently being converted to a men's prison—as subject to confiscation, because they were devoted to contemplation rather than social assistance.[85] According to the prefect, both were needed immediately "to provide for the custody of prisoners, whose number is always increasing because of the extraordinary influx of population to this City caused by the transfer of the capital."[86]

In the case of the Mantellate, the procedure was not completed until 1885. To initiate the transfer of property to the state, the Ministry of Public Works in 1873 sent an engineer, Filippo Annibale, and a notary to survey its lands and study its tax records. Totaling over 12,000 square meters, the majority of the property was comprised of gardens and orchards.[87] A second engineer, Luigi Garavaglia, was responsible for compiling a detailed map of the buildings and a list of their embellishments and contents.[88] The bulk of the inventory, which came to 245 pages, concerned the monastery itself and its adjacent church, S. Francesco di Sales.[89]

The expropriation of the Mantellate monastery was slowed by the resistance of the resident nuns. Upon the arrival of Engineer Annibale, Mother Superior Margherita Cati "protested against the act that he was about to carry out and did this in accordance to instructions from her spiritual superiors," although she finally admitted him into the monastery.[90] Six months later, however, the nuns demanded "a written order from the Prefect of the Province" before state officials could complete their work.[91] Although the outcome was never in doubt, government administrators hesitated—to forestall further conflict with the Church—to expel the nuns from their home. In addition, the Mantellate was serving temporarily as a refuge for the religious order that had recently been expelled from the neighboring monastery of Regina Coeli. Because of these practical problems, the transfer from Church to state dragged out for years. Although the Mantellate property was officially turned over to Gaetano Cardosa, the Director General of Prisons, in 1881, the last group of nuns moved out of their quarters only several years later.[92]

After its long struggle to expropriate the Mantellate monastery from the Church, however, the prison administration simply replaced one order of nuns with another. Instead of developing a secular model of female reform, the state immediately negotiated a contract with the Sisters of the Good Shepherd to administer the new women's jail. Signed by Doria, then director of Rome's penal institutions, and Maria di Santa Rosa, Mother Superior of the Sisters of the Good Shepherd, the short contract of 1895 differed little from the earlier agreement drawn up in 1872 for the management of incarcerated women at their own convent several blocks away.[93] It directed the nuns to follow the guidelines laid out in the Ordinance of 1891, but defined no clear mechanism of oversight. Most attention was paid to external security, which was to be provided by male prison guards. One additional article exhorted the sisters to pay taxes on all the goods manufactured in the prison, indicating that the state was more interested in the Mantellate as a financial resource than as a place of reform. In return for their services, each nun would receive 50 lire, only 5 lire more than in 1872. To perform the most "lowly tasks" the state promised to provide several female guardians to assist the nuns.[94] In an era when the Italian state was struggling against the Church to take control of other social institutions like schools and charities, it is striking that contracts for women's prisons did not more strictly require nuns to implement reforms infused with the liberal values of the new parliamentary order.

From its opening in 1884 until 1914, the Mantellate jail was usually filled to its official capacity of 120, and sometimes overcrowded. But this number does not offer an adequate sense of the high number of women who passed through its cells. Many such as prostitutes who were legally registered with police but had violated the myriad regulations imposed on them, were held for only a few days after arrest. These included prohibitions against soliciting in public, leaving their brothels at night, and frequenting certain areas of the city. A few days of incarceration might also follow arrest for disorderly conduct, drunkenness, or verbal brawls. In other cases, prosecutors lacked sufficient evidence for indictment so that half of all arrestees were quickly released without charge.[95] Only one third of all inmates had been convicted; those with longer sentences were transferred to Villa Altieri.[96] Because of the rapid turnover in the Mantellate, over a thousand Roman women passed through its doors each year. The frequency of incarceration among the lives of the poor may explain why the Mantellate came to hold a prominent place in the Roman imagination.

Like Villa Altieri, the new jail was not organized according to the latest principles of punishment. Rather than adopting the Philadelphia or Auburn model, the Mantellate housed inmates in dormitories that held eight to ten beds.[97] Their activities were regulated by a bell, which came to symbolize the larger institution for both inmates and Romans in general. While the mothers superior tended to hold long tenures as wardens, the staff under them shifted continually as both nuns and female guardians—often wives of male guards or police officers—frequently took sick leave or retired.[98] Thus transience characterized not only the inmates but also the personnel, who found multiple excuses to escape their work inside prison walls. The absence of organized programs of education or labor, neither of which was required in jails, compounded the instability of an institution characterized by the constant ebb and flow of prisoners, nuns, and guardians.

While the prison administration extolled the work of the nuns, episodes of resistance marked everyday life in the Mantellate. In a letter of 1905 to his superiors in the central administration, the director of Roman prisons denounced prostitutes as "the inmates who rebel most again disciplinary rules and are the continual cause of disorder, quarrels, and damage."[99] Characterizing them as "corrupt and fallen women, who have been hardened by vice and moral depravation and lack any shred of honesty or dignity," he held prostitutes to be impervious to the "elevated religious sentiment" espoused by the mother superior. In 1914, the male prison director again complained that prostitutes had defied "the normal disciplinary regime" and ignored the "orders and exhortations of the nuns."[100] Refusing to come out of their cells, they "indulged themselves in such an uproar" that he had to personally intervene. He feared to use force because rumors would soon reach Regina Coeli and possibly provoke a violent reaction among its male inmates. Therefore, he tricked the ringleaders into thinking that they were going to court and instead transferred them to the New Prison, where they were interned in isolation cells under police guard. This report provides evidence not only of inmate resistance but also of the inability of jail authorities to prevent communication between the female and male institutions.

Neglect and absence of government oversight were prominent among the factors that may explain periodic outbreaks of rebellion in the Mantellate. Disorder was likely when turnover was high and when neighbors from working-class districts, such as Trastevere near the Mantellate or Ponte near the New Prison, were imprisoned together. The prostitutes tricked into being transferred to the New Prison, for example, took advantage of their local ties once they found themselves in a holding cell. After the ringleader, Angelina Volpi, broke the window with her boot, they began to shout to friends on the sidewalks outside.[101] The general restlessness of these women, who may have undergone multiple arrests, was not necessarily unmotivated. One inspection in 1900 by Judge Enrico Albertazzi, for example, found fault with the Mantellate for dirty walls, infestations of insects, and inedible bread.[102] Only in 1904 were gas lights installed in the jail, an improvement that had already been made in the adjoining men's prison of Regina Coeli.[103] In 1905, eleven years after its opening, the director admitted that the Mantellate had not yet implemented the legal requirement to separate convicted prostitutes from women awaiting trial.[104] Only in 1910 did the prison physician request a professional nurse to tend the sick in the infirmary, a task previously carried out by untrained inmates. Rather than arguing that the prisoners had a right to professional healthcare, he criticized the inmate-nurses for "personifying the negation of hygiene and, furthermore, being temperamental."[105] Despite the antiquated and unhealthy conditions, the prison administration did little aside from praising the nuns for their "exceptional zeal and love" in carrying out their duties.[106] To solve institutional problems, the state increased the number of nuns from eight to nine in 1903 but never reconsidered its philosophy of punishment.[107]

The Mantellate continued to serve as the women's jail of Rome through the interwar period, when it became the place of internment for members of the anti-fascist opposition, and remained open during the first decades after World War II. In 1964, the female prisoners were transferred to Rebibbia, a large prison complex on the outskirts of Rome. Planned by Mussolini as a campus for male inmates, with only a small building reserved for women, Rebibbia was to constitute the jewel in the crown of a growing penal network dedicated to "human reclamation."[108] According to fascist propaganda, this new symbol of fascist modernity would contribute to molding the "new man," dedicated to war and loyal to the state. This gendered philosophy of punishment promised little for women, whose prisons continued to be administered by nuns even in the postwar era. When the Mantellate was closed in 1964, the Sisters of the Good Shepherd moved with their charges to Rebibbia.

The Mantellate has remained vivid in the Roman historical imagination to this day. In poor neighborhoods, many residents—or their friends or relatives—had experienced life within the jail and did not quickly forget it. For female political prisoners during the interwar period, the Mantellate had constituted the first stage of their journey through the fascist gulag and, after 1946, through the courts of the new Italian republic. Its memory was also perpetuated by a book entitled *Roma: Via delle Mantellate*, which purported to reconstruct everyday prison life.[109] Written by Isa Mari, it maps the three floors of the jail in 1953, which included separate sections for minors and petty offenders, common criminals, political criminals, and prostitutes. If such separations in fact were enforced, this would have represented a partial implementation of nineteenth-century exhortations to individualize punishment. Mari also mentions an elementary school taught by young women with university degrees, an innovative introduction of female lay personnel into the jail. But other characteristics changed little, such as the absence of work for most inmates, the small, internal courtyards for recreation, and the high rate of illiteracy among inmates. Most notable was the ever-present bell that tolled the hours and surveillance by the nuns, whom Mari portrays as moralistic although not sadistic.

In 1959, five years before its closing, a popular song immortalized the Mantellate. Recorded by Ornella Vanoni in Roman dialect, "Le Mantellate" adopts the perspective of a female inmate, who laments her internment in "an old convent" where, despite the presence of the nuns and the hourly tolling of the bell, "Christ is not within these walls." Sleeping on "a sack of straw instead of a bed," she receives only "a half loaf of bread and water from a bucket" for nourishment. On Sunday mornings, the nuns tell her to have "faith," but the old prison gates locked her into a life of "disgrace."[110] The bell mentioned in the song, which had become the symbol of the quasi-religious life of the inmates in the Mantellate, was conserved and is now on display at the Criminological Museum of Rome.[111] Today, only the prison church of San Francesco di Sales, which was restored and reopened in 2010, survives on the site of the former women's jail.

The National System of Female Punishment

Across the Italian peninsula, long-term penitentiaries and short-term jails for women shared many characteristics with Villa Altieri and the Mantellate, respectively. A certain uniformity derived from the centralized nature of the prison system, which was administered from Rome according to national regulations. On the other hand, the absence of strict government oversight offered each order of nuns a degree of autonomy in governing their own institutions. The state reserved only a few penitentiaries for women, who constituted about 4 percent of all long-term prisoners. After unification in 1861, with Rome not yet annexed to Italy, female inmates were divided among four institutions located in Florence (Ambrogiana), Turin, Aversa, and Trani.[112] Although the penitentiaries at Aversa and Florence closed during the early 1870s, the total number rose with the annexation of Venice and Rome, which had female prisons, and the opening of facilities in Messina and Perugia. In short, the number of female penitentiaries peaked at seven for much of the 1880s and the 1890s and then declined to three by the eve of World War I.[113] Various factors caused the closing of female prisons: conversion to male institutions, which were always a priority; the earthquake of 1908 that destroyed the penitentiary in Messina; and, after the turn of the twentieth century, the decline in the number of inmates.[114] In 1910, for the first time since unification, the state promised to build a new, modernized women's penitentiary but never carried out the plan.[115] The complicated and changing map of female institutions echoed the fate of women during the last decades of papal rule, who were frequently transferred among different prison buildings.

The closure of several female penitentiaries, including Villa Altieri in 1897, correlated with the downward trend in the number of women convicted of serious offenses. This arc of female incarceration—rising from 443 in 1863 to a peak of 1,384 in the 1891 and then falling back to 598 on the eve of World War I—echoed crime rates during the first fifty years after unification.[116] At the national level, the percentage of women in long-term penitentiaries convicted of violent crime was even higher than in Villa Altieri, averaging about 60 percent during the fifty years after unification and rising steadily after the 1880s.[117] Inversely, property crime fell over the same time period. Contrary to stereotypes about women's proclivity for sexual crime, this category accounted for only about 5 percent of all penitentiary inmates. Of course, incarceration rates do not reflect the amount of real crime but instead the inclination of state prosecutors and judges to target certain illegal behaviors as particularly dangerous to social order. Possibly the courts became more lenient by sentencing female thieves to short sentences in jails. But the rate of female incarceration for violent crime was extraordinarily high compared to other European nations of the same period.

In contrast to the small number of long-term penitentiaries on the peninsula, jails were significantly more numerous because they were attached to the local courts in each province. Thus their inmates resided, or at least had been arrested, in the same city or nearby villages. In large urban areas, nuns administered women's jails as they did the Mantellate; in smaller towns, female guardians staffed local jails under the supervision of male administrators. Averaging nationally two to three thousand, female inmates in jails far outnumbered those in long-term penitentiaries[118] (Graph 4.1). They also comprised 7 percent of the total jail population, a rate that exceeded the proportion in long-term penitentiaries and demonstrated their propensity of women to committing mostly minor offenses.

Like the Mantellate, jails across the nation admitted many more women than the daily average suggests. Mostly arrested for marginal offenses—such as begging, petty

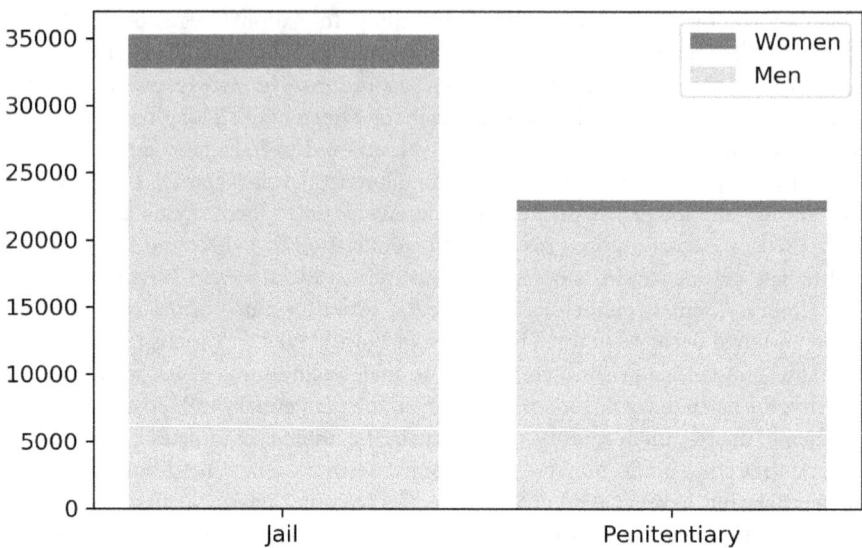

Graph 4.1 Average number of inmates by gender, 1863–1914. Source: Somm. Stat.

theft, disorderly conduct, and prostitution—twenty to forty thousand women passed through Italy's jails each year.[119]

Both women's penitentiaries and jails had female staff, a policy that had already been implemented in many parts of the peninsula before unification. The General Council of Prisons in Piedmont argued as early as 1851 that "it is intolerably abusive for men to carry out surveillance inside women's prisons and particularly to conduct personal searches of women to make sure that they are not carrying objects forbidden by the law."[120] Claiming that the prisons administered by nuns were "the best organized [and] the most clean," it urged that male guards be eliminated in all female institutions.[121] The regulations of 1861 on jails and 1862 on penitentiaries, both based on Piedmontese legislation, incorporated this principle by designating nuns and female guardians as internal staff while limiting male guards to tasks of external security.[122] Doctors, chaplains, and male directors could enter women's prisons during the day but never at night. Between 1871 and 1912, the number of nuns employed in women's penal institutions across Italy more than doubled from 61 to 143, partially due to their increasing presence in jails.[123] While early statistics are more difficult to find for female guardians, they numbered about two hundred after the turn of the twentieth century.[124]

The social profile of women prisoners at the national level for the most part corresponded to that for Rome. Most strikingly, at least two-thirds of all inmates, in both penitentiaries and jails, had been born in the southern provinces, a pattern that did not change between 1871 and 1914.[125] It is therefore not surprising that the majority of female prisoners came from the countryside, more typical of the South, than from urban areas. This preponderance of rural women declined over time, but remained over 50 percent into the 1890s, after which the state stopped collecting such information.¹²⁶ Data on profession confirms this pattern, with 40 percent of all female inmates having been previously employed directly in agriculture in both 1871 and 1903.¹²⁷ Domestic service also held steady at about 15 percent. The only major increase was in the confusing category of "worker," from 20 to 30 percent of all inmates, which reflected a slow urbanization of female criminality. Nevertheless, the largely rural origins of penitentiary inmates defies the stereotype of the nineteenth-century city, with its factories and freedom of movement, as a corrupting force for women.

Like Villa Altieri, other women's penitentiaries across the peninsula held mostly first-time offenders who were mature and integrated into families. Despite growing alarm about recidivism, the number of female inmates across Italy with previous convictions nevertheless remained below 10 percent until the 1890s, and then rose slowly to about 25 percent by 1914.¹²⁸ Experiencing prison for the first time, they were not the young and orphaned migrants whom criminologists warned were swelling the cities, but more often members integrated into poor rural families. Neither were they products of the many foundling homes across the peninsula that were thought to incubate criminality.¹²⁹ In 1871, only 2 percent had been illegitimate at birth, a rate comparable to the similarly low rate of 4 percent at Villa Altieri.¹³⁰ Also, the majority of women prisoners were married, with the rate rising from about 65 percent in 1871 to 78 percent in 1914.¹³¹ The number with children also rose from 46 to 58 percent. That most inmates had already formed their own families is compatible with their relatively advanced age. Between unification and World War I, at least two-thirds of female inmates in long-term penitentiaries were thirty years of age or older¹³² (Graph 4.2). The more stereotypical youthful criminal could instead be found in local jails, where the majority of inmates were under thirty.¹³³

Graph 4.2 Family status of penitentiary inmates, 1910–14. Source: Stat. Carc.

Upon admission, women across the peninsula entered a world similar in many ways to that of Villa Altieri. What united all women's long-term penitentiaries was their reliance on large dormitories; separate cells were reserved mainly for punishment.[134] In 1903, for example, regular individual sleeping cells numbered only five in Venice, nineteen in Perugia, ten in Messina, and were entirely absent in Trani. Only in Turin did a significant number of inmates, 159 out of 400, have access to single cells at night.[135] This failure to pattern female institutions on the Irish system meant that all categories of criminals were lodged together in violation of the Ordinance of 1891.[136] According to government statistics, overcrowding was not a problem as the number of female inmates rarely exceeded the official capacity of each institution.

Regulated on a strict schedule, a typical female inmate's daily routine emphasized the inculcation of religious obedience rather than secular education. While dropping from 88 percent in 1871 to 69 percent in 1914, illiteracy rates nevertheless remained significantly higher than in the general population; on the eve of World War I, the number of inmates who had completed elementary school had risen to barely 5 percent.[137] Prison schools enrolled only 12 percent of all female inmates across the peninsula between 1908 and 1914, demonstrating a glaring failure of the religious administrators to prepare women with the most basic skills of reading and writing before their release.[138] For those who could read, the dwindling number of books in prison libraries, which fell from a high of 806 in 1876 to only 332 in 1901, offered little opportunity for self-improvement.[139] Moreover, rates of borrowing from prison libraries, according to statistics collected by the state, were extremely low.[140]

In terms of work, women's prisons beyond Rome offered slightly more variety than Villa Altieri, but never in trades dominated by men in the outside economy. The percentage of female inmates participating in cloth manufacturing, one of the only jobs that also employed male prisoners, dropped from 25 percent in 1871 to 11 percent by 1903. The percentage of women who performed the mostly female tasks of sewing, knitting, and embroidery generally held constant at 30 to 40 percent (Illustration 4.2). The rest of the female prison population was dedicated to domestic service or other "small chores specific to the penitentiary."[141] And, whatever their occupation, female inmates were paid significantly less than their male counterparts, which allowed the nuns, who served as contractors in most women's institutions, to reap the profit.[142] Female inmates worked at much higher rates than men, which belies the common image of a dysfunctional prison system plagued by unemployment; under the management of the nuns, women were kept busy.

Loneliness characterized penitentiary life for women, most of whom had formerly lived in small villages with family and friends. Several types of statistics, collected by the prison administration beginning in 1901, demonstrate the meagerness of contact between female inmates and the outside world. On average, each inmate wrote, or dictated to a prison scribe, only nine letters each year and received thirteen in return.[143] Minutely regulated by sixteen articles in the Ordinance of 1891, a prisoner's letters had to be composed on official paper, never exceed a half page, employ "correct and respectful" language, and avoid any mention of prison conditions.[144] She could correspond only with members of her immediate family, and their responses were also opened and read by prison authorities. Most importantly, the law prescribed the

Lavori varii.

Illustration 4.2 Women and their work at the penitentiary of Perugia. Courtesy of Central Legal Library of the Ministry of Justice

number of letters by legal category: three per year for those with life sentences; four for those sentenced to reclusion; and twelve for those sentenced to detention.[145] Most female penitentiary inmates were subjected to reclusion, the penalty for most violent and property crimes, while those convicted of infanticide and abortion underwent the technically less serious punishment of detention. While these two legal categories were generally meaningless in women's prisons, which failed to provide the separate facilities required by law, they became important in the case of letter writing and explain the relatively small amount of inmate correspondence.

While letters were infrequent, visits from family members were even rarer. Each year between 1901 and 1914, only a tenth of female inmates received a visitor. That the vast majority of women lived for years without speaking to a relative can in part be explained by the restrictions in the Ordinance of 1891, which prescribed a maximum of two visits per year for those in reclusion and one per month for those in detention.[146] Family members failed to fulfill even these meager quotas for several reasons. As in the case of letters, myriad regulations discouraged relatives, particularly those who were illiterate or unpracticed in negotiating the state bureaucracy, from requesting a meeting.[147] To get permission to enter a prison, visitors had to show a certificate from the mayor of their home town attesting to their identity and close familial relationship with the inmate. Held in a special meeting room, visits were limited to a half hour and took place under the surveillance of a nun. She could suspend any conversations conducted in low voices or including "improper language or jargon unintelligible" to her.[148] For many poor villagers, who constituted the majority of inmates' relatives, a long journey to one of the few women's prisons required more money and time than they could spare for such a short meeting. Thus the infrequency of visits cannot be ascribed to lack of affection between prisoners and their families.[149]

That prisoners and their families exchanged monetary gifts attests to these continuing emotional ties. During the last decade before World War I, 63 percent of all female inmates received cash from relatives in order to supplement their meager meals with purchases at the prison commissary.[150] Averaging only 14 lire, these sums were small but demonstrate that bonds were not broken between incarcerated women and their families. Perhaps more surprisingly, during the same period, 31 percent of female prisoners sent an average of 6 lire each year to relatives. Even such tiny amounts represented a sacrifice for women earning little and a welcome gift to very poor families. By this circulation of financial resources, female prisoners and their families demonstrated both an anxiety about each other's economic destitution and continuing affection.

Prominent in the Ordinance of 1891 was a detailed list of punishments for prisoners who committed "infractions" or breaches of the rules. Composed of thirty-four articles, this section of the law minutely defined scales of prohibited behaviors with a corresponding list of penalties. According to official statistics, the percentage of women at the national level who broke the rules decreased over the decades. As at Villa Altieri, the most frequent violations across the peninsula involved insubordination and fights, a pattern suggesting a continuing level of tension.[151] While a minority of inmates received simply a reprimand as punishment, the majority were confined to an isolation cell on a diet of bread and water.[152] Although mostly focused on discipline, the Ordinance of 1891 offered more latitude to women awaiting trial and possible rewards for those already convicted. The former were permitted one letter and two visitors weekly, thereby creating the possibility of maintaining close contact with the outside world.[153] In line with the liberal nature of the Zanardelli Code, female suspects were free to confer frequently with their defense lawyers under the eyes, but out of earshot, of the nuns.[154] They also had the right to send sealed appeals to high officials, including the Ministers of Interior and Justice, as well as the Director General of Prisons.[155] While excluded from these benefits, convicts in penitentiaries could receive rewards for good behavior that ranged from the most modest, public praise from the director, to permission to buy books, send money to their families, write longer or more frequent letters, prolong their period of exercise or rest, have more visitors, or receive a small increase in their wages. Most importantly, the nuns could recommend their charges for parole or royal pardon.[156]

Because of the frequency of amnesties and pardons, it is difficult to estimate exactly how long women spent in penitentiaries. At trial, about one-third of all female inmates received sentences of up to five years in prison; another third of five to ten years; and the final third of more than ten years.[157] About 12 percent of the total faced life sentences. On the average, 5 percent of all inmates died during incarceration, with that percentage falling slowly over the fifty years after unification.[158] With the establishment of parole in 1889, the number of women released for good behavior was initially negligible but rose to 10 percent after the turn of the century.[159] Parole thus began to complement amnesties and pardon as mechanisms that allowed many female inmates to serve less than their proscribed sentences.

In conclusion, the convent prison continued to characterize female punishment long after it had lost its innovative character and become an anachronism in an age of secular liberalism. Religious orders managed the handful of penitentiaries throughout the peninsula, whose inmates were predominantly wives and mothers from rural villages. Mostly agricultural workers or domestic servants in their thirties, they had been convicted primarily of serious crimes against persons and property. Local jails, on the other hand, tended to hold younger women who had been arrested on urban streets for prostitution, begging, and petty theft. While inmates in jail remained physically close to their families, women in penitentiaries, allowed few letters or visits, were isolated from the outside world. Offering little education or job training, women's prisons failed to prepare their charges for citizenship in a modernizing society.

Belated Initiatives for Reform

It took almost fifty years before the neglected state of women's penitentiaries began to draw public attention. The voices calling for reform were disparate, never amounting to a movement and, in the end, achieved little. But at least the silence about female punishment was broken by a series of private and public revelations that forced the prison administration to turn its attention to two major problems. The first concerned the role of the nuns who, as both administrators and guards in female prisons, retained an independence that allowed them to violate the Ordinance of 1891 and deny certain prisoners' rights to women. The second issue, clearly related to the first, involved the conditions of everyday life for inmates, which were physically difficult and psychologically tedious, if not oppressive. In neither case had modernization, in terms of adopting international standards, made any impact on the stasis of women's penitentiaries and jails. While some grumbling came from inside the male prison administration, the most vocal critics were women in the fields of journalism, education, and social reform.

It is not coincidental that the belated call for reforms in female punishment came at the apex of the first wave of Italian feminism, which peaked after the turn of the twentieth century.[160] The roots of the feminist movement stretched back to 1848, when female patriots saw the Risorgimento as an opportunity to bring renewal to both sexes. Usually professing a Mazzinian faith in equality and democracy, early female emancipationists, as they were called, fought for gender equality in family law, education, and work. They also channeled their energies into the abolitionist movement that sought to free prostitutes from state licensing and police regulation. With the founding of the Italian Socialist Party in 1892, the movement began to split between bourgeois feminists, who continued to pursue legal equality, including the right to suffrage, and socialist feminists, who focused on improving the lot of working-class women. The early years of the twentieth century also saw the rise of Catholic feminism, a third strand of social reform that sought to improve women's status within the religious rather than secular sphere. In 1908, the first national conference of women brought all three groups together to discuss strategies for decreasing gender inequalities in literacy and law as well as protections for women and children in the workplace.[161] After a sharp dispute between Catholic and lay feminists over religious control of education, demanded by the former and rejected by the latter, unity among feminists began to decline. By the outbreak of World War I, tensions between bourgeois and socialist feminists had also increased markedly. Nevertheless, the early twentieth century witnessed the growth of a large and diversified movement of women who founded new organizations, petitioned parliament, and established a wealth of local institutions to improve the lives of women and girls. Often characterized as "practical feminism," this first wave was propelled by a new generation of middle-class women, who were taking degrees in law, medicine, education, and the social sciences, as well as working-class women, who were entering the industrial sector, especially the textile trade, in ever larger numbers.[162]

Yet, even with a history that stretched back to the Risorgimento, Italian feminists were tardy in turning their attention to the plight of women prisoners. Other nations boasted women of international stature within the prison reform movement, who were praised even by the *RDC*, whose articles usually focused unabashedly on men. It carried, for example, tributes to Mary Carpenter for her "uncommon energy" in focusing attention on institutions for women and youth in both England and India, and Donna Concezione Arenal, who, as an inspector of female prisons in Spain, was a "warm and indefatigable champion of reform."[163] Even though Italy had its own pioneer, Giulia di Barolo, whose biography was included in the *Acts* of the 1885 International Penitentiary Congress, her work to establish humane women's prisons in early nineteenth-century Turin seems to have been forgotten among the first Italian feminists.[164] Similarly, while the American women's movement lobbied energetically and successfully for the establishment of a system of female reformatories managed by educated lay women, its Italian counterpart was silent on the issue until after the turn of the twentieth century. Perhaps the employment of nuns as wardens and guards diverted the attention of Italian women to other institutions, such as schools, where they saw career possibilities. In any case, their early reform efforts in the area of penal law were focused on other issues, such as the abolition of regulated prostitution and the protection of children from sexual abuse.

In 1906, Regina Terruzzi was perhaps the first voice to break the silence about women's prisons, in her pamphlet entitled *A Visit to Women Inmates*. A teacher and writer, Terruzzi joined the League for the Protection of Women's Rights in the 1890s and the Socialist Party soon after.[165] As a socialist feminist, she fought for the rights of girls to attend secondary schools and for the salaries of female instructors to be raised to the level of their male colleagues. Branded as a licentious woman because she was a single mother, she endured a nasty campaign by her male superior to remove her from her post as director of a technical school.[166] Supported by feminist organizations and key socialist politicians, such as Turati, Terruzzi ultimately won the support of the Minister of Education and continued her teaching, writing, and participation in philanthropic activities. Her visit to the women's penitentiary in Turin touched all three aspects of her career and formed part of her broader initiatives to promote child protection, girls' education, and women's equality.

Terruzzi's description of the *ergastolo*, the wing of the Turinese prison reserved for inmates with life sentences, epitomizes the general tone of her critique: "In the section for lifers, I saw no *horrors* but neither did I see anything that would redeem, enlighten, or console them; I saw nothing of that rehabilitation promised by society."[167] She neither rails against the physical state of the building nor accuses the nuns of inordinate cruelty. However, she notes the multiple humiliations imposed on female prisoners, who were required to wear colored ribbons indicating their type of sentence; were forbidden from talking even during the hour of recreation; and had to eat on backless benches with their soup bowls in their laps. Under the strict discipline of the nuns, they embroidered, sewed, and knitted diligently but without enthusiasm. Illiterate and mostly from the South, the prisoners, according to Terruzzi, "seemed stunned as if they did not know where they were and spoke of their own villages as places very far away, an infinite distance from themselves."[168] Comparing imprisonment so far from home to "deportation," Terruzzi found that the inmates all have "the same thought: liberty. To be released from prison, to see people, streets, fields again ... ; to move around unobserved, to talk, cry, scream, be silent, laugh at will; to be master of themselves."[169] Instead, the hopelessness of their regimented life has reduced them to "children," who naively hope for a royal pardon. After her visit, Terruzzi called for short periods of punishment to promote "repentance and redemption" rather than long sentences of thirty years to life that demonstrated only the "presumptuousness, arbitrariness, and excessive power" of the state.[170] While she realized that radical transformation of women's penitentiaries would take much time and money, she counseled a series of small reforms that would make "daily life, characterized by basic and humiliating discomforts, less bitter."[171]

A second voice calling for reform of women's penitentiaries was that of Marchesa Zina Centa Tartarini, a journalist who had previously focused attention on the poor neighborhood of San Lorenzo in Rome by both supporting the railway workers' union and founding an experimental "school of civic education" for adults.[172] Although close to socialists such as Anna Kuliscioff, her feminism was more moderate and her view of the liberal state more benign. Nevertheless, under the pseudonym of Rossana, she wrote a scathing critique of women's penitentiaries in the widely respected magazine *Nuova Antologia*.[173] Her observations carried particular weight because they were based on her role as the only female prison inspector in Italy, a voluntary post that she held from 1903 to 1935. Published in 1912, her article drew from repeated visits to the three women's penitentiaries of that period in Venice, Perugia, and Trani. Its main accusation—that these were institutions of inexcusable pain and suffering—had already become familiar to the public through the performance of a play that she had written, "The House of Punishment," which told the story of a pregnant female prisoner who descends into madness after her baby is taken away immediately after birth.[174]

In place of the play's melodrama, Rossana's article methodically described the daily experience of women prisoners and enumerated the many ways in which they had been abandoned by the prison administration. She confirmed that women's prisons, hardly mentioned in the Ordinance of 1891, were governed by only weak contracts made between the director general and religious orders in various cities. Once the contract was signed, the sisters ruled over the quality of food, clothing, and medical care given to the inmates with little oversight from the central state. In most women's prisons, the sisters served as prison contractors and therefore held the power to stipulate types of work and rates of pay.[175] Like Terruzzi, she recounts how many inmates sent "small sums," earned through their "*forced labor*" for the nuns, to "*those far away*," living in "destitute houses deep in the Alps, hidden in forests, on river plains, or in the labyrinths of large cities." Although the Ordinance of 1891 required monthly meetings of a "discipline council" in each prison to rule on punishment for misbehavior and to recommend extra recompense for meritorious work, such councils rarely met in women's institutions. Instead, mothers superior unilaterally made such decisions. Most disturbing to Rossana was the absence of regular schools or well-stocked libraries in female prisons, even though both services were required by the Ordinance of 1891.

Because of neglect by state authorities, women's prisons were, according to Rossana, dilapidated and demoralizing. Situated in crumbling ex-convents, they lacked the architectural modernization typical of many male institutions. Women had to spend their daily hour of recreation in small paved courtyards rather than in the gardens or meadows more typical of men's prisons. Echoing Terruzzi, she characterized mealtime as humiliating, with some women having only a stool on which to eat. Afterwards, they all waited in line to wash their cups and bowls in the same pan of hot water which became "an unspeakable broth."[176] Such bleak surroundings and constant humiliation led to rebelliousness which, according to Rossana, took the form of "bad humor, despair, attempted suicide, or a flat and Jesuitical resignation" as well as simulated illness or madness.[177] To remedy these conditions that evoked the old regime, Rossana offered a simple solution: "treat women's prisons like men's prisons. That's it."[178] An admirer of the Director General of Prisons, Doria, she demanded that his reforming zeal be directed toward women's institutions.

Maria Rygier, a third critic, was more vociferous and unbending in her condemnation of the conditions in women's prisons and especially of their religious personnel. Born in Poland, Rygier moved at an early age to Italy with her family and, as a young woman, became involved with increasingly radical political organizations.[179] At first a socialist close to the feminists Sibilla Aleramo and Ersilio Majno Bronzini, by 1906 she began to espouse syndicalism and finally anarchism. Arrested in 1908 for preaching pacifism to soldiers, she was sentenced to five years in the Santa Veridiana penitentiary in Florence. After being released in 1909, as a result of socialist pressure in parliament, she began to denounce prison conditions for both women and girls in a series of articles and speeches based on her own experience and visits to other institutions.

Her most prominent article on women's institutions, entitled "Monasticism in Women's Prisons: The Penal Institution of Turin," was published in *Il Grido del Popolo* (*Cry of the People*) in 1909.[180] Claiming that "religious fanaticism knows no limits," she denounced the repeated kneeling and prayers required of inmates throughout each day of prison life.[181] She found only "clerical magazines and little newspapers" in the library rather than a wide choice of reading material. On Fridays, inmates were forbidden to buy meat at the prison canteen.[182] Out of seventy eligible women, only two were allowed to attend a special school on Sunday because, she claimed, they alone had promised to become nuns after being released from prison. Calling the discipline in the penitentiary "a regime of terror," Rygier accused the sisters of punishing any attempt by inmates "to affirm their liberty of conscience" with "horrible retaliation" including long terms in isolation cells.[183]

In addition to her denunciation of the "monasticism" in the prison of Turin, Rygier noted, as did Rossana, many violations of the prison Ordinance of 1891. Inmates were required to work twelve hours per day with no time for outside recreation in the winter and only a quarter hour in the summer. They were given no choice between two types of work—sewing by hand or making socks by machine—and were often cheated out of their wages by the sisters. The workshops, dining room, and even the infirmary were filthy; Rygier repeats Rossana's denunciation of the unhygienic procedure for dishwashing, adding that at Turin all the inmates drank from one container of water using the same ladle.

Rygier attributed these conditions to the greed and laziness of the nuns, whom she accused of increasing their income by skimping on food and furnishings and underpaying for work. Yet, as with Rossana, she also criticized the inspectors of the prison administration, who gladly accepted presents from the nuns and turned a blind eye to infractions of the law. Declaring "control by superior authorities over female prisons [to be] completely illusory," she upbraided the Minister of the Interior for failing to impose uniform rules on all female prisons.[184] She cited, for example, the varying regulations on permissible undergarments for inmates: the penitentiary in Perugia allowed women to wear petticoats but not underpants; that of Florence, underpants and not petticoats; and that of Turin, both petticoats and underpants if they were knitted rather than made out of woven cloth. Even such a seemingly trivial discrepancy was costly to inmates, who were often transferred among institutions, but profitable to the nuns who sold them the required undergarments. In short, Rygier argued that "the sisters command like absolute bosses" with the connivance of the state.[185] Unlike Rossana, who praised the work of specific nuns, Rygier called for their dismissal and replacement by lay personnel who would emphasize secular reform rather than religious conversion as the aim of female punishment.

A fourth woman involved in prison reform, Guglielmina Ronconi, exemplified the "practical feminism" that sought to bring small but important comforts to the life of female prisoners rather than engaging in theoretical debates.[186] By profession a teacher like Terruzzi, her work with the poor residents of San Lorenzo in Rome paralleled that of Rossana. In 1907, she founded the "Foundation for Moral Life" to spread popular education among the working classes, particularly women. The foundation also offered small donations for brides, prizes for clean houses, and articles of clothing. Local branches of organization were soon functioning not only in poor neighborhoods of Rome, such as Testaccio and Trastevere, but also in other cities including Florence and Bologna. Ronconi's frequent lectures, combining religiosity and patriotism with practical advice, were politically moderate and avoided denunciations of state officials. However, as a member of the National Council of Italian Women, she participated in the women's congresses of 1908 and 1914, and was a well-known supporter of votes for women. Working with other "Italian suffragettes" in the National Committee for the Vote, Ronconi, according to an admiring journalist, demonstrated a "combative spirit and admirable tenacity" in seeking to persuade parliament to act.[187] The campaign for female suffrage, which according to the same journalist was "serious and dignified," had garnered the support of many male deputies and seemed on the verge of victory. Thus despite her religiosity, Ronconi worked in secular organizations to pursue the expansion of women's rights.

In 1910, Ronconi extended her philanthropic work to the Mantellate jail, where she visited inmates, gave lectures, and promoted practical improvements. Unlike former charitable women who had visited prisoners only to save their souls, Ronconi paid attention, according to the feminist journalist Sofia Bisi Albini, to "their unclean bodies and everything that contributes to depression, rebellion, [and] desperation. Now new life, illuminated by modern science, has entered Italian prisons."[188] To alleviate the tedium and discomfort, she brought little presents, such as magazines, books, and candy, to female inmates.[189] Ronconi's first lecture—attended by Nathan, the mayor of Rome, as well as the district attorney, professors, and feminists—coincided with the inauguration of a library at the Mantellate. This event, covered by several newspapers, initiated a series of practical courses for women prisoners on "physical and moral hygiene" that touched on "pregnancy and childbirth, nursing and infant hygiene, the illegality of abortion, and the dangerous social effects of alcoholism."[190] Ronconi's prison work was encouraged and facilitated by Gina Mazza, the wife of republican deputy Pilade Mazza, who had already garnered subsidies for the prison library. That the library, as well as most of Ronconi's work, was nevertheless funded by private individuals demonstrates the meager resources allocated to women's prisons.

Most of Ronconi's fundraising as well as her good press came from the innovative "Cradle Project" that she began in Rome and then spread to other cities. As Ronconi recounted to the International Congress of Women in 1914, she was appalled to find female inmates at the Mantellate jails breastfeeding their babies while lying on dirty beds with colored striped sheets.[191] By sleeping with their mothers, babies risked being suffocated during the night or falling out of bed. According to Ronconi, 360 babies lived in Italian jails with their mothers. Her solution was to raise money from wealthy women, including the Queen Mother, to provide inmates with cradles for their babies. Covered in flowers and white veils, the cradles, according to Albini, introduced "a wave of purity among female murderers and thieves."[192] Clearly the symbolism of replacing striped prison sheets with white linens appealed to the public because of its sentimental and middle-class assumption that cleanliness was close to godliness. For Ronconi, cradles promised to redeem inmate mothers whom, she believed, still had charity in their hearts.[193] After the inauguration of the project at the Mantellate jail in 1910 with the presentation of twelve cradles, local chapters were founded in twenty-seven other cities. The Cradle Project also began providing local prisons with extra food for babies, such as eggs and milk, to improve their nutrition.

The response by Doria and the rest of prison administration to feminist demands for the reform of women's prisons varied according to the political stance and tone of each female critic. As an anarchist and radical feminist who had willingly violated the law, Rygier evoked the most indignation from prison officials and nuns alike. After the publication of "Monasticism in Women's Prisons," the mother superior of the Turinese women's penitentiary, Sister Alessandrina Lenti, wrote immediately to the director general in Rome to assure him that "this institution functions rather well" and that "the only accusation that can be brought against me is of excessive kindness."[194] That Rossana was sent by Doria to evaluate the veracity of Rygier's exposé demonstrates his preference for this more moderate feminist. In his yearly report to Prime Minister Giolitti, he praised Rossana as "a distinguished writer who unites acute powers of observation, broad erudition, and a profound understanding of the psychology of her sex."[195] The *RDC* included a positive notice of her play, affirming that its "skilled" author had been inspired by "the highest civic sentiments."[196] State officials were similarly supportive of Ronconi's "Cradle Project," sending representatives to its inauguration in the Mantellate jail. Through an official circular, the central prison administration in Rome encouraged local jail directors to take advantage of the "Cradle Project" to "make the life of newborns less pitiful and to alleviate the discomforts of the environment into which they had been born."[197] Ronconi also received praise for "raising the moral level of female inmates" through her lectures, according to a letter of thanks from its male director, Maldacea.[198] Awarding her a certificate, prison physician Alessandro Regnoli characterized himself as an "enthusiastic witness" to the same series of talks that treated "subjects that touch the heart of women and their maternal feelings."[199] In 1920, she was still offering lectures under the aegis of a new director general, Spano, showing the enduring interest of the state in her work.[200]

While feminist reformers gave public visibility to problems in women's prisons, complaints within the prison administration were also widespread. Internal reports of male inspectors, who—unlike Rossana—held high and permanent bureaucratic posts, documented a host of illegal practices in women's institutions. In 1906, for example, Inspector Gaetano Cardosa found "many irregularities and various problems" at the women's prison in Perugia.[201] The disciplinary committee had not met for over a year although, according to law, it was required to convene every four months. Two years later, the nuns in the Venetian penitentiary were faulted for multiple problems identified during a recent inspection. These included the bad quality of the school for inmates, which met only once per week, and the absence of a library. One prisoner who complained about the food had been demoted to a job with less pay and was subjected to "many unjustified punishments" by the sisters.[202] According to the inspector, fear of similar retribution discouraged other women from protesting bad conditions.[203] Such problems were not corrected for, in 1910, Inspector Cardosa was again critical of the religious administration in Venice, charging that some nuns used violence against the inmates; the food was below required standards; inmates received low pay for their work; rest periods in the courtyard were too short; and the penitentiary lacked a school or library.[204] Cardosa's criticisms disturbed his superiors in Rome who had expected him to contradict an earlier report by Rossana which had seemed to them "a bit exaggerated in its description of the existing problems."[205] Instead, his observations confirmed hers.

Prison administrators in Rome often attributed these problems to the lax supervision of women's prisons by the local male administrators, who nominally oversaw the religious personnel of female institutions. In 1910, the director general, for example, admonished Alfonso Cassella, the director of Venetian prisons, to visit the women's facility twice per week and exercise "regular and effective vigilance over the nuns and their work."[206] But, little must have changed because, in 1911, Inspector Cardosa reported that Cassella "does not exercise sufficient surveillance" over the nuns, especially over the quality of the food for the inmates.[207] Cassella was again ordered to inspect the prison several times per week rather than every ten to twelve days as was his custom. Violations of prison regulations stemmed not only from lax supervision by local male directors but also from resistance to secular oversight by religious orders. The nuns regularly tried to negotiate better terms when renewing contracts and sometimes adopted a combative tone in their correspondence with state administrators. In 1892, the mother superior of the women's prison in Venice refused to implement the guidelines of the Ordinance of 1891 on food, clothing, medicines, and wages until her present contract expired in 1894, even after the prefect gave her permission to make such changes "gradually in order to avoid disturbing in any way the management of the institution."[208] In 1907, the male director of Venetian prisons complained that he could find out nothing about the profit that the nuns extracted from their institution because "the Sisters ... repeat continually and without variation, the same sentences used during the negotiation for renewal of the contract."[209]

The intervention of feminists in women's prisons and the increasing willingness of internal male inspectors to record violations of the Ordinance of 1891 by religious administrators finally brought female institutions to public attention. For the first time, educated women—as prisoners, reformers, and inspectors—offered systematic critiques of a world that had been hidden and ignored. Feminists began to shine a light on institutions that had been marginalized in the concerted efforts of both Beltrani Scalia and Doria to implement prison reform. Although the Women's Congress of 1908 did not directly address the issue of female punishment, the subsequent meeting in 1910 established a special section devoted to "educational social work for incarcerated women and young offenders."[210] Led by the well-known lawyer and feminist, Teresa

Labriola, this subcommittee of the National Council of Italian Women declared itself "absolutely apolitical and a confessional" in its future work.[211] Such philanthropic efforts were endorsed both by Doria, which publicized Labriola's subcommittee in the *RDC*, and magistrates such as Lino Ferriani, who wrote extensively on female and juvenile crime.[212]

Yet, the new attention devoted to women inmates did not bring radical reform. Feminists advocated mostly for moderate improvements without calling for any fundamental structural change. Only Rygier forthrightly attacked the policy of employing nuns in female prisons and criticized the sentimental stereotype of women's nature as maternal. No programs were introduced to train women in more modern skills. The campaigns to fund libraries and provide cradles were laudable but also marginal, because they depended on private funding. Women, who lacked the right to vote or sit in parliament, could not sway the prison administration to invest more in female institutions. While Doria had agreed to open the doors of women's prisons to feminist reformers, he expected their efforts to be philanthropic rather than state-funded.

After 1914, the slow but steady momentum of feminist interest in female prisoners as a political issue, and the increasingly vehement private complaints of male prison inspectors, was derailed by the war and fascism. With the military crisis, prison reform was generally downgraded as a national issue and most bourgeois feminists threw their energies into supporting the troops. Some, like Rygier, became adherents of fascism in the 1920s; others, like Ronconi, were denied further access to women's prisons because of their refusal to support Mussolini.[213] Liberal and socialist feminist organizations alike were disbanded, and stasis again enveloped women's prisons for decades, a fact confirmed by the memoirs of anti-fascist women interned for their political activities. Only in the 1970s were women's prisons secularized and moderately reformed.

Conclusion

Citizenship was curtailed for female inmates in ways that were distinct from their male counterparts. While all prisoners lost fundamental freedoms, women were particularly and uniquely disadvantaged. Interned in institutions managed by religious orders, they did not enjoy the secular reforms that were hotly debated in parliament and instituted, at least partially, in male prisons. The state exercised little oversight to ensure the level of education, rehabilitative work, or even physical accommodations required by the Ordinance of 1891. Reform for women was narrowly conceived as religious conversion and sexual purification rather than as preparation needed to prosper after release in the rapidly changing society outside of prison walls. Lacking "negative rights" to equal treatment, female inmates found themselves enclosed in a religious and seemingly private sphere even though they were nominally wards of the state. Thus despite formal gender equality in the criminal code, its authorization of "special institutions" of punishment for women created a legal subordination similar to that in the civil code. Static and threadbare in conception and implementation, women's prisons represented one of the many ways that the new Italian state limited citizenship for Italian women during the five decades after unification.

5

Men: From Chains to the Penitentiary

In 1902, the Italian government abolished the use of iron shackles to restrain male prisoners. Such relics of the old regime had not disappeared with unification but had continued to be employed in the *bagni*, to which most men were sentenced. Even after the Zanardelli Code of 1889 closed the *bagni*, chains remained in place for prisoners who had been convicted to hard labor under the previous penal code. Although the 1902 decree thus affected only a minority of long-term inmates, its symbolic value was enormous because iron fetters continued to be identified with the old regime. When the patriot Duke Castromediano returned to his political prison after unification to reclaim his own chain, he surely expected such inhumane devices to disappear immediately during the transition to parliamentary rule. Instead, they remained legal instruments of punishment until the early years of the twentieth century.

Another turning point toward a general improvement in conditions of prison life for male inmates was the abolition of hard labor. The culmination of decades of debate within the prison administration, parliament, and the public, the Ordinance of 1891 finally replaced the old-regime punishments of hard labor and the death penalty with, at least on paper, an expanded and modernized system of men's penitentiaries. Opportunities for education and professional training widened for inmates, and conditions improved for the corps of male prison guards, who for decades had been underpaid and subjected to humiliating work rules such as the restrictions on marriage. While significant problems continued to plague men's prisons on the eve of World War I, changes in policy and to a lesser extent in practice, contrasted markedly with the stasis in female institutions.

The expansion of political rights for men, most significantly suffrage, and the increasing activism of trade unions and socialist organizations largely explain why men became the primary beneficiaries of the Italian wave of prison building and reform initiated by the Ordinance of 1891. Having been feared as the "dangerous classes" during the early decades after unification, working-class men were gradually recognized as citizens who were needed to build the new nation. Class anxiety, however, had not entirely disappeared. Instead, it shifted from crude repression of lower-class men to a project of reshaping them in accordance with middle-class values of industriousness, honesty, and domesticity. Prison reform was key to this normalizing process which, by the late nineteenth century, was predicated on positivist rather than Enlightenment principles. To implement individualization of punishment, for example, the Ordinance of 1891 recognized a variety of specialized male institutions, such as agricultural colonies for prisoners in the last stage of the Irish system and criminal insane asylums. An increasing number of male prisons were provided with individual sleeping cells, professional workshops, and large libraries. The new oversight and visiting committees, composed of individuals from outside the prison administration, were always inadequate but significantly more active in male than female penitentiaries.

Such reforms lessened but did not eliminate violence on the male body, which had continued without interruption during the transfer of power from the pre-unitary monarchies to unified Italy. Even after the abolition of hard labor, leg chains, and the straitjacket, disorder by inmates and excessive reaction by guards continued to characterize men's penitentiaries. Bolstered by positivist warnings about the atavistic impulses of born criminals, the prison administration defended repressive measures as necessary for security. By creating a new category of the "incorrigible" prisoner, or those considered irredeemable because of biological and psychological degeneracy, Doria attempted to resolve the conflict between his professed humanitarian reforms and the episodes of brutal repression that were publicized by an invigorated investigative press. Despite his assurances that only a minority of criminals were incorrigible, his obsession with disorderly inmates perpetuated the association of lower-class masculinity with violence. In the end, the outcome of prison reform for men was ambiguous; in a pattern promoted by positivist criminologists, it brought milder conditions for the majority of inmates and tightened discipline for those labeled as incorrigible.

Men in Criminal and Prison Legislation

Men possessed a higher legal status in united Italy than women although gender distinctions were not uniform across all types of statutes. As discussed earlier, the Pisanelli Civil Code awarded men authority over their wives and children; they also possessed markedly wider rights to dispose of their property and choose their profession than did women. In contrast, the Sardinian-Italian and Zanardelli criminal codes were fairly gender-neutral in terms of criminal responsibility and scales of punishment. Yet the prescription assigning women to "special institutions" meant that imprisonment in practice ran on two tracks: women continued to be confined in uniform and relatively unchanging convent prisons while men were subjected to a larger range of institutional arrangements. The most important were the hard labor camps or *bagni*, the agricultural colonies, and the penitentiaries, each of which were governed by separate administrative rules.

The *bagni*, organized according to guidelines that reached back to 1826, were criticized as outdated soon after unification by two parliamentary commissions. Initially refusing to close them, the state instead issued a new regulation in 1878 that was touted as a reform but harkened back to the old regime.[1] Upon admission, prisoners were "searched, shaved, made to bathe, clothed in a uniform, chained and put in solitary confinement."[2] After a minimum of a month, they were allowed to work in groups but continued to wear fetters on the left leg of varying weight depending on their sentence and behavior: from a nine-link chain of 3 kilos for the most rebellious to six links of 1.3 kilos for the most meritorious. Even patients in the infirmary were shackled unless gravely ill. When marching to and from the fields, inmates who worked outside were chained in pairs. During the night, prisoners were fettered to their beds. Calibration of restraints also permeated the different grades of internal punishment, which might require "double chains," "chains shortened to the third link," or "chains to the wrists."[3] Most severe was the straitjacket. Anxiety about escapes might have contributed to this obsession with bodily constraints but the degradation of prisoners was certainly its effect.

Inmates, however, were not entirely stripped of rights, although the law awarded directors wide discretion to waive them in everyday practice. After ten-hour workdays, *forzati* were granted a period of recreation with the right to smoke. They were permitted to read nonpolitical books, to send and receive letters under a system of censorship, and to have visits from relatives. Written complaints could be directed to the Interior Ministry in Rome although they were subject to prior review by the director. To supplement the prison guards, the most obedient inmates were eligible for relatively light tasks as monitors, scribes, and nurses. In sum, the guidelines for the *bagni* echoed to some degree those for regular penitentiaries. But the unusual autonomy of directors, the often backbreaking nature of the work, and the routine use of shackles were incompatible with international standards of prison reform. As the statesman, Scipio Ronchetti, remarked, the elimination of hard labor camps signaled the end of a "savage order of things which, far from rehabilitating the unfortunate individual expelled from society, instead lowered him to the level of a beast by keeping him chained."[4]

Agricultural colonies, whose number expanded after unification without any legal framework, had a more positive reputation. Regularized in 1887, new legislation proclaimed their purpose to be land reclamation and the construction of buildings and roads.[5] Although only those convicts with "commendable conduct … deserving of an award" were technically eligible for transfer to these institutions, forced laborers were also present during their early years. This blurring of the line between the *bagno*, with its reputation for gallery slavery, and the new notion of an intermediary institution to prepare prisoners for release, bedeviled the legislation and practical functioning of the agricultural colonies during the entire liberal period. On the one hand, the assignment of agronomists to the agricultural colonies offered a professional veneer absent from the *bagni*. Rules were relatively relaxed: inmates were not required to undergo an initial period of cellular confinement or maintain silence during recreational periods. The most meritorious might work alone at night without surveillance to tend flocks or to stoke kilns. On the other hand, all prisoners had to wear the striped uniforms typical of hard laborers, work at heavy tasks from dawn to dusk, and sleep in makeshift dormitories rather than in individual cells. Aside from the assumption that outdoor labor would banish habits of idleness, the Law of 1887 set out no specific philosophy of rehabilitation.

As editor of the *RDC* and director general, Beltrani Scalia championed adult agricultural colonies for promising a humanitarian approach to punishment as well as substantial benefits for the state.[6] He argued that the predominantly rural backgrounds of male inmates more suited them to outdoor work than factory labor. Their propensity for violent crime provided "an overabundance of energy, life, and force," which could be harnessed through "rigid and inflexible discipline."[7] After the necessarily repressive nature of the early stages of the Irish system, inmates would strive for transfer to an agricultural colony and its promise of relative freedom and finally full release. These low-security institutions were key to the process of rehabilitation by which "the transitory evil of today will become an enduring good for the future."[8] In a less utopian vein, Beltrani Scalia advocated agricultural colonies as potentially more profitable than regular penitentiaries. Italy lacked, or was unwilling to devote, the money necessary to equip their indoor institutions with modern industrial equipment and specialized technical personnel. Therefore, a large number of male inmates remained unemployed and sunk in the dreaded "*ozio*," or idleness, thought endemic to the dangerous classes.[9] Meanwhile, the new state needed labor to reclaim infertile lands, build roads, and even construct new prisons. A cheap alternative to the modern penitentiary, agricultural colonies had the added benefit of avoiding competition with free industrial workers, an increasingly controversial issue as the PSI gained strength.

The confused and belated legal codification of agricultural colonies did not prevent them from drawing broad support across party lines. Among the recommended reforms of the Commission of 1862, outdoor camps became a staple of parliamentary consensus. In 1875, Deputy Ruggiero Maurigi promoted them as "the elementary schools of agricultural," which were particularly suited to "an eminently agricultural country such as Italy."[10] During the yearly presentation of the proposed budget for the prison system, which was often contentious, a succession of interior ministers found ready support in parliament for the expansion of agricultural colonies.[11] In 1878, Deputy Augusto Elia called for the employment of "a good part of our convicts in agricultural development" in order that they not compete unfairly with urban manufacturing.[12] After the integration of agricultural colonies into the Zanardelli Code of 1889, they were increasingly touted as the most worthy alternative to solitary confinement, which was increasingly thought to "sap the constitution of inmates," and the industrial penitentiary, for which the funding was lacking.[13] In 1900, Justice Minister Emanuele Gianturco proposed a bill to reduce the initial period of cellular isolation for those sentenced to reclusion and allow them to be immediately reassigned to intermediate institutions.[14] While this bill failed, similar legislation was approved several years later that expanded eligibility for admission to an agricultural colony for all legal categories of male inmates.[15] Sponsored by Prime Minister Giolitti, who declared outdoor work to constitute, "one of the most effective methods of punishment and rehabilitation," the 1904 law crowned state efforts to define the agricultural colony for adults as Italy's unique contribution to penal reform.[16]

Despite the boast of the prison administration that "our Agricultural Colonies have no equal in foreign lands," only minimal expansion of outdoor work actually took place under the new law.[17] Doctrinal dissent cannot explain this stasis because agricultural colonies enjoyed support across the political and criminological spectrum. As Alfredo Gambardella has written, classical jurists were the earliest proponents of utilizing agricultural colonies as intermediary institutions to prepare prisoners for release.[18] There were quibbles within the group, with Lucchini, for example, opposing such broad use of outdoor labor as to violate sentencing guidelines, such as an initial period of solitary confinement.[19] But he supported the Law of 1904 and complained that it remained, a year after its passage, a "dead letter."[20] On the positivist side, while Lombroso never made outdoor work a focal point of his advocacy, he supported the Irish system and, more generally, any useful alternative to the traditional enclosed penitentiary for occasional criminals. Most notably, Ferri, who was utterly opposed to solitary confinement, included agricultural colonies in his proposed penal code of 1921.[21] In fact, rather than ideological quarrels, it was practical problems of financing that hindered the establishment of the new and more dispersed camps, particularly in the South. To make up the budgetary gap, Doria tried to close over ten small prisons in the early twentieth century but met with resistance from local interests who profited from them.[22] In essence, despite repeated requests from the prison administration, Giolitti never provided the funding to implement properly his own law and thus agricultural colonies remained limited in number throughout the liberal period.[23]

The Ordinance of 1891 regulated the penitentiaries which became the predominant institutions of male punishment after the abolition of the *bagni*. Men sentenced to reclusion, detention, and arrest were assigned to separate institutions, or separate sections within the same prison complex, and subjected to slightly differing regimes depending on the severity of the sentence. All inmates followed the same ritual of admission: shaving of the hair and beard; decontaminating baths; and the donning of prison garb. All were expected to work, have access to education and religious services, and be monitored by the new oversight and visiting committees composed of officials and citizens from the outside. Whether sentenced to life or only a few months of arrest, all convicts were liable to the same types of penalties and rewards in relation to their everyday behavior within prison walls.

Despite these commonalities, the Ordinance of 1891 imposed a scale of bodily restriction, which was highest for convicts sentenced for life and decreased proportionately for the lesser punishments of reclusion, detention, and arrest. For example, the duration of the first stage of the Irish system, solitary confinement, was seven years for lifers but only six months to three years for those in reclusion.[24] After admission to the second stage, inmates in these two categories were allowed to work and take recreational breaks in common but continued to be subjected to the rule of silence. The lesser sentences of detention and arrest did not require a first stage of complete isolation, and, during the daily hour of relaxation, these prisoners were allowed "to converse in a low voice."[25] Legal categories also determined the percent of their wages inmates received compared to the part retained by the state to subsidize their upkeep. The scale ranged from 30 percent for those in the *ergastoli* to 60 percent for those under simple arrest.[26] Similarly, the number of visits allowed each inmate or frequency with which he could send letters to relatives varied according to the types of custodial sentence. Such obsessive distinctions made the Ordinance of 1891 ungainly and difficult to enforce.

The Roman Context in the Liberal Era

As Rome transformed itself into a major European capital, several developments shaped, and in turn were shaped by, the spatial placement of male penal institutions. First, Via Nazionale was developed to link the old city with the new train station, which also involved a radical renovation of Piazza Esedra, an open area enclosed by the ruins of Diocletian's Baths. During the early nineteenth century, according to the memoirs of Manfredi Porena, this old piazza "seemed hardly urban" with its "huts and tents for menageries of wild animals, target practice, carousels, lotteries, and similar carnival games."[27] During the waning years of the Papal States, however, the enterprising priest, De Mérode, bought large swaths of real estate in Rome that included, in addition to Villa Altieri, much of Esquiline Hill. Envisioning "a radical development plan for Rome," according to another local observer, Emma Perodi, De Mérode sketched out the path of Via Nazionale and made a tentative contract in 1867 to sell the land, which included the piazza at Diocletian's Baths, to the papal government.[28] A canny businessman who was not averse to negotiating with the new Italian state, De Mérode demanded the same terms from the city council of Rome after the defeat of the papal regime. Despite reservations from anticlerical members who resented the profit to be made by De Mérode, the council approved a motion in 1871 to buy the land for the purpose of redeveloping the area near the station.[29]

Only in 1886, however, was an architectural plan approved for the redevelopment of the piazza. Submitted by Italian architect Gaetano Koch, the blueprint laid out two large semicircular porticos lined with imposing columns. Designed to follow the original shape of the "esedra" of Diocletian's Baths, the porticos offered an imposing facade for a section of the Roman ruins that housed a variety business and social institutions, including the prison. Although Koch's blueprint required expropriation of private land, including that of the Tiburina Bank, "for public utility," the city council approved the plan unanimously.[30] It suited their desire to have a "sumptuous and convenient" entrance to Via Nazionale for visitors entering Rome from the train station.[31] Across from the semicircular porticos, other sections of the ruins were preserved including the Basilica of Santa Maria degli Angeli that had been designed by Michelangelo. Construction of the ambitious Piazza Esedra, now designated the Pizza della Repubblica, was completed in 1901 with the grand Fountain of the Water Nymphs. Koch went on to design two other symbols of the new national capital, the Banca d'Italia on Via Nazionale and Piazza Vittorio near the train station.

A second change in the Roman landscape, which influenced not only the spatial distribution of its prisons but also the profile of the large numbers of local men that passed through its jails, was the expansion of it "popular" districts, that is neighborhoods of artisans, factory hands, and the poor. Trastevere remained, throughout the liberal period, a working-class neighborhood as well as the site of many charitable institutions to treat and house the sick, disabled, and abandoned. Employed mostly as artisans, shopkeepers, and day laborers, the local population also provided a workforce for the Tobacco Factory, a large neoclassical building situated in the middle of the district at Piazza Mastai. Erected by Pius IX in 1859, it was taken over by the Italian state, which retained a monopoly on cigarettes and cigars. One of the largest industries in Rome, the Tobacco Factory was unusual in employing women as well as men.

Another significant working-class district, Testaccio, was also located within the Aurelian Walls but did not see rapid residential development until after the annexation of Rome. A rural zone of country houses and wineries before 1871, its grottoes and Roman walls provided hiding places for political enemies of the Papal police.[32] Because of its large swathes of unbuilt land and its location on the Tiber, Testaccio was integrated into early city plans as a site of future industrial expansion and low-cost housing. As owner of most of the land, the state completed a number of projects during the last decades of the nineteenth century including a river port, public electric plant, train station, modern slaughter house, and central market. To attract labor to the zone, the state began to build subsidized housing as early as 1883 although the bulk of it was completed only after the progressive mayor, Ernesto Nathan, took office in 1907. His mayoral administration was also responsible for finally providing Testaccio with public baths, a washhouse, and a communal kitchen.

A study of Testaccio, based on a survey conducted by the philanthropist Domenico Orano, offers a detailed portrait of its working class in 1908.[33] In his published report entitled *How the Roman People Live*, Orano combated the image of Testaccio, held by the bourgeoisie and the police, as a district dominated by "organized crime" and "the hooligan."[34] Instead, he praised the local men for their "physical vitality and the flash of intelligence in their eyes" and the women for their "countenances of the highest and most genuine beauty."[35] However, he decried the living conditions of the poor, who were "crowded like chickens in a coop," with 38 percent of all families living in one room and another 30 percent in two.[36] Such high residential density produced mounds of garbage, bad air, and filthy toilets. With two-thirds of the family income needed for food, a high percentage of women worked in the Tobacco Factory in Trastevere, or as nurses, or as seamstresses at home. Boys and girls also sought employment rather than staying in school. Denouncing the frequency of abortion, illegitimacy, infant mortality, and alcoholism, Orano appreciatively cited Ferri's calls for penal substitutes, such as classes for the poor about hygiene and sexual planning. Although moralistic in tone, Orano offered a well-documented portrait of an impoverished population which was "working and modernizing itself."[37]

An even newer working-class neighborhood, San Lorenzo, was located outside the Aurelian walls behind the train station. Dating only to the 1880s, it housed a growing population employed in construction, including the expansion of the local Verano cemetery, transportation (railway and tram), and garbage collection.[38] Left out of early city plans, as were all the rapidly expanding neighborhoods outside the walls, San Lorenzo was even more disadvantaged than Testaccio. Only after the turn of the twentieth century was it equipped with sewers and then, under Nathan, with a washhouse, school, and market. Such extreme poverty attracted the philanthropic work of not only the prison reformer Ronconi but also Maria Montessori who established a series of elementary schools in this neighborhood.

A third development that was intertwined with practices of punishment, the campaign to eradicate malaria, was carried out mostly in the plains surrounding Rome called the Agro Romano. Although frequently characterized by nineteenth-century travelers as a desert, the Agro Romano supported a number of rural economic activities including the cultivation of wheat, grapes, and olives as well as the pasturage of buffalo and other migrating animals. The seeming emptiness of the agricultural ring around Rome derived both from its low density of population as well as large swings in seasonal migration. While the population of the Agro doubled between 1871 and 1900, the percentage of permanent residents accounted for less than a third of the total, while the remainder came mostly from other districts of Lazio, or from neighboring regions of the Abruzzi and the Marche, to take up temporary employment.[39] Few stayed through the summer, when malaria ravaged the wet and marshy plains typical of the Agro. Dubbed "Roman Fever" by Anglo-American tourists and novelists, malaria had plagued certain zones of the city since classical times, but was even more prevalent in the countryside and made travel outside the city particularly hazardous.[40] In his guidebook to Rome, for example, William Taylor Field warned that "death lurks in the stagnant pools, and the plain is desolate" south of the city. Approaching Rome from Naples by train, one of his traveling companions held a handkerchief to her nose "in an effort to strain the malarial influences out of the night air" while another took "sundry draughts from a flask in his breast-pocket, probably to fortify his system against the same insidious power."[41]

The problem of malaria—and more generally the impoverishment of the rural peasantry—elicited both public and private efforts to improve living conditions in the Agro Romano. The state focused on prevention through *bonifica*, or the draining of the swamps to alleviate the etiology of the disease, initially identified as miasma and, by the early twentieth century, as a parasite spread by mosquitoes. Beginning in the 1883, a number of bills on *bonifica* were proposed in parliament but only in 1904 was a moderately successful legislation passed. Progress was impeded by the owners of the *latifondi*, or large estates, who resisted the expropriation of the lands necessary to construct a drainage system.[42] Private efforts aimed more broadly at alleviating problems of not only health but also illiteracy, malnutrition, and substandard housing. Under the leadership of a group of prominent democratic and feminist intellectuals, such as Sibilla Aleramo and Giovanni Cena, over forty private secular night schools were established in the Agro Romano by 1910. Doctor Angelo Celli, a specialist in malaria, experimented with the use of screening and quinine to fight the disease and campaigned, as a member of parliament, to expand their use in the Agro.[43] Improvements in the lives of the peasants were so meager, however, that Cena and Celli organized a counter-exhibit in 1911 as a critique of the triumphal tones of the Grand Exposition in Rome celebrating the achievements of the first fifty years of unification.[44]

Roman prisons were not immune to the expansion and reshaping of the city during the Liberal period. Spatially, city planners were loath to situate penal institutions in middle-class neighborhoods and therefore looked to working-class districts and the Agro Romano. Despite improvements during the Nathan years, the miserable living conditions of Trastevere, Testaccio, San Lorenzo, and other impoverished zones made them the source of many of the inmates in local jails, whether native or immigrant. Beginning in the 1890s, waves of strikes by both industrial and agricultural workers drew attention to the plight of the poor and strengthened the campaigns of democrats and socialists for prison reform.[45] The state exploited convict labor power in schemes to solve social problems, such as malaria in the Agro, or to complete public works. Planning for new architectural projects to raise Rome's stature as a European capital came to encompass not only the more famous Piazza Esedra near the train station, Victor Emmanuel monument in Piazza Venezia, the Justice Ministry on the right bank, the walls of the Tiber, and statues to Risorgimento heroes such as Garibaldi and Cavour, but also a new men's prison.[46]

Men's Prisons in Rome

Rome offers a useful microcosm for tracing the experience of male prisoners during the five decades after the liberal state replaced the old regime monarchies. In contrast to the establishment of the convent prison at San Michele for women and children, policies of punishment for men changed little under papal rule. On the eve of unification, male prisoners in the Papal States were disbursed among a number of crumbling institutions. The liberation of Rome in 1870 and its subsequent annexation to the Kingdom of Italy brought significant, although not immediate, transformation in the geography of its male prisons. To refashion itself as the seat of Italy's new parliamentary government, Rome had to rid itself of its own bastilles, which had gained notoriety through the memoirs of political prisoners such as Paya. Castel Sant'Angelo, infamous for its treatment of liberal and nationalist opponents of the papal government, was immediately closed, while San Michele became an auxiliary jail to the New Prison. Although the old men's prison at Diocletian's Baths remained open for several decades, the state established two new institutions meant to signal a modernized policy of punishment: the agricultural colony of Tre Fontane and the radial penitentiary of Regina Coeli.

Diocletian's Baths

During its first few decades as Italy's capital, Rome continued to use the site of Diocletian's Baths as a penitentiary for men. While this papal prison did not harbor the unsavory reputation of former political dungeons such as Castel Sant'Angelo, its location nevertheless constituted an obstacle to the plans of both the city council and the national state for transforming Rome from a sleepy small town into a modern city. The prison occupied a wing of the vast ruins of the largest public bath in ancient Rome, dedicated to Emperor Diocletian in 306 CE. Able to accommodate over three thousand bathers, the original architectural complex of about thirty acres also included exercise rooms, libraries, and gardens.[47] It was so vast that it constituted "a sort of small city within a city and therefore completely self-sufficient and cut off from the external world."[48] The sense of enclosure was provided by walls around the entire complex, including an immense exedra or semicircular portico near the crest of the hill facing Rome. Abandoned during the Middle Ages, the baths had fallen into picturesque ruins by the renaissance, when a series of institutions began to be established within their walls. In the mid-sixteenth century, Pope Pius IV commissioned Michelangelo to design the Church of Santa Maria degli Angeli and a Carthusian monastery in one section of the ruins while Gregory XIII built a papal granary to store wheat and other staples that were distributed to the public to keep peace. In 1705, Pope Clement XI created a second granary that, after its closure in 1800, was transformed into a prison.[49] While the first inmates were women transferred temporarily from San Michele in 1827, Diocletian's Baths became predominantly and more permanently a male institution with the construction of dormitories for forced laborers in 1831 and for men convicted of minor crimes in 1834.[50]

After 1870, local and national officials no longer considered Diocletian's Baths to be an appropriate location for the major penitentiary of Rome. Earlier in the century, the ruins had offered several advantages for the construction of a prison because they were located far from the residential center on Viminale Hill, which enjoyed fresh air and plenty of water. This water, supplied by the Acqua Marcia, one of the Roman aqueducts restored by the Renaissance popes, had encouraged the building of summer villas by aristocratic families during the early modern period. Until mid-century, the area remained one of the many rural neighborhoods within the Aurelian walls that surrounded the small central city. In 1867, however, Pope Pius IX began the urbanization of this district by building the first railway station of Rome, which took the name "Termini" from the thermal springs that had fed Diocletian's Baths. Within a few years, the station became the primary entrance to the city, replacing the Flaminian gate to the north, which had traditionally welcomed travelers coming by foot, horse, and carriage into the Piazza del Popolo.

The juxtaposition of the railway station with the prison at Diocletian's Bath brought an immediate outcry after unification from the new city council of Rome. In 1873, one councilman lamented that "the erudite and diligent traveler, who, coming from beyond the seas or the mountains, journeys to Rome to explore the classical monuments of our ancestors" was immediately confronted with "the distressing and dispiriting spectacle of the prison at Diocletian's Baths."[51] Repelled by this "indecent, nauseating, and irksome sight," visitors would avoid Viminale Hill even though it was "one of the most breezy and salubrious of our city."[52] Because the prison at Diocletian's Baths was "unworthy of the leading city of monuments in the world," the councilman was pleased that the municipality was initiating discussions with the Director General of Prisons to move the institution to a different site.

Embarrassment about the placement of the prison at the entrance of Rome was not confined to the city council, but can be found in memoirs and parliamentary debates. According to Porena, travelers leaving the train station passed "barred windows" through which could be seen "convicts at work" who would greet the curious passersby with "words that were not always friendly and less often polite." For him, it was unimaginable that the prison remained at Diocletian's Baths for years after unification, offering "this spectacle as a welcome to the capital."[53] Deputy Giuseppe Mussi suggested moving the penitentiary to Viterbo because its location "offends the decorum of the capital" for visitors arriving on the train.[54] Such sentiments were echoed by L. Pavolini, an early director general of the prison administration when he asked, "Who could doubt that the hard labor prison at Diocletian's Baths must disappear?" Such an "unhappy structure" should be replaced by "elegant buildings that make the traveler happy as he enters the Capital of the Kingdom."[55]

The urgency to close the prison at Diocletian's Baths also related to its backwardness as an institution of punishment, according to city councilors. Housed within an early modern granary, itself constructed within the ruins of a Roman bath, it could never be remodeled to "achieve the twin goals of punishment, according to the teachings of the social sciences and ethics, which are to provide an example to the public and to reform the criminal."[56] In a modern prison, according to the minutes of the city council, this would be accomplished by "depriving the inmate of liberty without eroding his conditions of health."[57] Because the prison at Diocletian's Baths could not hope to reach this standard, Rome had fallen behind "her sister cities, which have had the fortune to precede us in the enjoyment of liberty, of which civilization is the first-born son."[58] In its place, municipal officials called for "a new majestic cellular prison" that would rival the model penitentiaries typical of other European capitals in humanitarian architecture.[59]

Critics were correct that Diocletian's Baths exhibited few characteristics of a modern penitentiary. Established in the early 1830s, the men's prison held about three hundred inmates at the time of unification and expanded within a few years to five hundred.[60] Rather than enjoying separate cells as advocated by reformers, prisoners slept in dormitories of thirty to forty beds. Punishment was frequent and mostly took the form of warnings. However, about a quarter of all infractions of the rules brought more serious retribution, specifically that of consigning the inmate to an individual punishment cell with a diet of bread and water. In an advance over the papal period, a school was established which, according to government records, increased literacy among its graduates. However, only a minority of inmates attended classes, which were large and lasted only a few months each year. A new library held fewer than 150 books, which were borrowed by only a small minority of inmates. Despite its location on Viminale Hill, the prison was not particularly healthy. On the average, most prisoners got sick at least once each year, with the most prevalent disease being scrofula, according to the long-time physician at Diocletian's Baths, Alessandro Casali.[61] Based on over thirty years' experience as a prison doctor, Casali claimed that hard labor outdoors was more healthy than the less strenuous indoor tasks because of the dark and dank conditions of enclosed workshops.

Inmates were divided into two juridical categories: serious criminals sentenced to the retribution of hard labor and minor offenders who were interned for the modern purpose of rehabilitation.[62] The first group worked outside in a variety of public projects including the completion of the railway station, the building of a ring of forts around Rome, and the expansion of the new cemetery of Verano. The second was employed mostly in textile production within prison workshops, making clothes for the guards and inmates of penal institutions throughout Rome.[63] Others served as shoemakers, carpenters, and ironmongers, with the most fortunate assigned to the printing press, established around 1840 to publish government documents.[64] As under papal rule, the first group, who labored in chains under the watch of mounted guards, was the largest. Despite the desire of administrators to make the prison financially self-sufficient, over 50 percent of all inmates of Diocletian's Baths were left without work in 1871, a proportion that declined slowly to 30 percent by the end of the decade and then dropped precipitously in the 1880s, when prisoners began to be employed in the experimental project of land reclamation at Tre Fontane. Although pay was low, employment allowed men to buy extra food at the commissary and to take savings home with them upon release.

Prisoner turnover was high at Diocletian's Baths, which lost one-third to one-half of its population each year, but admitted almost the same number. Transfer to another institution accounted for almost half of those leaving the penitentiary, while only a fourth gained release because they had served their entire sentence. Another fourth benefitted from personal pardons and mass amnesties, practices that had characterized the prisons of the old regimes and continued after unification.[65] Often proclaimed to celebrate a happy event in the royal family or a religious holiday, amnesties markedly shortened the sentences of many inmates and eased the burden of prison life. Liberals criticized the arbitrary nature of amnesties, which were thought to undercut respect for the criminal law and the principle of deterrence on which it was based.

Despite the sense of shame evoked by the men's prison at Diocletian's Baths, it remained in use until 1891under its long-time director, Martino Barrone. Its longevity can partially be explained by wider national problems, especially budgetary constraints during the first decades of unification. The delay in passage of a new penal code also complicated the designing of new prisons across the peninsula, because parliament was uncertain whether to model Italian penal institutions on the Pennsylvania, Auburn, or Irish system. At the local level, the transfer of executive, legislative, and judicial offices to Rome took precedence over the construction of new prisons. Furthermore, the search for a new site for the men's penitentiary was delayed by long negotiations between the city and the national state over the financing.[66] Once the prison at Diocletian's Baths finally closed in 1891, the space was offered by the Italian state to the Catholic orphanage of Santa Maria degli Angeli for charitable purposes.[67] Today it is the site of an elegant hotel, whose website mentions the former papal granary but not the penitentiary.

Tre Fontane

Instead of immediately replacing the prison at Diocletian's Baths, Beltrani Scalia opened an experimental and controversial project in 1880 attached to a monastery at Tre Fontane, situated in the *campagna* or countryside south of Rome. The penal institution of Tre Fontane combined the characteristics of a traditional *bagno* and a modern agricultural colony; both designations are used in official documents. Inmates were conscripted into the battle against malaria that plagued this low-lying area called the Agro Romano, which was dotted by ruins of Roman aqueducts and inhabited by the coastal cowboys known as *butteri*. Calling the reclamation of the Agro Romano "one of my few dreams," Beltrani Scalia developed a penal "experiment" at Tre Fontane to accomplish this end and claimed success in both national and international forums.[68] Even after closure of the Tre Fontane prison camp in 1895, he continued to lobby parliament for the reintroduction of convict labor into the war against malaria, whose success would constitute "the seal of our liberation—a favorable sign of our Risorgimento."[69]

In long articles in the *RDC* and presentations to parliament, Beltrani Scalia set forth the advantages of employing prisoners to reclaim the Agro Romano, which he characterized as a "project of civilization and progress."[70] Rather than copying the Northern European model of industrialization, he argued that Italy should recognize and exploit the agricultural character of its economy and its people. The nation had vast tracts of land in need of development and a potential convict workforce that came mostly from peasant backgrounds. Already a large economic enterprise, the prison system did not have sufficient funds to develop enough industrial workshops to employ its inmates. In any case, why would the state want to turn prisoners from rural backgrounds "into sedentary factory workers" whose life would be less healthy and who would compete unfairly, according to socialist and many liberal parliamentarians, with free labor?[71] Agricultural work not only cost the government less but was more appropriate for the countryside outside Rome, a city dominated by the administrative and service sector rather than manufacturing. As tracts of land were made habitable and healthy by convict labor, they would be turned over to poor but free colonists. Even prisoners would benefit from employment in the fresh air that, upon release, would provide them with skills useful for their return to rural life. As a result of his plan, Beltrani Scalia predicted that Rome would come to be "surrounded by a healthy atmosphere, fertile farmland, and thriving villages."[72]

While parliament was still debating the merits of land reclamation in the wider Agro romano, Beltani Scalia used his administrative muscle to initiate an experimental use of convict labor at Tre Fontane or "Three Fountains."[73] The site of an ancient Greek monastery dating to the seventh century, it marked the place where, according to legend, St. Paul was beheaded and, as his head bounced on the ground, three fountains sprang up. Each was memorialized by a small church, the most important of which has an oratory designed by the prominent renaissance architect Giacomo della Porta; the churches and monastery formed a picturesque cluster in the otherwise abandoned countryside[74] (Illustration 5.1).

Illustration 5.1 The monastery at Tre Fontane

Occupied and rebuilt by both the Benedictine and Cisturcian orders over the centuries, the monastery was entrusted to a group of French Trappist monks in 1868 by Pope Pius IX. To counter the malaria that threatened their lives, the monks began planting large numbers of eucalyptus trees in the mistaken belief that their roots would drain the soil and their aroma would sanitize the air. They also began to produce a eucalyptus liqueur, which was sold as an antidote to malaria. Early in his tenure as director general, Beltrani Scalia convinced the Italian state to sign a contract with the monks whereby they retained rights to a large expanse of land in exchange for paying rent, planting 10,000 eucalyptus trees each year, and building roads and houses for future peasant colonists. This contract offered him an opportunity to put his theories about the advantages of outdoor work to the test.

In 1880, Beltrani Scalia initiated his experiment of supplying prison labor to the Trappist monks. While the work was managed by the religious order, regular prison guards accompanied the prisoners to enforce discipline and maintain security. Both parties to this unusual partnership between Church and state were pleased with the results. In a report of 1882, Abbot Giuseppe Maria Franchino boasted that the planting of large numbers of eucalyptus trees had been so successful in combating malaria that "we are giving up drainage" of wetlands as unnecessary.[75] He praised the convicts, who "were more robust than most free workers, got ill less frequently, and ... were often more docile."[76] They were capable not only of heavy chores, such as breaking up the earth and constructing roads, but were surprisingly careful when carrying out the more delicate tasks of weeding and pruning the grape vines. According to Father Franchino, this outdoor work truly reformed the convicts, who arrived at the Tre Fontane as "almost brutes" but within a few weeks "became again men."[77]

Reprinted in the *RDC*, Father Franchino's enthusiastic report reached a larger public when it was quoted by Pietro Nocito, a lawyer and a member of the legislature, in the *Nuova Antologia*. In an article titled "An Excursion," Nocito recounted an investigatory visit by the parliamentary Committee on Criminal Statistics to Tre Fontane in 1882. The committee included Beltrani Scalia, Lucchini, Ferri, and Lombroso, the last of whom conducted his usual search for "criminal types" by questioning the prisoners and "touching their heads and their arms as a doctor would do with his patients."[78] Nocito was moved by the sight of the common work undertaken by the inmates and the Trappist monks, the former "condemned by law" and the latter "condemned by their own will" to live in toil and risk their lives to malaria.[79] Noting that "charity does not have political parties," he heartedly approved this cooperative effort of Church and state, which was symbolized by the juxtaposition of a portrait of Pope Pius IX and a marble bust of Luigi Torelli, a champion of the project in the Senate, in the reception room of the monastery.[80] In partnership with the Trappist monks, Nocito wrote, the state could obtain two objectives: reclaim the *Campagna romana* for future settlement while simultaneously transforming criminals into healthy and happy workers who rarely tried to escape. His reservations about the forced labor camp included the absence of a school and the infrequency of pardons for its inmates. But his sympathy was greatest for the guards, those "martyrs" who were exiled "to live in territories that were deserted and devastated by fever" with little prospect of professional advancement or public recognition for their sacrifice.[81]

The experiment at Tre Fontane, however, did not escape sharp criticism despite the glowing reports of Beltrani Scalia, Father Franchino, and jurists such as Nocito. The strongest denunciation came from Corrado Tommasi-Crudeli, a member of parliament, a physician, and a specialist in malarial research. A former follower of Garibaldi who had participated in the wars of unification, he objected vehemently to the contract between the Italian state and the Trappist monks, who were awarded a large tract of land previously owned by the convent of the Sisters of the Holy Sacrament. This transfer, according to Tommasi-Crudeli, contradicted the intent of the Law of 1865, which authorized the confiscation and secularization of certain monastic lands for the benefit of the state and its citizens. In the spirit of this legislation, fifty peasant families had submitted a proposal to establish a village on the land at Tre Fontane. Instead, the committee overseeing the liquidation of monastic land had chosen to return the land to a religious order and, even worse, to one that had been chartered in a foreign country. The result, complained Tommasi-Crudeli, was that "property, which had been confiscated from an Italian religious order, was withheld from a group of free workers and ended up in the hands of a French religious order. Those are the bare facts."[82] Rather than celebrating the cooperation of Church and state at Tre Fontane, as had Nocito, he took a more anticlerical and egalitarian stance in supporting the rights of poor workers in the new state.

Tommasi-Crudeli's training as a physician led to his second major denunciation of the penal experiment at the Tre Fontane. While he did not criticize the principle of outdoor work for prisoners and admitted that the "moral and economic conditions of the colony were excellent from the beginning," he found that "his illusions" about the benefits of agricultural labor as redemptive punishment were destroyed when he discovered high rates of malaria among the inmates and guards.[83] Few deaths had resulted because many of the sick were transferred to Rome and treated with quinine. But Tommasi-Crudeli pointed out the injustice of exposing prisoners to malaria, "a disease that may diminish their physical strength in order to benefit private industry," that is, the coffers of the Trappist order.[84] Malaria could also render prison guards unfit for work, an unjust burden that was not imposed on other state employees such as the security and finance police. Thus, Tommasi-Crudeli proposed on the floor of parliament that the work at Tre Fontane be suspended at least during the period from July through October when the risk of malarial infection was greatest.

Concerns about the conditions at Tre Fontane reached a wider public through the press. In a series of articles, Carpi, a participant in the Roman Republic of 1848–9 and a former parliamentary deputy, expressed his dismay at the employment of prison labor in land reclamation. While praising Beltrani Scalia for his "very sharp intellect" that had produced a "superb book on penitentiary reform," he nevertheless castigated him for forgetting the plight of free workers in favor of a project that reduced crime only minimally.[85] When more than eighty thousand peasants emigrated from Italy each year because of poverty, how could the prison administration ignore the larger moral and economic problems of the nation? Another newspaper of the capital, the *Rassgna Settimanale*, was generally sympathetic to outdoor work for prisoners, but was horrified at the high rate of sickness at Tre Fontane. Ridiculing the practice of giving inmates "*a cup of coffee with aniseed before going out to work and a glass of herbal liquor in the evening*" to prevent malaria, the journal suggested that "perhaps a bit of quinine would be better."[86] Was it "consistent with the principles of humanity" for the government "to force prisoners to work in such an insalubrious place where few, with only rare exceptions, preserved good health"?[87] The immorality of such a policy was only compounded by the fact that the profits of such work were enriching a private organization rather than the state.

Beltrani Scalia continued to defend the hard labor camp at Tre Fontane, reprinting both the critical newspapers articles and his replies in the *RDC*. To Carpi, he denied that he had ever maintained that "outdoor work had the potential to transform *forzati* into little lambs," but that idleness caused them irreparable harm.[88] By championing the working class, Carpi was sliding into "the most indulgent philanthropy" or even worse, a socialist advocacy "of national laboratories or phalansteries."[89] To the director of the *Rassegna settimanale*, he boasted that rates of disease were low and death almost unknown at Tre Fontane, a fact recognized by the International Congress of Hygiene, which had recently voted in support of his experiment. In parliament, the government vigorously defended the project at Tre Fontane against the denunciations of Tommasi-Crudeli, declaring that it had become "the terminus of a continuous pilgrimage of scholars, statesmen, journalists, and magistrates," who were fascinated by the coordinated efforts of the monks and the prisoners to reclaim the Agro Romano.[90] Even Prime Minister Depretis intervened personally in the debate to declare himself convinced that the project "had succeeded perfectly and that it must continue."[91] Tre Fontane also garnered international praise from the delegates who visited it during the International Penitentiary Conference in Rome as well as from several medical congresses, which judged that the positive effects on "general health and civilization" in the Roman countryside outweighed the mortality among prisoners.[92]

Despite continuing support from Beltrani Scalia and other criminologists such as Ferri, Tre Fontane was closed in 1895, partially doomed by the contradictions within its mission. On the one hand, assignment to Tre Fontane was touted as a reward to prisoners who had shown good behavior in their previous institutions and who were almost ready for release. By providing prisoners the opportunity to plant and tend eucalyptus trees in the open air, Tre Fontane did resemble in some aspects the "agricultural colonies" that began to be established, particularly in Tuscany and Sardinia, in the 1870s and which were subsequently reclassified as "intermediate" penal institutions in the Zanardelli code. On the other hand, Tre Fontane shared many characteristics with the traditional *bagni*, such as Civitavecchia, from which most of the prisoners were initially transferred.[93] Men convicted of violent crime got priority in admission, despite the general despair among statesmen and criminologists about Italy's high rate of illegal bloodshed in Italy. Beltrani Scalia, as well as many criminologists, preferred them to thieves because of their "superabundant energy, vitality, and strength" as well as their purported honesty.[94]

Furthermore, the abysmal living conditions at Tre Fontane contradicted any claims to the status of an innovative agricultural colony. Inmates numbered about three hundred, with most working for the monastery and the rest constructing a new labor camp at nearby Buttaro.[95] Wearing chains both day and night, they were kept under surveillance by mounted guards during daylight and by guards in "Turkish slippers made of cloth," which made no sound, during sleep.[96] Dormitories consisted of "mobile huts" that could hold up to eighty inmates.[97] The Regulation for the *bagni*, as opposed to that for the regular penitentiaries, prescribed food rations and other conditions of daily life.[98] Thus, despite the Beltrani Scalia's rhetoric of reform, which championed outdoor work as a reward for good behavior and an effective mechanism of redemption, Tre Fontane remained basically a penal camp of hard labor in chains.

Such contradictions between the theory and practice of outdoor prison work continued to characterize other agricultural colonies after the demise of Tre Fontane. Those in Sardinia, most notably the agricultural colony at Castianidis, also employed prison labor to reclaim malarial lands. But a penal project which subjected both inmate and guards to such high rates of disease could not be tolerated so close to the capital where it came under constant scrutiny from parliament and the press. In the face of such opposition, compounded by practical disagreements with the Trappist monks, the state closed the colony of Tre Fontane as a prison in 1895 although not without regrets. In 1899, Ferri continued to judge Tre Fontane as "an experiment that worked marvelously" while Beltrani Scalia, after being nominated to the Senate, introduced new proposals for using prison labor to reclaim the Agro Romano.[99] The most successful of these, approved in 1904, widened the categories of inmates eligible for employment in the reclamation of malarial lands throughout Italy. Even though Doria supported this measure, the size and number of agricultural colonies grew little during the ten years before World War I. Meanwhile, the Trappist monks remained in residence at Tre Fontane, and still today make eucalyptus liqueur, based on the original nineteenth-century recipe, for sale to tourists.

Regina Coeli

While the experiment at Tre Fontane was in progress, the Italian state finally began to construct a cellular prison for Rome, which promised to feature "architecture that has no equal in Italy or abroad."[100] Despite general consensus that the capital deserved a modern penal institution to complement other public works celebrating the newly unified nation, the project advanced slowly and required negotiations between the national government and the city council about two practical concerns: location and financing. The penitentiary at Diocletian's Baths, considered an embarrassing eyesore for travelers passing through the train station, had to be relocated. Furthermore, jail inmates were incarcerated in two dispersed and inadequate institutions—the New Prison and San Michele—which complicated administrative coordination and the transport of suspects to the courts during their trials. Therefore officials sought a location large enough to house both suspects and long-term convicts in adjacent cellular facilities.

Rather than readapt an old building, as was customary for many Italian prisons, national and local authorities proposed to erect an entirely new building that could be designed according to contemporary architectural guidelines. They explored two initial sites, both in the vicinity of the women's prison at Villa Altieri, but rejected each for different reasons. The first location, near the Church of Santa Croce in Gerusalemme, was ultimately judged as too unhealthy for a penitentiary, although the explanation was more complicated. In 1873, the state offered to sell two parcels of land, Diocletian's Baths and the New Prison, to the city in return for building a cellular penitentiary near Villa Altieri with local funds.[101] Municipal counselors were initially agreeable to the plan, which promised to provide "moral and economic advantages for Roman citizens."[102] Yet they worried that the old prison buildings were too small and unsuited for the public housing needed for the burgeoning population of Rome. Finding no resolution, the state subsequently identified a second possible site, the ex-convent of S. Fedele at Sette Sale, near the Basilica of San Clemente, as "perfectly suitable" for a cellular prison.[103] National officials ultimately balked at the price, however, because in this case the city owned the ex-convent. The collapse of these two projects meant that the new men's prison was not going to join Villa Altieri in the relatively rural district near the gate of San Giovanni. It also demonstrated the complicated property relations between national and local levels of government, both of which had benefitted from the expropriation of religious lands after unification.

Ultimately, the new cellular prison was built at Regina Coeli, the site of an ex-convent on the Tiber within the ancient working-class neighborhood of Trastevere. By choosing a parcel of land that it already owned, the state lowered its costs and avoided negotiations with the city council. Pronouncing the area to be healthy, it proposed building a "Palace of Justice," the new national court, nearby. The choice, however, was problematic because of the site's cramped location between the river in the front and the sharp rise of Janiculum Hill at the rear. As Vittorio Vidotto has written, the new prison blocked access from the new Mancini Bridge over the Tiber to the beautiful park above. Adorned with a statue of Garibaldi and busts of other heroes of 1848, this park was designed to celebrate the battles of the Roman Republic, fought nearby.[104] Ultimately, the parcel of land became too crowded to accommodate the national court, which was later built upriver north of the Vatican. But plans went forward for the cellular prison, reinforcing the status of Trastevere as a neighborhood of institutions for the poor, many of which were unwanted in the newer bourgeois parts of the city. Already the site of the Buon Pastore reformatory and San Michele jail, the river banks of Trastevere continued to serve as the prison zone of Rome. Thus in terms of spatial placement, Regina Coeli looked back to the past and increased the density of social institutions in a neighborhood that was too powerless to resist increased crowding.

The new prison supplanted the original monastery of Regina Coeli, which had been founded in 1655 by Princess Anna Colonna for the Discalced Carmelites (*Carmelitane Scalze*). Taking the name Chiara Maria della Passione after the death of her husband, this member of a prominent Roman family served as the first mother superior of the new religious complex, which included a church on the Via della Lungara facing the Tiber and a large expanse of gardens and fields within a walled enclosure.[105] According to a seventeenth-century observer, the church was "not very big, having only three altars ... but was adorned with stucco reliefs and marble balustrades" that made it worthy of the Virgin Mary, the Queen of the Heavens (Regina Coeli), to which it was dedicated.[106] However, because the Discalced Carmelites were not dedicated to social work, Regina Coeli, like the neighboring convent of the Mantellate, was expropriated in 1873 by the Italian state.[107] Government engineers immediately drew up a detailed survey, running twenty-two pages, of the elaborate buildings and agricultural grounds.[108] In the course of converting the convent into a penal institution, both the monastery and the church were demolished.

Regina Coeli was already being utilized as a temporary jail even before its choice as the site for a modern penitentiary. As early as 1872, the prefect of Rome requested the expropriation of the convent "to provide custody for prisoners, whose number is constantly rising in this City because of the massive influx of people related to the transfer of the capital."[109] By the following year, empty buildings in the convent complex were being used as a police lockup and for the new school for prison guards. Because Rome's jails were overcrowded, with space for only one thousand inmates, parliament devised a temporary solution of building a few modern radial wings on the Regina Coeli grounds[110] Once the decision was finally made in 1881 to locate the men's penitentiary at Regina Coeli, a series of laws approved financing for further expansion and for the modification of the urban plan for that section of Trastevere.[111] Support was almost unanimous from both parliament and the city council for "this new important institution," although financial restraints slowed construction.[112] But Prime Minister Depretis, who declared the cellular penitentiary to be "an issue of vital interest for the city of Rome," successfully won additional funding during the decade-long period of construction.[113]

Parliament also approved the use of "inmates themselves to build their own house," although this policy proved to be controversial.[114] Rather than resort to private contractors, as was usually the case, the state gathered a work force from hard laborers at Diocletian's Bath and convicts with construction skills from across the peninsula. The use of prison labor offered several advantages to the state: a remedy for the unemployment and resulting "laziness" of male inmates; a workplace already surrounded by a fence and occupied by the school and barracks for prison guards; and, most importantly, low labor costs without any threat of strikes. Proud of "experimenting on a vast scale," Depretis declared success based on reports from the chief engineer that "the convict workforce was very well-behaved, obedient, respectful, and loved—more than anyone had expected—every moment and type of work assigned to them."[115] Their rate of sickness was less than in penitentiaries, and they were leaning new skills from the free artisans hired from the outside to oversee the construction. In 1885, a delegate from the International Penitentiary Congress commented approvingly that, "if not for the surrounding walls and the prisoners' uniforms, one would believe oneself to be in the center of a vast construction site."[116]

However, the building of Regina Coeli did not escape criticism. Free workers, supported by leftist deputies in parliament, protested the employment of convicts in the type of construction work that formed the backbone of the Roman labor market. The state, which was saving about 43 percent by using convict labor, initially persisted until the economic recession of the 1880s raised unemployment to an unacceptable level. In 1890, the government announced that the final wing of the prison would be completed by "free," that is non-prison, workers.[117]

Despite the pride of Italian lawmakers and prison administrators that Rome finally possessed a radial prison, the architectural plan did not faithfully replicate the nineteenth-century ideal of a symmetrical star. Both because of the constraints of the site and the piecemeal process of construction, the final building consisted of three different sections.[118] The first—used for offices, the infirmary, chapel, and lodging for the guards—was rectangular and faced on the river; a second took the form of a partial star; while the third, on a skewed axis to the rear, that of a cross. The resulting eight wings of individual cells served the function of both a jail and a long-term penitentiary, with the latter housed near the back of the walled complex. Exercise yards shaped like pinwheels had internal barriers to ensure that prisoners would be segregated from each other even during recreation. Central towers allowed guards to monitor visually all the cells. Despite the disparate volumes and awkward placement of the three buildings, the modernity of Regna Coeli's radial design is immediately apparent from drawings or when viewed from Janiculum Hill. Its design contrasted with the architecturally old-fashioned women's jail of the Mantellate, located in the back of the same penal complex.

Great attention was devoted to the design of the cells in order to comply with modern standards. Depretis approved numerous studies to assure that the cells served "the requirements of hygiene and security and prevented any communication between inmates and the outside without imposing excessive severity."[119] Inspired by foreign examples of the Philadelphia model, Italian engineers designed each cell to have "a large window to admit light and air" covered by a special type of Persian blind made of glass, which prevented inmates from seeing the street.[120] A slit over the cell door allowed for cross-ventilation when the outside window was open. Uniquely Roman floors were designed using shards of earthenware from a hill in Testaccio, where ancient traders had disposed of broken oil and wine jars. A small hole in each door allowed guards to keep constant surveillance over inmates, who themselves could not see out. Only on Sundays did an ingenious lock allow doors to be cracked enough for inmates to watch the priest conduct Mass in the central tower. Although each wing was supplied with water taps, the prison was least modern in its lack of individual toilets. Instead, prisoners received clay chamberpots (*vasi fecali*) that were to be collected by guards and emptied into large latrines on each floor.

These uniform and rather innovative cells housed two different categories of inmates. The largest group, ranging from one to two thousand on the average, occupied the wings designated as a jail.[121] About one-fourth had been definitively convicted while the rest were suspects awaiting trial.[122] The penitentiary was much smaller, with 152 single cells for long-term inmates.[123] The number of personnel reflected the disparity in the size of the jail and penitentiary, with five times as many guards assigned to the former than to the latter.[124] As in the case of women, large numbers of men were jailed for short periods awaiting trial or serving only short sentences. In 1886, for example, over fifteen thousand men passed through the gates of Regina Coeli, a number that dropped to about eleven thousand in 1914.[125] Although some repeat offenders may have been admitted more than once during the year, these high numbers nevertheless reveal that incarceration was not an uncommon experience for Roman men.

While jail inmates remained in their cells all day, except for segregated exercise in the pinwheel yards, those in the penitentiary worked in groups both inside and out. During the early years, many prisoners participated in the construction of Regina Coeli, while others worked in blacksmithing, carpentry, and shoemaking. What most distinguished convict labor at Regina Coeli was its print shop, which in 1883 began to publish the *Official Gazzette* and the *General Calendar* for the national government. Over the years, the prison expanded its typographical operations to include other state publications such as the proceedings of the 1885 International Penitentiary Congress, the annual volumes of prison statistics, the *RDC*, and, after 1909, the yearly compilation of all Italian laws and decrees.[126] Because the print shop was located next to the adjacent women's jail, these volumes feature "Mantellate" on the title page. The press, as well as ancillary activities, such as bookbinding, employed about sixty inmates. Many of the machines had been transferred from the *bagno* at Civitavecchia, which had run a smaller operation.[127] During their tour of Regina Coeli, delegates to the International Penitentiary Congress admired the "vast and well-lit workshop," in which the presses were powered by gas engines.[128]

Because Regina Coeli competed with seventy other typographic establishments in Rome, it drew fierce criticism from leftwing members of parliament and organized workers.[129] Deputy Antonio Maffi, the first working-class member of parliament, charged that convict labor created unfair competition with free workers unless redirected to agricultural projects.[130] The large expenditures required to equip the workshop at Regina Coeli, he argued, should instead be used to improve the lot of the lower classes, whose living conditions were often worse than those in prison. In response, Depretis and subsequently Giolitti summoned a series of arguments to defend the print shop at Regina Coeli, the most obvious being the financial savings to the state and the ability to teach prisoners a skill. To answer more directly the objections of Maffi and other leftist deputies, they argued that convicts made up only a small percent of all printers in Rome and that, furthermore, the prison employed several free laborers as master artisans to oversee the work.[131] Finally, they pointed out that prisoners could not strike and therefore interrupt the daily publication of government documents, a perspective that demonstrated the fears of the state in the context of an expanding labor organization and socialist power.[132] In the end, Roman printers, unlike construction workers, constituted too small a group to successfully pressure the state to abolish the Mantellate press.[133]

A multifunctional complex, Regina Coeli also housed the school for prison guards. Founded in 1873, the school for guards constituted one of the major innovations immediately following unification, a period that otherwise saw little progress toward liberalizing penal law or practice. Because the guards came from the poorer and uneducated classes, the school combined basic instruction in reading, writing, and arithmetic with the rudimentaries of prison law.[134] On a practical level, the student guards learned to use weapons and underwent a trial period carrying out their duties. They lived in the prison barracks for three to six months of training which culminated in an exam. Although the courses were elementary, the school represented an innovative attempt to form a new generation of working-class personnel instilled with a secular and professional ethos corresponding to the liberal principles of the new state. In the 1890s, construction at Regina Coeli displaced the school, which moved to the New Prison after the turn of the century."[135] Generally satisfied with the functioning of the school, Doria was nevertheless ambivalent about the increasing political activism of its students, who no longer resembled "the old type of guard, who was rigid and faithful in carrying out his duties in an essentially mechanical way," but instead was influenced by "the new currents of thought that had infiltrated the social masses."[136] Having recognized and modestly improved their baleful working conditions, he nevertheless pined nostalgically for the more passive and obedient guards of the past.

As with earlier prisons, Regina Coeli became part of the urban fabric of Rome. Located in the dense and central neighborhood of Trastevere, it became the focus of complaints about noisy exchanges between prisoners and their families and friends, who called out greetings and news from the outside. In 1896, for example, Achille Girelli charged that people shouted from the upper balconies of his apartment building across the street to Regina Coeli "in a vulgar manner," particularly at dawn and dusk.[137] Through these vocal contacts, suspects awaiting trial were able to "prepare their defense and therefore trick the justice system."[138] Despite denials by prison administrators of "these calumnies," its engineers admitted that the streets around the prison were so narrow that prisoners could indeed see nearby buildings and agreed to modify the windows and heighten the perimeter wall.[139] The complaints continued, however, and even today, an urban legend persists that voices can be heard from the Janiculum Hill calling down to inmates below.

More substantial contact between the inside and outside of Regina Coeli came from the large number of local men who circulated, sometimes for only a few days, through its jail. So common has been the experience of incarceration that Regina Coeli has come to symbolize local urban identity. According to a popular *stornello*, or Roman song, those who have not mounted the steps of the prison can call themselves neither Roman nor *Trasteverini*, that is, inhabitants of the surrounding neighborhood.[140] During World War I, the government established a small munitions plant at Regina Coeli employing twenty inmates and offered amnesties to many others who enrolled in the military.[141] Under the fascist dictatorship, the innovative reputation of Regina Coeli was lost to memory as it became, together with the infamous jail in Via Tasso, a center for the interrogation and detention of political prisoners. Today, while long-term male inmates have been moved to the penitentiary at Rebbibia, Regina Coeli continues to serve as a men's jail.

The National System of Male Punishment

Because of the variety of male penal institutions in Rome, the capital generally reflected the larger prison system across the peninsula. Before the Ordinance of 1891, the *bagni* nationwide held 50–60 percent of all men with long-term sentences[142] (Graph 5.1). Even though early commissions recommended the abolition of these hard labor camps, their numbers grew throughout the period.[143] After the Zanardelli Code abolished the *bagni*, the number of male penitentiaries, which rose from twenty-five in 1862 to fifty-one in 1891, peaked at seventy-seven during the early twentieth century before declining slightly.[144] Inmate totals corresponded to this arc, rising from about 7,000 in 1863 to a peak of 24,500 in 1902 and then dropping to 15,000 on the eve of World War I.[145] Convicted men, constituting 96 percent of all long-term prisoners, greatly outnumbered women within the Italian penal system.

Men: From Chains to the Penitentiary 153

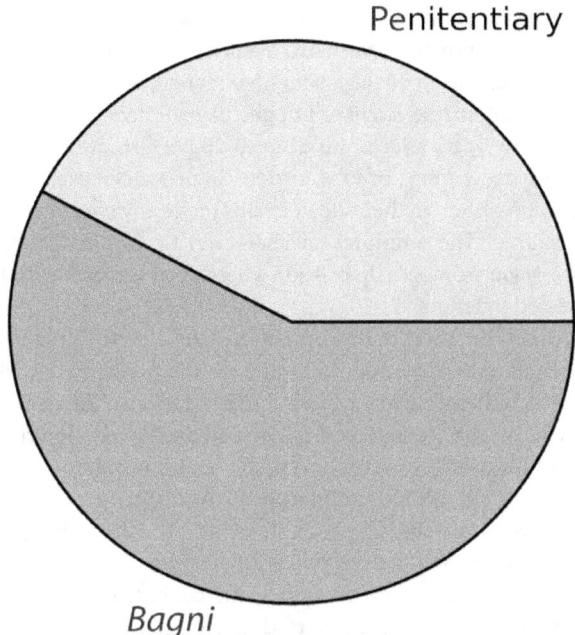

Graph 5.1 Men in penitentiaries and *bagni*, 1868–85. Source: Congrès pen.

Little information is available about everyday life in the *bagni* except for glimpses afforded by prison statistics. Although housed in antiquated and dilapidated buildings, dormitories were not overcrowded.[146] Contrary to the stereotypes of *forzati* as hardened criminals, rates of recidivism were 10 percent in the early 1870s and rose to only 25 percent in 1888.[147] More inmates were sentenced for violent than for property crimes, with the former increasing over the years and the latter falling.[148] A majority of prisoners, two-thirds of whom were southerners, came from rural areas.[149] Rather than loners, most had family ties: few had been foundlings, at least half were themselves married or widowers, and a third had children.[150] In terms of age, three-fourths were over forty, probably because of the long sentences meted out for hard labor.[151] During the 1870s and 1880s, a quarter of all inmates were sentenced for life and most of the rest to at least fifteen years.[152] Some hard labor camps had schools, although only 13 percent of all inmates attended classes sometime during the year.[153] They also had libraries, which grew during the 1870s and 1880s, but nevertheless contained only one book for every three to four prisoners. Because two-thirds of the inmates were illiterate, only a minority could take advantage of the opportunity to read during their leisure hours.[154] Overall, the most repressive aspect of life in the *bagni* remained the chains, which were worn day and night.

Despite their identification with earlier galley rowers, only about one-fifth of all *coatti* worked outdoors in agriculture, land reclamation, the salt mines, or construction. A slightly higher percentage was employed in manufacturing, organized either on a craft or industrial basis. Artisanal activities included carpentry, iron-mongering, shoemaking, and garment-making while industrial shops were concentrated in textiles. A small elite of inmates, less than 1 percent, were employed in typography.[155] As both Beltrani Scalia and many legislators bemoaned, a large number of prisoners remained without work in the *bagni* although the rate decreased sharply from over 50 percent in the early years after unification to 20 percent during their final year.[156] In contrast to the narrow range of jobs for female prisoners, even men in the *bagni* enjoyed an advantage, although their life in chains made any type of employment more painful and degrading. The omnipresent characteristic of physical restraint starkly differentiated the *bagni* from female prisons where even inmates with long sentences were never subjected to fetters.

Comparison between men and women in terms of their social profiles and everyday experiences is more straightforward for the penitentiary, where the same regulations applied to theoretically equivalent institutions. The conditions in men's penitentiaries were better than in the *bagni* and improved significantly over the fifty years after unification. In many ways, the social profile of male penitentiary inmates resembled their female counterparts. A majority of men—between 60 and 70 percent—were entering a penitentiary for the first time, although their rates of recidivism were higher than those for women.[157] In 1871, most had been sentenced for property crimes rather than violence, but in the 1890s this ranking began to flip.[158] As property crimes decreased sharply, homicide and assault persisted in a pattern that distinguished Italy from its northern neighbors. Southerners were not only overrepresented in the penitentiary population, but their percentage also increased from 50 percent in the 1860s to 63 percent in the years before World War I[159] (Graph 5.2). Similarly, men resembled women in coming predominantly from rural origins, a phenomenon that decreased only slightly by the 1890s, when the state stopped collecting this information.[160]

Male convicts, however, differed in other ways from their female counterparts. While rarely foundlings or orphans at birth, they were less likely to be married or have children. Like prisoners in the *bagni*, half were husbands or widowers (compared to at least two-thirds of all women), and only 30 percent had children. Male prisoners also tended to be younger than their female counterparts: 45 percent were under thirty

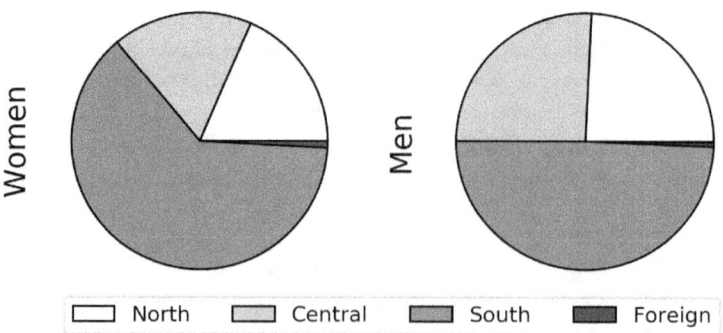

Graph 5.2 Birthplace of inmates by region, 1866–80. Source: Ann. Stat and Stat. Carc.

years of age in contrast to 30 percent of women.[161] In sum, while men in penitentiaries were more often young and single than women, nevertheless half were over thirty and enmeshed in family life. Such a social profile emphasizes the intermingling, rather than sharp distinction, between lawbreakers and other members of the popular classes.

Upon admission, male inmates were more likely to enter old-fashioned penitentiaries resembling Diocletian's Baths than radial prisons such as Regina Coeli. Despite the official adoption of the Irish system in the Ordinance of 1891, which required separate sleeping cells, the majority of men continued to live in dormitories with twelve to sixteen beds and, on the eve of the war, only one-fourth of all male inmates occupied single cells.[162] Like women, men suffered severe isolation from the outside world measured by the similarly small numbers of letters sent and received each year.[163] Prison regulations also discouraged visits from family members, which were even less frequent than for women, perhaps because of men's customary transfer to penitentiaries in distant parts of the peninsula.[164] The exchange of money constituted the strongest tie with relatives and demonstrated that prisoners were not forgotten by their families. In contrast to women, almost all men received small sums each year from their families to purchase extra food from prison commissaries although many fewer sent money home to relatives.[165] Despite these differences, loneliness must have characterized the lives of all prisoners, who were cut off from family and friends on the outside and largely forbidden from speaking to fellow inmates.

As in women's institutions, men's penitentiaries followed a strict schedule monitored by the clock and sometimes a bell. Religion played a much smaller role in daily life because secular administrators and prison guards, rather than religious orders, presided over the *bagni*, penitentiaries, and agricultural colonies. Despite their official status as auxiliary staff, chaplains occupied a relatively minor and sometimes disputed position in men's institutions. In 1888, for example, the papal newspaper, the *Osservatore Romano*, charged that the state had abolished religious services in the prisons of Rome.[166] The ensuing correspondence between national prison officials, who denied the allegation, and the Vicar of Rome, who recommended priests for its penal institutions, came down to money. The ensuing struggle over the appropriate pay for priests revealed continuing tensions between Church and state. Pleading for the centrality of religion to "the much debated problem of criminal rehabilitation," chaplains argued that "the prison must be first of all a hospital to cure moral diseases."[167] In his report to the director of Roman prisons, the chaplain Francesco Saverio Damiani boasted of his many victories over these "morbid infections" by increasing the number of masses and encouraging inmates to undergo the sacraments of confession, baptism, confirmation, and, for those living in "concubinage," marriage.[168] Nevertheless, religion was almost entirely absent from the pronouncements of prison administrators and treatises of criminologists about male punishment in contrast to its central role in female penitentiaries.

Opportunities for education were more widespread for men than for women, although the pattern was uneven. Felice Cardon, an early director general, actively promoted the expansion of primary education through a series of circulars to local wardens of male prisons. Noting that almost one-half of all male prisoners attended school in 1867, he suggested ways of increasing this percentage by raising the pay of teachers, rewarding inmates to attend classes, and creating a uniform curriculum across the peninsula so that transfers among penitentiaries would not impede learning.[169] By 1872, he declared that all penitentiaries possessed schools, which were fundamental to increasing literacy and "a principal instrument of rehabilitation."[170] The number of male inmates attending classes indeed continued to rise, peaking at 7,463 in 1878, but then fell to less than one thousand in 1914.[171] Such a steep decline, much sharper than the general contraction in the number of men sentenced to prison, may be partially explained by the voluntary nature of school attendance. As literacy increased from 39 percent to 63 percent of all male inmates, fewer may have needed the simple skills of reading, writing, and arithmetic taught in prison schools[172] (Illustration 5.2).

In contrast to the stagnant state of women's libraries, the number of books available to men rose from one per person in 1871 to 3.5 in 1914, and readership also increased.[173] Beltrani Scalia offered a prize for suggested readings for inmates that would "inspire in their soul moral health, love of their country, enthusiasm for work, [and] respect for the law" and recommended specific books to local prison wardens for their libraries, including *The Rehabilitation of the Prisoner* by Vitale Borba and Amilcare Pighetti and *The Prisoner's Book* by Giuseppe Miccoli.[174] He also edited a short-lived periodical for inmates, intended to "touch ... their hearts" without excessive moralism.[175] In spite of this official enthusiasm for reading, several men's penitentiaries reported as late as 1906 that their libraries were almost nonexistent, prompting several publishers to donate books to the prison administration.[176] Thus, although male inmates as a whole

Illustration 5.2 Classroom in a men's prison with "School is a Prize" written on the blackboard

enjoyed much larger libraries than their female counterparts, the funding for books was not always adequate.

Conditions of work improved significantly for men during the half century after unification because, after the abolition of the *bagni*, the majority of men were employed indoors. As Giulianelli has pointed out, Italian prisons before World War I were far from modern factories because the state did not invest the necessary resources for acquiring updated technology, buying sufficient primary materials, and training prisoners from rural backgrounds.[177] As late as 1913, only 11 percent of all male prisoners worked in the two main industrial occupations, textile production and typography, while 43 percent engaged in artisanal crafts such as garment and shoe making, carpentry, blacksmithing, bread-baking, and hand production from straw, jute, and horsehair.[178] Others were employed in outdoor gardens and domestic upkeep of the prison, while 22 percent remained unemployed.[179] To avoid competition with free labor, most of the finished goods supplied the prison network or the military and, in the end, were not particularly profitable. Administrators preferred direct state management of prison workshops, which brought a higher rate of profit and protected inmates from periodic abuse by private contractors. Nevertheless, outside businesses managed most of the production in the *bagni* and, even after the Ordinance of 1891 legally enshrined a preference for direct state control, continued to oversee at least half of the working inmates in male penitentiaries.[180] The profitability of prison labor was also curtailed by the large percentage of inmates who remained unemployed because of mental and physical health problems or, more importantly, the continuing failure of the state to provide enough jobs. In sum, men received training in a vastly larger range of jobs than did women, received higher wages, and had the opportunity to apply for outdoor work in the agricultural colonies as their third stage of punishment. But Italian prisons became factories only in the sense of paying wages for labor rather than in the organization of production.

Masculinity and Violence

The substantial reform of male punishment, with the abolition of hard labor and the death penalty, attenuated but did not eliminate the perceived relationship between violence and, in Lombroso's famous phrase, "criminal man." Positivist criminology codified in supposedly scientific terms early nineteenth-century prejudices against the dangerous classes, who were conceived to be more animalistic than their bourgeois superiors. Already represented as violent and bloodthirsty, male offenders were diagnosed by criminal anthropologists as biologically and psychologically atavistic and unable to restrain their inborn impulses toward murder and assault. While Lombroso and Ferri had little hope that crime would ever disappear, they predicted that it would become increasingly economic in nature with growing industrialization and urbanization. The characterization of Italy as a particularly violent nation, a conception propagated by both criminologists and members of parliament, was not incorrect, but simplified a complex issue. Although the Italian homicide rate was higher than that for northern Europe, it decreased over 50 percent between 1880 and 1914.[181] This dramatic drop in criminal violence among the general population, however, was not reflected in the make-up of the male prison population. Instead, long-term penitentiaries saw an increase in the proportion of inmates sentenced for murder and assault from 32 percent in 1871 to 56 percent in 1914.[182] This apparent contradiction can be mostly explained by the passage of the Zanardelli Code, which decreased or eliminated sentences of incarceration for many nonviolent crimes.[183] Thus many minor offenders remained in jails while those with longer sentences—often for violence—were concentrated in the penitentiaries.[184]

While historians have yet to fully explain the high rates of violent crime in Italy, recent research on masculinity and honor offer some fascinating initial insights. As Pieter Spierenburg has argued, ritual violence was widespread across early modern Europe among men, who took umbrage at perceived slights to their own masculinity or the honor of their families. Within the Roman working classes, such disputes took the form of knife fights carried out in bars or other public places, often fueled by alcohol. According to the French traveler Edmondo About, the "game of knives" was particularly prevalent in Trastevere where murder stemmed from "arguments incited by vanity or opportunism, competition in love, gaming, or drinking."[185] This folkloric characterization of Roman men as proud and disdainful of theft, but quick to draw the knife, has partially been confirmed by crime statistics. According to Daniele Boschi, unmeditated brawling between lower-class men, usually over trivial matters, accounted for most homicides in nineteenth-century Rome.[186] As Romans began to disparage such behavior and law enforcement improved, murder became less casual and widespread by the turn of the twentieth century. Increasingly, a small number of men with criminal records accounted for most violent crime. Thus, Boschi offers a suggestive explanation for the seemingly contradictory trends of a general drop in homicides with a rise in recidivism rates among the prison population, which, according to national statistics, increased from 30 percent in 1871 to 64 percent in 1914.[187] Disputes over masculine honor were also frequent among the middle classes but took the form of duels which, as Steven Hughes has argued, rarely led to death and were tolerated by police and prosecutors.[188] Thus few gentlemen (*galantuomini*), aside from political opponents of the state, saw the inside of a prison cell.

Violence permeated not only the earlier lives of male inmates but the routine of prison life itself. Most obviously, the requirement of wearing chains both day and night fatigued and sometimes wounded the bodies of all men sentenced to hard labor. After the abolition of fetters, the discipline in the penitentiaries remained rigid. Despite the myriad prison rules—which ranged from talking to fomenting revolt—less than a third of all prisoners committed infractions during each year and only about 20 percent more than once.[189] Yet punishment for this minority of inmates grew increasingly severe over the decades, with solitary confinement, rather than lighter punishments, such as a reprimand or deprivation of daily recreation, being levied in 79 percent of all cases in 1914 compared to only 44 percent in 1871.[190] To accommodate this "double imprisonment," the number of punishment cells reached one thousand by the turn of the century and almost doubled by 1910.[191] On the flipside of the increasingly severe punishment, the number of rewards tripled between 1900 and 1914 for prisoners with good behavior.[192] Thus discipline took a dual track of harsh repression for a small pool of inmates labeled as troublemakers and increasing leniency for the more docile majority.

Even if fewer prisoners underwent internal penalties, prison administrators never discontinued the use of exemplary violence as a means of discipline. As Mario da Passano pointed out, even the *RDC* had to admit that deaths occurred regularly within the prison system, a sign of the customary use of excessive force against rebellious or merely troublesome inmates.[193] One of the most egregious and publicly debated cases of the Giolittian era involved the sailor Giacomo D'Angelo, who died in 1903 while under arrest in Regina Coeli. After breaking a window in his holding cell, D'Angelo was put in a straitjacket and tied to his bed. Completely immobilized for two days, his screams were ignored until a guard found him dying during his morning rounds. The outcry in the press and parliament against this inexplicable death led to a trial of Regina Coeli's director (who had quickly been transferred), physician, and several guards. All were absolved, based on their testimony that confinement in a straitjacket was normal procedure. The defense claimed that D'Angelo was afflicted by "cerebral psychopathology" that was "presumably congenital" and, abetted by his heavy drinking before arrest, led to a nervous collapse.[194] Such a Lombrosian-inflected diagnosis, put forth by expert witnesses, offered the court sufficient evidence to protect the careers, if not the reputations, of Regina Coeli's personnel. As a vindication of the prison administration, Doria published the court's final sentence in the *RDC*.

The "D'Angelo case" displayed the growing power of the newspapers and public opinion to illuminate hitherto dark corners of the Italian criminal justice system. As with the exposés of the horrible conditions in women's prisons that began to appear after the turn of the twentieth century, investigations by journalists working for the numerous Roman newspapers, such as the *Messaggero*, *Giornale d'Italia*, and *Popolo Romano*, reached a public that included a growing and increasingly literate working class. Most critical of the state was *Avanti!*, the official organ of the PSI. Based on denunciations by socialist deputies, such as Turati, *Avanti!* repeatedly condemned episodes of violent discipline within Italy's prisons.[195] Because of widespread outrage, the "D'Angelo case" was instrumental to the passage of the 1903 regulation abolishing the use of the straitjacket in Italian prisons and the 1904 law expanding the categories of convicts eligible for the agricultural colonies, the latter of which were believed by many, including Ferri, to offer an antidote to cellular confinement. In addition, Doria, despite his satisfaction at the trial's verdict, launched a survey about prison discipline among administrators and criminologists.

Doria's study took the form of a "referendum" among "specialists in the fields of penal law, punishment, and anthropology"—both inside and outside of the prison system—about the best methods of keeping order among inmates.[196] The *RDC* published over twenty-five responses from criminologists such as Lombroso and Sergi; lawyers such as Ugo Conti and Alessandro Stoppato; psychiatrists such as Filippo Saporito and Augusto Sacozzi; various prison directors and doctors; and, as the lone female voice, Rossana. Taking the form of five questions, the open-ended survey focused on "incorrigible" prisoners, whom Doria claimed were becoming increasingly violent and rebellious following the softening of rules under the 1903 decree. As one respondent, Deputy Lorenzo Ellero, pointed out, Doria offered no empirical proof of increasing disorder in Italy's prisons and perhaps was simply seeking "a type of plebiscite approving a return to the past" characterized by harsher internal penalties.[197] Such an interpretation was consonant with Doria's declaration that the new "security belt," which had replaced the straitjacket, had not proven effective because guards had difficulty attaching it to recalcitrant prisoners and easy for the latter to wriggle out of.[198] However, the willingness to publish the results of the survey in the *RDC* indicated a certain degree of sincerity on the part of a prison administration that had often functioned more secretly in the past. Thin-skinned and quick to defend himself against journalistic and public criticism, Doria nevertheless employed the *RDC* in its best tradition, that of airing the views of experts in a variety of fields.

Not surprisingly, given the positivist proclivities of the *RDC*, Lombroso's answer to the referendum was published first. Most fundamentally, he insisted on the need to categorize inmates into groups according to their degree of dangerousness and apply different types of punishment to each. For occasional criminals, especially young offenders, he recommended probation, fines, outdoor work, or house arrest. He was critical of penitentiaries, which stifled inmates in cellular isolation or corrupted them in group dormitories. If occasional criminals were incarcerated, they should not be punished for drawing or singing; "humanitarian measures," such as gymnastics, lectures, and libraries should be provided to vary their routines.[199] Nevertheless, Lombroso praised the "the very great improvements" in the Italian prison system, including the abolition of those "wretched chains that evoked ancient slavery."[200]

Other respondents invariably repeated Lombroso's insistence on categorization and his plea that conditions be improved for the majority of prisoners, who were well-behaved and could be rehabilitated. According to the anthropologist, Sergi, a collaborator of Lombroso, "rigid and harsh treatment" understandably irritated inmates who instead deserved "really mild and always equal" management by guards.[201] Rossanda similarly suggested that the Italian prison system move further from "the ancient mosaic law of a tooth for a tooth" by "accommodating ... small demands" such as writing more often to their families, reading more books, and choosing their type of work.[202] Such calls for moderating the prison rules also came from internal administrators themselves. Cesare Polidori, the physician at the Viterbo penitentiary, pronounced most prisoners to be "tranquile, docile, respectful, and hard workers."[203] The doctor at the penal colony of Favignano, Emanuele Mirabella, recommended the use of names rather than numbers, so that each inmate would "feel himself lifted up, no longer feeling like a slave or an embarrassing material thing but instead a man."[204] As with several other respondents, Mirabella believed that prison disciplinary councils should have the power to shorten the sentences of well-behaved inmates, including those originally interned for life.

When referring to the smaller category of incorrigible prisoners, the language of respondents changed dramatically. Applying the Lombrosian label, Mirabella argued that born criminals "occupied the lowest step of the zoological ladder" because they were "degenerate ... amoral, [and] defective in reason and morality."[205] The psychiatrist Saporito suggested that jails be used as observation centers for identifying "the category of those for whom crime is a habit, an organic need that can be modified little or not at all and can erupt for any small reason."[206] In similar words, Gian Giacomo

Perrando, a professor of legal medicine in Catania, described incorrigible prisoners as "impulsive beings with an abnormal and immutable constitution."[207] Even the classical jurist Alessandro Stoppato, while avoiding positivist language, distinguished between convicts deserving encouragement and those who were "riotous and obstinate." For the latter, "we should be just but rigid in the application of punishment."[208]

For the most part, respondents to the referendum recommended similar remedies. For insane criminals, the simple answer was to expand the system of asylums managed by psychiatrists who were equipped to diagnose and treat mental disease. For penitentiaries, "sections for highly agitated" inmates were recommended by Rossana and Ferrandi among others. Doctors, preferably trained in psychiatry, should take responsibility for categorizing inmates and individualizing their punishment. Most respondents pinned high hopes on outdoor agricultural work, which Sergi, Mirabella, and Augusto Sacozzi, the director of the criminal insane asylum in Reggio Emilia, believed would physically exhaust and therefore soothe the bodies of overexcited prisoners. Dr. Carmelo Andronico, the physician at the women's prison in Messina, notably recommended field work also for incorrigible female inmates who, he argued, were too irritable to apply themselves to the usual monotonous female tasks of embroidery and lace-making.[209] Finally, most respondents were loath to resume the types of corporal punishment—labeled by Rossana as "the last vestiges of the Holy Inquisition"—that had been routinely applied before 1903.[210]

These replies to Doria's survey were emblematic of the real if limited transformation of the male penitentiary between unification and World War I. Even if the Zanardelli Code continued to prescribe universalistic sentences based on the crime, the prison system strove to individualize punishment for men based on criminal type. For the majority of inmates, who were considered amenable to rehabilitation, everyday life had improved significantly as chains and straitjackets were abolished; individual sleeping cells became more widespread; education and professional training improved; and rewards for good behavior became more common. The most coveted prize, advancement to an intermediate institution and subsequently parole, was built into the Irish system and integral to the Ordinance of 1891. For the minority of incorrigible prisoners, however, conditions were bleaker and marked by frequent and increasingly severe punishments. Diagnosed as biologically and psychologically damaged, they attracted little sympathy and were relegated to high-security facilities or to criminal insane asylums. Thus, the experience of male prisoners in Italy encapsulated both the promise and peril of the positivist agenda of social defense based on a rigid categorization of humanity as either degenerate or deserving of citizenship.

6

Juvenile Reformatories between State and Charity

The age of positivism promoted a particular focus on both the protection and discipline of youth across the Western world. A growing movement of "child savers" sought to model a separate theory and practice of punishment for juvenile delinquency, which was perceived as an explosive problem correlating with urbanization and industrialization. As a young and still fragile state, Italy was particularly preoccupied with molding its youth into productive citizens. Widespread anxiety about rebellious youth in the midst of a rapidly modernizing society had already been growing for several decades, as shown by the popularity of Carlo Collodi's children's book of 1883, *The Adventures of Pinocchio*.[1] In 1906, the socialist jurist and deputy, Antonio Guarnieri-Ventimiglia, repeated the widespread sentiment that "in this historical moment, juvenile crime and punishment constitute one of the greatest battles" of modern civilization.[2]

Although legislative efforts to reform legal institutions did not mature until the turn of the twentieth century, Italian experiments with special prisons for minors reached back to the seventeenth and eighteenth centuries. The most famous early penal institution for boys was San Michele, which prefigured the later Auburn model with its individual cells for sleeping and common rooms for work in the service of reeducation.[3] Florence boasted an even earlier asylum for troubled and troublesome youth, the Charitable House of Refuge, founded by Filippo Franci in the 1650s. Initially envisioned as a shelter for young male vagrants and beggars, it expanded after several decades to include individual cells for boys interned by their parents for misbehavior.[4] While not a prison for convicted delinquents, as was San Michele, this Florentine institution prefigured the complicated and ambiguous nature of "modern" reformatories in united Italy, which incarcerated both criminal and wayward youth. Thus, patterns of punishment for Italian children in Italy paralleled those for women, with incarceration beginning to replace corporal punishment long before the first wave of prison reform during the age of revolutions. Managed by a combination of secular and religious personnel, the early "convent" prisons for youth were inspired by ideals of Christian piety toward the weak rather than by the later Enlightenment humanitarianism based on reason and equal justice. Thus the variable of age, in addition to gender, complicates the search for the origin of the prison, which in Italy can be found in early modern Catholic culture and its model of chastising clergy with penitential confinement.

Despite these threads of continuity with the past, however, the modern Italian reformatory movement was given fresh and strong stimulus from three factors specific to the late nineteenth and early twentieth centuries. First, rapid demographic growth and economic change left children and adolescents increasingly vulnerable to poverty, hunger, and homelessness. With industrialization, patterns of child labor began to change. Although the majority of children remained in the unmodernized sectors of the economy, such as agriculture and domestic service, a significant number found employment in factories producing textiles, glass, and other commodities for the burgeoning cities. Others wandered the streets selling flowers, playing music, or simply begging.[5] Although the new Italian state passed legislation in 1877 requiring several years of schooling, many poor families evaded the law in order to retain their progeny's small income. As a result of widespread childhood poverty, as well as the perception that abandoned youth were flooding city streets, popular support began to grow for the modernization of reformatories for minors.

Second, positivist criminologists fueled these anxieties about the danger of uncontrolled children to both public security and the future health of the nation. Rejecting the eighteenth-century doctrine of Rousseau that held children to be essentially pure and innocent, they argued instead that babies lacked moral sense and displayed emotional traits similar to those of the born criminal: anger, cruelty, dishonesty, vanity, and idleness.[6] Writing in Ferri's journal, *The Positivist School*, Nicolo Pinsero argued that "the criminal impulse is almost always absolutely dominant" in children because of their mental underdevelopment.[7] This pessimistic perspective was counterbalanced by the belief that most children would mature at puberty into "normal" adults and therefore deserved moral and economic nurturing. A minority of youth, however, would remain a threat to future generations by passing down hereditary traits of family members tainted by syphilis, alcoholism, prostitution, insanity, or atavistic anomalies. Although Lombroso himself opposed incarceration as an answer to most cases of wayward and delinquent youth, the positivist obsession with degeneration directed attention to the need for institutions that could attenuate the threats posed by children to society.

Third, international experiments with new types of juvenile justice institutions inspired and sometimes shamed the Italian prison administration to explore radical changes to its own system of reformatories. Although Italy had been ahead of its time in separating children from adults, conditions in most convent reformatories, such as San Michele, had declined by the early nineteenth century. Thus, when the French judge and philanthropist, Frédéric-Auguste Demetz, founded an agricultural colony for boys at Mettray in 1840, it was heralded as a new model for child protection and discipline. Constructed to resemble a rural village, with a church and small dormitories arranged around a central green, Mettray was quickly copied by other European nations, such as the Netherlands and Belgium.[8] While San Michele had prefigured the main purpose of Mettray, which was to rehabilitate children through work and religion, the latter was distinctly nineteenth century in being located in a rural area, considered superior to the corrupt atmosphere of the burgeoning cities, and in requiring military exercises as training for male citizenship. As similar institutions spread throughout Europe and northern America, childsavers began to call for an additional experimental institution, the juvenile court, which was intended to shield minor defendants from the rigor and adversarial nature of adult tribunals. After the turn of the twentieth century, Italy's full engagement with this international movement was reflected in the pages of the *RDC*, where the number of articles on the protection and punishment of children increased dramatically.

Despite the professed commitment of the Italian state to juvenile justice reform, its implementation depended on several factors. To begin with, the large majority of reformatories in Italy were managed by private, usually Catholic, organizations with little government oversight. That religious orders resisted state guidelines is clear from the repeated circulars issued by prison administrators in Rome pleading for cooperation. The experience of interned children was also highly gendered, with public institutions serving almost exclusively boys. The only state reformatory for girls underwent little change, both because of defiance by the nuns who served as administrators and by lack of any real commitment to female reform on the part of the state. Its closure in 1909, after exposés of scandalous conditions, left all female youth in the world of private charity.

Further complicating this institutional grid was the division of juvenile inmates into three major legal categories: those convicted by the courts, those arrested on the streets for begging and vagabondage, and those consigned by their families for bad behavior. The latter two categories were not serving sentences as meted out in the criminal code but instead had been forcibly admitted by police or parents. Therefore, in contrast to adult prisons, youth reformatories blurred the line between criminal and civil law, public and private reform, and punishment and prevention. With a focus on the liminal status of youth reformatories, this chapter will open with an overview of penal and prison legislation for children and then map the world of charity with which it overlapped. As in previous chapters on women and men, Rome will provide the setting for short portraits of local institutions, in this case the private reformatory of the Buon Pastore for girls and the public institution of San Michele for boys. After exploring the network of juvenile reformatories at the national level, the chapter will return to the role of charity and the *patronati*, which were private societies that assisted prisoners, and particularly children, upon release.

Children in Criminal and Prison Law

Because of the mixed nature of youth reformatories, which straddled the line between the state and the family, the place of children was intertwined with civil and criminal law. According to the Civil Code of 1865, legitimate children fell under the rule of the father according to the traditional doctrine of *patria podestà*. Until their offspring reached legal majority at the age of twenty-one, fathers had the right to control their children's property, fix their place of residence, and make decisions about their education. With the permission of their fathers, daughters could marry at fifteen and sons at eighteen. Both could be emancipated by their fathers at the age of eighteen and thus reach legal adulthood.[9] While this dominance by fathers was typical in nineteenth-century European family law, one provision was more specific, although not unique, to Italy. According to Article 222 of the Civil Code, fathers who could not "restrain the perversions of their child" could make a judicial request for internment in an "educational or correctional institution" for the purpose of reform. Judges were not required to investigate the charges against the child but could accept a simple verbal petition from parents and expedite the admission of the child into a reformatory "without explaining his reasons in the decree."[10] As the legal basis for incorporating non-convicted children into the reformatory system, Article 222 aroused stormy debates in parliament and the press.

A second group of children, who had not undergone court proceedings but were also committed to preventive detention, were beggars, vagabonds, and abandoned children. Under the Public Security Law of 1865, police could arrest any minor under the age of sixteen, who was wandering city streets, on the suspicion of potential criminality.[11] Although the sanction of incarceration in a reformatory was technically "non-criminal," it mirrored the punishment for convicted juvenile delinquents. In fact, prison sentences following police arrest were often longer because, rather than being limited by the criminal code, they were indeterminate and could last until the age of majority. The subsequent Public Security Law of 1889 made these strictures harsher in order to counterbalance the concurrent Zanardelli Code, which had decriminalized begging. The new police law added more categories of youth who were subject to arrest, including the exclusively female category of prostitute, and extended the age limit to eighteen.[12] While many children were returned to their parents, others spent long periods of their adolescence in reformatories.

Finally, a minority of reformatory inmates had been duly sentenced by the courts under complicated provisions that differentiated treatment by age. All youth under twenty-one were eligible to have their punishment shortened or even abolished. The key concept was *discernimento*, or whether a child had the maturity to understand the difference between right and wrong. According to the Sardinian-Italian code of 1859, only minors under fourteen years of age were eligible for acquittal on the grounds of lacking *discernimento*, although this finding was not mandatory. Judges could convict children of any age if they were considered to possess the ability of moral choice as long as they received reduced sentences. Except for those over eighteen accused of homicide, parricide, or poisoning, all children were exempt from the death penalty and hard labor.[13]

Consonant with the increasing interest in child protection, the Zanardelli Code of 1889 was more liberal. All children under nine were recognized as incapable of *discernimento* and those between nine and fourteen remained eligible for acquittal if found incapable of understanding the illegality of their offense. However, because civil judges had the authority to levy "administrative" orders of confinement even after these cases were dropped, a small number of very young children continued to populate Italy's reformatories. For all other minors, the Zanardelli Code continued to offer reduced sentences and to exempt them from the most severe punishment, that of incarceration for life.[14] In 1904, the approval of probation redounded to the benefit of minors, who initially made up one-half of those diverted from prison sentences.[15] If eligible for suspended sentences, the courts were obliged to assign them temporarily to a reformatory, rather than an adult jail, during the trial itself.[16] The law on probation, therefore, added an additional, albeit small, category of internees to youth institutions.

This shift from punishment toward protection was even more pronounced in prison legislation, where the Ordinance of 1891 relabeled juvenile institutions of punishment as "reformatories" rather than "houses of custody." The early Regulation for Houses of Custody, promulgated in 1862 and emphasizing the centrality of labor, differed little from that for adult penitentiaries. In line with the Sardinian-Italian code, custodial prisons were not yet conceived as specialized institutions for youth but also admitted adults who were judged to lack a full capacity for moral discernment, such as the insane and the deaf. Although in practice very few adults were assigned to custodial prisons, the state clearly had not yet developed a coherent philosophy of youth reform. Like adults, minors underwent a period of isolation upon admission and were required to maintain the rule of silence after joining their peers in dormitories and workrooms. To keep in touch with their families, they were allowed only one visit and one letter per month. Five articles of the regulation outlined a long list of bad behaviors for which they could be punished ranging from lack of cleanliness and simple laziness to rebellion and attempted escape.[17] The former elicited mild punishments such as deprivation of recreation or one meal per day while the latter brought solitary confinement with a diet of bread and water. The most extreme measure was the *cella oscura*, or incarceration in a punishment cell deprived of any light.

In 1876 and 1877, two administrative decrees began to distinguish houses of custody from adult penitentiaries, although the steps were tentative.[18] While adults could still be assigned to houses of custody, they were to be strictly separated from minors. The purpose of internment was clearly stated to be "reform and moral education ... accompanied by elementary schooling and instruction in a craft or trade."[19] To this end, a new post of "tutor" (*istitutore*) was established to oversee teachers, whose status was raised to administrative rank.[20] This reordering of personnel was intended to strengthen the educational mission of the houses of correction, which had often been carried out on an ad-hoc basis by untrained chaplains. However, the innovation of the tutor was soon abolished and several other innovative features of the decrees, such as the promise of single sleeping cells and new agricultural colonies like Mettray, were never put into practice.[21] Neither was a requirement that the three categories of youth—those consigned by courts, the police, or parents—occupy separate quarters in each institution. In 1888, Beltrani Scalia partially remedied the last problem by designating that each boys' reformatory, whether public or private, admit only one legal category. No similar differentiation, however, was made among girls' institutions, in which the cohabitation of criminal and non-criminal internees—a practice universally condemned by all legal and criminological schools—remained in place. That Beltrani Scalia ignored the backward state of girl's reformatories cannot be attributed to their marginal number since they constituted 45 percent of all juvenile penal institutions. Instead, in a pattern that would be repeated throughout the following years, reformers devoted no particular attention to the needs of girls, who were not perceived as fundamental to nation building.

The Ordinance of 1891 constituted more of a break with the past by classifying reformatories as "special institutions of punishment" in contrast to "ordinary" jails and penitentiaries for adults.[22] Composed of only five articles, the section on reformatories sketched the broad principles for the internment of all three legal categories of youth. Directors of both public and private reformatories were to draw up "internal regulations" that would instill "a love of order, discipline, and respect for their superiors" as well as habits of "bodily cleanliness and sobriety of behavior and language."[23] Work and education were required "for the purpose of preparing children for an honest job appropriate to their own social class."[24] Rewards and punishments would "strengthen moral feelings and form character."[25] The only reference to gender regarded teachers, who were to be civil servants in public reformatories for boys and nuns in female institutions. The ordinance permitted reformatories to hire instructors in specialized areas such as drawing, music, and gymnastics, but this clause was implemented only in the case of boys.[26]

In 1904, Doria began to implement a radical reordering of juvenile reformatories by separating them administratively from adult prisons. As an initial step, he replaced prison guards in government institutions with civilian personnel who were to reform, rather than simply discipline, their charges.[27] The next step came with a 1905 decree that required all employees to be certified in primary education and promised to offer them specialized training in criminal law, pedagogy, and anthropology.[28] A brief decree of 1905 reorganized juvenile and adult penal institutions into two parallel bureaucracies under what was now renamed the General Division of Prisons and Reformatories.[29] Doria completed the process in 1907 by issuing a detailed "Regulation for government reformatories." This law defined the four categories of youth that were eligible for admission: "corrupted minors who have rebelled against paternal authority" under the age of twenty-one, beggars and prostitutes under the age of eighteen who had been picked up by police, all juvenile delinquents under the age of nine or those under the age of fourteen who acted without *discernimento*, and first offenders between nine and thirteen years at the recommendation of a judge.[30] All other convicted youth were now expelled from the reformatories and redirected to the adult penitentiary system. The regulation made few distinctions between the sexes, devoting only four articles specifically to girls and declaring that "the same system of education and discipline would be applied" in male and female reformatories.[31] However, to accommodate "the special necessities of the [female] sex," it made a few exceptions, which vitiated this equality in practice.[32] For example, girls over the age of fourteen had to learn "domestic tasks" by working "in the kitchen, in the laundry, in the supply room, in the storerooms, and in the general cleaning at the institution."[33] Boys were under no such obligation.

The formal reconfiguration of houses of custody into educational reformatories, initiated cautiously in the 1870s by Beltrani Scalia and completed by Doria in 1907, gathered almost unanimous support from legislators, criminologists, and jurists. Only Lombroso took the extreme stance, in a letter of 1876 to the *RDC*, of challenging the utility of reformatories of any type. While praising Beltrani Scalia as his "guide and maestro for everything concerning prison science," Lombroso argued that incarceration fostered "the most odious vices such as pederasty . . . and theft" in children because of the impossibility of preventing moral contamination of the innocent by the corrupt. He therefore called for the abolition of these "kindergartens of vice" and the placement of children under age twelve in special correctional day schools or with "moral families" in the countryside.³⁴ Still "malleable" in their habits and character, these prepubescent minors needed "fresh air and exercise and, above all, the care and closeness of mother and family which, once interrupted, can never be restored."³⁵ In response, Beltrani Scalia defended the reformatory system that, he reminded his "friend, prof. Lombroso," was needed to educate "the outcasts of civil society—many of whom harbor the germ of serious criminality and a rebellious instinct against society." To rescue them from the "social mud" of their environment, houses of custody needed to be improved but not abolished.³⁶ Lombroso's stance drew few adherents, probably because his more general theory of childhood depravity raised the specter of uncontrollable juvenile delinquency. Furthermore, the habit of looking to institutions of enclosure as the answer to social problems, which had its roots in the early modern convent prison, was reinforced by the popularity and promise of the modern penitentiary.

Rather than opposing reformatories per se, many of Doria's supporters strongly questioned the system of "paternal correction," which was overtaxing the prison system. Admissions based on parental request climbed steadily from 240 in 1871, or 19 percent of all children entering Italy's reformatories, to over 1,000, or 58 percent, by 1893.³⁷ The number was actually higher, because if parents failed to convince a judge to approve their petition under the guidelines of the Civil Code, they sometimes managed to intern their children as vagabonds under police regulations.³⁸ Such family determination to confine their children did not spare girls, who comprised over a fourth of all admissions for paternal correction.³⁹ Alarm over the rising number of parental requests, which outstripped the available beds in existing reformatories, produced an avalanche of publications speculating on the underlying causes. While concern centered on paternal correction as an indicator of moral breakdown in Italian society, government officials also emphasized the high costs of housing so many children.

Criticism focused not on children, who were often seen as innocent until corrupted by the experience of internment, but instead on their parents. According to an early study of 1883 by Salvatore Barzilai, a jurist and future member of parliament, most fathers who petitioned the courts were not "loving, disinterested, and humane" but were instead taking advantage of the state to unburden themselves of unwanted children.⁴⁰ Many were widowers, sometimes recently remarried, who falsely declared themselves "lacking in the means to support" their children economically or morally; women made the same argument after the death of their husbands.⁴¹ Once interned, according to Barzilai, a child from a moral home is "thrown together with petty thieves, swindlers, murderers, [and] little delinquents of every type."⁴² Quoting Ferri, his "beloved teacher and friend," he argued that the "maximum sentence" for minors not convicted by a court should be one year rather than indeterminate, as was customary.⁴³ In short, the state should severely restrict if not abolish altogether the right of fathers to incarcerate their offspring. Not all specialists agreed with Barzilai, as was clear from the debate and compromise resolution at the First International Congress for the Protection of Childhood, held in Florence in 1896. Giustino De Sanctis, the director of the male reformatory in Pisa, argued that the state needed to replace bad fathers; furthermore, 82 percent of his boys maintained good conduct after release. In its final vote, the congress voiced support for paternal correction only for "minors who were perverted and legally recognized as such," rather than in response to a simple parental petition.⁴⁴

While national prison administrators refrained from such a wholesale attack on the right of *patria potestà*, they agreed that too many children were being unnecessarily admitted to reformatories. In 1879, Beltrani Scalia argued that, while far from wishing "to undermine in the slightest paternal authority," he nevertheless felt a "sacred duty" to protect the rights of "a weak creature," such as a child, from unjust internment.[45] The state should require that fathers submit more detailed petitions and, if successful, reimburse the state for their child's room and board. Doria was equally suspicious of parents who, he argued, wanted to rid themselves of their children either "for unspeakable reasons" or "to shirk the care and expense" of their moral and practical upbringing.[46] To get the consent of the court, they "put themselves in the position of slandering their children ... by inventing multiple crimes" for which they were supposedly guilty.[47] To restrict the availability of paternal correction, Doria proposed several revisions to the Civil Code that, in the spirit of Beltrani Scalia, would protect minors from prolonged confinement at the will of their parents. Yet Article 222 remained intact on the eve of World War I, even though Doria's successor as director general, G. Girardi, continued to echo the same laments about the misuse of reformatories by "unscrupulous parents."[48]

Despite the failure to resolve the dispute over paternal correction, Doria's initiative to separate juvenile reformatories from the adult prison system met with widespread approval. In 1904, Lucchini, a member of the classical school long concerned with child protection, pronounced "his heart-felt congratulations for the reform of the reformatory system, which has drawn the applause of everyone."[49] His remarks were consistent with his support of probation, which he envisioned as primarily benefitting youth. The legal journal, the *Positivist School*, also praised Doria, although its editor, Ferri, continued to favor "penal substitutes" to prevent juvenile delinquency over internment.[50] The *RDC* happily reprinted a series of newspaper articles lauding the work of the prison administration, which was more accustomed to popular wrath; the only critical article warned that the meager salaries of the new tutors and teachers might cripple the practical implementation of the visionary reform.[51] Nominated as vice president of the seventh congress of the International Penitentiary Association, Doria also received recognition from his foreign colleagues, who were concurrently preoccupied with the perceived problem of rising juvenile delinquency.[52]

Mapping Roman Charity

Perhaps the long historical experience of charitable support for children explains the readiness of Italian parents to request sentences of paternal correction and of judges to approve them. According to Barbara Montesi, who has studied parental petitions, fathers used reformatories strategically to unburden themselves temporarily of unwanted children. Once their offspring had learned a trade and could contribute to the family income, parents would request their release. Rather than new, the recourse to paternal correction was consistent with a "culture of the poor" by which families survived by institutionalizing their weakest members.[53] Sometimes parents shared, perhaps unconsciously, the dominant discourse that labeled the misbehavior of their children as potentially criminal. But most simply considered the reformatory—like the foundling home, orphanage, and conservatory—to be "a philanthropic institution for the needy."[54] Rising rates of internment for paternal correction depended on a "complex web of complicity," which brought together not only parents and courts but also police, mayors, and priests who were quick to recommend "preventive internment" for naughty youth.[55] All parties to these negotiations considered confinement preferable to the streets, with their temptations and liberty of movement.

Such an interpretation is consistent with the early modern roots of Italian prisons for children. During the eighteenth and early nineteenth centuries, the complex of San Michele symbolized the strong ties between juvenile justice and charity, with its prison for boys annexed to a refuge for orphaned children. San Michele was just one of a large but confusing network of private charities that characterized the peninsula at the time of unification. In 1861, the number of philanthropic organizations, according to the first rough and approximate government survey, numbered over twenty thousand, two-fifths of which were administered directly by Catholic authorities. Others were sponsored by noble families, confraternities, or mixed boards of lay and religious members. The most important charities employed enclosure as a method to solve social problems; these included 955 hospitals, 1,265 foundling homes and orphanages, 265 poorhouses for adults, and 386 conservatories for unmarried girls.[56] After the annexation of Venice and particularly Rome, with its wealth of religious foundations, the number of philanthropic institutions became even larger.

Youth reformatories were one of many institutions that played a part in the struggle between the new Italian state and the Church for control over what were legally designated as *opere pie*, or pious works. While many charities were not directly controlled by the Church, they nonetheless tended to be inspired by Counter-Reformation piety, which had characterized the seventeenth and eighteenth centuries. In contrast, the new Italian state, with its avowedly secular constitution, sought to assert its authority over health, education, and other philanthropic sectors that were essential for molding a liberal citizenry. Its instruments were a series of laws that began to regulate a system that, in the words of Stefano Lepre, was "extremely fragile and backwards, only functional for a society based on religious and hierarchical principles."[57] Critics of traditional charities complained about the secret and irrational accounting practices that resulted in more money going to administrators than to the poor themselves. Original testaments, often centuries old, might require that assistance be directed to a problem that no longer existed. Many philanthropic institutions were organized around a monastic model, an approach now considered incompatible with individual rights and secular values. The state, however, was cautious in its efforts to rationalize and centralize a complicated network that benefitted, in terms and power and income, not only the Church but also notables and wealthy patrons who had endowed charities at the local level.

Between unification and World War I, a gradual series of laws enlarged, but never completed, the imposition of public direction over the multiplicity of *opere pie*. In 1862, the first national legislation placed the whole system theoretically under the Ministry of the Interior with financial oversight assigned to the prefects and provincial councils. However, the law forbade any governmental interference in the internal administration of each organization, and even the superficial measures to regularize internal bookkeeping were rarely enforced.[58] To ascertain a more exact number of the philanthropic bodies throughout Italy after the annexation of Venice and Rome, the state conducted a statistical survey in 1872, which came to the remarkable conclusion that the combined yearly income of all private charities equaled one-seventh that of the state.[59] After an even more rigorous "census of the poor" in 1880, Crispi won parliamentary approval for legislation that, in 1890, grouped philanthropies into thirty-two categories and concentrated similar types of institutions, such as hospitals, into local networks.[60] Not until 1904, however, was a "High Council of Welfare and Charity" created to oversee the entire system and expanded powers assigned to the provincial councils.[61] But because of continued resistance by Church and local officials as well as an underfunded administrative bureaucracy, even this "Giolitti" bill did not succeed in transforming Italy into a modern welfare state.

Secularization of charity ran into particular obstacles in the former Papal States, where clerical officials had directly administered both state and Church organizations before 1871. On the eve of unification, Rome was rich with charities to assist the poor, some of which were directly sponsored by the Pope and others by the many religious orders that congregated in the capital of Catholicism. Many of the roughly three hundred *opere pie* in the city, which were inherited by the new state, supported the poor "at home" by providing food, clothes, or dowries for young girls, the latter a particularly Roman tradition.[62] Others were large institutions, such as the specialized and internationally renowned hospitals of Santo Spirito in Sassia for acute diseases in men, San Giovanni for women, San Giacomo for surgery, San Rocco for childbirth, San Gallicano for skin and venereal diseases, and Santa Maria della Pietà for the mentally ill.[63] In addition to the ancient foundling home annexed to Santo Spirito, Rome also boasted a number of orphanages and homes for the aged.

Like other Italian cities, Rome was populated by a multitude of conservatories that, according to Morichini, were dedicated to saving the honor of unmarried girls by offering them Christian education in domestic skills.[64] Although the oldest, S. Caterina della Rosa de' Funari, dated back to the mid-sixteenth century, the majority had been inspired by the counter-reformation impulses of the subsequent two centuries.[65] On the eve of unification, they numbered about twenty.[66] As Angela Groppi argues in her incisive portrait of Roman conservatories, their function had changed over time from early modern refuges for poor and abandoned girls, often rescued from the streets, to nineteenth-century educational institutions for lower-middle-class families.[67] With this shift, admission came to depend less on recommendations by parish priests and other local authorities than on requests by families thrown into crisis by the death of a parent, remarriage, or simply economic problems. The typical internee was no longer a destitute child beggar but an older "respectable" girl in need of education. With the change in the class base of their internees, conservatories also began to de-emphasize productive work, such as textile manufacturing, in favor of knitting, sewing, and other domestic skills to prepare girls to become good housewives. The length of internment became a subject of negotiation between institutional authorities and parents, who sometimes requested the return of their daughters after the resolution of a family crisis.

The parallels between the "archipelago" of Italian conservatories, in Groppi's phrase, and juvenile reformatories are unmistakable.[68] Based on a monastic model, both institutions responded to requests from policing authorities and parents to remove children from supposedly adverse environments. In a "game" among the various parties transacting the terms of admission, the charitable organization or, in the case of public reformatories, the state agreed to relieve families of their responsibilities for the purpose of preserving order in families and society. The specific mission of several Roman conservatories underlines their close relationship to the world of the prison: S. Caterina de' Funari had been founded to take in the daughters of prostitutes and the Refuge at Santa Maria in Trastevere to house female convicts after release from prison. While the number of charitable institutions for "endangered" or "fallen" girls exceeded those for abandoned boys, the reformatory at San Michele demonstrates that, in the case of minors, the overlapping of penal and charitable institutions had not been completely gendered in Papal Rome. What is striking is the dynamic of change in this relationship after unification, as the state refocused its mission on boys, with the purpose of remolding even the most wayward into reliable workers, soldiers, and citizens.

Juvenile Reformatories in Rome

Rome offers a case study of juvenile justice that had its roots in the early modern tradition of the conservatory and convent prison. In the case of girls, the new capital inherited a conservatory, which housed a mixture of criminal, repentant, and endangered girls under the management of the religious order of the Buon Pastore. In contrast, boys were interned in a series of institutions that were managed directly by the state. This peripatetic history began during papal rule, when the inmates of San Michele were transferred to an annex of the New Prison in 1827, to the Santa Balbina monastery in 1854, and finally to Tivoli, outside of Rome, in 1880. In 1904, San Michele was refurbished and reopened as a model reformatory and a showcase in the capital for Doria's reforms. This gendered pattern of interning girls in private, charitable institutions and boys in public reformatories was typical of the larger peninsula.

Buon Pastore

The history of the Buon Pastore, or the Good Shepherd Reformatory, encapsulates the Italian tradition of disciplining women, which was characterized by uncertain borders between the polarities of public/private, penal/extrajudicial, and protection/punishment. Originally named Santa Croce della Penitenza alla Lungara, this charitable institution was founded in 1615 to take in "women who had fallen into dishonest ways and to protect them without the obligation to take religious vows and with the freedom to leave for the purpose of becoming a wife or nun."[69] Like many conservatories, it drew support from both religious and lay patrons, in this case father Domenico of the Carmelite order and Baldassarre Paluzzi, a Roman nobleman. Originally a refuge for women labeled as sexually deviant—including prostitutes, unwed mothers, and adulterous wives—Santa Croce later began to accept endangered girls needing moral and economic assistance. While passing through periods of shifting administrative arrangements, the conservatory retained its mixed character on the boundary between the Church and secular society. By the early nineteenth century, when the number of internees began to decline, it was managed by a lay staff of philanthropic noblewomen and teachers under the oversight of the parish priest.[70]

In 1838, Pope Gregory XVI brought the sisters of the Good Shepherd of Angers, a French order of nuns, to revive its mission to protect and discipline both women and girls. Like the order of the Divine Providence, which had similarly been summoned by the papal government to administer the women's prison at Diocletian's Baths, the nuns of the Good Shepherd were dedicated to charitable work rather than to monastic reclusion. Founded in 1829 by Marie-Eufrasie Pelletier, the new order spread quickly around the world to staff female refuges and prisons.[71] Once submitted to religious control, the Roman conservatory initially housed two groups in separate quarters: young girls requiring assistance and adult penitents who had been interned by husbands, fathers, or brothers for supposedly immoral behavior.[72] In 1854, Pope Pius IX enlarged the complex to include a prison for women convicted of sexual offenses. In his survey of Roman charitable institutions on the eve of unification, Morichini reported that the penitentiary wing held sixty women, half of whom were serving long sentences for infanticide. Kept completely separate from the other two groups, these inmates watched the mass through grates installed behind the altar. They spent their days in work and were allowed to keep one-half of their wages.[73]

Pope Pius IX may have singled out the Buon Pastore conservatory, as opposed to the many others in Rome, as suitable for a women's prison because of its location. As signified by its original name, the church and monastery faced on Via della Lungara, an ancient road built by the papacy to facilitate travel by pilgrims from the Ripa port to St. Peters Basilica. Beginning in the south at San Michele, whose wool factory utilized the shipping facilities at the port, Via Lungara followed the banks of the Tiber toward the Vatican and Castel Sant'Angelo, which served as a political prison during the decades before unification. The road bordered Trastevere, the working-class quarter that was the site of many other charitable institutions for the poor, including the hospital and founding home at Santa Spirito in Sassia, the mental asylum of Santa Maria della Pietà, the hospital for skin and venereal disease at San Gallicano, and the conservatory of Santa Maria in Trastevere. The Buon Pastore was also conveniently located across the Tiber from the New Prison, from which the first female convicts were transferred.[74]

Immediately after the annexation of Rome by the new Italian state, the monastery of the Good Shepherd, with its adjacent conservatory and prison, came under review by two levels of public officials. One was the city council, which, according to the new legislation on charities, was to oversee all institutions of philanthropy for the sick or poor. In November, 1871, the council voted to give the Buon Pastore legal status as an officially recognized *opera pia* on the basis of its social mission "to take in deviant women, both single and married, and to offer them every type of assistance."[75] As the prefect informed the mother superior, this declaration applied only to the two oldest sections, the conservatory for girls and the refuge for adult women consigned by their families.[76] He requested copies of the charter, financial records, and internal rules of the institution for review by local authorities while leaving the buildings in possession of the order. A new lay commission, composed of the prefect and four city councilors, was created in 1876 to oversee the work of the nuns, although the latter retained substantial autonomy.[77] Designated a private reformatory, the Buon Pastore began to admit girls consigned by their parents or by police according to the legal codes of the new state.

Meanwhile, the central state seized the penitentiary wing of the Buon Pastore complex on the grounds that it had been erected by the Pope Pius IX "for a purpose that is eminently a state function, that is, the punishment and incarceration of women sentenced according to the criminal laws of that time."[78] Reclassified as a jail by the prison administration, it began to admit only women awaiting trial or serving short sentences. Despite protest against the loss of this wing of their institution, several nuns accepted employment as guardians in the jail and, like the sisters at Villa Altieri, received a salary.[79] In 1895, they followed the inmates to the new Mantellate jail, which was only a few blocks away. The Buon Pastore convent, however, retained its role as the only girls' reformatory in Rome.

Tensions flared up between Church and state when the mother superior, Maria di Santa Modesta, petitioned Beltrani Scalia for the return of the prison building that, she argued, had been illegally confiscated in 1870.[80] Her request was supported by the president of the lay council overseeing the reformatory, which needed additional space for "the complete moral and intellectual education of the interned girls" as well as an infirmary.[81] In a note to the director general, the prefect agreed and warned that "in the case of contagious disease, it is not possible to isolate the sick."[82] In the face of such pressures, Beltrani Scalia, clearly unwilling to give up property controlled directly by his administration, dragged out the process by equivocating about the price to be paid for return of the property. Some officials wished to give everything over to the nuns for free, others to offer them the buildings if they paid for the land. After the prefect sent a second, this time personal, letter to Beltrani Scalia assuring him that the sale of the old jail buildings "would not in any way damage the interests of the state," the director general finally gave in.[83] This protracted negotiation demonstrated the complexity of relations between Church and state: in the case of the former, the nuns of the Good Shepherd persisted in defending their property while accepting employment in the women's jail; in terms of the latter, officials were divided in their attitudes to religious claims for restitution. In the end, it was to the advantage of the prison administration to give up the buildings and ensure the viability of the Buon Pastore reformatory.

The nuns of the Buon Pastore were also combative about the periodic contracts that defined relations between the state and their private institution. Having no clear policy for negotiating contracts with the nuns, the prison administration usually took the easy route of simply renewing the old ones.[84] Despite this loose approach, S. Maria di S. Giovanni, the mother superior in 1902, complained that the recent contract devoted far too many articles to the lay oversight commission and only one to her as the "Director." She objected particularly to the commission's proposal to appoint "female inspectors" to exercise "vigilance over the civil, professional, and scholastic training of the interned girls."[85] Insisting that only the ministry or prefecture had the authority to order an inspection, she demanded that the director general "do whatever he could to decrease the number of bosses; furthermore, it has been proven that, when we are left to ourselves, things go better."[86]

Despite its status as a private *opera pia*, the Good Shepherd reformatory received public funding for upkeep of the girls and therefore was required to submit standard statistical reports. These show that the reformatory grew over the years, from 125 beds in the nineteenth century to 250 after 1906. It was rarely filled to capacity, however, which confirmed official reports that female reformatories were less crowded than their male counterparts.[87] Although holding two legal categories of inmates—those arrested by police as vagabonds and children interned by their parents—the institution failed to provide for the type of separation required for boys. In the early years, the rate admitted for paternal correction was very low, but after the turn of the twentieth century it reached 50 percent.[88] Thus Roman parents seem to have increasingly employed reformatories instrumentally to unburden themselves of costly or troublesome daughters. During the decade before World War I, inmates between fourteen and sixteen comprised the largest age group with very few girls admitted under ten years old. Fourteen percent were over eighteen years of age, which demonstrates the tendency of the nuns, with the complicity of state authorities and parents, to prolong the enclosure of girls in a pattern that replicated traditional conservatories, where a significant number of internees stayed for life[89] (Graph 6.1). Despite its monastic model, however, the Buon Pastore had to comply with secular legal codes and, according to its contract, release its inmates at the age of twenty-one.[90]

Even though they had not been convicted of any crime, girls at the Good Shepherd reformatory followed a similar schedule to prison inmates. Only the very youngest were excused from work while the majority spent their days employed in hand sewing or knitting. These tasks conformed to the contract, which stipulated that the "pupils" should be trained in "women's work" such as cooking, laundry, ironing, and cleaning the institution.[91] They received only one-fourth of their wages with the rest retained by the nuns. According to the contract, the nuns were required to provide only the lower grades of education to their "pupils."[92] Thus, at the turn of the twentieth century, only two-thirds of the inmates could read, fewer could write, and only a handful had completed primary education.

In other matters, the reformatory was supposed to conform to national legislation, yet girls slept in dormitories rather than the separate cells required by Doria's reforms.[93] Limited statistics suggest that each inmate, on the average, was punished only once per year, often with a reprimand and less often with solitary confinement. However, the increase in the number of punishment cells—from one during the early decades to seventeen by 1907—casts doubt on the nuns' official claim to employ only mild methods.[94] Before 1911, the internees received few "rewards," but after that date the mother superior became more generous.[95] Most girls remained in the Buon Pastore for one to four years; only about 20 percent were released annually.[96]

Because of the paucity of inspections, it is difficult to evaluate the conditions in the Good Shepherd reformatory. A ministerial report of 1884 rated the hygiene at the institution as good, although it noted the absence of bathtubs and an infirmary. Other facilities included a workshop, school, chapel, and courtyard to take the air.[97] Four years later, after being appointed as president of the oversight committee, the lawyer Niccola Bartoccini sketched a darker picture of the institution, describing it as "more than miserable in terms of both hygiene and culture."[98] Finding that the girls spent

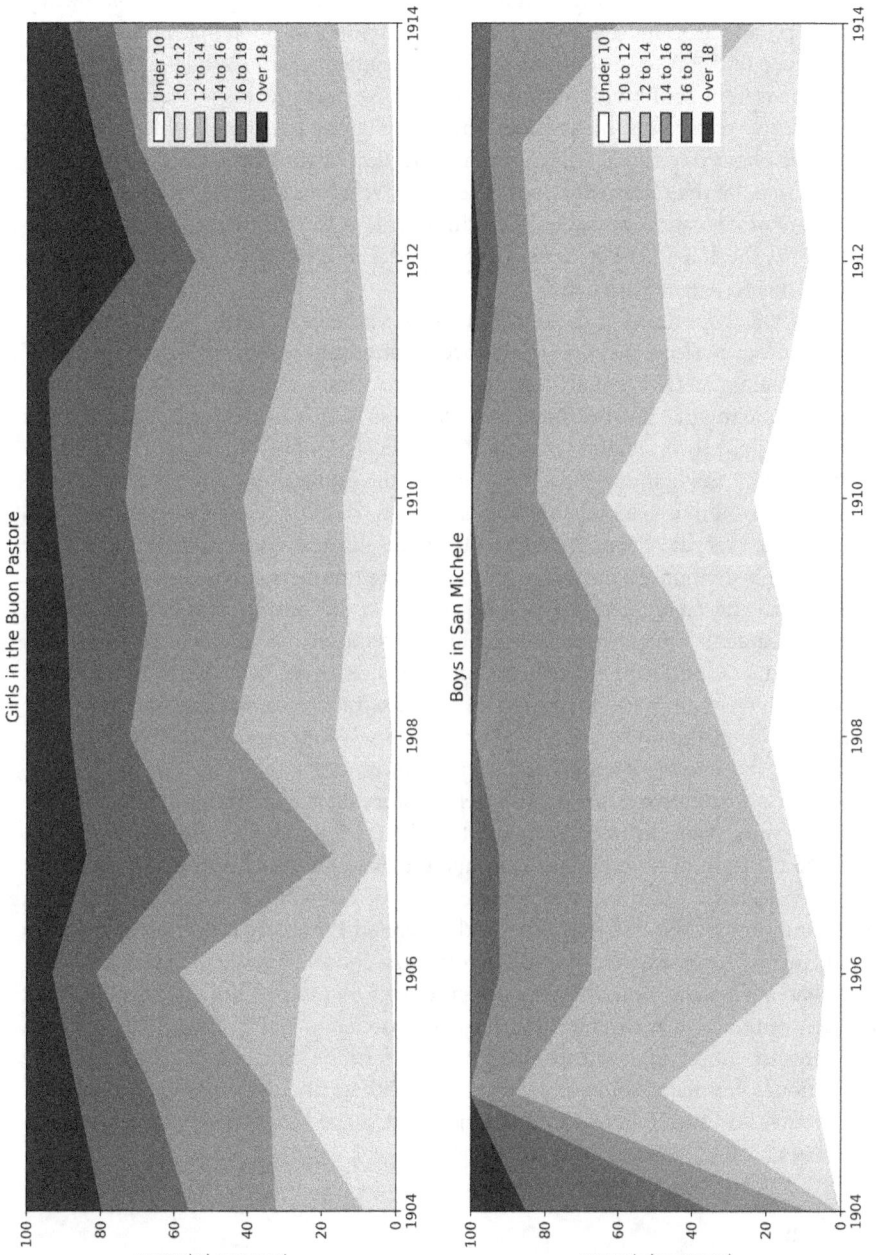

Graph 6.1 Age of children in Roman reformatories, 1904–14. Source: Stat. Rif.

most of their time "knitting stockings and reciting prayers," he argued that they needed professional training.[99] He insisted that the nuns, who refused to hire lay teachers, should at least get licensed in education. He also initiated training in washing, sewing, embroidery, and ironing since the inmates' skills were so poor that he feared they would never find jobs even as domestic servants after release. While criticizing the low compensation paid by the state for each girl, he nevertheless put most blame on "*the absolutely retrograde*" management by the religious personnel, which resolutely resisted his plans for change.[100] In 1895, an inspection by the provincial doctor praised the cleanliness of the reformatory but noted that "religious sentiment dominated" the three years of education available to the inmates.[101] Clearly little changed under the direction of the religious personnel despite periodic efforts by a few conscientious commissioners such as Bartoccini.

After 1908, inspections of the Buon Pastore became more frequent and judgments generally more positive. Reports of the oversight commissions tended to praise the nuns for their maternal and selfless management. Improvements were noted, such as the remodeling of the workshops and school so that they were more orderly and filled with light. Yet complaints continued about the lack of bathtubs, which forced the girls to wash in the laundry sinks.[102] Only after the publication of a "severely critical article" in a local newspaper, penned by a woman, did Doria ask for any substantial change in the everyday life of the reformatory: the elimination of grates in the visiting room. He now denounced the grates for preventing "mothers and other relatives from seeing clearly their daughters, their blood-relations, and getting close to them, to hug them."[103] Although the grates were immediately removed, the incident clearly shows how close the Good Shepherd reformatory remained, even in 1910, to its monastic model in which grates were standard. The 1902 contract remained in place despite the pointed advice of the prefect that the Buon Pastore would do well to model itself on San Michele, the "so meritorious" counterpart for boys.[104]

The Good Shepherd remained a girls' reformatory through the fascist period and the two world wars. After the establishment of the Italian Republic in 1946, the institution ceased to function as a prison but continued for several decades to house programs of social assistance managed by the same order of nuns. In 1983, the city of Rome, which had bought the building years earlier, ended the many centuries of religious management. The ex-convent was turned over to a consortium of ten feminist groups, which had been occupying a house across the river on the street of Governo Vecchio. Despite continued controversy over the city's decision, the building was restored by a feminist consortium with partial funding from the city. In 2002, it became the International Women's Center of the capital.[105] With its library and conference rooms, the center restores to memory an institution that shaped the lives of Roman women for 500 years.

San Michele

San Michele ceased to house a boys' reformatory in 1827, over a century after its original establishment within a larger charity complex on the Tiber River. The boys were first transferred across the river to an annex of the New Prison, on Via Giulia, where they continued to spin wool as a branch of the San Michele manufacturing enterprise.[106] Furnished with only forty rooms, this new facility quickly became so overcrowded that the boys were again moved in 1854 to the Santa Balbina monastery on the Aventine Hill, near the Baths of Caracalla. During this period, the Aventine, although not far from the Tiber River, maintained a rural character with little domestic housing.[107] De Mérode brought in a Belgian order of monks, the Fratelli di Nostra Signora della Misericordia, to manage the institution. Attached to an ancient monastic church, the reformatory at Santa Balbina continued to admit a mixture of boys convicted by the courts or interned by their parents. After unification, the number of boys in Santa Balbina grew to over 150, very few of whom had actually committed a crime.[108] In 1880, the internees were transferred outside of Rome to a larger public reformatory in the nearby hill town of Tivoli. For the next twenty-four years, the capital no longer hosted a penal institution for boys.

During these early decades after unification, the historic boys' reformatory of San Michele remained only a memory. The wool factory, which had employed all able-bodied inmates, had been closed in 1861 when De Mérode sold off the machinery at "a really cheap price," according to a critic on the Roman city council in 1871.[109] Nevertheless, the state inherited workshops for tapestry weaving, engraving, and other specialized crafts.[110] After being declared an *opera pia*, the city council appointed a board that reorganized the charity wing.[111] No longer supported by the popes and income from other religious properties, the refuge for orphaned boys invited artisans to rent parts of the complex and teach the boys carpentry, hat-making, metalwork, and other crafts while the more advanced pupils learned the arts of painting, carving in wood and marble, and tapestry.[112] In the meantime, the prison wing, which had incarcerated political opponents of the Papal States during its last few decades, became a jail after unification and, in 1895, a police lockup for new arrests.[113]

Only in 1904 did San Michele again resume its historic role as a boys' reformatory.[114] Its reopening coincided with Doria's earliest legislation to transform juvenile institutions into schools and, in the case of San Michele, to provide the capital with the most shining example. In terms of its location and architectural structure, San Michele differed little from its original incarnation in 1703, although the Ripa port was in decline and therefore the piazza bordering the prison on the south was no longer bustling with merchant ships. The Tiber, too shallow to accommodate most modern steamers, but prone to floods, had been sheathed in embankments that reached San Michele in 1887 and blocked direct access to the river.[115] Thus, San Michele, the southern point of Trastevere's prison zone, remained cut off from direct contact with central Rome. Only after World War I was a bridge, the Ponte Sublicio, completed to link San Michele with the burgeoning working-class neighborhood of Testaccio across the river.

To mold the new institution according to his vision of juvenile rehabilitation, Doria transferred the warden of the state reformatory in Tivoli, Giuseppe Ricchi, to Rome. An experienced administrator, Ricchi was immediately faced with the detailed work of hiring the administrative staff and filling the positions for "proctors" (*censori*) and "tutors" (*istitutori*) required by the new legislation. The low pay made it difficult to hire a chaplain, a position filled from the outside, and extra, specialized teachers.[116]

Ricchi was unsuccessful in keeping peace with the proctors and tutors, who resented their meager compensation and the many restrictions imposed on them as live-in employees. Required to have a teaching certificate and to manage the boys by persuasion rather than punishment, they expected, upon arrival, to occupy a well-remunerated and respected rank.[117] However, the salaries of tutors barely exceeded those of prison guards, with the former averaging 1,500 lire per year in 1907 versus 1,200 for the latter.[118] Furthermore, a protest broke out in 1906, which spread to several other reformatories, against wearing the prescribed uniforms. Calling the protest "useless, illegal, and unjustified," Doria ordered that the ringleaders among the tutors be punished and the proctor, who had expressed sympathy, be transferred.[119] That agitation among tutors recurred periodically throughout the peninsula demonstrates that Doria's reforms were inherently circumscribed by the hierarchical nature of the reformatories. In short, despite their avowedly educational mission, juvenile institutions retained many characteristics of the prison.

For the most part, however, conditions in San Michele were more consistent with international standards for juvenile justice than in the old houses of custody. With an official capacity of about 170, it was full but not overcrowded.[120] By utilizing both of the original eighteenth-century prisons—one of which had been for boys and the other for women—and building additional cells in an adjacent section, all the boys slept separately at night.[121] They were overseen by one proctor, two assistant proctors, and seventeen tutors, all of whom had teaching licenses. The building contained two elementary schools, several workshops for training in various crafts, and three courtyards for recreation and military exercises.[122] San Michele held only boys interned by their parents, who were mostly aged ten and sixteen.[123] Notably, very few were over sixteen years of age compared to the many girls who were left in the Buon Pastore until their twenty-first birthday. Upon admission, the staff employed the latest anthropometric instruments—including a dynamometer for measuring musculature and strength, and calipers to establish the shape of the head—thus setting a baseline for gauging the development of each boy.[124] Unlike adult prisoners, boys in San Michele were overwhelmingly urban in origin, perhaps demonstrating that farm families were reluctant, or too in need of labor, to request placement of their sons in an institution. But these juvenile prisoners mirrored older inmates in their tendency to come from the South, and in this case, the neighboring province of Campagna.[125]

Ricchi energetically sought to equip San Michele with resources necessary to reform his charges through education, work, and physical exercise. In 1903, in preparation for the inauguration of the reformatory, he submitted to his superiors a long list of needed personnel: elementary school teachers, instructors in gymnastics and music, and master artisans to train the boys in design, ironwork, carpentry, woodcarving, shoemaking, and tailoring. Meeting resistance from the prison administration to his insistence on two elementary school teachers, he argued that San Michele should incorporate "the newest maxims and healthy principles" of education. Rather than being limited to "*plain, bare,* and *sterile* lessons," the instructors should have the time to study "the character, temperament, and heart" of each boy by taking them on educational excursions to monuments and art museums.[126] In fact, after only a few months of overseeing the new reformatory, Ricchi requested a third teacher for internees under twelve years old, who were too young to work but could be prepared for future crafts. Displaying his knowledge of international developments, he pointed out that this type of training had been successful in France. He also negotiated with the prison administration over the daily schedule for the younger boys, recommending more school and less work than regularly required.[127]

Different types of sources attest to the successful implementation of the new programs at San Michele. In 1905, Ricchi reported the "the results of the exams taken by the internees were better than expected" despite the short time that the reformatory had been open.[128] While official statistics demonstrate that 42 percent of the boys were illiterate, this number dropped to less than 20 percent by 1908, and the number completing primary education rose.[129] Seeking "to furnish the worker with a certain culture and capabilities," classes were offered in advanced subjects such as technology, science, literature, French, recitation, and singing.[130] By 1909, the reformatory had instituted a special course in the telegraph, in which students learned the basics of electricity and how to send messages in Morse code.[131] Regular classes were supplemented by lectures from outside speakers, such as Ronconi, who sponsored the "cradle project" at the Mantellate women's jail.[132] The equipment for gymnastics included a vaulting horse, seesaw, football, and muskets for military exercises[133] (Illustration 6.1). In its varied curriculum, San Michele clearly went beyond fundamental literacy training in an attempt to mold modern male citizens through scientific and technical skills. It also prepared them, through military exercises, to become soldiers, a role required of all young men under Italy's universal draft law and one that many boys took up directly upon release.

Like other prisons, San Michele required its internees to work and disciplined their lives through punishments and rewards. All boys underwent manual training, with carpentry (24 percent), blacksmithing (18 percent), and shoemaking (18 percent) comprising the largest categories.[134] Discipline was maintained through a sliding scale of punishments from simple warnings to exclusion from recreation to solitary confinement. According to San Michele's doctor, Ernesto Persichetti, the last was imposed mostly on boys who fought among themselves. While rare, displays of violence were not surprising, he argued, using criminal anthropological language, "in those individuals who exhibit stigmata of degeneration" and therefore lack of self-restraint.[135] Official statistics indeed show a significant decline in the rate of punishment per boy from eight per year in 1905 to three in 1914.[136] That San Michele was shedding its punitive nature is also confirmed by the annual rate of rewards received for good behavior, which rose from roughly twenty to forty per internee. While many of these were small, such as books or additional food, they nevertheless displayed the eagerness of the administrators to use kindness rather than reprimands to encourage good behavior. In his praise of San Michele, Doria was particularly enthusiastic about the school outings, many of which were awarded as prizes. He reported that the boys, when permitted to take part in "excursions for both pleasure and learning," were greeted with "admiration and enthusiasm by citizens and municipal officials" of small towns and larger cities through which they passed.[137] Such festive occasions resulted in telegrams of congratulations to government officials including the prime minister. In short, life

Illustration 6.1 Boys exercising at the reformatory of San Michele

for boys in San Michele was much richer in opportunities for education, work, and recreation than for girls in the Buon Pastore. Furthermore, periods of internment were shorter in San Michele, with two-thirds of the boys being released within three years and only a small number remaining for more than six.[138] Once they passed their qualifying examinations for a trade, which meant that they had "completely achieved the purpose for which they were confined," Ricchi was eager to send them back to their parents.[139]

Inspected more often than its female counterpart, San Michele received almost unanimous applause from outsiders. Criticisms were few, although Ricchi himself admitted a rough beginning with the first boys in 1904, who shocked the staff by crying and "calling for their mammas."[140] A later inspector found Ricchi to be "often excessively indulgent" with the boys, although he praised his dedication to their education.[141] Raffaele Calabrese, a member of the royal commission that toured San Michele as part of its project on juvenile courts, noted the remaining bars gave San Michele the air of a prison rather than an educational institution.[142] Nevertheless, he noted the cleanliness and abundant ventilation of the building.

More often, however, the Roman reformatory received high praise. Based on a recent inspection, Doria lauded Ricchi for "dedicating a loving solicitude" to his duties and recommended him for an official commendation along with the vice-director, Vincenzo Damiani, and Dr. Persichetti. Received by the entire staff and two of the boys from the "Honor Council," the new prefect of Rome, Angelo Annaratone, was so impressed that he recommended similar reformatories for each region of the nation "for the purpose of getting so many youngsters out of Prison, which completely demoralizes them."[143] The most noteworthy visitor was Maria Montessori, who pronounced San Michele to be "a masterpiece worthy of providing an example to the whole world." Acclaiming Ricchi as the "perfect director" and the teachers as "pearls," she applauded their educational methods for combining the most modern principles from Northern Europe with those of Italian criminal anthropology.[144] By individualizing the treatment of each boy, beginning with a "psychological-physical examination" at the time of admission, San Michele was applying the "new pedagogy" that was sadly absent in other Italian schools.[145] Montessori's positive assessment was widely publicized through frequent articles in the daily press and her own lectures at the University of Rome.

In 1912, in response to one of Doria's last requests as director general, Giolitti named all nine public boys' reformatories after a prominent pioneer of pedagogy.[146] Now officially known as the Reformatory Aristide Gabelli, after an esteemed nineteenth-century educational administrator and writer, San Michele appeared to have become the model reformatory worthy of the capital. Its only rival in terms of reputation was its counterpart in Turin, now renamed after Ferrante Aporti, the founder of the first nursery schools in Italy. Both won the highest honors at the international Exposition in 1911, a widely attended world's fair held in Turin to mark the fiftieth anniversary of Italian unification. Based on a display of the products produced by the boys of San Michele, Ricchi won a gold medal and four of the teachers bronze medals.[147] According to an article in the journal, *Professional Teaching*, the high quality of the objects exhibited in Turin derived from the "sense of art" instilled by the boys' teachers, who guided them from simple to more complicated skills "with loving assistance" rather than as "exploiters of their strength for the purpose of making money."[148] Doria, who was often irritated by Ricchi's constant demands for more personnel for San Michele, sent the director a warm letter expressing "his congratulations for this very high honor, one that no similar governmental institution received, which makes the victory even more significant."[149]

When Doria retired from his post as director general in 1912, his legacy was already enshrined in the main hall of San Michele. Beside a plaque dedicated to one of the lay founders of the original institution in 1703, Francesco Albani, a second praised Doria as an "illustrious student of the disciplines of modern social pedagogy."[150] These plaques were hung among portraits of Italian kings and poets, and, most notably, of Edmondo de Amicis, author of the famous children's book, *Cuore*. As an ensemble, these decorations symbolized Doria's intended goal, that is, education as the foundation of citizenship. San Michele remained open as a boys' reformatory until 1927, although the adjoining charity wing was mostly abandoned. After the internees were transferred to a new juvenile institution at Casal San Marmo, on the outskirts of Rome, the entire complex underwent periods of renovation by the state and now houses various offices of the Ministry for Culture and Tourism. Because its rows of separate cells have remained intact, the wing that had housed the boys' reformatory was utilized as a set for over ten films during the 1970s and early 1980s.[151] Now completely restored to its eighteenth-century appearance, it hosts periodic exhibitions of art, while the nearby women's prison is still under renovation. Perhaps because of its historical reputation as one of the first juvenile reformatories in Europe, San Michele is unique among Roman prisons, in being carefully preserved as a site of carceral memory.

Reformatories at the National Level

Between the annexation of Rome and World War I, the annual population of Italian reformatories across Italy averaged 5,000–6,000.[152] The only significant exception occurred during the years 1895–1905, when totals increased slightly in correlation with temporarily rising rates of juvenile crime. Across the peninsula, the number of boys' reformatories ranged from thirty-eight to forty-eight between 1871 and 1914. After the 1890s, girls' institutions became more numerous, but, because they tended to be smaller, boys continued to make up a majority of the total inmate population.[153] Nonetheless, the rate of incarcerated girls was substantial, rising from 14 percent of all juvenile inmates in 1871 to 40 percent by 1895.[154] The rate of incarceration for girls under twenty-one, therefore, was much higher than that for adult women, which averaged only 4 percent over the same period. This disparity can partly be attributed to the wide discretion of police and courts to punish minors for "status crimes," or behavior that was legal for adults but considered deviant in children. Behaviors tolerated in boys, such as playing in the streets or staying out at night, were criminalized as sexually deviant and indicators of prostitution in girls and often led to arrest.

On an average, public reformatories made up only one-fourth of all juvenile institutions between 1871 and 1914. The other 75 percent were managed by private, usually religious, organizations[155] (Graph 6.2). The imbalance was most striking in the case of girls, who had access to only one public reformatory, in Perugia, before its closure in 1909. In contrast, boys benefitted from the opening of new state institutions, such as San Michele, after the passage of the Ordinance of 1891 and subsequently the reforms of Doria. The rate of boys in public reformatories thus rose from 23 percent in 1871 to almost 50 percent in 1914.

The variation among juvenile reformatories was further complicated by the division among legal categories of internees, which, in the case of boys, determined their placement in specific institutions. On an average, about one-half of all admissions between 1871 and 1914 were for paternal correction, although the rate was much lower in 1871, and then tripled by 1914. The increase was steepest for girls whose families, before the mid-1880s, rarely turned to the criminal justice system—as opposed to conservatories and other traditional charities—to discipline their daughters. Arrest by

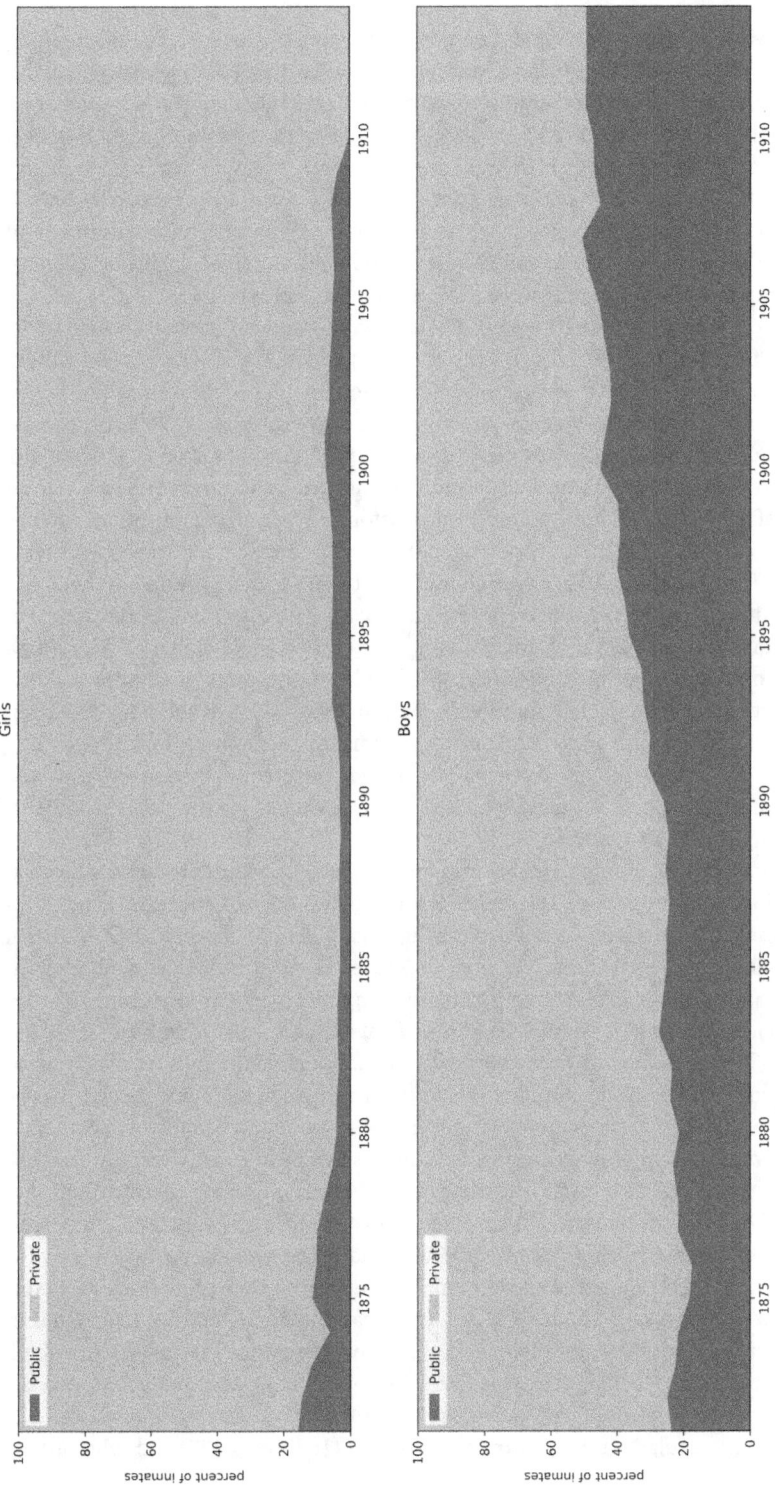

Graph 6.2 Inmates in public and private reformatories by gender, 1871–1914. Source: Ann. Stat.

police for vagabondage, begging, and prostitution accounted for most of the remaining admissions for both boys and girls. Court conviction accounted for very few children in reformatories; in 1901, for example, out of almost 2,000 children admitted, only 27 had been tried and absolved because of extreme youth and another 89 had been convicted of an offense in the criminal code.[156] In 1907, minors in the latter category were banished from reformatories as part of Doria's reform and transferred back to traditional "houses of correction."[157] This cleansing of the new reformatories of all "criminals"—that is, youth who had been tried and held morally culpable by a court— further emphasized their nature as semi-charitable institutions

Because of this complicated system of classification, juvenile reformatories varied widely in terms of the everyday experience of internees. By the twentieth century, state institutions for boys were equipped with separate sleeping cells while private reformatories relegated both sexes to communal dormitories.[158] Male internees had access to more outdoor space for recreation, including military exercises, while girls were often confined in a monastic fashion to internal courtyards.[159] After Beltrani Scalia's reform of 1888, boys entered reformatories specializing in either paternal correction or the rehabilitation of vagabonds, with the former reserving special treatment for paying inmates from rich families. In either case, young boys who had been acquitted or were awaiting trial were strictly separated from older inmates. And after Doria's reforms, staff at all-male institutions carried professional or educational titles. In contrast, female institutions accepted all legal categories of inmates and held them together in a completely undifferentiated mass.[160] Most of the personnel were simply designated "nuns in general" on governmental accounting forms, and these employees received strikingly lower pay than their male counterparts.[161] Nuns were assisted by volunteers, a fact cited by the state as an excuse for the paltry number of paid staff in girls' reformatories.[162]

The social backgrounds of child inmates in some ways differed from those of adults. Most significantly, almost three-fourths of both boys and girls came from urban rather than rural families, a pattern that changed little between 1862 and 1914. Heavy policing of the cities, and therefore widespread arrest of juvenile vagabonds and beggars, may offer one explanation for this striking divergence from the mostly rural origins of adult prisoners. Another factor may have been the unwillingness of peasant fathers to lose the labor of even the most rebellious children in contrast to urban parents, where the family economy was breaking down and children were perceived as an economic burden. Furthermore, parents in cities would have been more acquainted with the practice of interning unwanted children since most charity institutions, with their many resources, clustered in urban areas. A second factor that distinguished children from adults concerned their place of birth. From 1870 to 1880, 76 percent of all children came from northern or central Italy, the more urbanized regions of the peninsula.[163] During the decade before the outbreak of war, this rate dropped to 60 percent as increasing numbers of southern parents began placing their children in reformatories, such as San Michele. But even on the eve of World War I, juvenile inmates were much less likely to come from the South than their adult counterparts.

Rituals of admission, followed most closely in public reformatories for boys, were laid out in the early regulations on the houses of custody (1862 and 1877) and subsequently the much expanded reformatory law of 1907.[164] Upon arrival, new internees were required to bathe and don a uniform. They then met the director who, in the words of Doria's law, was to "comfort and encourage them" and offer "paternal advice about how to correct their shortcomings and become good citizens."[165] The doctor filled out their medical charts, including "anthropological and anthropometric" measurements.[166] Their photograph was attached to the "biographical dossier" that would follow them through their career at the reformatory. New internees underwent up to ten days of observation during which they were taught "new habits" and prepared for their "new life."[167] Once integrated into the life of the reformatory, they were required to remain silent during work, school, and religious services but allowed to talk and encouraged to play during hours of recreation. As in adult prisons, personnel had to be addressed with the formal form of address (*lei*) while the children employed the informal *tu* among themselves.[168]

During their internment, children did not have much contact with their families. While this differed little from adults, children must have felt particularly lonely once institutionalized; Doria, like Ricchi, noted the frequency of crying by young children during the night. It is difficult to generalize about the average age of juvenile internees both because early statistics failed to count private institutions and age categories changed in the yearly volumes of statistics. But in general, about two-thirds of all inmates were aged twelve to eighteen with the rest almost evenly split between younger and older groups.[169] As in the case of Buon Pastore and San Michele, the population of female reformatories tended to be older because many girls were not released until the legally required age of twenty-one. In contrast to adult penitentiaries, no limits (at least after 1907) were put on the number of letters that children could write or receive from their family and in fact the staff was supposed to encourage such correspondence. However, when families could not afford stamps, the state paid for only one postcard per month.[170] All letters were read, and presumably censored, by the director. That boys sent and received, on average, ten to fifteen letters per year and girls half that amount demonstrates the infrequency of correspondence in general and the relatively greater isolation of girls.[171] According to Montesi, the letters from children interned for paternal correction expressed primarily a wish to return home and, secondarily, requests for money. Rather than blaming parents for their internment, children promised to reform.[172] Boys and girls in private reformatories received more visits from family members than those in public institutions, where the directors considered them an indulgence.[173] In any case, few children received more than one yearly visit. Because only about 10 percent of juvenile inmates were orphans, this shocking lack of contact with the outside world seems to indicate family indifference.

Everyday life in reformatories centered on education and work. During the first few decades after unification, schools varied widely in quality with chaplains and nuns—rather than certified teachers—in charge of classes for barely literate students. As reformers began to enunciate the principle that "the State must be the great educator," schooling began to occupy more of the day and, at least in boys' institutions, became more professional.[174] Although the majority of the students continued to cluster in the first three grades after Doria's reforms, the years 1904–14 showed clear improvement in reading and writing. For example, the students who completed the first grade increased from 74 percent to 80 percent for boys and from 54 percent to 73 percent for girls.[175] Of those released in 1914, illiteracy had dropped from 80 percent to 3 percent between admission and release, and one-third had completed elementary school.[176] Although the improvement in female internees was more dramatic than that of boys, they nevertheless remained behind in rates of literacy and completion of elementary school.

Girls were more markedly disadvantaged in two related areas of learning. First, by the turn of the twentieth century, boys had access to a range of "special schools" in design, instrumental music, singing, gymnastics, public speaking, and even, at one government reformatory, firefighting. By the early twentieth century, the craze for gymnastics was so great that Doria sent a professor of physical education, Michelangelo Ierace, to inspect the classes at boys' reformatories and suggest a long list of improvements.[177] Ierace preached the particular utility of gymnastics for offering "an unobstructed outlet for the natural energies of youth for whom, in the conditions of enclosure, movement is the greatest need."[178] While the participation of male internees in these extracurricular courses was higher in public than private reformatories, all boys took advantage of them. The same was not true of girls in the state reformatory of Perugia, who lacked any opportunities for specialized training. Private female institutions offered only special classes in singing, a traditional activity of convent nuns.[179]

Second, male reformatories supplied a much larger number of books in their reading rooms, facilities required by the Regulation of 1907.[180] The state reformatory for girls at Perugia probably never had such a room, since official statistics list no books there. Some private female reformatories had libraries, but in 1900, for example, they held a total of 765 books while male reformatories boasted 7,641.[181] This disparity is particularly striking in light of the fact that girls constituted over a third of all reformatory inmates during that year. According to Gino Bernabò-Silorata, the secretary of the Turin reformatory, boys loved the reading room in his institution. Based on a survey of five hundred boys over two years, he found a preference for books "that succeeded in appealing to their fantasy" about travel, battles, and perilous adventures. He argued that such books "corresponded best to that savage nature and those criminal traits, which form the substratum of all their psychic functions."[182] Echoing Lombroso's theory of juvenile atavism, Bernabò-Silorata encouraged institutions to buy these types of modern books—by authors such as Jules Verne, Émile Zola, and De Amicis—in order to encourage reading. Girls, on the other hand, had access mainly to religious texts.

Girls were also disadvantaged compared to boys in terms of work. As early as 1871, male houses of custody employed boys as blacksmiths, carpenters, shoemakers, straw-workers, typographers, and musicians.[183] Although the state never established the promised agricultural colonies for juveniles, boys with rural backgrounds worked in gardens attached to reformatories. In contrast, girls were clustered in two categories: "seamstress," which included embroidery and knitting; and "other," which meant cleaning and laundry. As the experience of inmates in the Buon Pastore and San Michele demonstrated, little changed over the decades in terms of the gendering of job categories. That girls had fewer choices of employment did not mean that they were idle; on the contrary, they worked at higher rates than boys in both public and private institutions.[184] For example, in 1901, about 80 percent of girls held paid jobs in reformatories in contrast to 72 percent of all boys. By 1914, the director general claimed that 94 percent of all internees had learned a skill by the time of release.[185]

In terms of discipline, no clear gendered pattern emerges. Male inmates committed more infractions of institutional rules and therefore endured more punishment than girls. For example, between 1896 and 1903, on the average each boy broke the rules six times per year while the rate for girls was only three. Immediately before the war, rates began to converge at two to three infractions per internee, mostly for disobedience to staff and teachers.[186] As part of Doria's reforms, punishments became milder; in 1914, two-thirds were what Director General Girardi termed "moral," that is, reprimands and suspension of recreational privileges, while the rest were "corporal" or isolation in a punishment cell.[187] After 1907, children could no longer be deprived of food as a punishment, although some individual reformatory directors continued to do so.[188] To mitigate tensions in the reformatories, inmates had the right to request individual hearings to air their grievances. Between 1910 and 1914, this practice was encouraged most strongly in state reformatories, where each boy, on the average, met eight times each year with the director; in contrast, boys in private reformatories secured only two annual audiences and girls only one.[189] Girardi glossed over this disparity by citing "reasons of tradition and different structure."[190] Punishments were balanced by "rewards," which rose at a steep rate after the publication of the Regulation of 1907. While in the 1890s, most children received only one or two prizes annually, by 1914 the rate had risen to thirty-two for boys and eighteen for girls.[191] These were comprised mostly of trips outside of the reformatory, with those for boys more often being long excursions while girls simply took weekly walks.[192] In short, after Doria's reforms, punishments declined and prizes increased for all juvenile inmates although more markedly for boys.

The impulse to lighten punishment cannot be entirely attributed to a state that was increasing preoccupied with protecting children and constructing useful citizens. A spate of reformatory revolts occurred during the 1890s and early 1900s that brought embarrassing publicity to the prison administration. In a stinging indictment, published in 1902, of Italy's system of punishment for minors, Guglielmo Curli and Alessandro Bianchi documented fifty-two uprisings in public and private juvenile institutions.[193] Arguing that Italy's reformatories "created and multiplied delinquents," they reprinted the opinions of a number of experts about the causes of such frequent disorders.[194] Giulio Benelli, director of the government reformatory in Bologna, blamed both administrators, who needed to learn more about child psychology and rehabilitative pedagogy, and guards, who considered "the youngsters less like students to educate than as little criminals of the future."[195] He considered the standard complaints about the food as a pretext, asserting that in state institutions it was sufficient and healthy although possibly less adequate than in their private counterparts. De Sanctis, the director of the state reformatory in Pisa, lamented the mixture of violent boys—"in whom the stigma of degeneration or of hereditary culpability is profoundly impressed"—with those who were younger and more innocent.[196] He also blamed bad administrators, as did Ottaviano Morici, the director of a private institution in Ancona, who warned against discipline that was either too severe or too lax. Like many of their informants, Curli and Bianchi emphasized the need for turning reformatories into educational institutions and replacing prison guards with teachers. The impact of their book and its reviews in the press put pressure on Doria to institute his reforms.

Unlike adults, few juvenile inmates had fixed sentences and therefore could not foresee the year of their release. From 1897 to 1914, over 95 percent of all children were given either indeterminate sentences or, until the practice was discontinued in 1910, incarceration until adulthood.[197] In the former case, release depended on a determination by prison directors that the child was reformed or on a request by parents, who often wanted their progeny, particularly boys, to return home and contribute to the family economy. Neither case worked to the advantage of girls, who remained enclosed in reformatories for longer periods of their lives. From 1902 to 1914, a third of all girls had already served four years as compared to only 11 percent of all boys.[198] Ultimately, most children returned to their families, although boys were encouraged to join the military.[199]

Despite his lauded reforms, Doria left office with two issues unresolved. The first involved the inadequate number of public institutions that, despite their increasing quality, held only a minority of inmates. As early as 1883, Depretis admitted that private reformatories rarely separated their inmates by legal category, a problem that had not been solved by government inspections.[200] Clamor for more state institutions accelerated after the turn of the twentieth century when Doria took up the cause. In a report to Giolitti in 1904, he accused private reformatories of failing in their mission, "either because of insufficient funding, the unfitness of their personnel, or for the imprecision of their pedagogic and didactic direction and aims."[201] Six years later, he was still lamenting the use of "antiquated methods" by "simple attendants rather than teachers" in private institutions.[202] Although Doria repeated his call for the state to take over and unify the entire network of reformatories, successive prime ministers considered the proposal too expensive.

The second problem, the particularly decrepit state of girls' reformatories, was forced into public view by a revolt in 1908 at the state institution at Perugia.[203] In parliament, Eugenio Chiesa, a leader of the Republican party, denounced Doria for allowing the reformatory doctor to lock up the rebellious girls for up to thirty days in "therapeutic" isolation. Confined to punishment cells, the girls were kept in "absolute darkness, like a tomb," and in some cases tied down by leather straps that constituted "a real instrument of the inquisition."[204] Not only did these methods of punishment exceed the limits of the law, they had been applied not to convicts but to "unfortunate girls who had fallen low and needed to be pulled up and reborn."[205] Prime Minister Giolitti responded that "collective madness" had broken out among the girls, who "*broke everything* [and] assaulted the nuns."[206] Unlike boys, whom he considered to be "easily rehabilitated," these girls were "very depraved" and "absolutely degenerate persons."[207] With this Lombrosian analysis, which emphasized the propensity of women to hysteria and sexual malfeasance, he defended both Doria and the reformatory doctor.

Chiesa's critique went beyond the Perugia reformatory to indict the religious management of all girls' institutions. According to Chiesa, the state had handed over too much power to the nuns, who made money off provisioning the reformatory and contracting the work. As a result, the girls received "measly pay" in line with the "starvation type of labor regime typical of female monastic orders."[208] During the next few years, a debate ensued for the first time over the adequacy of religious personnel for the rehabilitation of girls. Bernabò-Silorata, while claiming not to be anticlerical, questioned whether nuns, who had deliberately chosen to withdraw from the world, understood the proper pedagogical principles for training children. He argued that female teachers should be acquainted with "all the instincts of maternity" and offer practical knowledge, including sex education, to the girls.[209] Writing in the *RDC*, Stanislao D'Alessandro agreed that religious personnel were incapable of instilling "a healthy modesty, without hypocrisy" that would prepare young inmates for love of their future husbands.[210] Another critic pointed to the monotony and sedentary nature of embroidery and lace-making in girl's reformatories, which lacked the industrial schools provided for boys.[211] For all these writers, the answer was to secularize female reformatories and extend to them the principles of the 1907 Regulation.

Not surprisingly, Rossana, the only female inspector of prisons, took an active and public part in this discussion through lectures, articles, and finally a book published in 1911 and devoted to the problems of girls' reformatories.[212] As is clear from its title—*Subject to the Rod: Pain, Poverty, and Female Degeneration*—the book combined criminal anthropological, sociological, and feminist perspectives. Rossana offered a severe critique of the system but laid only moderate blame on the nuns. Boasting that "no lay woman before me, with full authority and strength of spirit, has entered [these] convents where enclosure has reigned for centuries," she combined practical advice with melodrama in her reporting.[213] In describing the inmates, she repeated many positivist truisms: for example, that incarcerated girls had weak nerves, tended to mass crying or anger, and were dominated by their lower, sexual, instincts. Devoting an entire chapter to puberty, she emphasized the centrality of the uterus and ovaries for explaining the marked differences between female and male internees; early sexual development of girls from the South, she maintained, placed them closer to Africans than those from the North. Citing Lombroso, she warned against the tendency to lesbianism, which in his view characterized all institutions for women, including reformatories, brothels, conservatories, and even convents. Because of the importance of physical and psychological traits for analyzing the individual inmates, she warned that "not even the most generous and energetic soul will succeed in transforming these female Reformatories without the aid of the science of criminal anthropology"[214] (Illustration 6.2).

Despite this biological bent, Rossana also pointed out the multiple privations to which the girls were subjected. Most reformatories, located in old convents, lacked light, fresh air, and heating as well as facilities for bathing, since nuns discouraged disrobing as immoral. Food was scarce and gymnastics practically unknown. Work was monotonous, old-fashioned, and often not paid. Illiteracy was still widespread among confined girls, and, "no one tries to equip them with a conscience and a sense of their own will," in contrast to the training for independence typical of boys' reformatories.[215] In short, Rossana depicted the typical female reformatory as dirty, dark, stifling, and filled with hungry, joyless, and ignorant internees.

Despite her sharp indictment of the state of girls' institutions, Rossana was loath to join the growing chorus of voices promoting secularization. As in the case of adult women, she simply recommended that Doria, whom she admired immensely, convince the nuns to change their ways and implement the Regulation of 1907 by providing

Illustration 6.2 Inmates of a girls' reformatory

separate sleeping cells, bathtubs, plentiful and healthy food, gymnastics and outdoor recreation, certified teachers, and a variety of job training to prepare girls for release. To those who called for banishment of the nuns, she replied that "very few lay women would have the patience, sense of self-sacrifice, and heroic perseverance" to live amidst "these diseased and depraved individuals."[216] With their mystical ideals and humility, only religious women were tough enough to maintain discipline. She even pronounced the few lay teachers recently hired by a few reformatories as ill-equipped for their jobs, although her resentment was clearly piqued by their resistance to her demands to observe their classes. Yet she offered little practical advice for impelling the nuns, with their "primordial existence," to adopt modern principles of reform.

The revolt at Perugia prompted an escalating public debate about the neglect suffered by incarcerated girls. Erminia Montini, on behalf of the National Council of Women, took a more radical stance than Rossana and denounced the hegemony of nuns over girls' reformatories.[217] Yet, Doria took only limited action. In 1910, he simply closed—rather than secularized—the Perugia institution, leaving Italy without any female state reformatory. The courts ceased sentencing children, mostly girls, to confinement until adulthood. Admitting that the nuns were reluctant "to change their traditional methods," Doria planned to establish, during his last few years as director general, a new lay reformatory for girls in Turin but never secured the government's approval.[218] His less energetic successor, Girardi, dropped the plan, concluding in 1914 that "the results obtained in private reformatories can, in general, be considered satisfactory."[219] The outbreak of war interrupted further secularization of reformatories for either girls or boys.

Prisoner Aid Societies

On the eve of World War I, charity remained closely intertwined with the public sphere of juvenile reform. Private, religious institutions continued to outnumber those administered directly by the state, with the latter available only for boys. Further blurring the border between charity and criminal justice were the prisoner aid societies, called *patronati*. Recognized in both the Ordinance of 1891 and the Reformatory Regulation of 1907, these organizations did not form part of a public welfare system but instead were staffed by volunteers. Over the decades, a series of government ministers, such as Nicotera, Depretis, and Crispi, had urged prefects to encourage the establishment of *patronati* in concurrence with repeated resolutions at the International Penitentiary Congresses.[220] Despite widespread sympathy for aiding prisoners after their release, the activities of such societies waxed and waned over the years. In response to Nicotera's efforts, which included state subsidies in some cases, the number of *patronati* rose from three to twenty-two between 1876 and 1878, only to decline during the next decade.[221] Another wave of interest developed in the 1890s, continuing until the beginning of the war. The targets of assistance also varied, as adults benefitted most in the nineteenth century and minors in the decade before the war, at the height of the child protection movement. As the state tightened its regulation of charities, confusion ensued about the legal status of *patronati*, and, as a consequence, their charters varied from city to city and over time.[222] Rome's history in this regard offers a glimpse into the diverse albeit limited efforts by private volunteers to aid prisoners.

Traditional confraternities, whose legal status was uncertain after unification, were the first Roman organizations to offer assistance to the condemned and their families. Although officially abolished after unification, confraternities could register as *opere pie* if they carried out philanthropic activities. For example, the city council of Rome was inclined to order the closing of San Girolamo della Carità in the early 1870s, because its main function—to provide free defense in court for the poor—was no longer needed under the new liberal law codes. In the end, however, the city council approved its status as an official charity because it continued to give clothes and other subsidies to prisoners "in that terrible moment, after leaving prison and facing serious obstacles to gaining their bread through honest work, they could easily fall back into a life of crime."[223] A second confraternity, San Giovanni Decollato, was also in peril because its major role of accompanying prisoners to their executions became unnecessary once the Zanardelli Code abolished the death penalty. But again its mission, as approved by the prefect of Rome, was redefined to emphasize its other philanthropic activities, which included assisting prisoners and their families as well as providing dowries to "honest girls" who could produce a "certificate of good behavior."[224] While these organizations did not appear in official national lists of *patronati*, it is clear that local authorities encouraged the transformation of these types of confraternities into prisoner aid societies rather than simply repressing them as a token of the retrograde past.

After Nicotera's circular of 1876, new secular and religious organizations were founded to assist prisoners, although they were often short-lived. In 1878, a group of Roman notables, with the support of Lucchini, published a statute for a *patronato* committed to helping ex-convicts get jobs and planned to establish workhouses for both men and women throughout the province of Rome.[225] Little is known, however, about its activities. In 1882, the Refuge of the Holy Family, near the Church of San Giovanni in Laterano, became the site of another private *patronato*. Subsidized by the ministries of Public Education and the Interior as well as the king, banks, and wealthy individuals, it supported both abandoned children and twenty to thirty men and boys after their release from prison.[226] It closed in 1896 after running out of funds. More enduring was the refuge of Santa Margherita, founded by Padre Simpliciano in 1879, "with the intention of preventing the corruption of young women and of helping them redeem themselves from vice."[227] Located first in Testaccio, the refuge moved in 1886 to Santa Balbina, which had earlier served as a boys' reformatory. In this old monastery, women released from the penitentiaries of Villa Altieri and Perugia, as well as "endangered" girls in need of protection, did agricultural work, on the still rural Aventine hill, as well as the more common tasks of washing, knitting, sewing, and needlework. Registered as an *opera pia*, Santa Magherita received annual subsidies from the Ministry of the Interior. In return, the refuge provided the prison administrative with detailed reports on its activities and finances. In 1904, it was one of thirty societies for ex-prisoners that received a state subvention.[228]

During the decade before World War I, a number of new, and in most cases secular, *patronati* for children were established in Rome as part of the child protection movement that has been described by Carl Ipsen.[229] The most innovative organization, the Charity for Youth on Probation, sought to institute an American approach that offered social services to convicted children with suspended sentences.[230] Founded in 1905 by Lucy Bartlett, an English feminist and prison reformer living in Italy, this *patronato* offered several types of assistance: job placement, legal representation in court, and cash subsidies for the very poor.[231] It also planned to open libraries, evening schools, and recreational facilities in the future. According to its *Statuto*, the *patronato* was supported by a long and prestigious list of members including Ottolenghi, the director of the national police school; Prince Augusto Torlonia, a member of one of the most prominent aristocratic families in Rome; Countess Cora Di Brazzà Sarvognan, an American woman married to an Italian nobleman and explorer; and Eugenio Trompeo, a lawyer and city councilor of Rome who had a special commitment to child protection. In an interesting link between traditional and more modern forms of charity, S. Girolamo della Carità, which had its roots in the old system of religious confraternities, devoted financial support to this entirely secular organization.[232] The *patronato* worked closely with a special section of the Roman criminal court, which had taken over the cases of minor defendants in anticipation of a national law instituting children's tribunals. Although no such law was approved before World War I, the magistrates sent information to Barlett's organization about each boy or girl released on probation. However, according to its first president, Raffaele Calabrese, follow-up visits by volunteers often found the children missing from their official residences or unwilling to accept any aid.[233]

The number of secular *patronati* expanded not only in Rome but throughout the nation during the years before the war. In 1913, Barlett's organization, now with branches in Turin, Florence, Milan, and Bologna, held a national conference to organize its work. In Milan, Professor Antonio Martinazzoli founded the "Institute of forensic pedagogy" to assist wayward boys and "to study each minor that is admitted using the anthropological method."[234] In Turin, a "Council for the defense of youth" was founded by a local judge, Giuseppe Cesare Pola, to provide abandoned and convicted minors of both sexes with legal and medical help. In Rome, lawyer Raffaele Maietti established

"The Refuge" with workshops, one of which was located in Regina Coeli, to employ criminal youth in making toys; in 1914, he began to publish a related bulletin, *For Social Defense*.[235] As with their earlier religious counterparts, many of these secular *patronati* were short-lived because they relied on the money and enthusiasm of volunteers. Despite the praise that they received from Doria and Beltrani Scalia, who himself founded an organization to aid the children of inmates, prison-aid societies received only minimal subsidies from the state and remained in the sphere of private charity.[236]

Feminists played an important role in the child-saving movement, although they focused mostly on prevention of sexual abuse of young women rather than post-incarceration assistance. For example, the Council against the White Slave Trade, founded in 1901 with branches in several Italian cities, helped poor girls find jobs and housing so that they would not have to resort to prostitution. As part of its mission, its national director, the socialist feminist Majno Bronzini, established the Mariuccia Home in Milan, which cooperated with police by taking in young female vagabonds and prostitutes. As Annarita Buttafuoco has cogently demonstrated, this innovative institution sought to equip young women with a "new female identity" based on secular values and training in modern industrial work rather than domestic service.[237] In 1913, Gina Mazza, who worked with Ronconi to provide libraries in female penal institutions, opened her own institute in Rome to assist women and girls after release from prison.[238] But, despite these feminist initiatives, Rossana lamented at the National Women's Conference in 1917 that most Italian *patronati* were still managed by men and assisted mostly male prisoners, a claim supported by official statistics.[239] Even at the peak of the child-saving movement, girls released on probation or paroled from reformatories received little attention or assistance. Citing examples of other nations, Rossana proposed that through "private initiative and the intelligent energies of modern women," workshops should be established to "educate and redeem ... those female powers that could be of such great utility to the country and to human life."[240] Many *patronati* survived the war, but a significant gender gap remained in assistance to minors involved in the court system.

The history of prisoner aid societies encapsulates the contradictions in Italy's movement for juvenile justice reform. On the one hand, the coercive nature of the old houses of custody had drawn public criticism and prompted a wave of new charities funded by private individuals through religious organizations or, increasingly after 1900, secular patrons. However, the *patronati* were small and their activities depended on the enthusiasm and financial generosity of volunteers. Receiving only small governmental subsidies, they represented one end of a spectrum of juvenile justice institutions that blurred private with public initiatives. Meanwhile, religious reformatories for girls and boys, while nominally under the supervision of the Director General of Prisons, in fact retained an autonomy that defied the tenets of Doria's regulations. Only the state reformatories for boys approached his ideal of turning prisons into schools, although their public nature was undercut by the admission procedures. Rather than convicted criminals, the immense energies and relatively lavish funding for these model institutions benefitted mostly troublesome, unwanted, or homeless youth, at the behest of parents or police. Similarly, children awaiting trial and undergoing punishment, were mainly sent to jails even as late as 1914. Complaints about the plight of minors held in local jails, whose size and disorganization often defied reform, had been sparked in the 1860s by the muckraking book of Bellazzi and continued for fifty years.[241] While Doria and Girardi defensively claimed that juveniles were strictly separated from adults, they could not deny the fact, reported in their own statistics that, in 1913, over 2,300 children were incarcerated in jails staffed by guards rather than teachers.[242] Thus, while Doria was rightly proud of his reform of government reformatories for boys, the majority of criminalized youth, particularly girls, were denied, in Laura Guidi's words, "the earliest forms of a specific type of 'citizenship' for children."[243]

7

Prisons on the Margins: Police Camps and Criminal Insane Asylums

The Italian network of incarceration extended beyond the standard prisons for women, men, and children to include two additional institutions: police camps and criminal insane asylums. Located on islands off the southern coast of Italy, police camps held "suspicious" persons who were considered dangerous to social order and therefore deserving of banishment from the mainland. Although this type of internal exile, called *domicilio coatto*, was initiated by police, the camps themselves were mostly staffed by prison guards. Criminal insane asylums, while labeled as hospitals by the Italian state, were directly subordinate to the penitentiary rather than public health administration. That punishment, rather than simply prevention, was the primary function of police camps and criminal insane asylums is clear from their inclusion in the annual government volumes of prison statistics. Relatively invisible to the public, both institutions swept additional individuals, who had not necessarily been sentenced by the courts, into a life of confinement and demonstrate the elasticity of the prison system on its margins to punish groups possessing little right of self-defense.

Despite their similarity as exceptional branches of the prison network, police camps and criminal asylums had different origins and were inspired by radically divergent philosophies of punishment. The island colonies for *domicilio coatto* carried the retributive flavor of the old regime in which banishment and exile had played a prominent role in penal law. Harsher than the *bagni*, the camps did not even provide for the basic needs of the *coatti*, as the inmates were called, leaving them frequently without work, sufficient food, or adequate shelter. Admission came at the order of police rather than through normal court procedures. In contrast, the criminal insane asylum encapsulated the modern positivist principle of individuation, whereby punishment was to be tailored to each prisoner. According to this medical model, the insane criminal deserved a special hybrid institution that combined the security of a penitentiary with the curative power of a hospital. Unlike the police camps that served only a custodial function of isolating "dangerous" individuals, the criminal asylums promised treatment and rehabilitation based on the most recent scientific principles.

During the fifty years after unification, these two liminal types of Italian penal institutions were gendered, according to different logics, as male. The police camps—a form of corporal punishment like the *bagni*—were not considered appropriate for women, who were, by the nineteenth century, instead enclosed in convent prisons. Only the male criminal, who symbolized the incarnation of violence during the heyday of anxiety about the dangerous classes, was a candidate for police exile. However, while being shielded from the harsh and arbitrary punishment of internal exile, female inmates were also excluded from the potential benefits of medical care in the new criminal insane asylums. Thus, as recipients of the new principle of individualized punishment, men experienced both the most repressive and possibly most advantageous forms of incarceration. In a seemingly contradictory way, the police camps and criminal asylums addressed two types of masculinity: the former, the traditional violent member of the dangerous classes and the second, the new male citizen deserving of treatment and rehabilitation. This chapter will examine each of these marginal penal institutions at the national level in terms of legislation, the social profile of inmates, and prison life.

Police Camps (*Domicilio Coatto*)

At first glance, the network of outdoor police camps that dotted the southern islands of Italy was an anomaly in nineteenth-century Europe. While the Hapsburg Empire had employed a similar policy of internal exile in the previous century, by the time of Italian unification the radial penitentiary dominated discourse about punishment.[1] While its geographical neighbors were seeking to replace hard labor with rehabilitative reclusion in sanitary, indoor environments, Italy created the seemingly archaic punishment of *domicilio coatto*, or what Daniela Fozzi has labeled "an Italian specialty."[2] Yet in a broader, transnational context the Italian island colonies mirrored the policies of overseas transportation employed by many European nations to rid the metropole of recidivists and other seemingly incorrigible prisoners. That Italy debated the deportation of convicts to overseas colonies only underscores the parallels between Italy's police camps and the penal colonies established throughout Asia, Africa, and the Americas by European powers. If Italy's imperial ambitions had been fulfilled earlier, the police camps very likely would have been transferred from the mother country to its overseas colonies. Thus, *domicilio coatto* reminds us that despite the triumphant narrative of the birth of the prison, many nations retained a hybrid system of incarceration that included outdoor penal colonies alongside the modern penitentiary.

Debates about Deportation

Transportation, in the classic sense of the deportation of convicted criminals to colonial territories, came under serious consideration by the new Italian state in the years immediately following unification. It seemed to offer an alternative to the death penalty, which had already been abolished in Tuscany during the eighteenth century and which was widely unpopular within parliament after Italian unification. During three decades of long and heated debates about the principles of a new criminal code, statesmen searched for an alternative to capital punishment that would be severe enough to prevent crime, and many found the answer in deportation. One of the major stumbling blocks, however, was the hard fact that Italy did not possess any foreign colonies in the immediate post-unification period. Rather than dropping the option of transportation, the state entered into a series of negotiations with other European powers to acquire an appropriate territory "outside the Mediterranean," in the words of Justice Minister Paolo Vigliani. Thus ensued talks with Portugal, to acquire a parcel of land in Mozambique, the Congo, or Angola; and with England, Denmark, and Russia for access to their possessions.[3] In addition, several officials were dispatched to Asia to locate an uninhabited island that might serve as a penal colony, and follow-up reports suggested the acquisition of the Nicobar Islands in the Indian Ocean (1864) or the occupation of a territory off the coast of Sumatra (1867). In the subsequent years, Emilio Cerruti, a law professor and passionate supporter of deportation, negotiated several conventions of dubious legality with local rulers for ownership of islands near the coast of New Guinea or Australia. The failure of these absurd expeditions, however, did not put an end to the debates about transportation, which continued until the passage of the Zanardelli Code in 1889 and beyond.

Proponents of deportation varied in the scope of their proposals. Adolfo de Foresta, a magistrate who was later nominated to the Senate, published a series of articles in 1873 supporting a narrow application of transportation for only the most serious crimes.[4] Deportation would provide an intimidating but relatively humane substitute for both the death penalty (with, in his words, its "executioner and its scenes of blood") and for the Philadelphia model of cellular confinement, which he branded a "barbaric American invention."[5] On the other hand, Cerruti envisioned a wider application of transportation to be applied to four categories of prisoners with sentences of two years to life so that Italian penitentiaries would be emptied of half their inmates. Mainland prisons could then be converted to the Pennsylvania model, which he favored in contrast to de Foresta, and penal colonies could, on the Australian model, become sites of future settlement.[6]

Cerruti was most enthusiastic about the islands off the west coast of New Guinea, which he declared to be "today perfectly free, really *res nullus*, only a den of very barbarous tribes of cannibals; it would be glorious for Italy to replace them with a civilized population even if selected from the most vicious prisoners."[7] Thus for Cerruti, "free" did not refer to the indigenous inhabitants, whom he considered less than human, but to the claims of other European powers. In fact, the proximity of "man-eating tribes" on the islands would provide a handy disincentive for prisoners contemplating escape. Furthermore, subjection of the indigenous peoples would be easy and cheap, requiring "only one company of European troops accompanied by two small canons."[8] After citing England and Holland as examples of successful and profitable policies of transportation, he admitted that Italians were often considered unfit to be colonizers. But had not Italy been one of the first nations of explorers? For centuries a major seafaring nation? Now a nation of emigrants who traveled long distances to the Americas? While he longed ultimately for a wider commercial empire, Cerruti pronounced that penal colonization could take place at once.

Despite his claim to represent majority opinion, Cerruti and other supporters of deportation were opposed by a phalanx of jurists and criminologists from both the classical and positivist schools. Pessina, a prominent voice of the former, argued that transportation would stigmatize prisoners in a manner that was unjust even for those sentenced to capital punishment or hard labor. Instead, modern penitentiaries should provide a uniformity of punishment applicable to all serious crimes.[9] Lombroso, despite the overtly racist nature of his criminal anthropology, opposed the acquisition of colonies for any reason. Most importantly, Beltrani Scalia declared himself "an open adversary" of deportation in a series of articles in the *RDC* as well as in his well-respected book, *Prison Reform in Italy*.[10] For Beltrani Scalia, the experience of other European countries did not constitute a persuasive model, as England had already discontinued transportation and France had recently experienced a prisoner revolt in New Caledonia. He opposed deportation on both moral grounds, in that it introduced inequity into the scale of punishment, and on the practical issue of high costs. According to his estimate, Italy would have to spend twice as much to deport prisoners than to keep them in mainland penitentiaries, an impossible price for a new nation struggling with poverty and depleted public finances. The opponents of deportation claimed victory in 1889, when the Zanardelli Penal Code omitted it from the scale of punishments. After Italy began to acquire small colonies in Eritrea (1890) and Libya (1912), advocates again published tracts extolling transportation and tried to reopen the debate, but Beltrani Scalia and his successor, Doria, successfully opposed all but one short-lived experiment in Assab.[11]

Domicilio Coatto in Law and Legislation

From the time of unification, Italian police exercised wide discretion in applying "administrative measures" to control or punish behavior deemed too petty for a court trial. Most controversial of these administrative measures was *domicilio coatto* (forced internal exile), which could be applied to suspicious persons even if they had not been convicted of any crime. First formalized in the infamous Picca Law of 1863, internal exile was primarily to be used against "brigands," as southern separatists were labeled, and secondarily against vagrants, beggars, and *mafiosi*. Meant to constitute a temporary measure to impose order while the new Italian government extended its power over the disparate territories of the peninsula, internal exile was nevertheless incorporated into the first national police law of 1865. It quickly became a permanent feature of the Italian criminal justice system that was directed during certain periods against common criminals and at others against political opponents, such as anarchists and socialists. Thus the liberal state handed an instrument of extrajudicial confinement to the fascist dictatorship which, in 1926, changed its name to *confino* and expanded its scope to ever widening groups of political and social "outcasts."

Many victims of internal exile had simply violated the conditions of a milder administrative measure called *ammonizione* or legal warning. The procedure for applying *ammonizione* was left mainly to police and involved the magistracy only marginally. After arrest, the accused were granted summary hearings before local judges (*pretori*) and almost invariably "warned" not to engage in certain behaviors for a period of two years. Vagabonds and the unemployed had to find work immediately, establish a fixed address, and advise police authorities of their whereabouts. Reputed criminals were admonished "to live honestly, respect persons and property, avoid suspicious behavior, and remain in their present neighborhoods."[12] Police regulations prescribed curfews for both groups and forbade them to carry arms, hang out with bad characters, or frequent taverns and brothels. Any infraction of this long list of regulations would lead to arrest.

Over the years, grounds for being sent into internal exile varied slightly with successive modification of the police laws but remained substantially two. First, violations of the myriad rules surrounding judicial warning could land "suspicious persons" in an island penal colony. Thus even after the Zanardelli Code decriminalized begging and vagabondage, police substituted administrative measures to continue disciplining the homeless and poor. As Lorenzo Benadusi has pointed out, *domicilio coatto* also became the fate of many homosexuals, who had become a special focus of criminal anthropological study by the late nineteenth century.[13] Although the criminal code seemed to tolerate same-sex behavior by failing to list it as a crime, police acted on the moral panic raised by the press to send homosexuals and transvestites to island colonies.[14] Any individual with a criminal record could also be subject to arrest simply for suspicious behavior and then sentenced to *domicilio coatto*.

The second target of *domicilio coatto* was political crime, whose definition changed over the decades.[15] During the 1860s and 1870s, the new state used this tool against southern brigands, who were labeled as traitors plotting to undo unification. It was also directed against members of the Sicilian mafia and the Neapolitan Camorra, although the label was applied loosely by officials who could not yet clearly identify such organizations.[16] During the 1890s, a series of "exceptional laws" turned *domicilio coatto* against anarchists and socialists involved in the waves of strikes and protests that swept Italy from south to north.[17] With the dramatic increase in the number of prisoners on the islands, socialists in parliament, always critics of police powers, compared *domicilio coatto* to a "malignant tumor, because it is poisoned by arbitrariness, suspicion, and injustice."[18] Thus internal exile became a parallel type of summary police punishment of both common and political criminals that continued to coexist with a liberal court system dedicated to the protection of individual freedom under the Zanardelli Code.

The large majority of individuals condemned to *domicilio coatto* served their sentences in island colonies although a few were banished to small towns in a pattern that became more common under fascism. Numbering seven to eight during the fifty years after unification, the most permanent penal colonies were located on the islands of Favignana, Lampedusa, Lipari, Pantelleria, Ponza, Tremiti, Ustica, and Ventotene. Several, such as Tremiti and Ventotene, had previously served as prison islands under the Bourbons and were redeployed after the passage of the Pica Law in 1863.[19] Prisoners slept in makeshift dormitories or old castles managed either by police officials or prison administrators. During the day inmates were free to wander the island without supervision. While expected to work, many passed their time drinking and gambling in local taverns. A few brought their wives and children; others struck up relationships with local women. Jobs were difficult to find, low-paying, and unskilled; most *coatti* could find employment only as agricultural workers or porters.[20] The islands, typically volcanic and mountainous, were too small and poor to provide a living for the majority of prisoners. Those without work received a daily pittance from the Italian government to buy food and other necessities. Internal exile, therefore, was a strange hybrid system that combined restriction with freedom. It met none of the standards of modern penal reform, that is, cellular separation, rehabilitative work, or a healthy diet and living environment.

Immediately upon their establishment in 1863, the island penal colonies became the target of criticism from the political Left and an embarrassment to a liberal state intent on burnishing its image as modern and progressive. As in the case of deportation, members of both the classical and positivist schools called for the abolition of *domicilio coatto*. Predictably many classical jurists abhorred any punishment that did not result from a court trial. Clearly, the application of legal warnings and internal exile for behavior that did not violate the criminal code was an anathema to jurists steeped in the Beccarian principle of the presumption of innocence. More surprising was the strong condemnation of the positivist school, which might be expected to welcome *ammonizione* and *domicilio coatto* as necessary tools of social defense against born criminals. Yet, in his book, *On the Increase in Crime*, Lombroso declared these two administrative measures as "not particularly legal and not particularly useful" and "like palliatives in general, always ineffective and sometimes harmful."[21] Those subjected to *ammonizione* were "slaves in the hands of police officers," liable for arrest if they simply greeted a fellow suspect or missed their nightly curfew.[22] *Domicilio coatto* was even worse, since the islands offered little opportunity for work, which was the essential component of rehabilitation.

Ferri agreed that *ammonizione* was "absolutely inefficacious in protecting public order" although it lulled citizens into feeling safe.[23] More than many of his positivist colleagues, he worried about civil rights, arguing that it was inappropriate for a civilian government at peace to maintain "this exceptional institution in quite normal times."[24] Yet he boasted that he opposed *ammonizione* from an "absolutely practical point of view."[25] First, those under police warning could rarely find a job, because employers routinely turned down such applicants as untrustworthy. Rather than being reformed through steady work, the condemned had to turn to crime in order to survive. Second, *ammonizione* discouraged serious investigations by police, who simply took a name off the list of those under warning rather than going after the real suspects. That 50 percent of all criminal cases had to be dropped in the first phase of the trial, for lack of evidence, proved that keeping a phalanx of men under surveillance did not help police solve crimes.

Exposés in the press, as well as information collected by the Ministry of the Interior, attested to the dismal conditions in the island colonies. For example, Jessie White Mario's investigative reporting during the 1890s included visits to several police camps.[26] Although a democrat and feminist, White Mario did not blindly condemn the entire Italian prison system but was appalled at the conditions that she found on the island of Favignana. She described the men condemned to *domicilio coatto* as "the most vile and despicable mixture of human beings that I have ever set eyes on."[27] They roamed the island, "without discipline and without work," terrorizing the inhabitants and preying on each other.[28] In an interview with Giuseppe Alongi, a high police official and ex-warden of a penal colony, she learned that his charges had spent most of their time in drinking and gambling. The strong had transplanted the methods of the *camorra* to the island, shaking down the weak after the distribution of the daily allowance.[29] White Mario also noted the disproportionately high percentage of Sicilians in the penal colonies, many of whom were political detainees whose revolt in 1894 had been brutally suppressed by the central government.[30] She concluded that the system of *domicilio coatto*, "while evil in and of itself and harmful to all, is deadly for Sicilians."[31]

Official reports echoed the criticisms of White Mario. According to a letter of 1913 from the Prefect of Agrigento to police headquarters in Rome, only 60 of 200 inmates on the island of Lampedusa had found jobs, although almost all of them were able-bodied. The work, primarily in agriculture or on the docks, was unskilled and seasonal, paying only about 1 lira per day. Over 50 percent of the men were alcoholics, 15 percent having acquired their bad habit since arriving at the colony. Drunkenness was punished with banishment to an isolation cell, but—by his admission—"such measures are for the most part totally useless."[32] About 10 percent of the convicts had tuberculosis or syphilis, exacerbated by the filthy dormitories that needed disinfecting. Fights between inmates were frequent, including "violent acts typical of the Camorra, that is, of organized crime."[33] He concluded pessimistically that the colony of Lampedusa was "a preparatory school for the perpetuation and execution of future crimes since the infectious germ of criminality is disseminated with the exchange of ideas."[34] He asked for more dormitories, in order to separate the prisoners, and funds for disinfecting them weekly.

Not surprisingly, Beltrani Scalia supported the campaign to abolish the island colonies, which bore little resemblance to his vision of a rehabilitative prison. As early as 1879, he impatiently proclaimed to have criticized *domicilio coatto* "from its birth" for gathering "a few hundred of the worst riff-raff" on islands without work or sufficient sustenance.[35] The "bitter fruit" of this absurd system was to spread "corruption and disgrace" among the free population whose communities were turned into a type of hell. Humanitarianism figured little in Beltrani Scalia's critique, which characterized the typical *coatto* as "the worst sort" of criminal marked by "evil wiles."[36] Instead, he denounced the impracticality of a police measure lacking two main components of the Irish system: an initial disciplinary stage of cellular isolation and subsequent rehabilitation through work. Uneasy with a system of punishment not fully under his control, Beltrani Scalia attempted throughout his career to rid Italian police legislation of this hybrid institution.

In response to the widespread feeling of shame about the island colonies as constituting a blot on Italy's project to build a liberal state, parliament entertained a series of measures to modify or even abolish *domicilio coatto*. The Finocchiaro-Aprile–Pelloux proposal of 1899 substituted indeterminate relegation to isolated agricultural or industrial prisons or exile from Italy entirely for *domicilio coatto*, while the Gianturco plan of 1900 suggested relegation or deportation for an indeterminate time. In 1904, the Ronchetti proposal echoed that of Gianturco but added parole as a mechanism to encourage good behavior and rehabilitation on the part of inmates. Wide discretionary power was to be left in the hands of judges who, on the advice of prison administrators and other experts, would determine when—if ever—a recidivist was sufficiently normalized to rejoin society.

As none of these plans was approved by parliament, Prime Minister Luigi Luzzatti proposed a further variant to the Chamber of Deputies in 1910. He retained the principle of indeterminate sentencing, which could be "prolonged in perpetuity for incorrigible criminals, thus putting into practice the eliminative principle of natural selection as society has been demanding."[37] Luzzatti was unwilling to give up the hope of deportation, since "current criminology," meaning criminal anthropology, taught that "individuals unable to adapt to our civilization will adjust and feel at home in a semi-savage environment."[38] Adopting the positivist equation of criminals and "barbarians," he suggested sending convicts and their families to colonize Africa, a plan that would provide the maximum social defense of Italian society at a minimum cost. Anticipating objections that such forced colonization would punish innocent family members, Luzzatti quoted the positivist maxim that "inborn criminality is almost never limited to one member of a family but rather affects the entire stock."[39]

Realistically, however, most habitual criminals would not be sent to Africa but to six new "colonies of confinement" (*colonie di relegazione*) that would replace the present facilities for *domicilio coatto*. Luzzatti did not clearly define how the new colonies would avoid the abuses of the old, except to insist that they be situated where work would be available to all inmates. He trusted that steady employment in agriculture or commerce would rehabilitate some recidivists and at least keep them from harassing the local "honest and free population."[40] He argued that convict labor would not depress wages on the capitalist job market, if the new colonies were located in areas such as Sardinia, Basilicata, and Calabria where emigration had emptied rural villages. To placate whatever population was left, the proposed law forbade convicts from frequenting public places.

Consistent with its earlier pattern, parliament failed to pass this modification of *domicilio coatto*. The proposal was doomed both by outright opposition from many on the Left, who insisted on total abolition of the colonies, and by bickering among moderates over the shape of a new institution to replace them. After the fall of Luzzatti's short-lived government, successive prime ministers could not summon the political will to abolish a policy that bolstered the power of the State to discipline its opponents. As the war interrupted further discussion of the issue, *domicilio coatto* as well as *ammonizione* remained on the books until the fascist seizure of power, when both police measures were eagerly appropriated by the new regime. The new Public Security Law of 1926 changed the name of *domicilio coatto* to *confino*, or internment, and weakened the scraps of due process contained in the old law. It also explicitly identified political opponents as legitimate targets of *confino*, so that the island colonies became integral to the totalitarian aspirations of the fascist state.

Life in the Penal Colonies

Several types of sources, including prison statistics and memoirs of political prisoners, confirmed the intolerable conditions of everyday life in the penal colonies. Statistics on *coatti*, while not as extensive as those for inmates in the regular prison system, offer a general profile of those men banished to island camps by police. The total number of individuals serving sentences of internal exile ranged from 1,000 to 5,000 per day over the period from 1876 and 1914, with averages falling between 2,000 and 3,000.[41] While it is true that the number of individuals assigned to the colonies declined drastically

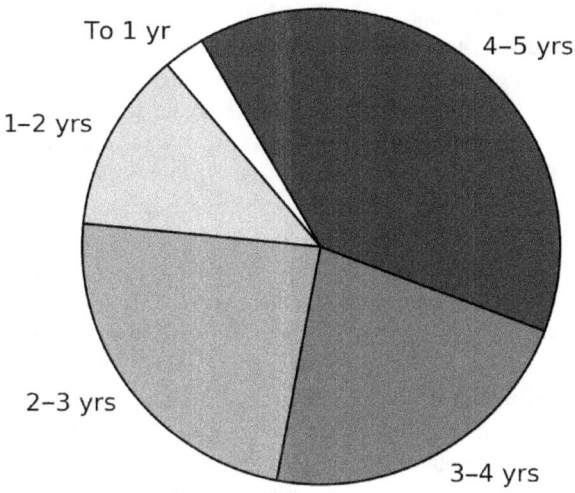

Graph 7.1 Length of sentence for inmates in penal colonies, 1900–11. Source: Stat. Carc.

during the 1880s and again after 1900, the island camps remained crowded because of the long sentences imposed on most *coatti*. In the 1890s, for example, almost half of the prisoners were serving sentences of four to five years, the longest possible under the police law. While this percentage declined to 32 percent by 1911, the large majority of inmates were still serving sentences of more than two years[42] (Graph 7.1).

During the same era, most *coatti* were aged over thirty, making them older than male prisoners in general and demonstrating the intrusion of internal exile on the lives of mature adults. That almost two-thirds of men in exile were single demonstrates their social marginality as a group, compared to their compatriots in regular penitentiaries or even the old *bagni*. Yet most of those who were married or widowed had children, demonstrating that *domicilio coatto* broke many families apart. As with other groups of prisoners, the majority of *coatti* were from the South although the percentage dropped over the decades from 66 percent in 1878 to 54 percent in 1888, 50 percent in 1898, and 44 percent in 1908.[43] Only future research will reveal whether decreasing crime rates or less repressive policing in the South contributed to this downward trend. But the fact remained that the northern provinces were underrepresented in the older group of men who spent long periods of their lives in police exile.

Unlike male penitentiaries, the island camps provided neither education nor job training to *coatti*. While some colonies provided elementary schooling to a small percentage of inmates during the 1870s, this practice, and any pretense of reform, disappeared soon after. Work was scarce, with the percentage of unemployment oscillating over the decades between 16 percent and 62 percent with only a slight improvement after 1906.[44] The more fortunate found jobs as agricultural day laborers or porters and thus learned few new skills. Artisans, such as shoemakers, and even constructions workers found less demand for their crafts. Wages were not guaranteed, even at the low minimum paid by penitentiaries, since *coatti* had to find their own work. Thus the majority subsisted on the meager pittance distributed daily by colony authorities.

Even though men subjected to internal exile roamed the islands during the day, they were nevertheless subjected to punishment for breaking a variety of rules. In fact the most frequent offenses—drunkenness and gambling—were facilitated by their freedom to escape surveillance and mingle with the local community. Other misdemeanors included disobedience to camp officials and absence at the nightly roll call, while the vague charge of "*camorra*," or being involved in a criminal organization, was more serious. Infractions of any type were typically punished by solitary confinement, usually aggravated by a diet of bread and water and/or chains. Only about 10 percent received the lighter penalties, such as a verbal warning. The frequency of punishment increased over the decades from a yearly average of one per prisoner to double that number during the two decades before World War I. Concurrently, release on parole decreased over the same period indicating a tightening of discipline in the island camps. Conditions in the penal colonies improved only in terms of health with fewer *coatti*, according to official statistics, needing hospitalization after the turn of the twentieth century.

A final source for information about everyday life on the island penal colonies comes from political prisoners, who sometimes left memoirs and letters about their experience. While most common criminals remained illiterate or able to write only in dialect before World War I, anarchists and socialists came often from the middle or lower-middle classes and were eager to denounce the state that had arrested them. For example, Ettore Croce, one of the socialists arrested during the turbulent 1890s and by profession a journalist, authored a series of short books about his experience at Tremiti and Lipari. By labeling these islands *Cayenne*, the name of the capital of French Guiana, Croce explicitly compared *domicilio coatto* to transportation.[45] His account graphically describes the inhuman conditions at the camps that included insufficient food, rags for clothes, and hot and insect-infested dormitories. Unlike regular prisons, there was little work so that *coatti* lived in a state of "forced idleness," a play on the term forced labor. Praising the honesty, intelligence, and social commitment of his fellow political prisoners, he bemoaned the fact that they had to live among common criminals and were even chained to them during the night. For Croce, the common criminals were all *camorristi* who were covered in tattoos, talked in criminal jargon, and dedicated to alcohol and masturbation. Jensen, however, has shown how relationships between political and common *coatti* were sometimes more positive; the artisan Amedeo Boschi, for example, was wrongly arrested for subversive activity in 1894, but, after meeting anarchists in the colonies of Tremiti, Lipari, and Pantelleria and absorbing their message, he actually became anarchist.[46] The freedom of *coatti* during the day allowed them to meet for political discussions, conduct courses on foreign languages, and even publish a little newspaper. Boschi's memories remind us of the complexity of inmate experience but constitute an exception to the generally dark picture of internal exile painted even in official documents.

Overall, *domicilo coatto* exemplified the most extreme and in some ways puzzling gap between discourse and practice within the Italian penal system. Even though reformers of all legal schools preached the benefits of work for both the rehabilitation of inmates and the state budget, most *coatti* remained idle (Illustration 7.1). Instead of

Prisons on the Margins: Police Camps and Criminal Insane Asylums   207

I COATTI ASPETTANO LA « MASSETTA »

Illustration 7.1 Group of men exiled to a penal colony

profiting from convict labor or even submitting inmates to bourgeois discipline, the Italian state created an inexplicably chaotic system of internal exile that encouraged all the vices thought by contemporaries to lead to crime—sloth, drinking, and gambling. Several hypotheses may explain this seeming irrationality of national policy. Ironically, the general theory of the born criminal bolstered the fear of wild barbarians living in the midst of civilization despite the condemnation by Lombroso and his colleagues of *domicilio coatto*. Yet parliamentary debates about internal exile employed many of the tropes of criminal anthropology to excuse the practice. Perhaps more importantly, prime ministers from both the right and the left were loath to let go of such a handy mechanism for banishing their enemies—whether political or common criminals—without submitting to the principles of due process. Avoiding the increasing publicity of famous trials and the gaze of journalists, police could secretly transfer troublesome individuals to unpopulated and nearly invisible islands. In the meantime, the admirable Zanardelli Criminal Code remained the public face of a nation striving to be modern on the model of its neighbors in Northern Europe.

Police Exile in Africa

Italy's establishment of a police camp in Africa only underscored the close relationship between its policy of *domicilio coatto* and overseas transportation as practiced by other nations. After acquiring its first colony in Eritrea, in 1890, members of parliament began to draw up proposals for deporting Italian prisoners.[47] Among their rationales was the desire to punish incorrigibility more harshly, to secure cheap labor for economic development, and to assure a supply of settlers upon the completion of inmates' sentences. Opponents argued that transportation would violate prisoners' rights, by compounding their punishment, and contradict Italy's "civilizing mission" in Africa. Plans were also interrupted by the passage of the Zanardelli Code in 1889, which withheld approval for deportation as a legal punishment, and the preparations for the campaign against Ethiopia, where Italians were defeated 1896. Two years later, Prime Minister di Rudinì revived the project but with a twist: rather than regular prisoners, the deportees would come from the island penal colonies. The latter were extremely overcrowded following harsh repression of leftist protests throughout the 1890s, which culminated in a military massacre in Milan in 1898. Citing the "murderous influence" of this "class of the worst sort of delinquent," he transported 196 *coatti* from the port of Naples to the highlands of Assab in Eritrea.[48]

Lasting less than a year, the penal colony in Assab was a complete failure. In his careful reconstruction of its short history, Marco Lenci has identified several factors leading to the demise of this experiment in punishment. First, the inmates themselves "were well conscious of their rights" and began protesting when they passed Sicily and discovered that they were being transported overseas. As the revolts continued after landing in Africa, Director Ferdinando Caputo and his staff of prison guards were unable to keep order. Second, both the *coatti* and the prison guards began to sicken from excessive heat, inadequate diet, and infectious disease. Within six months, almost a third of the prisoners had died or been sent back to Italy for medical treatment. Thirdly, public opposition swelled as legislators and the press, particularly on the Left, denounced the deportation as an extreme punishment aimed at political opponents of an increasingly dictatorial government. As in the case of Tre Fontane, deputies such as Ferri charged that inmates in Assab were effectively being sentenced to capital punishment, which had been abolished in the Zanardelli Code. By the early months of 1899, even Prime Minister Luigi Pelloux, a general who had imposed martial law in Italy, withdrew his support from Assab and the colony was closed. Because of the disastrous nature of this penal experiment, the later fascist regime hesitated and finally refused to establish overseas prisons after its conquest of Ethiopia in 1936.

Instead, the penal entanglement of Italy and Africa took an unexpected turn: the deportation, beginning in 1911, of Libyan prisoners to the Italian metropole. Initiated during the Italian campaign to conquer Libya from the Ottoman Empire, this unusual practice accelerated during World War I and then continued at a slower pace until 1943. Such an anomaly, as Francesca Di Pasquale has written, seemed to overturn the traditional hierarchy of colonizer and colonized by importing, rather than exporting, groups considered undesirable.[49] She argues that this extraordinary reversal of the usual pattern of transportation demonstrated the weakness of the Italian army which, unable to control Libya, shipped local rebels and troublemakers indiscriminately out of their native lands. Initiated by Giolitti and lasting through Mussolini's dictatorship, up to six thousand Libyan "hostages" were admitted to twenty-one—mostly southern Italian—penal facilities. The majority, those who had not yet been tried, were sent to island police camps, such as Favignana, Ustica, and Lipari, while a smaller number of convicted inmates were distributed among regular penitentiaries. Those brought from Libya on Italian ships included women, who were interned in the female penitentiary at Trani, and the mentally ill, who became inmate-patients at the criminal insane asylum at Aversa. The South became the favored destination for Libyan prisoners both because of prejudice, encouraged by positivist racial theories, and of its status as the region of police camps and agricultural colonies. The arrival of African prisoners incited local protest and interracial tension, particularly on the islands where *coatti* were free to roam and mingle with the local population.

In the global context, the Italian history of *domicilio coatto* and reverse transportation are a reminder of the failure of the modern penitentiary to triumph completely over supposedly pre-modern forms of enclosure. Within Western Europe, Italy was unusual for employing internal exile as a punishment in the late nineteenth century, although other versions were practiced simultaneously by Russia in Siberia, Japan in Korea, and some nations in Latin America. Similarly, colonial powers transported indigenous prisoners within their empires, such as the British practice of shipping Indian convicts to the Andaman Islands. As for Italy's policy of importing Libyans to the metropole, historians have as yet to find similar examples. However, the Italian experience demonstrates that outdoor work camps never disappeared in modern Europe and had a dialectical relationship to colonial penal colonies. Despite the triumphal narrative of the birth of the prison and the real building programs that ensued throughout the nineteenth century, older forms of confinement remained intact and subsequently resurged during and after World War I. On a transnational scale, outdoor camps multiplied in the interwar and postwar periods to detain and discipline political, social, and ethnic "enemies of the state" as well as prisoners of war, displaced persons, and migrants. In Italy, hard labor did not die with the abolition of the *bagni* but survived in the police camps that gained new life under the fascist dictatorship and continued to flourish alongside the positivist prison.

Criminal Insane Asylums

On May 8, 1924, Ferri brought a group of students from the University of Rome to visit the criminal insane asylum of Aversa outside of Naples. According to the director of the asylum, Filippo Saporito, Ferri and his students were taken first "to observe the spectacle of a large number of patients of every legal category and of the most varied psychological types—from healthy to mentally ill—involved in work that was useful both to them and to the prison administration."[50] The visitors then toured the entire institution, stopping periodically to discuss specific patients and "their psychopathologies as revealed by their rooms, their clothing, and their manual and intellectual pastimes" as well as to see the "scientific laboratories" for the clinical study of these same patients. At the end of his visit, Ferri signed the required register and noted the great progress of the criminal insane asylum of Aversa toward reconciling "the need for social defense with that for human compassion."[51] The Director proudly attached a copy of these favorable comments to his report to the Ministry of Justice as well as an article from a Neapolitan newspaper on Ferri's visit. According to the newspaper, Ferri lectured during the tour of Aversa on "the concepts and postulates of the positivist school [of criminology]" and declared himself "delighted to see, in the evening of his life, the germination of the seeds of his ideas and the affirmation of his theories and his methods."[52]

As this anecdote makes clear, members of the positivist school were essential proponents of the criminal insane asylum, a penal institution born after the founding of the unified state. As a lawyer, Ferri fought to incorporate the principle of individualization into criminal law so that the psychological state of each criminal would become central to sentencing by the courts. As a doctor, Lombroso rallied his fellow psychiatrists to lobby for the establishment of a new hybrid institution, which would combine incarceration with mental therapy and be managed by doctors rather than prison administrators. A willing ally, Beltrani Scalia used his considerable administrative power within the Ministry of the Interior to begin opening special prisons for the insane in 1876 even without parliamentary approval. Ferri's crusade to rewrite criminal law according to positivist principles was less successful, as exemplified by the Zanardelli Code. Nevertheless, the criminal insane asylum—a symbol of scientific progress during the liberal era—became a longstanding feature of Italy penal system. This section will analyze the birth of the criminal insane asylum in terms of the concept of insanity in Italian criminal law, parliamentary legislation, and conditions of life for inmates.

Criminal Law and the Insanity Plea

Legal debates about the relation of mental illness to criminal responsibility stretched back for centuries but intensified during the revamping of European criminal codes during the revolutionary era. After the defeat of Napoleon in 1815, many of the restoration states in Italy retained some version of Article 64 of the French Penal Code of 1810, which absolved defendants who, at the time of their crime, were insane or compelled by an "irresistible force." This was true of the 1859 Piedmontese code, which held that "no crime exists if the accused was in the condition of absolute imbecility, insanity, or morbid fury when he committed the act or if it is a question of a force which he could not resist."[53] Article 34 of the Tuscan code, however, was more simple and elastic, shielding from indictment anyone who had acted without "consciousness of his acts or freedom of choice."[54] Both of these definitions remained in force until the passage of the Zanardelli Code in 1889.

Thus for thirty years, jurists and psychiatrists argued over the merits of each definition and the appropriate wording for a new national concept of legal responsibility. The classical school accepted the need to exempt the insane from indictment, but believed that judges should retain control of such decisions. Its proponents held criminal behavior to be voluntary and excusable only when reason and free will were compromised and therefore adhered to a circumscribed definition of insanity, typical of the early nineteenth century, as a delirium that interrupted the proper functioning of intelligence. The positivist response emphasized the special expertise of psychiatrists to assess the mental capacity of individual defendants during courtroom proceedings. They therefore proposed a more expansive definition of insanity that could include a variety of conditions arising from either inborn constitutional defects or degenerative disease. Criminal anthropologists, therefore, wanted the article of the new code pertaining to mental capacity to adhere more closely to the Piedmontese wording, with its medical terminology, while the classical school championed instead the Tuscan code with its philosophical language.

In the end, the Zanardelli Code of 1889 hewed more closely to the Tuscan than the Piedmontese code in its definition of the necessary conditions for acquittal under the insanity defense. According to Article 46, a defendant was not "punishable" if "at the moment in which he committed the act, he was in such a state of mental illness that he was deprived of consciousness or freedom of action."[55] Such a formulation retained the Enlightenment notion of free choice, fundamental to the Tuscan code, and excluded the list of specific mental incapacities found in the Piedmontese code. Thus this article, and the Zanardelli Code in general, has been judged by most legal historians as a triumph of the classical over the positivist school. However, Article 46 offered a few openings to proponents of the new psychiatry. By employing the term "punishable" rather than the more common "indictable," the authors of the code avoided a word that, in Italian, has a close association with the philosophical notion of individual responsibility. Furthermore, the term "mental illness" was broad enough to include "any state of mind which, straying from a normal equilibrium, could constitute mental illness whether congenital or acquired, habitual or transitory" according to Antonio Raffaele, a Neapolitan forensic doctor.[56] Thus he and many other positivists interpreted Article 46 as only a partial defeat, because the law left room for an evolution of the definition of "mental illness" in tandem with psychiatric advances.

Notably absent from Article 46 was any mention of "morbid fury" or "irresistible force," conditions expressly listed in the Piedmontese code as a type of insanity. According to the prominent jurist Vincenzo Manzini, by the late nineteenth century, the "irresistible force" of emotions was no longer considered a sign of mental illness and therefore held to be inadequate for excusing criminal behavior.[57] Only violent passions arising from a morbid state, such as epilepsy, could constitute grounds for the denial of legal responsibility. However, the old notion of irresistible force crept back into the code in Article 51, which reduced punishment for anyone who acted "in an outburst of anger or from intense pain caused by an unwarranted provocation."[58] As the noted jurist Pessina explained in his annotations to the code, this rather vague article most often referred to violent male crimes provoked by the seduction or rape of wives and daughters, although it gave wide latitude to judges to consider other provocations as equally worthy of excusing violent reactions.[59] Thus in a contradictory manner, the Zanardelli Code managed to uphold a classically inflected definition of insanity in Article 46 while re-enforcing one of the most traditional aspects of Italian law, the mitigation of punishment for "crimes of honor," in Article 51. Psychiatrists were similarly ambivalent about Article 47 of the Zanardelli Code, which allowed the judge to reduce penalties in the case of diminished mental capacity. This recognition of "partial insanity" appeared an absurdity to many psychiatrists, whose biological model taught that constitutional atavism and degenerative disease affected the entire organism including the mind. Furthermore, their rejection of free will denied the possibility of semi-responsibility on the part of defendants.[60] However, parliament spent little time discussing this article, perhaps because a similar provision had been included in both the Piedmontese and Tuscan codes.[61] For classical jurists, humanitarianism required a middle position or else, in the words of Carrara, judges would find themselves caught "in the terrible crossroads between the gallows and absolution."[62] Again, while criticizing the notion of partial insanity in theory, psychiatrists realized its practical value in expanding their role in the courts.

This role consisted primarily in giving expert testimony (*perizia*) on the mental capacity of defendants as outlined in the Code of Criminal Procedure (CCP) of 1865. Because the CCP regulated the conditions under which psychiatrists were allowed access to the courtroom, Ferri pronounced it more important than the penal code to the positivist goal of recasting punishment as an arm of social defense rather than of retribution.[63] According to the CCP, experts might be called to testify during both the preliminary investigation (*istruttoria*) and the trial (*dibattimento*), but according to different rules. During the preliminary investigation, which was closed to the public, only the judge had the right to nominate and question psychiatric experts. According to Marco Nicola Miletti, positivists were most interested in changing this phase of the judicial procedure because judges were thought to lack the medical expertise to choose specialists who were trained in the latest criminological theories. As an alternative, psychiatrists called for the nomination of experts based on qualifying examinations. During the early decades after unification, most psychiatrists were less interested in appearing in open court during the second part of the trial, because of the sensationalist nature of the exchanges between experts chosen by the prosecution and the defense. By the end of the nineteenth century, however, with increasing journalistic and public interest in courtroom drama, psychiatrists learned to use this public phase of the trial as a mechanism for advertising new advances in psychiatry and its relationship to legal responsibility. Expert testimony in famous trials—often reprinted in newspapers, journals, and books—became, in the words of Renzo Villa, "the true public face" of psychiatry in late nineteenth-century Italy.[64]

Despite their limited authority within the courtroom, psychiatrists honed their skills by publishing a series of guides for the expert witness. The most famous was written by Lombroso, who counseled his readers to

> gather the results of tests on height, weight, and urine, of the examination of general anthropological characteristics, of the skin and cutaneous processes, of the skull, limbs, etc., then the data on sensitivity to weather, to touch, to pain, to drugs, on affectivity and emotionality, on feelings, [and] on the association of ideas ... so that, in the end, based on all these characteristics, you can offer a synthesis that will illuminate the judge.[65]

Other guides were written by lesser-known practitioners of legal medicine such as Raffaele, whose *Practical Guide to Expert Testimony* exhorted his colleagues to include a case history, physical measurements, and a psychological examination based on an interview and handwriting analysis. For both authors, mind and body were so closely linked that physical anomalies became clues to mental instability. Expert testimony based on these positivist assumptions did not always convince judges, as in the famous case of Carlo Grandi, arrested in 1875 for the murder of four children. His trial became an early example of the increasingly frequent courtroom duels between the classical and positivist schools. Led by the young Enrico Morselli, a disciple of Lombroso, the team of expert witnesses for the defense declared Grandi to be a congenital imbecile marked by multiple physical and psychological anomalies and therefore not responsible for his violent behavior. The prosecution, however, won a conviction by arguing that Grandi's skills as a cartwright and his premeditation of the murders (he dug graves in advance) proved his ability to reason and distinguish right from wrong.[66] Despite the failure of positivist strategy, the Grandi case nevertheless brought the new fields of psychiatry and legal medicine to public attention.[67]

Psychiatry and Civil Asylums

While Ferri led the positivist campaign among lawyers to modify the legal codes, Lombroso was more influential in setting the agenda for Italian psychiatrists. Lombroso himself was a specialist in psychiatry and had served as director of the mental hospital in Pesaro before turning to criminology. In the first two editions of *Criminal Man*, he used statistical data that he had previously collected on the insane as a control group for born criminals and concluded that the latter harbored more physical anomalies. For Lombroso, this relative absence of atavism among the insane confirmed his assumption that their disease was transitory and liable to cure.[68] Born criminals, on the other hand, were congenitally atavistic and therefore permanent throwbacks on the evolutionary scale. He thus initially resisted the common prejudice that the mentally ill as a group was dangerous. By the third edition of 1884, however, Lombroso announced that new research on moral insanity had persuaded him that the line between mental illness and criminality was more blurred than he had previously thought.[69] Like atavism, moral insanity was incurable and posed a dire threat to society. He soon added epilepsy to the mix, arguing in the fourth edition that

> the difference among epilepsy, moral insanity, and born criminality is only a matter of degree ... Overall, the three phenomena are similar, and since two things that resemble a third thing are therefore identical to each other, it is clear that congenital criminality and moral insanity are nothing but special forms of epilepsy.[70]

In the same edition, he also identified specific subgroups of insane criminals: the alcoholic criminal, the hysteric criminal, and the *mattoid*, a religious or political megalomaniac. Lombroso's elaboration of the insane criminal was daring in its scope, but at the same time consistent with the generally organicist stance of early Italian psychiatry. This materialist approach was not unusual in nineteenth-century Europe, but was less contested and more long-lived in Italy where scientists had to battle traditional Catholic hegemony over intellectual life. Not yet an autonomous discipline in 1839, when scientists from across the peninsula had begun to hold congresses for the purpose of setting an Italian agenda of research, psychiatry gradually separated itself from general medicine and philosophy. In 1852, Andrea Verga, considered the father of Italian psychiatry, founded *The Psychiatric Appendix*, the first periodical dedicated to mental diseases.[71] Verga and other pioneers in this new field began to meet in 1862 as a special section of the annual scientific congresses until they formed their own independent association, the Italian Society of Phrenology, in 1873. Dedicated to positivism in its general sense, that is, the application of experimental methods, the new Society sought to turn Italian psychiatry into a science.

Within the young field of psychiatry, little dissent existed on the need for a new institution, the criminal insane asylum, for which Lombroso initiated a campaign in 1865 that continued throughout the five editions of *Criminal Man*.[72] For the insane criminal, Lombroso argued that "liberty is dangerous, but prison would be unjust."[73] Because the law gave no guidance in such cases, "judges rule unfairly or imprudently. When madness is obvious, they acquit or reduce the punishment. But just as often they convict, even applying the death sentence."[74] The answer was the criminal insane asylum, which would combine the security of a prison with the therapy of a mental hospital. In answer to critics who worried that criminals would escape punishment by employing the insanity defense, Lombroso denied that he was motivated by "a sentimental pity that might threaten the well-being of others. Criminal insane asylums are more a precautionary than humanitarian measure" since they would have the power to intern insane criminals until cured.[75]

The campaign in favor of criminal insane asylums fit into the wider program of the psychiatric community, which supported internment as the primary response to the problem of mental illness. Like schools, hospitals and prisons, modern asylums were considered a necessary tool to "make Italians," that is, to construct a new Italian citizen through humanitarianism and discipline. Thus the number of public mental hospitals increased from twenty-seven in 1866 to forty-three in 1898 and finally fifty-nine in 1918, with overcrowding always a major problem.[76] Medical directors of civil asylums were often prominent psychiatrists who also held university chairs, and they tirelessly conducted studies of the physical and psychological characteristics of their patients. Yet this same positivist approach, which denied the existence of a mind separate from the body, meant that they spent little time with their patients and were resistant to new clinical techniques developing elsewhere in Northern Europe.[77] Instead, they believed that the best therapy derived from the isolated and moral environment of the asylum, with its hygienic atmosphere, frequent baths, and the discipline of work.

In 1904, a new national law on mental asylums finally standardized rules for the treatment of the mentally ill across the nation. Before that, legal and institutional arrangements differed widely throughout the peninsula, with procedures for admission and conditions within asylums depending on the local regulations and funding.[78] The Law of 1904 continued to leave financial support of civil asylums to the provinces, but dictated that forced admittance could be initiated by relatives, judicial authorities or, in an emergency, by the police. Most notoriously, the law established "dangerousness" and "public scandal" as the major grounds for admission, criteria that have been criticized by many historians as buttressing the popular stereotype of the madman as a social threat.[79] It also gave psychiatrists almost total control of mental hospitals, a step that was cheered as a victory by asylum doctors who bemoaned previous disputes with non-medical administrators over medical programs and funding.

Criminal Insane Asylums: Legislation

Lombroso was joined by other psychiatrists such as Tamburini, Gaspare Virgilio, Serafino Biffi, and Carlo Livi in lobbying the parliament for legislative approval for criminal insane asylums. They argued that such institutions would strengthen the young and fragile nation and bring its social policy into line with England, Ireland, France, Germany, and the United States where special facilities for the criminally insane had already been established. This appeal to the merits of criminal insane asylums for state-building rested on two important but sometimes contradictory principles of criminal anthropology. On the one hand, positivists argued that the internment of dangerous criminals—including the criminally insane—would protect Italy from enemies of the state that included not only brigands and *mafiosi* in the southern provinces, but also atavistic criminals from all regions. Embarrassed and frightened by Italy's high rates of violent crime, legislators should welcome an institution where professional psychiatrists used their expertise to identify born criminals and intern them for life.[80] On the other hand, criminal insane asylums would illustrate Italy's commitment to liberal reform by rescuing insane criminals from penitentiaries and offering them medical treatment. Imbued by a social conscience that led most of them to membership in the Italian Socialist Party, positivist criminologists exhibited a humanitarian impulse toward the criminally insane that often coexisted uneasily with their passion for social control.

Tamburini, an eminent psychiatrist who became the director of the civil asylum in Reggio Emilia in 1877, was Lombroso's prime collaborator in the campaign for the new institution. His description of the ideal criminal insane asylum of the future explicitly recognized its contradictory role as both a defense again social disorder and a progressive hospital for benevolent cure. According to Tamburini, the new institution would have to reconcile both "the discipline of the prison and the security of a fortress with the comfort of a family, offering all possible security against the dangers posed by these patients as well as a most attentive and affectionate treatment of the diseases that make them dangerous."[81] Citing the English asylum of Broadmoor as an example, he recommended a militarized staff of guards to watch over inmates who, during the day, would be divided into small groups according to their degree of dangerousness and, at night, would sleep in separate cells. He promised that inmates would enjoy "fresh air under the open sky with access to meadows, gardens, the vital warmth of the sun, and purity of an air invigorated and perfumed by plants and flowers."[82] Work, schooling, and recreation would complete their therapy with the goal of "restoring disciplined behavior and curbing their impulses, even those arising from disease."[83] To accomplish these multiple and often conflicting goals, Tamburini insisted on the need for new buildings rather than the conversion of older and ill-adapted structures

Even staunch opponents of Lombroso, such as Lucchini and Carrara, were amenable to the establishment of criminal insane asylums for carefully defined groups of defendants. Debate centered on three legal categories of possible inmates for such institutions: convicted criminals who became insane in prison; suspects in jail who became mentally unstable while awaiting trial; and defendants acquitted on the grounds of insanity. Agreement was strongest on the suitability of an alternative to incarceration for the first group, convicted criminals who became insane after sentencing. Positivists and classicists were in accord that mentally ill inmates deserved treatment and therefore transfer to some type of hospital as long as they were released at the end of their sentence. The two criminological schools were in less accord over the second category, inmates of jails who became insane while awaiting trial. According to positivist logic, such individuals should be admitted to criminal insane asylums for observation and, if found to harbor atavism, moral insanity, or epilepsy, be interned until cured. Members of the classical school held all persons awaiting trial to be innocent and therefore not subject to admission to a mental hospital, particularly one that could hold patients indefinitely. Concern over individual rights also shaped attitudes to the third group, defendants acquitted on the grounds of insanity. For classicists, the state had no right to detain anyone, even in a hospital, not charged with a crime, while positivists again argued that their expert opinion alone could separate the born criminals from the innocuous neurotic or imbecile defendant.[84] Lombroso and his followers believed that born criminals, even if acquitted, should be interned for life in the name of social defense.

Because of such differences, the incorporation of the criminal insane asylum in legislation came slowly despite the near unanimity among psychiatrists for its need. At its first congress in 1876, the Italian Society of Phrenology appointed a commission, composed of Lombroso, Virgilio, and Biffi, to study the issue. In 1881, its members were united in their support of a proposed law on treatment of the mentally ill, introduced into parliament by the Minister of the Interior Depretis, which required the establishment of the criminal insane asylum.[85] When legislators failed to act on this initiative, proponents of these institutions—including both psychiatrists and positivist jurists—set their hopes on the new criminal code that had been debated for decades. Yet, they were disappointed. Although the penultimate draft authorized judges to intern defendants in criminal insane asylums, the final text of Article 46 made no specific mention of these institutions. In his commentary on the final wording of this article, the forensic physician Arrigo Tamassia lamented that "academic sentimentalism" among classical jurists had defeated "the only serious concession to the positivist school" in the criminal code, that is, the criminal insane asylum.[86] All was not lost, however, for the subsequent Regulation on Prisons and Reformatories of 1891 outlined the procedures for the forced commitment of all three categories defined by positivists as requiring internment: convicted criminals and suspects who became mentally ill in prison as well as defendants acquitted on the grounds of insanity.[87] Such wide jurisdiction was subsequently cut back in 1904, however, when the law on mental hospitals directed that only convicted criminals and the most dangerous defendants awaiting trial be interned in criminal insane asylums.[88]

Only a few historians have begun to reconstruct the birth of the criminal insane asylum in Italy, and they doubt the humanitarian motives of Tamburrini and his colleagues. According to Villa, the call for this new institution "did not reflect a real social necessity in terms of public order or health, or in terms of a hypothetical imperative of social defense."[89] Instead, criminal insane asylums were championed by positivist psychiatrists because of their mania for classification and their determination to extend the power of their new profession into the judicial system. Valeria Babini agrees, although she puts more emphasis on the theoretical conundrum in late nineteenth-century Italian psychiatry of reconciling the new notion of congenital mental conditions—most notably moral insanity—with the more traditional understanding of mental illness as temporary and treatable. Thus, the creation of the criminal insane asylum offered an institutional solution that disguised continuing theoretical confusion.[90] An additional factor, it could be argued, was the everyday experience of many Italian psychiatrists as asylum doctors. Whatever the shortcomings of the criminal insane asylums, they promised to relieve the regular mental hospitals of unruly convicts who had been transferred from prison. As almost 80 percent of convicts in criminal insane asylums had committed violent crimes, psychiatrists were not necessarily exaggerating the problems of mixing them with other categories of the mentally ill.[91] Furthermore, archival records show that civil asylums had trouble collecting payment for criminals forcibly admitted by prison wardens.[92] After years of wrangling, the Council of State finally ruled in 1907 that the central state should pay for the initial period of observation in civil asylums, after which the province would pick up the cost for extended treatment, but the central prison administration continued to object.[93] Consequently, directors of civil asylums—which were overcrowded, underfunded, and dependent on the provincial governments—had strong motives for supporting the establishment of a companion institution that, because of its classification as a prison, would be paid for by the national state. Thus criminal insane asylums came to be seen as necessary on both theoretical as well as practical grounds.

Criminal Insane Asylums: Practical Conditions

Despite the delays in legislative authorization, criminal insane asylums were nevertheless established under the aegis of Beltrani Scalia, who used the *RDC* as a promotional tool. He was able to take advantage of his power over a highly centralized administration to establish three criminal insane asylums in the last quarter of the nineteenth century: at Aversa, where a special "section for lunatics" (*sezione per maniaci*) was opened in 1876; Montelupo Fiorentino in 1886; and Reggio Emilia in 1897.[94] The priority of security over medical treatment is clear in their subordination to Beltrani Scalia rather than to the Director General of Health. Even after the Law of 1904 substituted psychiatrists for prison officials as directors, prison guards were not replaced by nurses. Although punishment, according to official statistics, was less frequent than in regular penitentiaries, inmates were nevertheless restrained by means of bedstraps, straitjackets, and isolation cells.[95]

The number of inmates in the three asylums grew dramatically from 118 in 1881 to 735 in 1901, after which totals remained in the range of 650–750 until World War I. According to the prison administration, the institutions were rarely full, housing slightly fewer patients than their official capacity in most years.[96] Crowded sleeping quarters were most typical of Aversa, an old monastery outside Naples, which was ill-adapted for the individualization of treatment. Until a scandal and subsequent investigation forced the state to renovate and enlarge Aversa in 1906, each dormitory held about thirty inmates, a number that dropped to nine by 1909. In contrast, Montelupo Fiorentino placed an average of only six inmates in each dormitory, with more than 100 provided with a private sleeping cell. Housed in a large and handsome

Illustration 7.2 A postcard of the criminal insane asylum at Montelupo Fiorentino

villa, inmates at Montelupo Fiorentino spent their days together in workshops, dining halls, and gardens[97] (Illustration 7.2). Reggio Emilia could not boast individual cells, which were the ideal of psychiatrists, but succeeded in limiting each sleeping room to three inmates. Each of these early institutions also had isolation cells for prisoners undergoing punishment or, more often, defendants awaiting trial who in theory were not to be mixed with convicted criminals.[98]

A social profile of the inmates in criminal insane asylums reveals that they were all men, a bit older than male prisoners in general, and mostly poor. The absence of any sections for women, who were relegated to penitentiaries administered by nuns, is indicative of a general disinterest by the prison administration in female inmates. The male population of the criminal insane asylums clustered between twenty and forty years of age, with the larger group over thirty; very few were minors but significant numbers were over fifty. This age structure may have reflected the long sentences of most inmates. Over two-thirds were single and, even after the turn of the twentieth century, 40 percent were illiterate. In terms of class, the largest category, between 31 and 55 percent, were from rural areas and had labored in agriculture or mining before admittance.[99] A smaller but growing number worked in Italy's burgeoning cities, although rarely in factory jobs because of the slow pace of industrialization. Thus most male urban workers were artisans, shopkeepers, construction workers, and servants. The number of middle-class inmates (including clerks) dropped from 11 percent to 4 percent of the total between 1894 and 1907, perhaps because the 1904 law forbade the internment of defendants acquitted by reason of insanity. Wealthy enough to hire good lawyers and private psychiatrists as expert witnesses, middle-class defendants were most likely to be acquitted and sent to civil asylums, whether public or private. Thus, the population of the criminal insane asylum, which was not particularly young but nevertheless impoverished, badly educated, and unmarried, represented a marginal sector of the working classes.

Inmates of the criminal insane asylums were somewhat isolated, in poor health, and serving long sentences. In 1911, only a quarter of them received a visitor, a number that was even lower in the previous years.[100] They wrote and received, on the average, five letters per year in 1904 though that number increased to eight by 1913.[101] Most inmates received money from the outside, probably to buy extra food, and an average of 18 percent sent small sums to their families saved from their modest wages.[102] On the average, each inmate was admitted to the infirmary once or twice per year while yearly rates of death were high, dropping slowly from 8 percent in 1901 to 4 percent in 1914[103] (Graph 7.2). By both measures, the criminal insane asylums were less healthy than regular prisons. Statistics show that very few inmates earned early release, either through pardons or parole even though 80 percent had been sentenced to at least ten years of punishment.[104] If pronounced cured of mental illness, convicts were returned to regular penitentiaries to serve out the balance of their sentences; indicted prisoners sent to jails to await trial; and acquitted defendants usually transferred to a civil asylum. It was not easy to escape institutionalization.

Although work—or ergotherapy, in medical terminology—was the central pillar of treatment in all Italian mental hospitals, statistics for the period preceding World War I show low rates of employment in the criminal insane asylums. On June 30, 1895, only 14 percent of all inmates were working, a rate that increased to 16 percent in 1904 and finally 23 percent in 1907.[105] Unlike inmates in regular penitentiaries who were often employed by private contractors, those in criminal insane asylums worked almost exclusively for the state as bricklayers, carpenters, shoemakers, textile workers, or servants. Idleness was not relieved by education, despite the ideal model proposed by Tamburini. As official statistics show no evidence of the type of schools and libraries found in other prisons, inmates seem to have received little academic or professional training for life after release.

Despite the generally dismal life of a typical inmate, conditions were not static and each asylum had its own particular history. For example, a scandal at Aversa in 1905–6 provoked significant improvements. The oldest and most crowded of the three institutions, Aversa had previously served as a poorhouse and prison. In 1905, after denunciations from inmates about abuse from the staff and spoiled food, the public prosecutor of Naples opened an investigation of conditions in Aversa. In his defense, Director Virgilio, a prominent pioneer of Italian psychiatry, pointed out that he had taken control of the institution only eight months before, in line with the Law of 1904 requiring medical administrators. He blamed his predecessor for the physical condition of the building, which was "little suitable and in fact dangerous" for inmates and therefore not surprisingly "a theater for deplorable and unfortunate incidents."[106] He had done his best to make improvements, but it was impossible as long as "the rooms for the patients resemble less a hospital than a cauldron of physical and moral putrefaction" and the personnel was composed of "*guardamatti criminali*," that is, convicts from a nearby prison. An Oversight Commission sent from Rome confirmed that Aversa "resembled in no way a [civil] insane asylum either in its physical structure or in its technical organization."[107] Its architecture did not allow for the separation

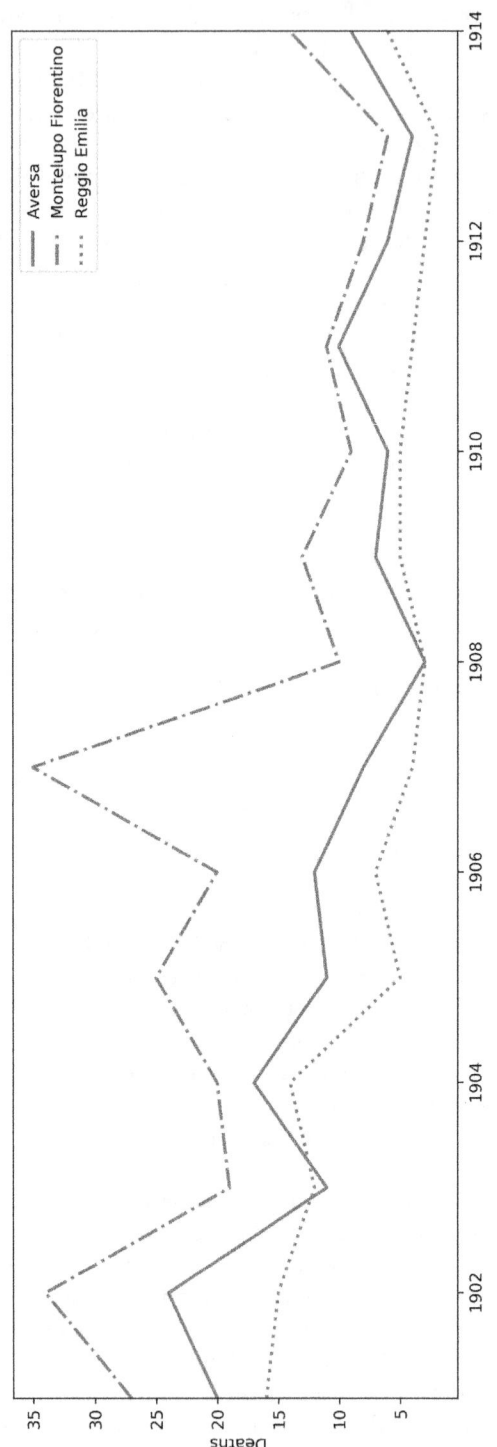

Graph 7.2 Annual deaths in criminal insane asylums, 1900–14. Source: Stat. Carc.

of different categories of patients or for common spaces and dining areas; it did not provide therapy through work and baths, nor laboratories for clinical research. Because convicts were used as guards, "methods of coercion have been too widely adopted."[108] The commission recommended the abandonment of Aversa in favor of building a new criminal insane asylum elsewhere in Italy.

Aversa was not abandoned, but Virgilio was hastened into an honorable retirement in 1906 and replaced by his assistant Saporito, who remained the director at the time of Ferri's visit in 1924. Young, energetic, and idealistic, Saporito radically renovated Aversa. His dream was to turn criminal insane asylums from "bad prisons" to "general hospitals of criminality" with laboratories for scientific research.[109] Within three years, another oversight commission, led by Tamburini, pronounced a "real satisfaction with a transformation that embodies the good, the useful, and the rational."[110] Inmates were now separated into nine different categories (those in observation, those who were dangerous, those who were calm, etc.); hygiene was improved (gas lighting, hydraulic toilets, new bathtubs and showers); and a hospital diet replaced prison food. Other changes were not as complete. Only one-third of all inmates were employed in new workshops. Physical restraints were used less often, although the straitjacket had not been abolished. The convict *guardamatti* had been replaced by prison guards who, while receiving special training for their role, were clearly not professional nurses. Even though Tamburini pointed to the need for additional improvements, he concluded that "this institution will really bring honor to Italy and debunk the common view, also expressed in foreign newspapers, that the Italian judicial insane asylums are built and organized like prisons and therefore represent the negation of science and humanity."[111] Tamburini's pride in the renovation of Aversa led him in 1912 to feature drawings of its floorplans, pictures of its garden, and photos of its inmates it in the psychiatric section of the International Exposition of Social Hygiene, of which he was chair.[112]

Postscript

Scholarly evaluation of Italy's experiment with criminal insane asylums is overwhelmingly negative and holds that their main purpose was to expand the power of psychiatrists rather than to treat mental health. In many ways, this is an accurate analysis of an institution whose priority was social control over a group of poor and uneducated men who had been admitted under dubious diagnoses. Isolated for long periods from their families and the outside world, inmates were offered little therapy aside from work and baths. Suspects could be held for long periods of observation and, until the Law of 1904, those acquitted on the insanity defense could be interned indefinitely. The use of physical restraint was widespread while education was absent.

However, such a wholesale condemnation of the early criminal insane asylum is simplistic and perhaps colored by their degradation during the fascist and postwar periods. The example of Aversa illustrates that their history was not static but subject to change at the instigation of government inspectors or new administrators. Leading psychiatrists such as Lombroso, Virgilio, Tamburini, and Saporito were honest enough to denounce conditions at Aversa before 1906 and to call for its closure. The appointment of Saporito as director significantly improved the material life of inmates in Aversa, who began to enjoy increased physical comfort and freedom of movement within the institution. While therapy in all three institutions was minimal and ill-conceived, it nevertheless resembled the treatment employed in civil asylums. The prominent psychiatrists who served as resident doctors and directors were well-trained and eager to turn their institutions into symbols of modernity through empirical investigation of the physical and psychological characteristics of the inmates, the results of which they proudly disseminated in professional journals. While the resulting data are of little scientific value today, they are typical of the research carried out in hospitals and prisons throughout the country in this period in order to further the national project of turning psychiatry and criminology into sciences. In short, a more nuanced portrait of the criminal insane asylum, while not meant to excuse their repressive nature or to obscure the absurdities of positivist theory, shows the need for further study of the evolution of each institution, particularly to evaluate whether they fared better after 1904 when put under the direction of medical professionals.

The existence of parliamentary government after unification, with its attendant freedom of speech, was an important factor in limiting the reach, and therefore the repressiveness, of the criminal insane asylum. Despite its many faults, such as the failure to approve a national criminal code until 1889, parliament had the merit of allowing for lively debate between opposing factions. Thus members of the classical school, many of whom were members of parliament, were able to curb Beltrani Scalia's power in 1904 by limiting admission to the criminal insane asylums to indicted and convicted criminals. Criminals acquitted for insanity could be interned only in civil asylums and at the discretion of the courts rather than of psychiatrists. Clearly classical jurists were defending their power over the courtroom, but at the same time their writings enshrined a firm belief in individual rights that had its roots in the Enlightenment and inspired the Risorgimento revolt against autocracy and foreign rule.

With the advent of fascism, positivism lost its humanitarian edge and parliament its power. At first glance, the Rocco Criminal Code of 1930 seems little different from the previous Zanardelli Code in its treatment of the insanity. According to Article 88, defendants were released from responsibility for their crimes if mental illness deprived them of "the capacity to understand or will."[113] However, while the wording of this article seemed to indicate a triumph for the classical school, it was counterbalanced by a new section on "security measures" applicable to individuals thought to be a threat to social order, even if they had not been convicted of a crime. In the positivist spirit of social defense, judges were given the power to declare defendants, acquitted on the grounds of insanity, to be "socially dangerous" and interned in criminal insane asylums.[114] Listed under the new rubric of "security measures," this provision was technically not a punishment but instead an "administrative" regulation and thus did not theoretically contradict the definition of legal responsibility. Nevertheless, the fascist introduction of security measures represented a reversion to the situation before 1904, when Beltrani Scalia had opened the criminal insane asylums without parliamentary approval and admitted defendants acquitted as insane. In the Rocco Code, these individuals were to be interned in criminal insane asylums for two to ten years despite the objections of many jurists that judges have no grounds for determining the length of incarceration when there has been no crime.[115]

As a corollary to its doctrine of social defense, the fascist dictatorship increased the number of criminal insane asylums, opening three more in Naples (1922), Barcellona Pozzo di Gotto (Messina, 1925), and a third at Castiglione delle Stiviere (Mantua, 1939). In 1931, the first criminal section for women was established at Aversa as fascism stretched a web of internment over an ever larger portion of the population.[116] This doubling of the number of criminal insane asylums paralleled a marked expansion in the number of the mentally ill interned in civil asylums, which jumped from 60,000 in 1926 to 96,000 in 1941.[117] Although Italy closed itself off from international developments in psychotherapy and psychoanalysis during the interwar period, it continued experiments in the biological tradition. New therapies included the use of drugs and most notably electric shock, which was invented by Ugo Cerletti in 1938, bringing him applause from the fascist regime and international fame. As yet, historians have not explored whether these new technologies were introduced into criminal insane asylums. Undoubtedly work remained a central goal of fascist administrators who were urged to turn the carceral institutions into tools for "human reclamation."[118]

Despite the fall of fascism, the postwar period saw the retention of the Rocco Code, with its provision for imposing security measures after acquittal on the insanity plea, and the criminal insane asylums, with an additional institution for women opening in Pozzuoli (near Naples) in 1955. By the 1970s, with the expanding political movement for deinstitutionalization, the criminal insane asylums also came under scrutiny. According to critics, these institutions were characterized by physical abuse, unhygienic conditions, a shortage of doctors, and the absence of therapy. Only Castiglione delle Stiviere was staffed by nurses rather than prison guards, but even here, according to one journalist, the patients endured "a violent and bestial life."[119]

This same journalist noted that a large portrait of Lombroso hung in the director's office at Montelupo Fiorentino.[120] While it is not uncommon to honor founders of an institution, this image of Lombroso also symbolizes the long historical shadow that late nineteenth-century positivist criminology threw on the development of forensic psychiatry in Italy. Many Lombrosian tenets—the biological basis of mental illness, the dangerousness of the insane criminal, and the necessity of criminal insane asylums to protect social order—have had a long life, enduring the change in types of government from liberal to fascist to republican. Criminal insane asylums even outlived the famous and radical "Basaglia law" of 1978, which ordered the closure of all civil mental institutions in Italy.[121] Relabeled "judicial psychiatric hospitals," (*Ospedali psichiatrici giudiziari* or OPG), they continued to decline and were officially shut only in 2015. Aversa, Montelupo Fiorentino, and Reggion Emilia, which were among the last six OPGs, now stand as empty monuments to a failed penal experiment.

Conclusion

In several ways, police camps and criminal insane asylums lay at the margins of the Italian prison system. Both interned a mixed group of individuals, many of whom had never been convicted by the courts. They occupied the opposite ends of a penal spectrum that uneasily combined discipline and reform. Entirely repressive, the colonies of *domicilio coatto* made no pretense of rehabilitation or even humane treatment. In that sense, they carried on the worst characteristics of old-regime justice: pure retribution and the failure to provide for the most basic bodily needs. At the other end of the scale, criminal insane asylums claimed to be hospitals where the most advanced therapies would restore physical and mental health to patient-inmates. The former remained untouched by any principles of the positivist age, even in its most expansive definition, while the latter had been conceived and subsequently managed by psychiatrists wedded to Lombrosian criminal anthropology. Yet the liminal position of police camps and criminal insane asylums did not detract from their centrality to the lives of thousands of mostly lower-class men who endured their strictures between unification and World War I. Like jails for suspects awaiting trial and reformatories for paternal correction, both institutions widened the web of punishment over large sections of the population that had not been afforded due process in the courts. This penal network would grow exponentially during the interwar fascist dictatorship.

8

Laboratories of Criminal Anthropology

In 1878, Dr. Andronico published a study of the 122 inmates in the women's penitentiary in Messina. Inspired by Lombroso, the prison physician viewed his institution as a "clinic of crime" where "every delinquent constitutes a new book in the modern anthropology of disease."[1] While he admitted that his study was small, he was eager "to increase further the number of practical facts" that facilitated modern anthropological and psychiatric research.[2] The largest categories of crime for which the prisoners at Messina had been sentenced were homicide, theft, assault, and infanticide. For his report, he recorded the anthropometric measurements of each inmate, including the circumference of their heads, the height of their foreheads, and the angle of their faces. In addition, he noted their physical anomalies, such as asymmetrical facial features or protruding ears, as well as their dispositions, which he characterized as nervous, imbecilic, melancholy, hysterical, or even epileptic. Of the 122 women, he concluded that fourteen "represent a damaged and degenerate type" that was close "to animals."[3] While he sympathized with their poverty and lack of education, he pronounced these fourteen inmates to be insane and, therefore, human evidence of the close relationship between criminality and madness. Citing the psychiatrist Virgilio as an inspiration, Andronico endorsed criminal insane asylums as a sign of social progress and the appropriate institutions to treat such inmates.

Andronico's report encapsulates the close relationship between the birth of criminal anthropology and prison reform in post-unification Italy. Writing only two years after the publication of *Criminal Man*, he exemplified the many prison physicians who were already eagerly utilizing anthropometric machines and psychological interviews to produce scientific data as a basis for policy proposals. This concluding chapter will pull together the strands of positivist theory and practice that pervaded Italy's prison system. Both Beltrani Scalia and Doria encouraged prison administrators, such as Andronico, to carry out biological and psychological research on their patients, and the *RDC* published the results. They also facilitated visits by positivist criminologists and lawyers to the nation's penal institutions and provided them with a mouthpiece for their theories in the *RDC*. To participate in the new national program of "scientific policing," established by Lombroso's student, Salvatore Ottolenghi, prisons installed equipment for criminal identification through anthropometry, forensic photography, and fingerprinting. Ottolenghi also chose Regina Coeli, the jewel in the crown of Italian prisons, as a classroom for both police officers and prison guards. Using inmates as living human material, he taught successive courses every year in classifying criminals based on biological and psychological measurements. Prisons also became sites for collecting "totems" of deviancy, which ranged from body parts to cultural products of inmates, which were transferred to new criminological museums throughout the peninsula.

The purpose of this concluding chapter is to document the close, but not exclusive role, of criminal anthropology in the founding of the modern Italian penitentiary. As the preceding chapters have demonstrated, several overlapping periods of prison reform shaped the peninsula's penal system as it took shape between unification and World War I. The earliest use of enclosure as a form of punishment, dating to the early eighteenth century, was formulated solely for women and children. Based on the Catholic preference for penitence over corporal mutilation, the premodern convent prison promoted moral reform through religion and work. This model continued to shape institutions for women and girls throughout the liberal period, during which nuns meted out female punishment with little government oversight. For men, the movement to replace corporal punishment with incarceration began in the late eighteenth and early nineteenth centuries. Dubbed by Foucault the "birth of the prison," the construction of widespread networks of new penal institutions in Northern Europe and the United States was inspired primarily by Enlightenment values of secular humanitarianism as well as an impulse to normalize and discipline the national citizenry. After Italian unification, this earlier period of reform, which had already significantly influenced the old regime states of Tuscany and Lombardy, manifested itself in the legislative requirement, mostly unfulfilled, that jails adopt a cellular structure. The Ordinance of 1891 also incorporated priorities of this first wave of modern penal reform, such as humane physical conditions in terms of ventilation, light, sanitation, and medical care for inmates and the provision of primary education and professional training. Such measures were implemented most widely in men's penitentiaries and public reformatories for boys.

Overlaying and intermingling with these earlier stages of prison reform were the new positivist initiatives of the late nineteenth century, which shaped the organization and daily regimes of different types of Italian penal institutions to varying degrees. What was common to all, however, was their role in generating new science that purported to identify the essential physical and psychological character of the criminal. In Foucauldian terms, prisons not only subjected inmates to "power" but also extracted "knowledge" from their bodies. In Italy, this dialectic between power and knowledge was essential to the construction of criminal anthropology and, more specifically, the notion of the born criminal. As Neppi Modona has brilliantly pointed out, the prison functioned as a "special theater" for Lombroso and his positivist colleagues, whose research would have been impossible without access to the captive bodies of inmates.[4] The resulting "knowledge" about the true nature of the criminal—which was disseminated to popular audiences through books, magazines, newspapers, and even novels—was reliant on a series of interactions between the Italian penal administration and the burgeoning field of criminal anthropology.

Knowledge

The most obvious point of contact between positivism and prisons was Lombroso himself, who served as the doctor in the large and important cellular jail of Turin. Beginning in 1885, Lombroso had full access to one of the largest penal institutions in Italy as a laboratory for his research. As Gina Lombroso reported in her biography of her father, he went "every morning to *his prison*, even when he was sick, tired, or even melancholy, because *his prison* always had the power to restore excitement and joy to his life."[5] His double role as a professor and a practitioner was not unusual in a period when many criminologists held posts as resident directors or physicians of prisons or insane asylums. Admired by Beltrani Scalia and Doria, both of whom proclaimed themselves disciples of scientific facts, Lombroso was a frequent contributor to the *RDC*, which published installments *Criminal Man*.[6] While he disagreed with some of Lombroso's specific policy recommendations, Beltrani Scalia seconded the "unanimous and well-merited praise" received by the book.[7] The *RDC* also published a series of "criminology clinics" in which Lombroso, sometimes in collaboration with colleagues, analyzed specific prisoners in biological and psychological terms. His subjects included the authors of famous crimes, such as Vincenzo Verzeni, Achille Agnoletti, and Giovanni Cavaglià as well as anonymous delinquents, such as "G.E.," whom Lombroso and his student Camillo Golgi, a future Nobel recipient, diagnosed as a case of "criminal mania."[8] This close relationship served the interests of both Lombroso, who retained daily access to human research material, and of the prison administration, which strengthened its reputation for modern policy through association with the newest sciences.

Criminal anthropology was a group effort, and the *RDC* went beyond Lombroso in publicizing new advances in the field. It hosted, for example, a series of comparative articles on degenerative characteristics in criminals and the mentally insane by Giuseppe Sergi, a founder of the Institute of Anthropology at the University of Rome.[9] In its pages, positivists, such as Ferri and Garofalo, reviewed each other's works in an arrangement that was clearly meant to result in positive evaluations.[10] Accounts of foreign research were also included, such as that of the Russian scholar Pauline Tarnowsky, the only woman besides Gina Lombroso to be invited into the inner circle of Italian criminal anthropology.[11] Psychiatrists who joined Lombroso in the campaign to establish criminal insane asylums, such as Tamburini and Virgilio, were also frequent contributors to the *RDC*.[12] Citing the "really productive relationship between Lombroso's work and our subject," that is prison science, the *RDC* urged its readers to attend the International congresses of criminal anthropology.[13]

Prison administrators did not simply constitute a passive readership for criminal anthropological articles but they themselves took part in constructing the new discipline. Repeating the truism that penitentiaries were "clinics of crime," Leopoldo Rosi, the prison doctor at San Gimignano, praised their potential to yield "a rich harvest of facts" relevant to anthropology, physiology, medicine, and public health.[14] Tamburini was also enthusiastic about the "invaluable and voluminous material," that is inmates, that could be found in penal institutions.[15] Proclaiming criminal anthropology to be a group endeavor that required large amounts of data to reach valid conclusions, several local prison officials sought to standardize their results. In 1885, Benelli, Director of the House of Custody in Reggio Emilia, proposed a form to be used by all prison doctors in their research on inmates. Noting that Lombroso and his colleagues had studied 3,839 criminals, he sought to raise the total number "to 10,000, 20,000, 100,000" using uniform criteria.[16] Examination of prisoners would involve psychology, physiology, anthropometry, craniometry, and anomalies. While Benelli's idea was not immediately adopted, it prefigured the "biographical-anthropological dossiers" that were later developed by Ottolenghi for use by police and prison officials. In the meantime, both Beltrani Scalia and Doria called for more positivist research in Italy's penal network.[17]

Many administrators met their challenge with enthusiastic projects to prove their scientific credentials. One of the most prominent was Antonio Marro, Lombroso's predecessor as the physician at the Turin jail, whose book, entitled *The Characteristics of Criminals: An Anthropological-Sociological Study*, won an award from the *RDC*.[18] Published by Bocca, an editorial house that specialized in criminal anthropology, Marro's book received a glowing review from Virgilio as "a patient, conscientious and intelligent collection of the smallest facts that the author learned from his long contact with prisoners."[19] Over the years, the *RDC* hosted the results of a series of medical studies conducted in the jails at Bologna and Alessandria, the penitentiary at Santo Stefano, and elsewhere.[20] While the majority focused on men, physicians also had access to female institutions, where they both treated and conducted research on inmates. For example, Giovenale Salsotto, the doctor of the women's penitentiary in Turin, subjected female prisoners to elaborate anthropometrical and biological tests as well as questionnaires about their family heredity for the purpose of identifying differences among categories of criminals.[21] Like Lombroso, he produced detailed tables that were short on analysis but succeeded in adding to the stockpile of minute measurements so prized by criminal anthropologists. Such accretion of the facts was expected to bring criminal anthropology ever closer to a more accurate—and predictive—definition of the born criminal.

Inmates provided research material for not only internal personnel but also specialists from outside the prison. In general, it was extremely difficult for anyone except members of parliament, the judiciary, and the police to gain access to Italian penal institutions. Only a few semiprivate groups—such as the visiting and oversight committees as well as the prisoner aid societies—were authorized to enter these closed institutions. Even relatives were barred by law from frequent conversations with inmates and had no privacy when doing so. However, the Ordinance of 1891 named one exception to the strict ban on outside visitors and that was "for reasons of study."[22] Lest the intent be misunderstood, a later circular from Doria clarified that "special permission" would be granted exclusively to university professors or well-known scholars of "penal law, anthropology, legal medicine, and pedagogy."[23] This broad definition of course included classical jurists such as Lucchini, who shepherded a group of students to the Volterra penitentiary in 1881. While not completely rejecting the future possibilities of criminal anthropology, they sensibly reported to have observed among the inmates "physiognomies that appeared idiotic or very smart, facial features that were sympathetic or repulsive, similar in sum to what you can see anywhere."[24] But more celebrated and frequent were the visits of positivist criminologists, who collaborated with students on research or conducted classes on the human material in the prison network. Ferri's visits, frequently reported in the press, resulted in different findings from those of Lucchini. After touring several penal institutions in Emilia, for example, he criticized legislators who, "from a desire for metaphysical symmetry and uniformity, refuse to adapt criminal law to those organic and indelible differences that nature has established among the various categories of the criminal world."[25] Ferri became so well known that several inmates asked permission to consult with him, requests sometimes granted by Doria.[26]

As letters to the central administration demonstrate, permission for research was routinely granted for medical or anthropological studies but rarely for sociology, which was suspected to have journalistic and muckraking intent. In some cases, such as that of a student of psychiatry and criminal anthropology who petitioned to conduct research in 1893 at the penitentiary on the island of Procida, the director general specified that inmate participation be voluntary.[27] This was also a condition for Dr. Lorenzo Giunti, who wanted to test mineral water, from his nearby thermal springs, on inmates in the jail of Cagliari.[28] Of course prisoners, whose rewards in the Irish system depended on good behavior, may not have felt themselves free to refuse. Results of criminal anthropological studies, by both doctors and lawyers, were sometimes presented on standardized forms, demonstrating the passion for "facts," whose import was thought to be self-evident.[29] Such reports became fodder for Lombroso, who amalgamated studies of individual criminals from all over Italy as the basis for sweeping generalizations about the typical signs of deviancy.[30]

To carry out their studies, internal and external scholars needed specialized anthropometric instruments, which became a field of lively rivalry among inventors. As David Horn has written, the process of measuring criminals revealed "how the body was imagined and mapped through tools."[31] While quantification involved the whole body, the focus remained the head, whose size and features were purported to reveal psychological and mental health. Skulls, which were easily measured, filled the laboratories of Lombroso, Sergi, and other positivist criminologists but were only helpful for counting anomalies after death. Researchers eagerly sought after cadavers, which were legally available for research if inmates died while in prison. But most useful for assessing the "dangerousness" of living offenders were anthropometric measurements taken by police and, increasingly, prison doctors. Certain calculations were required by the Ordinance of 1891 for admission registers; after 1905, the new Central Identification Office asked for even more data. Eager to standardize the process, Doria issued a circular inquiring whether prison directors had the necessary "anthropometric instruments" to measure "the length and width of the head, the length of the forearm and of the middle finger, etc."[32] (Illustration 8.1).

Minors, including those interned by parents and therefore not convicted of any crime, were a particular target of study by the prison administration for the purpose of classification and predicting future delinquency. For each child, reformatory doctors had to note four head measurements, degenerate characteristics such as facial asymmetry and protruding jaws, and tattoos.[33] Such requirements provoked requests

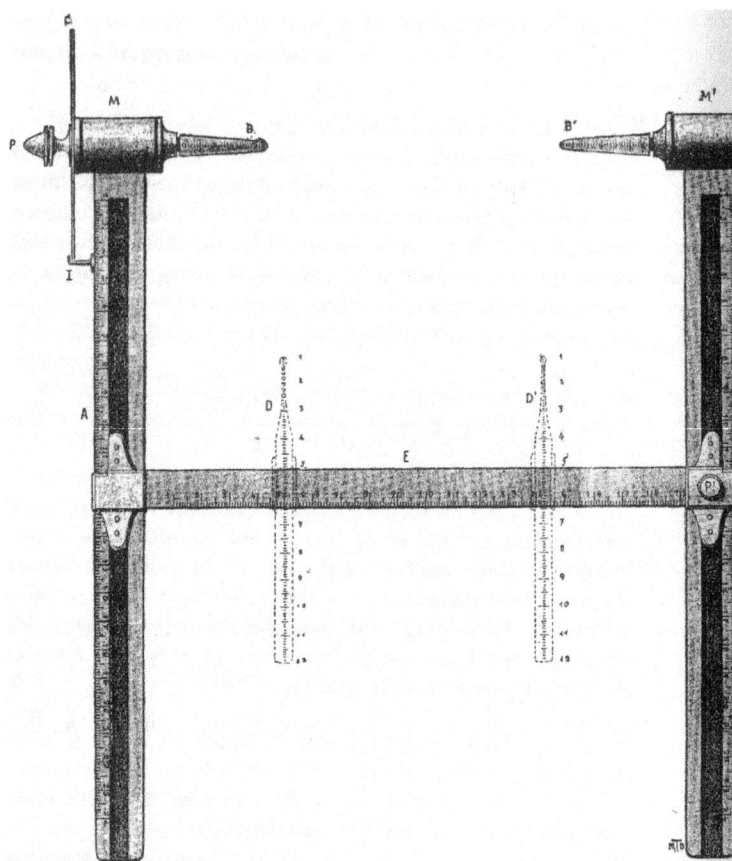

Illustration 8.1 A cephalometer, an instrument for measuring the head

from the director of San Michele and other institutions, for the necessary equipment.[34] Such procedures were approved in 1912 by the second Congress of prison-aid societies, which listed the "anthropological exam" as an important means of preventing crime among youth.[35]

The *RDC* welcomed articles by inventors of new anthropometric instruments, which promised to be useful in categorizing inmates. Cosimo Binda, for example, promoted the merits of his new cephalometer, a tool for measuring the diameter, curves, and angles of either a skull or living head.[36] Boasting that it was easier to use than earlier versions, Binda, a specialist in legal medicine, offered a detailed description of its various functions accompanied by a drawing of the device. Other authors described how they used certain apparatus and interpreted the results. The psychiatrist Gaetano Perusini presented readers of the *RDC* with a detailed article, accompanied by drawings, about the best "chewing" machines to calculate the size of the jaws and the teeth. Comparing criminals with ancient and modern "racial" groups, he found the former to rank lower than natives of Hawaii but higher than African

Zulus on this important measure. His results demonstrated a variety of anomalies in offenders, some of which signaled "a clear *atavistic reversion*" to the level of "apes and the lowest human races on the anthropological scale."[37]

Researchers sometimes asked to photograph the physical features of inmates, but the central administration was less enthusiastic about these requests than those for anthropometric studies. In 1908, for example, the penitentiary doctor in Civitavecchia requested permission from Rome to photograph "some anomalies of the skeletal and organic structure that are frequent among the prisoners who form the object of his study."[38] The reply from Rome was equivocal, approving the procedure only if the identity of the inmates could be protected. A similar request from the Director of the Perugian women's penitentiary was rejected "for obvious considerations of order and prison discipline," indicating an ambivalence about the propriety of making images of the female body.[39] For police purposes, however, prison directors themselves began to use photography as early as 1882 to identify recidivists. New government regulations ordered that over ten categories of inmates be photographed three times: upon admission to jail; after conviction; and upon release. The categories ranged from suspects indicted for serious crimes such as homicide or counterfeiting to those who had simply violated judicial warnings.[40] A subsequent circular added the categories of convicts sentenced to capital punishment or hard labor to those required to be photographed.[41] While both of these circulars left prison officials the freedom to choose the position of the photographic subject, a directive of 1898 finally sought to make the procedure uniform. In correlation with international standards, Beltrani Scalia insisted that convicts faces be photographed from the front and right profiles.[42] In 1910, Doria ordered prison directors to add fingerprints to prisoners' photographs and promised to send the necessary new equipment for this modernization of identification techniques.[43]

Ottolenghi, a student of Lombroso and professor of legal medicine at the University of Rome, provided the main impetus for introducing photography and fingerprinting into the prison system. Founder of the Advanced School of Scientific Policing, Ottolenghi oversaw the specialized training for the administrators of the urban Public Security force. Besides crusading to extend new methods of identification from the police to the prisons, he had other close ties with Doria. First, his police school was located in Regina Coeli so that prisoners could be brought from their cells to illustrate lessons in criminal anthropology. According to Giovanni Gasti, one of the instructors, these "live demonstrations and exercises" had the enthusiastic approval of Doria, who had offered space for not only a classroom but also the necessary anthropometric and photographic instruments.[44] Second, the *RDC* published a series of lessons by Ottolenghi and his assistants, under the title "Anthropological Types of Delinquents," in a tradition that went back to Lombroso's earlier "criminal clinics." The case studies, adapted from the curriculum at Regina Coeli, included "a homicidal type," "a hereditary epileptic," "a rapist and self-styled amnesiac," and "a quick-witted professional thief."[45] Ottolenghi regarded the prison administration as another fertile field for positivist research and identified prison doctors as key to the individualization of punishment by applying the new insights of "forensic psychology and criminal anthropology."[46] They would be instrumental in carrying out his plan to have his new biographical-anthropological dossier follow each arrestee from police to prison, meanwhile accumulating ever more physical and psychological data.[47] By 1914, Ottolenghi had capped his mission to strengthen the role of criminal anthropology in prisons by devising a special course for prison guards. This intermingling of the police and prison administrations continued through the war and into the era of fascism.[48]

Although criminal anthropologists are best known for gathering data from the bodies of criminals, they also examined their minds. The most widespread method was the interview, which occupied a central place in clinical reports by Lombroso, Ottolenghi, and many of the prison doctors who conducted research on inmates.[49] Lombroso appended examples of his interviews to the second edition of *Criminal Man* while Ottolenghi featured interviews in his class lectures published in the *RDC*. Based on these interrogations, often in front of classes, positivist criminologists constructed colorful "personal narratives" for subjects that emphasized both diseased inheritance and the psychological traits reputed to typify criminals, such as vanity, vindictiveness, cupidity, ferocity, and laziness.[50] These stories seemed to lead inexorably to a Lombrosian diagnosis of atavism, epilepsy, or moral insanity.

Perhaps less well-known was the interest of criminal anthropologists in criminal culture, which was judged equally revealing of delinquent psychology. Again, Lombroso was the most active but not the sole prison doctor to scour his institution for examples of prisoners' writing, drawing, and sculpture. As Gina Lombroso wittily remarked, her father was "a born collector," who supplemented his accumulation of artifacts from the Turin jail with gifts from colleagues employed throughout the national penal system.[51] In 1892, the Ministry of Justice offered him a valuable group of objects from Regina Coeli, which would subsequently amass its own collection. Lombroso was proud of his assemblage of tattoos, art, poems, and furniture made by prisoners, which he used to illustrate his books and to furnish a museum, opened in 1896, for the purpose of research by fellow criminologists.[52] He was not the only collector of criminal artifacts; other assortments of body parts and objects culled from prisoners were assembled at the University of Naples, by Pasquale Penta and Angelo Zuccarelli, and at the mental hospital in Reggio Emilia, under the guidance of Tamburini.

Among the many types of artifacts gathered by Lombroso, two can serve as examples of how criminal anthropologists appropriated prisoner subculture to undergird their theories. The first was a collection of short writings by men and women incarcerated in the jails of Turin and nearby Alessandria.[53] Lombroso was resourceful and innovative in his research: he copied down the lyrics of prison songs; graffiti on prison walls; scribbles on the margins of books in prison libraries; tattoos on inmates' bodies; and embroidery on their clothes. Characterizing himself as a paleographer of the prison, Lombroso promised "a serious and experimental study" of these traces, which he published in a book titled *Prison Palimpsests*.[54] Despite his denigration of prisoner artifacts as signs of atavism, Lombroso, as Pierpaolo Leschiutta has pointed out, must be seen as a pioneer of urban anthropology. While early Italian folklorists were scouring rural villages for vestiges of supposedly pure popular traditions, Lombroso instead focused on collecting products of a criminal culture in the process of urbanization and modernization.[55]

Despite the extreme heterogeneity of the 809 examples of male prisoner writing collected in the *Palimpsests*, Lombroso pretended to turn them into scientific data by dividing them into statistical categories. According to his computations, 21.5 percent of them referred to the inmate's crime, 18.3 percent to his fellow prisoners, 15.2 percent to his punishment, and 10.1 percent to his fate and future. In total, 65 percent of the writings expressed the preoccupation of inmates with their legal travails. These scribblings included protestations of innocence ("I've been in prison for two months without being told my crime"), imprecations against informers and police ("I'm inside because of a lying informer. Death to all informers and police"), and complaints about prison life ("In this cell, it is hard for those who do not have money").[56] Only 11.8 percent referred to either "lust" or "other vices" and only 2.4 percent were "dirty." In a semblance of scientific methodology, Lombroso compared these numbers to a "control group" of graffiti collected by his assistants from "walls, public toilets, military barracks, and finally books" outside of prison.[57] Of course the "external" writings dealt little with criminal justice but to Lombroso's surprise contained many more "dirty" comments than those by prisoners. Nevertheless, despite his own evidence that only a small minority of prisoners exhibited depravity in their writings, Lombroso continued to insist that prisoners were "a species of earthly demons."[58]

Lombroso gives short shrift to graffiti by female inmates, of which he found far fewer examples. He was surprised to find the walls in women's prison cells most often blank, even though many of their occupants had served long sentences. The exception were prostitutes, whose jottings were mostly sexual and included references to cunnilingus and lesbianism. He used these findings to prop up his famous pronouncement, that "the prostitute represents the female born criminal" while most women who committed non-sexual crimes were simply "criminaloids [or] occasional criminals," who had been corrupted mainly by an evil environment.[59] His search for a control group of graffiti by "normal" women, in private Turinese boarding schools, came up with so little that he could confirm one of his other intuitions, that women's "faculty of speech is more developed than that for writing," a reference to their low intelligence.[60] That prostitutes showed more inclination for this mental activity simply derived from their custom of inscribing their names and those of their pimps in public places.

A second, more material type of prison artifact collected by Lombroso were ceramic water jugs and pitchers. The eighty water jugs, which constituted the larger group, had been decorated secretly—in violation of prison regulations—by adult prisoners who scratched pictures and words on their surfaces. Often biographical in nature, they featured the inmate's name, birthplace, and crime, as well as anger at police and judges, protestations of innocence, and longing for mothers and girlfriends. Several prisoners, such as the famous murderer, Cavaglià, expressed such despair at prison conditions that they presaged their own suicides by hanging (Illustration 8.2).

The smaller group of pitchers came from one of the oldest Italian reformatories, "La Generala," which Doria renamed after Ferrante Aporti, a pioneer of childhood education. Permitted to use paints as part of their rehabilitation, juvenile inmates created more elaborate and colorful designs. One pitcher even featured a portrait of Lombroso observing a group of "psychiatric subjects for alienists," the nineteenth-century designation for asylum doctors.[61] This remarkable image acknowledges

Illustration 8.2 The water jug of the prisoner Cavaglià with a picture prefiguring his suicide

the consciousness of prisoners about their role as research subjects for criminal anthropologists. Despite Lombroso's dismissal of the scratched and painted representations as merely pictographs, typical of savages, Luca Spanu more accurately suggests that the unconscious intent of the prisoner artists was to "personalize the bare and mute environment of their cell" and "leave a sign of their own passage through prison."[62]

Rome also established its own museum, but was hindered by rivalry with Lombroso in acquiring artifacts from penitentiaries throughout the peninsula. With the founding of the school for prison guards in 1873, the faculty began to collect instruments of restraint and punishment, models of prisons, and products manufactured by inmates.[63] These were displayed at the International Penitentiary Congress, held in Rome in 1885, as well as other conferences over the decades. But much of this material was handed over to Lombroso in 1892, against the will of Beltrani Scalia. After the establishment of the School of Scientific Policing at Regina Coeli, Ottolenghi began again to collect objects for use in his classes. Only after the death of Lombroso in 1909, however, did prison directors throughout Italy begin to send documents, photographs, weapons, and objects fashioned by inmates more often to Rome rather than to Turin. In the words of the *RDC*, "the penitentiaries, inexhaustible mines of information about crime," enriched Ottolenghi's collection, which subsequently formed the nucleus for the national Criminological Museum in Rome.[64] Even though the *RDC* announced its establishment in 1913, the museum became a reality only in 1930, under the orders of the fascist Minister of Justice, Alfredo Rocco. That it occupied the premises of the New Prison confirmed the strong and enduring ties between criminal anthropology and Italy's inmate population.

Power

Positivist criminologists used the knowledge that they wrested from prisoners to exert power within the prison administration and among the public at large. Arguably their greatest success was the claim to have discovered a universal criminal type when at most they simply described the traits of marginalized and incarcerated Italians during the first decades after unification. A reverse image of the ideal citizens of the newly united nation, Lombroso's born criminals were short, dark, and disfigured. Barely literate, they wrote graffiti in dialect and decorated their bodies and water jugs with pictographs rather than words. Often resorting to prostitution to survive, female offenders failed to blush when reminded of their "crimes." Graffiti on jail walls and jottings in the margins of prisoners' books revealed resentment against police, the courts, and prison guards, as well as anxiety about their families. But, in fact, these traits of the born criminal were no more than characteristics of the Italian poor, and particularly the southern peasant, during the first decades after unification. Malnourished, ravaged by diseases such as malaria, tuberculosis, and pellagra, living in often appalling conditions, and working at heavy labor, large numbers of lower-class Italians would have failed Lombroso's many physical and psychological tests for normalcy. Nevertheless, the fictitious category of the born criminal permeated international criminological discussions, surfaced in parliamentary debates, was appropriated by journalists and novelists, and gripped the popular imagination. Despite its many, often derisive critics, the notion that criminals, and other "deviant" groups, can be identified by their physical features grew only stronger after Lombroso's death.

To defend society from the purported threat posed by atavistic delinquents, Italian criminal anthropologists advocated a number of changes in the process of punishment, some of which were new and others that dressed traditional ideas in scientific garb. On the whole, positivist policies deviated in two overarching ways from those of Beccaria, Howard, De Toqueville, and other first-wave prison reformers of a century earlier. First, the central principle that punishment must be individualized contrasted sharply with the Enlightenment belief in equality before the law based on natural rights. In place of the classical theorem that punishment should equal the crime, positivists placed criminals, with their heterogeneous physical and psychological traits, in the center of the equation. Firmly convinced of their ability to categorize criminals based on their potential "dangerousness" to society, criminal anthropologists rejected the homogenization of the earlier Philadelphia and Auburn models in favor of an array of specialized prisons. Most emblematic of this medical model was the criminal insane asylum, to be administered by doctors with wide discretion over the type and length of treatment of inmates. Biology and psychology, factors absent from Enlightenment view of punishment, also shaped positivist proposals for distinctive institutions for incorrigible, alcoholic, or chronically ill offenders. For occasional criminals, not considered innately atavistic or degenerate, positivists favored "penal substitutes," including alternatives to prison such as parole and probation. Second, positivists broke with classical penology by singling out certain groups as distinctive in their biological predisposition to crime. Even though Enlightenment thinkers had not been immune from implicit or unconscious sexism or racism, criminal anthropologists explicitly emphasized difference rather than equal rights. Based on social Darwinist assumptions and supposedly scientific methods, positivists proposed vastly different policies for biologically defined groups that purportedly held lower positions on the evolutionary scale than white men. From this perspective, children constituted a potential social threat because they could inherit degenerative traits from their parents and pass them to future generations. Until puberty, they mimicked the worst features of the born criminal. Believing, however, that most children would successfully mature into law-abiding adults, positivists advocated mostly liberal measures of education and job training within the environment of families or the new reformatory. While not unique in supporting the transformation of the traditional houses of custody into schools, criminal anthropological warnings about the threat of born criminality among children and the inheritable potential of degenerative weakness such as alcoholism, syphilis, and insanity raised anxiety about juvenile delinquency and re-enforced the child-saving movement.

Women clearly represented another group whom criminal anthropologists defined by their biology. Asserting that prostitution was typical of early human society, they identified sexual deviancy, rather than violence, as key to female delinquency. At the same time, official statistics showed lower rates of crime among women than among men, and even Lombroso admitted that environmental, rather than biological, factors accounted for most female lawbreaking. However, the outpouring of research on criminal women during the 1890s, most famously encapsulated in Lombroso's *Criminal Woman, the Normal Woman, and the Prostitute* (1893), was not matched by concrete proposals to individualize punishment, modernize inmate education and work, or expand probation and pardon for women. Lombroso, a secular Jew, even applauded the role of the nuns for trying to transform sexual desire into religious piety by playing on women's emotional "susceptibility."[65] Refusing to challenge traditional stereotypes about female nature, positivists gave short shrift to prison reform for women and girls.

Thirdly, criminal anthropology contributed to the general redefinition of race as a physical attribute that determined moral, mental, and psychological differences. For Lombroso, race was the subject of one of his earliest books, *White Man and Colored Man*, which accepted the recent Darwinian notion of evolution but added a corollary— that black, brown, and yellow "races" were closer to apes.[66] During his lifetime, he focused most of his racial research on differences within Italy, as did colleagues such as Sergi and Niceforo. Despite their recognition of social inequalities in the South, they singled out its history of invasion and resulting ethnic intermingling with northern Africans to explain the predominance of "atavistic" violent crime over economic offenses more typical of the more civilized North. By offering pseudoscientific backing for older stereotypes of backward southerners, positivists indirectly contributed to their overrepresentation among penitentiary inmates.

After Italy began acquiring small holdings in Eritrea and, more importantly, defeated the Turkish Empire in Libya in 1912, criminal anthropologists turned their attention to black Africans, held to be the least evolved and therefore the most criminal of the races. In a series of articles in the *RDC*, Emanuele Mirabella, doctor at the criminal insane asylum of Aversa, shared the results of his research on Libyans who had been deported to the island colony of Favignana during the imperialist war. Insisting on the necessity of studying not only the moral but also the physical characteristics of these new African prisoners, Mirabella subjected them to the usual anthropometric measurements, emphasizing the head, and to the inspection of their anomalies, tattoos, and levels of sensitivity. Comparing his data with that for Italians, he concluded that

> the Libyan constitutes an anthropological variety all to himself, which has special pathological, degenerative, and atavistic characteristics; he has something that differentiates him from a normal man, almost as if he belongs to an intermediate zone between healthy men and monkeys! To what race does [the Libyan] belong?[67]

In his introduction to this long and multipart article, Mario Carrara, the son-in-law of Lombroso and director of his museum, praised Mirabella for such detailed proof that a criminal type could be found among "primitive peoples and savages."[68] Criminal anthropologists had indeed doubted whether Africans, whom they placed at the bottom of the evolutionary ladder, could exhibit their own type of biological anomalies.

These criminal anthropological theories, which emphasized individual and group differences, were implemented more fully in some types of Italian penal institutions than in others. Perhaps because they carried no historical baggage, criminal insane asylums came closest to the positivist ideal of empowering medical specialists at the expense of the judiciary. Public reformatories for boys, the object of lively debates and relatively generous funding, radically changed their focus from repression to education, which was consonant with the criminal anthropological focus on the child. The proliferation of different types of men's penitentiaries, as well as the intensification of educational and professional training within them, gestured toward the ideal of individualization although financial resources were limited. Stasis instead defined the condition of institutions for women and girls, which echoed the absence of any innovative positivist proposals for reforming female punishment. Within Italy's web of penal institutions, the police camps were least touched by criminal anthropology, until the arrival of Libyan prisoners after 1912. During the previous fifty years, the positivist school had consistently assailed the institution of *domicilio coatto* as inhumane and ineffective in reforming inmates or protecting society. However, no particular protest accompanied the arrival of the African prisoners, who were not thought to merit humane or individualized punishment. In short, criminal anthropological research simply validated the limits on citizenship for Italian women and colonial subjects; neither were granted the "negative" right to serve their sentences in modern penitentiaries.

Transnationally, Italy's experience between unification and World War I encapsulated many of the sometimes contradictory aspects of the second wave of prison reform. In theoretical terms, the medical model prevailed in Europe, sometimes under the guise of degeneracy theory; in South America, where Italian criminal anthropology was widely imitated; and even in some Asian countries, such as China and Japan, where local criminologists studied positivist doctrines. Model prisons, based on the principle of individualization and recognizable from their radial patterns, spread throughout the world. The international movement of child-savers resulted in the multiplication of innovative reformatories in Europe and North America, which emphasized education and professional training. Even in countries where biological theories were challenged by sociological schools of criminology, psychology became ever more central to the project of sorting prisoners and fashioning punishment. Increasingly elaborate categories of offenders led to additional repression for some but more humane alternatives to incarceration, such as probation and parole, for others.

As in Italy, however, the positive project had its limits and failed to thoroughly transform global regimes of punishment. Most obviously, most nations refused to invest the necessary financial resources to implement a theory that required individual sleeping cells, medical and psychiatric examination of each inmate, advanced education, and professional, well-paid types of prison work. Neglect fell mostly on less favored groups for whom individualization did not seem theoretically appropriate or economically advantageous. Many nations transported their "incorrigible" criminals and recidivists to work camps that little resembled the modern penitentiary. Like Italy, Russia and several Latin American nations employed an alternative tactic, that of "internal transportation," or shipping undesirables to penal colonies separated from populated centers by large expanses of water or land. Gender also permeated penal policies, with women languishing in unreformed penitentiaries in Europe and Latin American and facing even more repression—including sexual exploitation—in the colonies than men. Only the United States, with its movement to establish a network of female reformatories after the turn of the twentieth century, constituted an exception to the general silence on women. Finally, in the age of empire, the ruling classes relegated subordinate ethnic and racial groups to punishment that were little different from the old-regime hard labor camps. With profit as their goal, this type of harsh and undifferentiated confinement was most typical of colonial administrations but also continued in western societies, such as the American South. The age of positivism, therefore, produced a mixed map of global punishment that deprived the many prisoners of promises of reform. The penal camp survived the era of positivism only to make a decisive and horrifying return during the interwar period and beyond.

Conclusion

Today, few of the many prisons that dotted the nineteenth-century Roman landscape are remembered by tourists or even city residents. Only Regina Coeli, on the right bank of the Tiber River, continues to function as a penal institution although the women's section, the Mantellate jail, has been closed. The boys' prison at San Michele has been meticulously restored but accessible only during special exhibitions and generally missing from most travel guidebooks. Instead, they limit their descriptions of Rome's prison history to the Mamertine, which forms part of the archeological complex of the Roman forum, and to Castel Sant'Angelo, an ancient ruin which has been transformed into a museum. The buildings that housed the penal institutions at Diocletian's Baths, Villa Altieri, Tre Fontane, and the Buon Pastore still stand but serve other purposes and are rarely identified in popular memory as former sites of punishment. Nevertheless, the history of this constellation of nineteenth-century penal institutions illuminates the complex and contradictory process by which the new Italian state sought to transform its penal policy according to the dictates of political liberalism and modern science.

The Italian state's struggle to shape a modern prison system that reconciled liberty and order challenges, or at least revises, certain standard interpretations of Italian state-building after unification in 1861. Because the transition in punishment occurred over several centuries, the experience of liberal Italy must be contextualized within a longer period stretching back to at least the seventeenth century. Certainly radical political change marked the decade after 1861 as a written constitution, and a parliamentary form of government was implemented across the peninsula. But several continuities characterized both the pre-unitary monarchies and the liberal state, most importantly the model of the convent prison for women and children. Administered by Catholic orders, this hybrid institution blurred the lines between public and private justice at the stage of punishment. In the form of private charities, religion also continued to play a role in the state's strategy of inmate rehabilitation. Prisoner aid societies, rooted in or inspired by traditional confraternities, were integrated into prison legislation as partners of the state. While religious precedents affected most directly women and children, another vestige of the early modern period, forced labor, continued to shape the life of adult male inmates until the passage of the Zanardelli Code in 1889. In short, unification constituted less a pivotal turning point than one of several important markers in the long Italian transition from corporal punishment to the prison.

The liberal era witnessed additional markers of change, accelerating during the twenty-five years before World War I and demonstrating the increasing vitality of prison, and more generally social, reform. This reality of slow but significant improvements in prison life, while limited to specific demographic groups, defies the common stereotype of the Italian criminal justice system, and penal policy in particular, as stagnant, provincial, and merely repressive before World War I. Often based on credible evidence of violent suppression by the state of political opponents, the traditional view is not wrong but too simplistic. Common criminals constituted the large majority of inmates and the main focus of prison reformers, who sought to bring Italian policy into line with principles enunciated at the International Penitentiary Congresses and implemented to differing degrees in Northern Europe and America. As Director General of Prisons during the early decades after unification, Beltrani Scalia drew Italy into transnational debates by his high-level participation in these congresses, one of which was held in Rome. He founded the *Journal of Prisons Sciences* to encourage dialogue with foreign experts by printing their articles and reviewing their books. Although holding strong opinions himself, Beltrani Scalia encouraged lively and sophisticated interchange across disciplines about not only punishment but also criminology and penal law.

The advent of social-reform legislation, under the aegis of the Left-liberal administration of Crispi in the late 1880s, provided the conditions for turning many of Beltrani Scalia's ideas into state policy. As part of the package of "Crispi laws," the Prison Ordinance of 1891 constituted a limited but nevertheless significant step toward social justice in punishment to accompany companion reforms pertaining to local administration, public health, prostitution, emigration, and charities. Attention to prison reform resumed after the turn of the twentieth century with Prime Minister Giolitti participating actively in parliamentary debates in support of Doria's initiatives to abolish chains and mitigate discipline in men's institutions, institute probation, expand agricultural colonies, renovate old penitentiaries, transform boys' reformatories into schools, and improve the working conditions of prison guards. The effectiveness of Doria's program was limited by both restricted budgets and his own gendered vision of reform, which almost entirely excluded women and girls. But increasing outcry in the press and feminists' activism might have pressured the state to begin addressing inequities for female prisoners if not for the outbreak of war.

Italian prison history is instructive not only for internal national historiography but also for addressing transnational issues of punishment. The timing and circumstances of the birth of the prison around the globe varied widely, but several characteristics of the Italian experience encapsulated global trends. First, the transition from corporal punishment to the modern penitentiary took place over an extended period of time rather than at a specific turning point. As a result of a process of successive and overlapping waves of reform, modern prisons systems are more hybrid than uniform in nature. Not just the absence of adequate funding, but also the persistence of older reform impulses, have prevented the realization of the penitentiary ideal within nations and across regions. Furthermore, premodern forms of internment continued to coexist with new penitentiary networks even in the pioneering nations of the first wave; England and France, for example, established penal camps in their colonies while the United States maintained chain gangs in Southern states. The triumph of the prison, therefore, has been uneven and incomplete.

Second, the Italian example points to the importance of gender and age for explaining the irregular chronology of prison development and the disparities among types of institutions within national prison networks. In Rome, women and children were the first beneficiaries of early-modern Catholic initiatives to extend the convent model into the penal realm. In place of hard labor or corporal punishment, the institution of San Michele experimented with enclosure for the purpose of reform through work and prayer. Rather than disappearing after the first wave of enlightened prison reform during the age of revolutions, convent prisons in Italy, as well as many other Catholic countries in Europe and Latin America, were given a new lease on life by the introduction of religious orders during the nineteenth century to oversee the punishment of women and girls. At the same time, the modern penitentiary became masculinized as men were withdrawn from forced labor and became the prime subjects of prison reform as part of state building. To shape future citizens of the new liberal state, boys' reformatories became laboratories of educational, professional, and military training. Current research suggests that this Italian developmental pattern was most typical of the Catholic world, in which the monastery was traditionally identified with repentance, and enclosure employed to protect and discipline women and children. While different chronologies have been reconstructed for other geographical regions, the integration of gender and age is essential to revising the grand narrative of the birth of the prison.

Finally, as the birthplace of positivist criminology, Italy is essential to the exploration of global practices of imprisonment during the late nineteenth and early twentieth centuries. Of course, Lombroso's theories were not entirely new; he acknowledged his debts to earlier theorists of phrenology, moral statistics, and moral insanity. Less consciously, he drew on popular stereotypes, such as the purported violence of lower-class men, the sexual nature of women, and the inferiority of non-white races, to guide his research. Although his resulting criminological insights, most particularly that of the explanatory power of atavism, were not universally accepted, they constituted the fulcrum of debate among criminologists in Europe, the Americas, and Asia during the age of increasingly strident nationalism and imperialism. It was during this era that Italy, and the majority of nation-states and colonial regions across the globe, adopted the modern penitentiary as a sign of progress. As in Italy, this second wave of prison reform produced contradictory and sometimes repressive policies that varied according to gender, age, and race. Nevertheless, the power of Italian positivist criminology promoted a common transnational project that no longer sought the etiology of crime in society but in inmates' bodies themselves. In Italy, this approach yielded some substantial improvement in conditions and rights for prisoners during the liberal era but contained a repressive potential that was unleased under the subsequent fascist dictatorship.

Notes

Introduction

1. See Charles Klopp, *Sentences: The Memoirs and Letters of Italian Political Prisoners from Benvenuto Cellini to Aldo Moro* (Toronto: University of Toronto Press, 1999). Klopp argues for an Italian "tradition" or even a "literary genre" of prison letters and memoirs in which their authors spoke to each other across the centuries (p. xii). His fascinating analysis of this genre concentrates on the moral and psychological torment of imprisonment rather than its physical deprivations.
2. Michel Foucault, *Discipline and Punish: The Birth of the Prison* (New York: Vintage, 1977); French edition, 1975.
3. For example, see Christian De Vito and Alex Lichtenstein, eds., *Global Convict Labor* (Leiden: Brill, 2015), and Clare Anderson, ed., *A Global History of Convicts and Penal Colonies* (London: Bloomsbury, 2018).
4. Cesare Beccaria, *On Crimes and Punishments* (Indianapolis: Hackett, 1986).
5. Cesare Lombroso, *Criminal Man*, trans. Mary Gibson and Nicole Hahn Rafter (Durham, NC: Duke University Press, 2006); Cesare Lombroso and Guglielmo Ferrero, *Criminal Woman, the Prostitute, and the Normal Woman*, trans. Nicole Hahn Rafter and Mary Gibson (Durham, NC: Duke University Press, 2004).
6. Eugenio Garin, "Il positivismo italiano alla fine del secolo XIX fra metodo e concezione del mondo," *Giornale critico della filosofia italiana* serie 5, vol.1, no. Jan.–Dec. (1980): 4.
7. In addition to Foucault, see David J. Rothman, *The Discovery of the Asylum: Social Order and Disorder in the New Republic* (Boston: Little, Brown, 1971) and Michael Ignatieff, *A Just Measure of Pain: The Penitentiary in the Industrial Revolution, 1750–1850* (New York: Columbia University Press, 1978).
8. For an analysis of the common themes of the revisionist school by Ignatieff, see "State, Civil Society, and Total Institutions: A Critique of Recent Social Histories of Punishment," in *Social Control and the State*, ed. Stanley Cohen and Andrew Scull (New York: St. Martin's Press, 1983).
9. Foucault, *Discipline and Punish*, 26.
10. Pieter Spierenburg, *The Prison Experience: Disciplinary Institutions and Their Inmates in Early Modern Europe* (New Brunswick, NJ: Rutgers University Press, 1991).
11. The phrase comes from Norval Morris and David J. Rothman, eds., *The Oxford History of the Prison: The Practice of Punishment in Western Society* (New York: Oxford University Press, 1998).
12. Joanna Innes, "Prisons for the Poor: English Bridewells, 1555–1800," in *Labour, Law and Crime: An Historical Perspective*, ed. Francis Snyder and Douglas Hay (London: Blackwell, 1987); Paul Griffiths, *Lost Londons: Change, Crime, and Control in the Capital City, 1550–1660* (Cambridge: Cambridge University Press, 2008).

13 Patricia O'Brien, *The Promise of Punishment: Prisons in Nineteenth-Century France* (Princeton: Princeton University Press, 1982).

14 Maria Soledad Zárate Campos, "Vicious Women, Virtuous Women: The Female Delinquent and the Santiago de Chile Correctional House, 1860–1900," in *The Birth of the Penitentiary in Latin America: Essays on Criminology, Prison Reform, and Social Control, 1830–1940*, ed. Ricardo D. Salvatore and Carlos Aguirre (Austin: University of Texas Press, 1996), 84. See also Lila Caimari, "Whose Criminals Are These? Church, State, and Patronatos and the Rehabilitation of Female Convicts (Buenos Aires, 1890–1940)," *The Americas* 54, no. 2 (1997).

15 See, for example, Lucia Zedner, *Women, Crime, and Custody in Victorian England* (Oxford: Oxford University Press, 1991) and Nicole Hahn Rafter, *Partial Justice: Women in State Prisons, 1800–1935* (Boston: Northeastern University Press, 1985).

16 For an overview, see Mary Gibson, "Global Perspectives on the Birth of the Prison," *American Historical Review* 116, no. 4 (2011).

17 Dario Melossi and Massimo Pavarini, *The Prison and the Factory: Origins of the Penitentiary System*, trans. Glynis Cousin (New York: Macmillan, 1981); Italian edition, 1977.

18 Guy Geltner, *The Medieval Prison: A Social History* (Princeton: Princeton University Press, 2008).

19 Anna Capelli, *La Buona Compagnia. Utopia e realtà carceraria nell'Italia del Risorgimento* (Milan: Franco Angeli, 1988).

20 Simona Trombetta, *Punizione e carità. Carceri femminili nell'Italia dell'Ottocento* (Bologna: Il Mulino, 2004).

21 Guido Neppi Modona, "Carcere e società civile," in *Storia D'Italia*, vol. 5, pt. 2 (Turin: Einaudi, 1973); Roberto Giulianelli, *L'industria carceraria in Italia: Lavoro e produzione nelle prigioni da Giolitti a Mussolini* (Milan: Franco Angeli, 2008). For a short overview in English, see Susan B. Carrafiello, *"The Tombs of the Living": Prisons and Prison Reform in Liberal Italy* (New York: Peter Lang, 1998).

22 See Michael R. Ebner, *Ordinary Violence in Mussolini's Italy* (Cambridge: Cambridge University Press, 2006) and Ilaria Poerio, *A scuola di dissenso: Storie di resistenza al confino di polizia (1926–43)* (Rome: Carocci, 2016). On fascist prison policy, see Giovanni Tessitore, *Carcere e fascistizzazione. Analisi di un modello totalizzante* (Milan: Franco Angeli, 2005).

23 James Q. Whitman, "The Transition to Modernity," in *The Oxford Handbook of Criminal Law*, ed. Markus D. Dubber and Tatjana Hörnle (Oxford: Oxford University Press, 2014), 100.

24 A major research project in France called "Enfermements," or enclosures, has been exploring the close relationship between monasteries and prisons, with an emphasis on the Cistercian Abbey of Clairvaux which now serves as a prison. See http://enfermements.fr/ (accessed July 6, 2018) for the project's publications. See also Norman Johnston, *Forms of Constraint: A History of Prison Architecture* (Urbana: University of Illinois, 2000), 17–27.

25 Foucault, *Discipline and Punish*, 173.

26 On total institutions, see Erving Goffman, *Asylums: Essays on the Social Situation of Mental Patients and Other Inmates* (New York: Doubleday, 1961).

27 For an exception, which focuses on prison labor, see Giulianelli, *L'industria carceraria in Italia*.

1 Punishment before Italian Unification

1. Fiorella Bartoccini, *Roma nell'Ottocento. Il tramonto della "città santa". La nascita di una capitale*, 2 vols. (Bologna: Cappelli, 1985), 1: 121.
2. The Senate of ancient Rome, destroyed during barbarian rule, was reestablished in 1144 CE. Although it never regained its former power, it represented the ancient prerogative of municipal self-rule by the secular nobility.
3. Michele Di Sivo, "Il popolo e il suo giudice. Studi sui documenti del Tribunale Criminale del Senatore di Roma (1593–1599)," in *Popolazione e società a Roma dal medioevo all'età contemporanea*, ed. Eugenio Sonnino (Rome: Il "calamo", 1998), 616. The city government began to lose autonomy as early as 1469, when Pope Paul II took over the power to nominate the Senators; in 1580, the number of judges on the Capitoline Court was reduced to three, all appointed by the Pope.
4. On the Vicar's court, see Gabriella Bonacchi, *Legge e peccato. Anime, corpi, giustizia alla corte dei papi* (Rome-Bari: Laterza, 1995).
5. Irene Fosi, "Il Governo della Giustizia," in *Roma moderna*, ed. Giorgio Ciucci (Rome-Bari: Laterza, 2002), 122.
6. Ibid.
7. For the different types of torture employed by the courts of the Papal States, see Luigi Cajani, "Pena di morte e tortura a Roma nel Settecento," in *Criminalità e società in età moderna*, ed. Luigi Berlinguer and Floriana Colao (Milan: 1991), 517–18.
8. Catherine Brice, *Storia di Roma e dei romani da Napoleone ai nostri giorni* (Roma: Viella, 2009), 15.
9. The phrase "penal signs" is borrowed from Daniel Botsman's marvelous description of nineteenth-century Tokyo. See Daniel V. Botsman, *Punishment and Power in the Making of Modern Japan* (Princeton: Princeton University Press, 2005), 28.
10. Carlo De Paolis, "Galere, ciurme e forzati nella Civitavecchia pontificia," *Lazio ieri e oggi* 16 (1980). Most other European states abolished the galley earlier than the Papal States, replacing them with sailing vessels. On galley slavery in Spain, see Ruth Pike, *Penal Servitude in Early Modern Spain* (Madison: University of Wisconsin Press, 1983).
11. Prisoners of war were usually Muslims; unemployed men were free workers and therefore received wages, better food, and the right to wear their own clothes rather than the prison stripes.
12. Roberto Benedetti, "Tribunali e giustizia a Roma nel Settecento attraverso la fonte delle liste di traduzione alla galera (1749–1759)," *Roma Moderna e Contemporanea* 12, no. 3 (2004): 523–4.
13. Ibid., 508–9.
14. Capelli emphasizes the centrality of forced labor to the penal policy of the Papal States in the decades before unification. See Capelli, *La Buona Compagnia*, 84–5, 335.
15. For the employment of *forzati* at Ostia Antica, the ancient Roman port that silted up after the founding of modern Ostia, see Arturo Pittaluga, "Galeotti agli scavi di Ostia Antica," *Lazio ieri e oggi* 11, no. 1 (1975). Excavations at Ostia Antica began in 1803 under the direction of Giuseppe Petrini, a classical scholar assigned by the papal administration.
16. George Head, *Rome: A Tour of Many Days* (London: Longman, Brown, Green and Longmans, 1849), 80–1. I wish to thank Richard Wittman for pointing out this

source. For images of "*galleotti* at work" see Pittaluga, "Galeotti agli scavi di Ostia Antica," 173.

17 Guy Geltner, "*Detrusio*, Penal Cloistering in the Middle Ages," *Revue Bénédictine* 118 (2008): 94. Women were particularly subjected to *detrusio*. See Geltner, "A Cell of Their Own: The Incarceration of Women in Late Medieval Italy," *Signs* 39 (2013): 32–3.

18 Roman secular jurists, such as Prospero Farinacci, also began to accept imprisonment as punishment. See Romano Canosa and Isabella Colonnello, *Storia del carcere in Italia dalla fine del'500 all'unità* (Roma: Sapere 2000, 1984), 18.

19 Angela Groppi, "Roman Alms and Poor Relief in the Seventeenth Century," in *Rome-Amsterdam: Two Growing Cities in Seventeenth-Century Europe*, ed. P. van Kessel and E. Schutte (Amsterdam: Amsterdam University Press, 1997), 182–3.

20 Brice, *Storia di Roma e dei romani da Napoleone ai nostri giorni*, 91. The first Roman confraternity was that of the Gonfalone, founded in 1264; two hundred more were established during the Renaissance and early modern period. For confraternities dedicated to prisoners in Bologna, another city in the Papal States, see Nicholas Terpstra, "Confraternal Prison Charity and Political Consolidation in Sixteenth-Century Bologna," *Journal of Modern History* 66 (1994).

21 A. Bertolotti, "Le prigioni di Roma nei secoli XVI, XVII e XVIII," *Rivista di Discipline Carcerarie* 20 (1890): 535. A slightly earlier date is given by Giuseppe Adinolfi, *Storia di Regina Coeli e delle carceri romane* (Rome: Bonsignoli, 1998), 31. On the prisoners assisted by the confraternity of San Giovanni Decollato, see Silvana Di Mattia Spirito, "Nazionalità e condizione sociale dei condannati a morte assistiti dall'arciconfraternità di S. Giovanni Decollato di Roma (1497–1527)," in *Popolazione e società a Roma dal medioevo all'età contemporanea*, ed. Eugenio Sonnino (Rome: Il "calamo", 1998).

22 Cited in Vincenzo Monachino, ed. *La carità cristiana in Roma* (Bologna: Cappelli, 1968), 270.

23 Carlo Cirillo Fornili, *Delinquenti e carcerati a Roma alla metà del '600: Opera dei Papi nella riforma carceraria* (Roma: Editrice Pontificia Università Gregoriana, 1991), 95. The Confraternity of S. Girolamo played an important role in the spiritual and material workings of Tor di Nona since its founding in 1520. The Pietà dei Carcerati was established in 1575.

24 Monachino, *La carità cristiana in Roma*, 269. On the Committee for Prison Inspection, see also Antonio Parente, "Il tribunale della visita," *Rassegna Penitenziaria e Criminologica* 1, no. 1–2 (1997). "Foreigner" (*straniero*) designated any person who had been born outside of Rome, whether in Italy or Europe more generally.

25 For examples of prisoner complaints, see Bertolotti, "Le prigioni di Roma nei secoli XVI, XVII e XVIII," 645–9.

26 Ibid., 649.

27 Brice, *Storia di Roma e dei romani da Napoleone ai nostri giorni*: 77.

28 On the Papal police, see Fornili, *Delinquenti e carcerati a Roma alla metà del '600*, Chapter 5.

29 Michele Di Sivo, "Sulle carceri dei tribunali penali a Roma: Campidoglio e Tor Di Nona," in *Carceri, carcerieri, carcerati. Dall'antico regime all'Ottocento*, ed. Livio Antonielli (Soveria Mannelli: Rubbettino, 2006), 16. These figures come from the records of S. Girolamo della Carità.

30 Christopher Hibbert, *Rome: The Biography of a City* (New York: Viking, 1985), 202.

31 The Capitoline prison, which was also called the prison of the Campidoglio, Senator, or the Conservators, has been studied most closely by Michele Di Sivo. See Michele Di Sivo, "Il tribunale criminale capitolino nei secoli XVI–XVII: note da un lavoro in corso," *Roma moderna e contemporanea* 3 (1995) and "Il popolo e il suo giudice. Studi sui documenti del Tribunale Criminale del Senatore di Roma (1593-1599)."
32 Historical sources confirm the presence of Paul in Rome but do not clearly confirm the Christian tradition of Peter's martyrdom in the city. This tradition forms the basis for the Catholic claim that the popes are descended from Peter. On the Mamertine prison, see Ludovico Gatto, "Le carceri nell'antichità," *Roma ieri, oggi, domani* 7, no. 72 (1994): 62.
33 Nathaniel Hawthorne, *Passages from the French and Italian Note-Books* (Boston and New York: Houghton, Mifflin, 1892), 11.
34 The existence of the Capitoline prison can be documented back to at least 1198. See Giuseppe Adinolfi, *Storia di Regina Coeli e delle carceri romane* (Roma: Bonsignori, 1998), 11.
35 The Hospital of SS. Salvatore retained the management of the Capitoline prison until 1833; for a short period before its abolition in 1847, it was overseen by the Camera apostolic, a high papal council.
36 Bertolotti, "Le prigioni di Roma nei secoli XVI, XVII e XVIII," 534. The Borgo prison was located near the Church of Santa Maria in Traspontina, later torn down to make the Via della Conciliazione.
37 Hadrian's tomb was built between 130 and 199 CE. It was given its name by Pope Gregory the Great when, in 593, he claimed to see the Archangel Saint Michael at the top of the mausoleum proclaiming the end of the recent plague. Restored and fortified by a number of popes over the centuries, Castel Sant'Angelo was linked, after 1500, to the Vatican by a covered passageway that allowed the popes special access to the fortress in times of danger.
38 On the antiquity of Castel Sant'Angelo as a prison, see Adinolfi, *Storia di Regina Coeli e delle carceri romane*, 19. For accounts of famous prisoners such as Cellini, see AAVV, ed. *Le prigioni più rinomate d'Italia* (Florence: A spese degli editori, 1859). That political prisoners were interned in Castel Sant'Angelo is common knowledge among opera fans who are familiar with the final scene of Tosca, in which the revolutionary hero, Cavaradossi, is interned in Castel Sant'Angelo and shot at dawn.
39 Hawthorne, *Passages from the French and Italian Note-Books*, 137.
40 Little research has been done on the Savelli court/prison, whose date of establishment varies among sources. For brief overviews see Gatto, "Le carceri nell'antichità," 63; ManfredoTafuri, "Le 'Carceri Nuove' e la casa di correzione per i minorenni," in *Via Giulia: una utopia urbanistica del 500*, ed. Luigi Salerno, Luigi Spezzaferro, and Manfredo Tafuri (Rome: Aristide Staderini, 1973), 360–1; Assunta Borzacchiello, "Modi e luoghi della giustizia a Roma al tempo di Beatrice Cenci" (paper presented at the Mostra sul quattrocentenario della morte di Beatrice Cenci, Fondazione Basso, Rome, 1999), 24–5.
41 Borzacchiello, "Modi e luoghi della giustizia a Roma al tempo di Beatrice Cenci," 24.
42 For the most recent research on the Tor di Nona prison, see Di Sivo, "Sulle carceri dei tribunali penali a Roma: Campidoglio e Tor Di Nona."
43 Ibid., 9.
44 Giorgio Ciucci, ed. *Roma moderna* (Rome-Bari: Laterza, 2002), xvi. Rome had shrunk precipitously since the height of the Roman Empire when the population had

reached over a million and buildings covered most of the area within the Aurelian walls, erected in 264 CE. Despite its modest population, Rome continued to be defined politically and legally by its ring of Roman walls, punctuated by fortifications and gates. The walls measured 20 kilometers and, at the time of unification in 1870, had twenty gates, seven of which had been closed since Roman times. See Felice Giordano, *Cenni sulle condizioni fisico-economiche di Roma e suo territorio* (Florence: Stabilimento di Giuseppe Civelli, 1871), 171.

45 For example, see the floor plan of the Savelli prison reproduced in Tafuri, "Le 'Carceri Nuove' e la casa di correzione per i minorenni," 361.

46 Although the name is plural in Italian (*Carceri Nuove*), New Prison is less awkward in English.

47 For example, see Elvira Grantaliano, "Le Carceri Nuove (1658–1883)," in *Carceri, carcerieri, carcerati. Dall'antico regime all'Ottocento*, ed. Livio Antonielli (Soveria Mannelli: Rubbettino, 2006), 23–4.

48 Scanaroli, whose book was titled *De Visitatione carceratorum libri tres* (Rome: Camera Apostolica, 1655), is termed an unjustly "forgotten writer" by Canosa and Colonnello. See Canosa and Colonnello, *Storia del carcere in Italia dalla fine del'500 all'unità*, 37. On the importance of Scanaroli, see also Fornili, *Delinquenti e carcerati a Roma alla metà del '600*, 101–32. That his book was published by a Vatican press shows that it received implicit papal approval.

49 For a list of the legislation regulating the work of the Committee for Prison Inspection between 1548 and 1612, see Canosa and Colonnello, *Storia del carcere in Italia dalla fine del'500 all'unità*, 38–9.

50 The phrase is from Grantaliano, "Le Carceri Nuove (1658–1883)," 24. For other positive evaluations of the New Prison, see Fornili, *Delinquenti e carcerati a Roma alla metà del '600*, 100; Adinolfi, *Storia di Regina Coeli e delle carceri romane*, 29; Borzacchiello, "Modi e luoghi della giustizia a Roma al tempo di Beatrice Cenci," 28–9.

51 Carlo-Luigi Morichini, *Degli istituti di carità per la sussistenza e l'educazione dei poveri e dei prigionieri in Roma* (Rome: Edizione Novissima, 1870), 688.

52 This plaque still exists on the building, which now serves as the headquarters of the anti-mafia unit of the Ministry of Justice.

53 Wolfgang Braunfels, *Urban Design in Western Europe: Regime and Architecture, 900–1900* (Chicago: University of Chicago Press, 1988), 5.

54 Tafuri, "Le 'Carceri Nuove' e la casa di correzione per i minorenni," 360.

55 Because Antonio del Grande appears to have been only a master builder rather than a distinguished architect, historians tend to credit Virgilio Spada, a priest close to the Pope, with the conceptualization and general design of the New Prison. See for example Grantaliano, "Le Carceri Nuove (1658–1883)," 23.

56 Howard quoted in Fornili, *Delinquenti e carcerati a Roma alla metà del '600*, 29; Adinolfi, *Storia di Regina Coeli e delle carceri romane*, 29.

57 Laura Chiarotti, "La popolazione del carcere nuovo nella seconda metà del XVII secolo," *Archivio della Società Romana di Storia Patria* 115 (1992): 153.

58 The entire complex of was officially named the Ospizio Apostolico di San Michele (Apostolic Poorhouse of San Michael). The papal complex grew out of a private philanthropic refuge that had been founded by the nobleman Carlo Tommaso Odescalchi to shelter abandoned and runaway boys in 1650 and was moved to the Ripa port in 1689. See the excellent history of the entire complex (with an appendix of

key documents) by Francesco Sisinni, ed. *Il San Michele a Ripa Grande* (Rome: Istituto Poligrafico e Zecca dello Stato/Editalia, 1991), 130.

59 For a learned analysis of papal policies of charity, especially for the aged, see Angela Groppi, *Il welfare prima del welfare: Assistenza alla vecchiaia e solidarietà tra generazioni a Roma in età moderna* (Rome: Viella, 2010). Begging was legal for individuals who wore a specific garb that identified them as having been certified as unable to work.

60 Capelli, *La Buona Compagnia*, 90. On San Michele before Italian unification, see Thorsten Sellin, "The House of Correction for Boys in the Hospice of San Michael in Rome," *Journal of Criminal Law and Criminology* 20, no. 4 (1930); Melossi and Pavarini, *The Prison and the Factory*; Luigi Cajani, "Sorvegliare e redimere: La Casa di Correzione di S. Michele a Ripa di Roma (secoli XVIII e XIX)," in *Criminalità, giustizia penale e ordine pubblico nell'Europa moderna*, ed. Luigi Cajani (Milan: Unicopli, 1997); Capelli, *La Buona Compagnia*; Sisinni, *Il San Michele a Ripa Grande*.

61 This decree, the "Motu proprio di Clemente XI sul regolamento della Casa di Correzione e sul trattamento dei ragazzi delinquenti che vengono ospitati (14 november 1703)," is reprinted in Sisinni, *Il San Michele a Ripa Grande*, 271–2.

62 Motu proprio of 1703 in ibid., 271.

63 Quoted in Melossi and Pavarini, *The Prison and the Factory*, 80.

64 Motu Proprio di Clemente XI (1703) in Sisinni, *Il San Michele a Ripa Grande*, 271.

65 Until recently, there has been less interest in the women's than the boys' prison at San Michele. On the women's prison, in addition to Capelli and Sisinni, see G. M. Sirovich, "Correzionale del San Michele e istanze di reclusione a Roma (XVIII–XIX secolo)," *Ses* 50 (1990); Trombetta, *Punizione e carità. Carceri femminili nell'Italia dell'Ottocento*; Chiara Lucrezio Monticelli, "*Donne dietro le sbarre. Il carcere femminile nella Roma dei secoli XVIII e XIX*" (Tesi di laurea, Università di Rome-La Sapienza, 2002–3). For a more general analysis of the role of gender in "enclosed spaces" such as monasteries and prisons, see Isabelle Heullant-Donat et al., eds., *Enfermements III. Le genre enfermé: Hommes et femmes en milieux clos (xiiie-xxe siècle)* (Paris: La Sorbonne, 2017).

66 Morichini, *Degli istituti di carità per la sussistenza e l'educazione dei poveri e dei prigionieri in Roma*, 706.

67 Hawthorne, *Passages from the French and Italian Note-Books*, 65.

68 For example, see the guidebook by Walter Taylor Field, *Rome*, 2 vols. (Boston: L. C. Page, 1904), vol 1: 32.

69 For a history of transportation on the Tiber during the last two centuries, see Rita D'Errico, "La navigazione sul Tevere a valle di Roma dall'Unità al secondo dopoguerra," *Roma moderna e contemporanea* 12 (2004).

70 Sisinni, *Il San Michele a Ripa Grande*, 48, 51. The smaller upstream port, the Ripetta, serviced boats from inland regions like the Sabina carrying wine and oil. See Armando Ravaglioli, *Roma la Capitale, immagini di cento anni*, 2 vols. (Rome: Edizioni del Banco di Roma, 1970–1971), 1:30.

71 For a photograph of the floating mills in the Tiber, see Maria Ludovica Lenza Andreucci, ed., *Roma: Cento Anni (1871–1971)* (Florence: La Nuova Italia, 1971), Plate 1. For reprints of rules for bathing in the Tiber, posted by the Papal Minister of Police, see Franco Migliori, ed. *Testimonianze di vita romana dell'800*, vol. 3 (Florence: La Nuova Italia, 1969), docs. 1 and 2. Only men were allowed to swim

off the public and private platforms floating on the river; swimmers were "strictly forbidden from being naked either in the water or on the banks of the Tiber for any reason." so that "public decency and morality, which form an important measure of a people's civilization, be respected everywhere and especially in cultured Rome."

72 The population of the ghetto grew from about 3,000 at the beginning of the nineteenth century to about 4,500 at the time of unification. See Bartoccini, *Roma nell'Ottocento*, 1: 87.
73 Ibid., 84–5. She also points out that, at the same time, the Tiber was an enemy during the times of floods.
74 Beccaria, *On Crimes and Punishments*. On Beccaria, see Marcello Maestro, *Cesare Beccaria and the Origins of Penal Reform* (Philadelphia: Temple University Press, 1973); Giovanni Tessitore, *Cesare Beccaria: l'uomo e il mito* (Milan: Franco Angeli, 2008).
75 As in other parts of Europe, various regions of Italy experienced uprisings in 1820, 1830, and 1848.
76 Grantaliano, "Le Carceri Nuove (1658–1883)," 40–1.
77 On the architecture of this annex, which was designed by Valadier, see Tafuri, "Le 'Carceri Nuove' e la casa di correzione per i minorenni," 367, 69.
78 Sui delitti e sulle pene, 20 settembre 1832.
79 Regolamento disciplinale per le case di condanna. (Roma: Stamperia della Rev. Camera Apostolica, 1830) located in AV, Atti della Segretaria del Vicariato, Pachetto 26, Plico 118 (f) E3.
80 Ibid.
81 Enrica Ormanni, "L'estensione a Roma dell'ordinamento giudiziario italiano," in *Studi in occasione del Centennario* (Milan: A. Giuffrè, 1970), 87. In 1847, before the Roman Republic, Pope Pius IX finally granted the city of Rome its own municipal assembly (*consiglio municipale*) of laymen, whose members retained the old titles of senator and conservator. Although not elected, the committee was notable for replacing ecclesiastical with secular control of city government for the first time in centuries (except for parentheses provided by the short-lived Roman republics of 1799 and 1849 and the Napoleonic era).
82 Luigi Cajani has found that executions in eighteenth-century Rome, where learned jurists were swayed by Enlightenment philosophy despite the papal ban on Beccaria's treatise, were not numerous. See Cajani, "Pena di morte e tortura a Roma nel Settecento." This trend toward clemency, however, was reversed during after the restoration in the early nineteenth century.
83 On another notorious execution, that of Giuseppe Monti and Gaetano Tognetti in 1868, see Aldo De Jaco, *Antistoria di Roma Capitale: Cronaca inedita dell'Unità d'Italia* (Rome: Riuniti, 1970), 263–5. De Jaco includes their portraits and a rare photo of the guillotine, which was set up on Via dei Cerchi near Circus Maximus (between pages 224 and 225).
84 Capelli, *La Buona Compagnia*, 30. On the architecture of the House of Correction, see Marta Ghidoli, "La pena detentiva e i suoi spazi architettonici. La Casa di correzione nel sistema carcerario milanese di metà Settecento," *Rivista online di ricerca storica, letteratura e arte*, no. 13 (2010): 1–5.
85 Melossi and Pavarini, *The Prison and the Factory: Origins of the Penitentiary System*: 73–4.
86 Capelli, *La Buona Compagnia*, 77–8. On the Tuscan criminal code of 1786, see Giovanni Berlinguer and Floriana Colao, eds., *La "Leopoldina" nel diritto e nella giustizia in Toscana* (Milan: Giuffrè, 1989).

87 Antonio Parente, "Architettura ed archeologia carceraria: Santo Stefano di Ventotene ed il "Panopticon,"" *Rassegna penitenziaria e criminologica* 3, no. 1 (1999):102.
88 Examples include the Casa di forza in Padua (1807) and the Casa di correzione in Venice (1811). See Capelli, *La Buona Compagnia*, 31.
89 For a short biography of Volpicella, see the *RDC*, 11 (1881): 421-2.
90 Carlo Ilarione Petitti di Roreto, *Saggio sul buon governo della mendicità, degli istituti di beneficenza e delle carceri*, 2 vols. (Turin: Giuseppe Bocca, 1837), 2: 597.
91 Ibid., 453.
92 Ibid., 423-4.
93 Carlo Peri, *Notizie sulla riforma delle prigioni in Toscana*, 2nd ed. (Florence: Tipi della Stamperia nel Carcere delle Murate, 1850), 5.
94 Ibid., 6.
95 Ibid., 8.
96 Ibid., 7-8.
97 Cited in Giovanni Tessitore, *L'utopia penitenziale borbonica. Dalle pene corporali a quelle detentive* (Milan: Franco Angeli, 2002), 175.
98 Ibid., 181.
99 Quoted in Donato Palazzo, "A proposito di 'Riforma delle prigioni' nella prima metà del secolo scorso," *Rassegna di Studi Penitenziari* 20 (1970): 697.
100 Prisons were on the agenda of the scientific congresses of 1841 (in Florence), 1842 (in Padua), and of 1843 (in Lucca).
101 Capelli, *La Buona Compagnia*, 6.
102 Trombetta, *Punizione e carità*, 74, and "Public vices, private remedies in nineteenth-century Italy: Giulia Falletti di Barolo Colbert and Le Forzate," *Journal of Modern Italian Studies* 7, no. 1 (2002): 56-73.
103 For those with life sentences, cellular isolation lasted for the first twenty years.
104 Capelli, *La Buona Compagnia*, 312. The phrase was coined by Ubaldino Peruzzi, a prominent politician and statesman who had represented Tuscany at an early Prison Congress held in 1847 in Brussels.
105 Roberto Didi, *Correggere e non punire. Medicina e carcere nel Risorgimento: Carlo Morelli e il laboratorio di Volterra* (Manduria: Piero Lacaita, 2006), 50.
106 Tessitore, *L'utopia penitenziale borbonica*.
107 The Ucciardone replaced the old Vicaria Prison of Palermo, which was notorious for overcrowding and filth. See Pina Catalanetto, "Il carcere patogeno: Malattie e repressione nella Palermo di primo Ottocento," in *Malattie, terapie, e istituzioni sanitarie in Sicilia*, ed. Istituto di storia moderna della Facoltà di Lettere e Filosofia dell'Università di Palermo (Palermo: iso, 1985).
108 Tessitore, *L'utopia penitenziale borbonica*, 151-2.
109 These *Istruzioni ministeriali* were issued on October 26, 1844, and have been reprinted in ibid., 216-22.

2 The Failed Revolution in Punishment

1 Klopp, *Sentences*, 187.
2 This was partially a misreading of Pellico's memoir, which caused controversy from the time of its publication because he dwelt on his conversion to Christianity rather than defending his political beliefs and those of his fellow *carbonari*.
3 Silvio Pellico, *Le mie prigioni* (Milan: RCS Libri, 1984), 176, 94.

4 For instances of suicidal thoughts, see ibid., 114, 56, 205.
5 Ibid., 224. In another passage, Pellico also uses a similar phrase—"being buried in a prison"—to convey his sense of solitude and hopelessness (51).
6 Leone Carpi, "Prigioni di Stato Borboniche/Prigioni di Stato Austriache," in *Il Risorgimento Italiano: Biografie storico-politiche d'illustri italiani contemporanei*, ed. Leone Carpi (Milan: Antica Casa Editrice/Dottor Francesco Vallardi, 1884), 3: 545. Italics in the original.
7 Ibid.
8 Ibid.
9 On Settembrini, see Klopp, *Sentences*, 87–92.
10 Sigismondo Castromediano, *Carceri e galere politiche: Memorie del Duca Sigismondo Castromediano*, 2 vols. (Lecce: Editrice Salentina, 1895), 1: 11.
11 Ibid., 165.
12 Ibid., 12.
13 Ibid., 318.
14 Ibid., 315.
15 Carpi, "Prigioni di Stato Borboniche/Prigioni di Stato Austriache," 3: 531.
16 Ibid., 532.
17 William E. Gladstone, *Two Letters to the Earl of Aberdeen on the state prosecutions of the Neapolitan government* (New York: J. S. Nichols, 1851), 26. Gladstone did not visit Montefusco and Montesarchio, where conditions were much worse.
18 Jean-Baptiste Paya, *Les Cachots du Pape*, 2nd ed. (Paris: Achille Faure, 1865), 57.
19 Ibid., 62.
20 Ibid., 65.
21 Fiorenza Tarozzi, "I giorni e le notti dalle lunghe ore nel Carcere di San Giovanni in Monte nell'Ottocento," in *Criminalità e controllo sociale a Bologna nell'Ottocento*, ed. Giovanni Greco (Bologna: Pàtron, 1998), 59.
22 Ibid., 57.
23 John Davis, *Conflict and Control: Law and Order in Nineteenth-Century Italy* (Atlantic Highlands, NJ: Humanities Press, 1988), 1.
24 Steven C. Hughes, *Crime, Disorder and the Risorgimento: The Politics of Policing in Bologna* (New York: Cambridge University Press, 1994), 3.
25 On negative tropes in the national discourse about Italian character, see Silvana Patriarca, *Italian Vices: Nation and Character from the Risorgimento to the Republic* (Cambridge: Cambridge University Press, 2010), 14.
26 Alberto M. Banti, *La nazione del Risorgimento. Parentela, santità e onore alle origini dell'Italia unita* (Turin: Einaudi, 2000).
27 Martino Beltrani Scalia, *Sul governo e sulla riforma delle carceri in Italia: Saggio storico e teorico* (Turin: G. Favale, 1868), 395–9.
28 Technically, Italy was a nation of three criminal codes until 1889; Naples remained under the jurisdiction of a third code that will not be discussed here because it closely resembled the dominant Piedmontese code.
29 A modified version of the Sardinian-Piedmontese code of 1859 was extended the formerly Bourbon territories by the Decreto luogotenenziale 17 febbraio 1861.
30 Mario Sbriccoli, "La penalistica civile: Teorie e ideologie del diritto penale nell'Italia unita," in *Stato e cultura giuridica in Italia dall'unità alla repubblica*, ed. Aldo Schiavone (Rome-Bari: Laterza, 1990), 149.
31 James Q. Whitman, *Harsh Justice: Criminal Punishment and the Widening Divide between America and Europe* (New York: Oxford University Press, 2005), 103–7.

32 Crimes were divided into three categories according to severity: *crimini* (serious crimes) and *delitti* (less serious crimes) were adjudicated by courts while *contravvenzioni* (misdemeanors) were punished by police. Reclusion and relegation were punishments for crimes falling into the first category.
33 The sentence of relegation, to be carried out in forts and castles, invoked a medieval notion of honor because of its origins as an aristocratic punishment. In fact, Italian places of relegation were often as dark and dank as institutions for common criminals.
34 Prisoners sentenced to temporary terms of forced labor were exempt from this public humiliation if they had not committed the crimes of armed robbery, extortion, kidnapping, theft, forging of public documents, counterfeiting, or slander (Art. 23).
35 The death penalty, originally abolished in 1786, was restored in Tuscany during the restoration. Used rarely, especially after 1830, it was again abolished in 1859.
36 Capelli, *La Buona Compagnia*, 340–1.
37 Luigi Lacchè, *La giustizia per i galantuomini: Ordine e libertà nell'Italia liberale. Il dibattito sul carcere preventivo (1865-1913)* (Milan: A. Giuffrè Editore, 1990), 34.
38 Both were more serious than a third category of offense, the misdemeanor (*contravvenzione*).
39 Lacchè, *La giustizia per i galantuomini*, 31.
40 On political consciousness among the poor, see Domenico Rizzo, *Gli spazi della morale: Buon costume ed ordine delle famiglie in Italia in èta liberale* (Rome: Biblink, 2004), 192.
41 RD 29 novembre 1866 extended Italy's prison legislation to Rome.
42 Ann. Stat. (1905–7), 378. This total does not include the individuals exiled to island penal colonies by police order, who numbered between three thousand and four thousand but were not included in penal statistics until 1876 (ibid., 379).
43 The number of minors in the prison system exceeded 5 percent because many were held in jails even after conviction because of the insufficient number of reformatories.
44 Ann. Stat. (1881), 530–1; 534–5; and 538.
45 *RDC*, 9 (1879): 333 (Beltrani Scalia).
46 For an excellent analysis of Italy's judicial structure, see Antonella Meniconi, *Storia della magistratura italiana* (Bologna: Il Mulino, 2012).
47 In 1871, 60 percent of jail inmates were suspects and 40 percent convicted criminals. Overall, jails held 61 percent of the prison population in Italy. See Ann. Stat. (1881), 528.
48 Stat. Dec., 112. For the number of *bagni*, see *Actes du congrès penitentiaire de Rome, Novembre 1885*. (Rome: Mantellate, 1887–9), 3 (pt. 1): 601.
49 Ibid.
50 Ibid., 601, 629, and 633.
51 Ann. Stat. (1903–5), 379.
52 Richard Bach Jensen, "Italy's Peculiar Institution: Internal Police Exile, 1861–1914," in *Essays in European History*, ed. June K. Burton (Lanham, MD: University Press of America, 1989).
53 Ann. Stat. (1881), 528–9.
54 Federico Bellazzi, *Prigioni e prigionieri nel Regno d'Italia* (Florence: G. Barbèra, 1866), 13.
55 Ibid.
56 Ibid., 20–1.
57 Ibid., 23.
58 Ibid., 28.

59 *RDC*, 3 (1873): 501 (Atti parl.).
60 RD 19 settembre 1860 (forced labor camps); RD 27 gennaio 1861 (jails); RD 13 gennaio 1862 (penitentiaries); RD 23 agosto 1862 (prisons of relegation); RD 27 novembre 1862 (reformatories). A ministerial decree (Decreto 23 dicembre 1863) regulated Pianosa, the sole agricultural colony inherited from the old regime.
61 Legge sui provvedimenti speciali di pubblica sicurezza 6 luglio 1871.
62 The commission was appointed by RD 16 febbraio 1862.
63 Quoted in Beltrani Scalia, *Sul governo e sulla riforma delle carceri in Italia*, 484.
64 Martino Beltrani Scalia, *Lettera al Sig. Cav. Federico Bellazzi sul libro Prigioni e prigionieri* (Florence: Tipografia delle Murate, 1867), 486.
65 For long-term prisoners, the period of solitary confinement would cease after fourteen years.
66 Beltrani Scalia, *Sul governo e sulla riforma delle carceri in Italia*, 506. The law, Legge 28 gennaio 1864, n. 1653, allowed prisoners to leave their cells for recreation but only in yards where they would continue to be segregated from each other (Art. 1).
67 For the parliamentary committee debates about the Law of 1864, see CD Arch, DPLIC, v. 49, AC 113, 357–86.
68 *RDC*, 2 (1872): 595 (Atti parl.).
69 Ibid., 593. In 1875, Senator Giorgio Tamajo again invoked the name of Gladstone in denouncing the "the stench and lack of air" in several overcrowded Neapolitan prisons. *RDC*, 5 (1875): 69.
70 *RCD*, 2 (1872): 58 (Atti parl.).
71 *RDC*, 5 (1875): 504 (Atti parl.).
72 *RDC*, 6 (1876): 346 (Atti parl.).
73 *RDC*, 5 (1875): 497 (Atti parl.).
74 Bellazzi, *Prigioni e prigionieri nel Regno d'Italia*, 22.
75 Ibid., 38.
76 Ibid. Bellazzi provides a table with the prisoner number (*numero di matricola*) of each boy.
77 Ibid., 28.
78 *RDC*, 5 (1875): 79 (Atti parl.).
79 RD 7 marzo 1878, n. 68.
80 Bellazzi, *Prigioni e prigionieri nel Regno d'Italia*, 27.
81 *RDC*, 5 (1875): 496 (Atti parl.).
82 *RDC*, 5 (1875): 75 (Atti parl.).
83 For example, see *RDC*, 7 (1877): 324–36 (Atti parl.).
84 According to Deputy Speciale, "no civilized country in the world has as many escapes as Italy." (*RDC*, 5 (1875): 80 (Atti parl.)). See also Bellazzi, *Prigioni e prigionieri nel Regno d'Italia*, 86–94.
85 For example, see *RDC*, 5 (1875): 71–113 (Atti parl.).
86 Giovanna Tosatti, "Il Ministero dell'Interno," in *L'amministrazione centrale dall'unità alla Repubblica. Le strutture e i dirigenti*, ed. Guido Melis (Bologna: Il Mulino, 1992), 42–3.
87 The only exception to this continuity was the temporary abolition of the General Direction of Prisons in 1878 (RD 24 febbraio, n. 4306), an administrative gap that lasted less than a year.
88 Regolamento generale per le case di pena del regno, 13 gennaio 1862, Articles 8–14 (hereafter Prison Regulation of 1862).

89 RD che rimette alle facoltà dei prefetti alcuni affari riguardanti il servizio carcerario, 4 febbraio 1877.
90 Ann. Stat. (1881), 548.
91 Ann. Stat. (1881), 548. Of twenty-four hard labor camps, twenty had resident wardens; of thirty-seven penitentiaries, twenty-seven had resident wardens.
92 RD 10 marzo 1871, n. 113, Quadro A. The salary of deputy wardens ranged from 2,500 to 2,800 lire.
93 Salaries ranged from 1,200 to 2,000 lire.
94 Ann. Stat. (1881), 548. Only 39 clerks were employed in jails as compared to 70 in hard labor camps and 102 in penitentiaries.
95 RD 10 marzo 1871, n. 113, Articles 7–13.
96 Ann. Stat. (1881), 548–9.
97 Prison Regulation of 1862, Articles 52–64.
98 In 1871, teachers were paid between 200 and 600 lire; by 1906, their salaries had risen to 1,400–1,500 lire. See RD 10 marzo 1871, n. 113, Quadro A and Legge 30 dicembre 1906, n. 649, Tabella A.
99 For 1871, see Ann. Stat.(1881), 549; for 1912, see Ann. Stat. (1914), 149.
100 RD 10 marzo 1871, n. 133 (serie 2).
101 Prison Regulation of 1862, Article 116, confirmed by the Regolamento pel corpo delle guardie carcerarie, RD 27 luglio 1873, n. 1511, Article 3.
102 The term of enrollment, established as six years under the Regulation of 1862 (Art. 118), was raised to eight years in the Regulation of 1873 (Art. 5).
103 Regolamento per la istituzione di scuole per le guardie carcerarie, RD 27 luglio 1873, n. 1510, Articles 1 and 5.
104 Ann. Stat. (1881), 548–9 and RD 10 marzo 1871, n. 113 (serie 2).

3 Prison Consolidation and Reform

1 For a political biography of Crispi, see Christopher Duggan, *Francesco Crispi: 1818–1901: From Nation to Nationalism* (Oxford: Oxford University Press, 2002).
2 Legge 30 dicembre 1888, n. 5865.
3 Legge 22 dicembre 1888, n. 5849.
4 R.D. 29 marzo 1888, n. 5332. In fact, many lock hospitals were attached to prisons and administered by the prison director.
5 Legge 30 dicembre 1888, n. 5866.
6 Lette 17 luglio 1890, n. 6972.
7 On Lombroso, see Renzo Villa, *Il deviante e i suoi segni: Lombroso e la nascita dell'antropologia criminale* (Milan: Franco Angeli, 1985); Delia Frigessi, *Cesare Lombroso* (Turin: Einaudi, 2003); and Mary Gibson, *Born to Crime: Cesare Lombroso and the Origins of Biological Criminology* (Westport CT: Praeger, 2002).
8 Although classical and positivist criminologists agreed on certain practical issues, they held fundamentally different philosophical principles, employed divergent methodologies, and defined themselves as adhering to opposing juridical camps. I therefore disagree with Paul Garfinkel's recent claim that the two categories are meaningless. See Paul Garfinkel, *Criminal Law in Liberal and Fascist Italy* (Cambridge: Cambridge University Press, 2016), 9–10.

9. Beltrani Scalia served as Director General of Prisons during 1879–85, 1887–91, and 1895–8.
10. On Beltrani Scalia's early career, see Gabriella de Strobel, "La concezione penitenziaria nel pensiero e nell'opera di Martino Beltrani Scalia" (University of Bologna, 1981–2), 9–15, and Stefano Rodotà's entry in the *Dizionario Biografico degli Italiani*, v. 8 (1966) available at http://www.treccani.it/enciclopedia/martino-beltrani-scalia_%28Dizionario-Biografico%29/ (accessed February 5, 2014).
11. Guido Melis, *Storia dell' amministrazione italiana: 1861–1993* (Bologna: Il Mulino, 1996), 49.
12. *RDC*, 21 (1891): 613 (Beltrani Scalia).
13. The earlier journal, *Effemeride Carceraria* (1865–70), was also divided into these same two parts but the "unofficial" section was written mostly by the editor, Inspector Napoleone Vazio, and hewed closely to the policies of the Director General of Prisons.
14. *RDC*, 1 (1871): 3 (Beltrani Scalia).
15. The name of the journal fluctuated after the turn of the twentieth century, sometimes modified to *Journal of Prison and Rehabilitative Sciences* with the subtitle lengthened to include "sociology" and/or "criminal, administrative, and civil law, criminal procedure, and scientific policing."
16. For a list of contributors with their comments on the "Program" see *RDC*, 16 (1886): 9–17.
17. For example, see *RDC*, 8 (1878): 534–58 and 9 (1879): 97–9.
18. *RDC*, 21 (1891): 40 (Beltrani Scalia). For the editorial stance of the journal, see also *RDC*, 22 (1897): 3–7 by Beltrani Scalia and *RDC*, 30 (1905): 1–2; 32 (1907): 1–4; and 33 (1908): 1–2 by Doria.
19. For example, see Beltrani Scalia, *RDC*, 8 (1878): 480 and *RDC*, 9 (1879): 315.
20. For excerpts of *L'uomo delinquente* (1 ed., 1876), see *RDC*, 5 (1875): 113–26; 375–95; 441–8; 516–22. For the reference to Lombroso, see *RDC*, 4 (1874): 117. For the list of "collaborators," see *RDC*, 16 (1886): 9–17.
21. *RDC*, 14 (1884): 126–30 (Beltrani Scalia).
22. *RDC*, 21 (1891): 611–2 (Beltrani Scalia).
23. Beltrani Scalia, *Sul governo e sulla riforma delle carceri in Italia*.
24. *RDC*, 1 (1871): 145–51, 193–205, and 241–51; *RDC*, 2 (1872): 169–75, 247–67; *RDC*, 3 (1873): 105–20, 145–65 (Beltrani Scalia).
25. On Beltrani Scalia's role in the International Prison Congresses, see *RDC*, 34 (1909): 92–5 (Doria); de Strobel, *La concezione penitenziaria nel pensiero e nell'opera di Martino Beltrani Scalia*, 31–8.
26. Before World War I, the International Penitentiary Association held eight congresses: 1872 (London), 1878 (Stockholm), 1885 (Rome), 1890 (St. Petersburg), 1895 (Paris), 1900 (Brussels), 1905 (Budapest), and 1910 (Washington, DC). The congresses continued after World War I with the ninth returning to London in 1925.
27. *RDC*, 29 (1904): 442.
28. *RDC*, 15 (1885): 270 (Pierantoni). Parliament approved 40,000 lire of financial support for the congress.
29. Ibid., 267 (Pierantoni).
30. Opened in 1883, the Palazzo delle Esposizioni di Belle Arti was designed by the Roman architect Pio Piacentini and located on the new artery of Via Nazionale that was built to link the center of Rome with the train station. It was the first Italian building dedicated solely to temporary art exhibitions and still serves that purpose.

The current renovation includes plans to restore the "glass room." See https://english.palazzoesposizioni.it/categorie/categoria-14.
31 Quoted in Epaminonda Querci-Seriacopi, *Il passato, il presente e l'avvenire dell'Amministrazione delle carceri in Italia (Memorie storico-critico-aneddotiche)* (Rome: Tipografia delle Mantellate, 1925), 26.
32 For lists of delegates to both conferences, see *RDC*, 15 (1885): 607–14 and 686–8. Attendance at the Penitentiary Congress (234 official delegates) was much larger than for the Congress of Criminal Anthropology (108).
33 *RDC*, 15 (1885): 57–8 (Canonico).
34 *NA*, 84 (1885): 421 (De Renzis).
35 *RDC*, 15 (1885): 606.
36 *NA*, 84 (1885): 421 (De Renzis).
37 Ibid., 424.
38 *Actes du congrès penitentiaire de Rome, Novembre 1885*, v. 2, pt. 1, 184.
39 Ibid., 185.
40 For a synopsis of Italy's participation in the first six congresses, see *RDC*, 29 (1904): 433–7 (Doria).
41 Cesare Lombroso, *La medicina legale delle alienazioni mentali studiata col metodo sperimentale* (Padua: Prosperini, 1865).
42 *RDC*, 2 (1872): 115 (Lombroso).
43 *RDC*, 6 (1876): 443–4 (Tamburini).
44 At Aversa, only the annex (*sezione per maniaci*) of an existing mental hospital was initially devoted to the criminally insane; after 1890, the entire institution was converted to a full-fledged criminal insane asylum.
45 Stat. Carc. (1904–7), 340–1. The criminal insane asylum was approved as part of a more general regulation on mental hospitals.
46 The Ordinance was 50 percent longer than the Penitentiary Law of 1862 with its 558 articles.
47 Foucault, *Discipline and Punish*, 26. In the Ordinance of 1891, the second section on inmates was composed of 346 articles compared to 218 in the Penitentiary Law of 1862.
48 Ibid., 141.
49 The number of articles in the financial section jumped from 114 in the Penitentiary Law of 1862 to 526 in the Ordinance of 1891.
50 For an overview of the Criminal Code of 1889, see Pietro Nuvolone, "Giuseppe Zanardelli e il codice penale del 1889," in *Giuseppe Zanardellli*, ed. Roberto Chiarini (Milan: Franco Angeli, 1985).
51 Carlo Ghisalberti, *La codificazione del diritto in Italia, 1848–1948* (Rome-Bari, 1994), 171. Beltrani Scalia objected to this complicated hierarchy and instead advocated a "single mode of punishment." See "Addio ai nostri Associati," *RDC*, 21 (1891): 609 (Beltrani Scalia).
52 Sbriccoli, "La penalistica civile: Teorie e ideologie del diritto penale nell'Italia unita," 193.
53 *RDC*, 9 (1879): 190 (Beltrani Scalia).
54 Ibid., 191.
55 Ibid.
56 Ibid.
57 Beltrani Scalia, *Sul governo e sulla riforma delle carceri in Italia*, 11–13.

58 Lombroso, *Criminal Man*: 140. On Lombroso and prison policy, see Mary Gibson, "Cesare Lombroso, Prison Science, and Penal Politics," in *The Lombroso Handbook*, ed. Paul Knepper and P. J. Ystehede (New York: Routledge, 2012): 30–46.
59 Lombroso, *Criminal Man*: 144.
60 Ibid., 143.
61 Ordinance of 1891, Articles 21–8.
62 Ibid., Articles 46–53.
63 Ordinance of 1891, Articles 29–45. The Prison Regulation of 1862 mentions aid societies only briefly in its section about release (Art. 423).
64 Ordinance of 1891, Article 30.
65 Ibid., Article 43.
66 Ordinance of 1891, Article 253; Prison Regulation of 1862, Article 5.
67 The numbers indicated their chronological position in the admission files (Ordinance of 1891, Art. 249).
68 Ordinance of 1891, Tabella G, Annotazioni 5–8.
69 Ibid., Article 249.
70 Ibid., Article 254.
71 Ibid., Article 359. For the list of infractions, see Articles 359–63.
72 Ibid., Article 332.
73 Ordinance of 1891, Articles 366–90.
74 Querci-Seriacopi, *Il passato, il presente e l'avvenire dell'Amministrazione delle carceri in Italia (Memorie storico-critico-aneddotiche)*, 44.
75 *RDC*, 30 (1905): 2 (Doria).
76 *RDC*, 33 (1908): 1 (Doria).
77 *RDC*, 30 (1905): 2 (Doria). Doria emphasized the importance of criminal anthropological studies in his general report to Giolitti in 1904 on the prison system. See *RDC*, 29 (1904): 74.
78 *RDC*, 30 (1905): 1 (Doria).
79 Transcripts of Ottolenghi's lessons were reprinted in a regular column entitled "Figure antropologiche di delinquenti"; see for example *RDC*, 33 (1908): 377–86 and 472–6; 35 (1910): 20–30 and 443–7; and 36 (1911): 155–9, 176–9, and 334–8.
80 *RDC*, 32 (1907): 2 (Doria).
81 On the legal history of pardons, see Monica Stronati, *Il governo della 'grazia': Giustizia sovrana e ordine giuridico nell'esperienza italiana (1848–1913)* (Milan: Giuffrè, 2009). The Criminal Code of 1889 reconfirmed the practice of pardons and amnesties in articles 86–7 and 89.
82 *RDC*, 27 (1902): 166 (Forni).
83 In 1914, the director general continued to complain that the government bypassed the authority of wardens by issuing large numbers of royal pardons. See *RDC*, 39 (1914): 500 (Girardi).
84 The legal term for parole in Italian is *libertà condizionale* (and occasionally *libertà provvisoria*).
85 Criminal Code of 1889, Art. 16. Those who were incarcerated for minor crimes (*detenzione*) could apply after serving half of their sentence.
86 Ordinance of 1891, Article 500.
87 For the use of the word "passport," see *RDC*, 7 (1877): 243 (Atti parl.).
88 Criminal Code of 1889, Article 17 and Ordinance of 1891, Article 502.
89 *RDC*, 6 (1876): 313 (Atti parl.).
90 Ibid.

91 *RDC*, 7 (1877): 159 (Atti parl.).
92 Ibid., 239.
93 Ibid., 153–6 and 253.
94 *RDC*, 8 (1878): 418 (Nocito).
95 Ibid., 420.
96 *RDC*, 7 (1877): 219 (Atti parl.).
97 Ibid., 235.
98 Ibid, 230.
99 Ibid., 238, 243.
100 Ibid., 239, 244.
101 Legge 26 giugno 1904, n. 267, Article 1. Those sentenced to small fines were also eligible for probation.
102 Ibid., Articles 1 and 7. In place of jail, children without families could be assigned to a charity institution before trial.
103 Ibid., Article 5.
104 Ibid., Article 3. Probation could last no more than five years.
105 For a list of international resolutions advocating probation, see *RDC*, 29 (1904): 97 (Atti parl.).
106 Ibid., 106.
107 Ann. Stat. (1905–7, 1911, 1914).
108 *RDC*, 22 (1897): 626, 631 (Beltrani Scalia).
109 Mass amnesties were promulgated almost yearly and designated certain categories of criminals as eligible for reductions of their sentences or early release. For example, see RD 4 giugno 1899, n. 503; RD 31 dicembre 1899, n. 467; RD 11 novembre 1900, n. 366; and RD 1 giugno 1901, n. 187. Individual pardon was much more difficult to obtain; in 1897, only 10 percent of pardon requests were successful. See *RDC*, 23 (1898): 132.
110 *RDC*, 34 (1909): 67.
111 Ibid., 110.
112 Ibid., 120.
113 ACS, M. GG, DGIIP, AA (1896–1905), b. 256, f. 9.
114 *RDC*, 32 (1907): 2 (Doria).
115 In 1905, Doria enumerated his reforms in a report to the International Penitentiary Congress held in Budapest. See *RDC*, 30 (1905): 171–5 (Doria).
116 ACS, MGG, DGIP, AA (1896–1905), b. 256, f. 9 (Doria). New regulations on inmate transfer were outlined by RD 20 dicembre 1906; increase in prison pay by RD 12 febbraio 1911. On his acceleration of inspections, see *RDC*, 29 (1904): 71–2 (Doria). For a long list of Doria's achievements, see *RDC*, 38 (1913): 159–62 (Ferri) and Querci-Seriacopi, *Il passato, il presente e l'avvenire dell'Amministrazione delle carceri in Italia (Memorie storico-critico-aneddotiche)*, 59.
117 *RDC*, 38 (1913): 159–62 (Ferri).
118 RD 2 agosto 1902, n. 377.
119 Criminal Code of 1889, Article 558, which reformed the prescriptions of RD 7 marzo 1878, n. 4328, Articles 21 and 22.
120 *RDC*, 29 (1904): 72–3 (Doria).
121 Querci-Seriacopi, *Il passato, il presente e l'avvenire dell'Amministrazione delle carceri in Italia (Memorie storico-critico-aneddotiche)*, 44.
122 RD 14 novembre 1903, n. 484.
123 For a further discussion of the "D'Angelo case" (*fatto D'Angelo*), see Chapter 4.

124 ACS, MGG, DGIP, AA (1896–1905), b. 256, f. 9.
125 RD 14 novembre 1903, n. 484, Article 5.
126 Ferri wrote approvingly of the elevation of the status of prison doctors in *RDC*, 38 (1913): 160 (Ferri).
127 Italy, CD., *Disegni*, Legis. 21:2 (1902–4), 6: 20–1.
128 "Habitual criminal" was one of Ferri's famous five categories of criminality, and the label was adopted by Lombroso and the rest of the positivist school.
129 Anthony Platt, *The Child Savers: The Invention of Delinquency* (Chicago: University of Chicago Press, 1977).
130 RD 29 novembre 1877, n. 4190 replaced the original Law of 1862 on houses of custody.
131 Legge 3 Luglio 1904, n. 318.
132 RD 24 marzo 1907, n. 122, Article 24.
133 RD 14 luglio 1907, n. 606.
134 The law made an exception for boys under thirteen, who were too young to be held responsible for their illegal behavior.
135 Italy, CD, *Disc.*, Legis. 23:1 (1909–13), 7:7854.
136 Ibid., Legis. 24:1 (1913–19), 3:2433.
137 Doria circulated this draft ordinance to all prison wardens by Circolare 5 novembre 1911 and incorporated some of their opinions into the final draft presented to the Council of State. See ACS, M. GG, DGIP, Studi per la riforma penitenziaria (1897–1930), b., 1, f. 1.
138 Querci-Seriacopi, *Il passato, il presente e l'avvenire dell'Amministrazione delle carceri in Italia (Memorie storico-critico-aneddotiche)*, 61
139 Nominated by DM 3 marzo 1923, this commission was chaired by the Minister of Justice, Oviglio, and included the Director General of Prisons, Giuseppe Spano, and Deputy Enrico Ferri. See ACS, M. GG, DGIP, Studi per la riforma penitenziaria (1897–1930), b. 3, f. 10.
140 Ann. Stat.
141 Gibson, *Born to Crime*, 12–13.
142 Ann. Stat.
143 Ann. Stat. (1909).
144 This figure underestimates the number of minors in the prison system since many continued to be held in adult institutions.
145 In 1910, 62 percent of men and 73 percent of women in long-term penitentiaries had been born in the South. See Stat. Carc. (1910), 90.
146 *RDC*, 39 (1914): 509 (Girardi).
147 Luigi Lucchini, ed. *Il Digesto Italiano. Enciclopedia metodica e alfabetica di legislazione, dottrina e giurisprudenza* (Turin: Unione Tipografico-Editrice, 1906–12), vol. 18, pt. 2, 81–2. DM 16 giugno 1891 outlined the new categories of penal institutions.
148 The special prisons were at Pianosa and Soriano nel Cimino (for the chronically ill) and Montesarchio (for the tubercular). *RDC*, 34 (1909): 11 (Doria).
149 Ann. Stat. and Stat. Carc.
150 Ann. Stat. and Stat. Carc.
151 Congrès Pen., Prosp. Stat, Ann. Stat., and Stat. Carc.
152 The number of forced labor camps rose from twenty-eight in 1871 to forty in 1886 and then declined to thirty-three in 1891, the year of their closure. Some of these were subcamps, which explains their high number.

153 Congrès Pen., Prosp. Stat., Ann. Stat., and Stat. Carc.
154 Stat. Rif. (1912).
155 The number of individuals interned in island penal colonies dropped from 4,011 in 1876 (the first year for which the prison administration published statistics on internal exile) to 1,464 in 1914. See Ann. Stat.
156 Querci-Seriacopi, *Il passato, il presente e l'avvenire dell'Amministrazione delle carceri in Italia (Memorie storico-critico-aneddotiche)*, 55. The office was established by DR 24 giugno 1888. The number of engineers was reduced to five in 1904.
157 Jessie White Mario, "Il sistema penitenziario e il domicilio coatto in Italia," *Nuova Antologia* 154–5 (1896–97): v. 68, p. 697.
158 Ibid., v. 68, p. 698.
159 *RDC*, 23 (1898): 102.
160 *RDC*, 29 (1904): 68.
161 ACS, M GG, DGIP, Studi per la riforma (1897–1930), b. 3, f. 9. This report lists the new jails and reformatories initiated mostly during Doria's administration.
162 *RDC*, 29 (1904): 68 (Doria).
163 The number for both years was forty-seven; for 1871, this number includes the directors of the forced labor camps. In 1914, 69 percent of all penitentiaries had their own wardens compared to 70 percent in 1871.
164 Ann. Stat. and Stat. Carc. By 1912, the penal system employed 5,300 guards; the number for 1871, about 4,200, is less certain because official statistics do not distinguish between male guards and female guardians.
165 Laws of 1871, 1875, 1876, 1877, 1904, 1906, 1907, 1911.
166 An example of the lowly position of prison guards was the requirement that they, like registered prostitutes, undergo weekly medical examinations for venereal disease. Low-ranking soldiers were the only other male group subjected to similar medical control. *RDC*, 18 (1888): 98–9 (Beltrani Scalia).
167 RD 27 luglio 1873, n. 1511, Article 61. In 1873, the salary of guards ranged between 560 and 750 lire per year, far lower than the required 3,000 lire in property required for marriage.
168 *RDC*, 3 (1873): 261 (Cantelli). The Civil Code of 1865 secularized marriage by transferring the power of licensing marriage from the Church to the state.
169 RD 24 marzo 1907, n. 150, Article 11. Alternatively, a wife's wages from a steady occupation could replace the minimal property requirement. Before 1907, the director general suspended the dowry requirements several times. For instructions on suspending the dowry requirement, see M. Int., DGC., Circolare 24 aprile 1901, 8 agosto 1903, 30 gennaio 1905, and 31 agosto 1906.
170 Andrea Marinelli, *Memoriale sull'ordinamento del Personale di Custodia degli Stabilimenti Carcerari e dei Riformatorii Governativi del Regno*, 2nd ed. (Catania: Giuseppe Russo, 1899), 4, 9. Italics are in the original text.
171 *RDC*, 31 (1906): 478 (Doria) and 32 (1907): 150–2.
172 *RDC*, 39 (1914): 494 (Girardi).
173 RD 24 marzo 1907, n. 150, Article 123.
174 Ibid., Article 119.
175 *RDC*, 35 (1910): 346, 348 (Conti).
176 David J. Rothman, *Conscience and Convenience: The Asylum and Its Alternatives in Progressive America* (Boston: Little, Brown, 1980), 5. For a darker interpretation of this new "therapeutic" approach to crime, see Edgardo Rotman, "The Failure of Reform: United States, 1865–1965," in *The Oxford History of the Prison: The*

Practice of Punishment in Western Society, ed. Norval Morris and David J. Rothman (New York: Oxford University Press, 1998).

177 Sean McConville, "The Victorian Prison: England, 1865–1965," in *The Oxford History of the Prison: the Practice of Punishment in Western Society*, ed. Norval Morris and David J. Rothman (New York: Oxford University Press, 1998), 131.

178 For France, see Robert Badinter, *La prison républicaine (1871–1914)* (Paris: Fayard, 1992) and O'Brien, *The Promise of Punishment*.

179 For example, see Carlos Aguirre, *The Criminals of Lima and Their Worlds: The prison experience, 1850–1935* (Durham NC: Duke University Press, 2005), Frank Dikötter, *Crime, Punishment and the Prison in Modern China* (New York: Columbia University Press, 2002), and Botsman, *Punishment and Power in the Making of Modern Japan*.

180 For example, see Peter Zinoman, *The Colonial Bastille: A History of Imprisonment in Vietnam, 1862–1940* (Berkeley: University of California Press, 2001) and Florence Bernault, ed. *A History of Prison and Confinement in Africa* (Portsmouth, NH: Heinemann, 2003).

181 On Spain and Portugal, see Tiago Pires Marques, *Crime and the Fascist State, 1850–1940* (London: Pickering & Chatto, 2013), 23–4; on Russia, see Bruce E. Adams, *The Politics of Punishment: Prison reform in Russia, 1863–1917* (DeKalb: Northern Illinois University Press, 1996).

4 Women and the Convent Prison

1 Civil Code of 1865, Article 131.
2 For the prescriptions of *autorizzazione maritale*, see Civil Code of 1865, Articles 134–7. According to Article 135, part 3, female merchants were exempted from most of the limitations on carrying out financial transactions. These exceptions are spelled out in the Commercial Codes of 1865 and 1882.
3 Civil Code of 1865, Articles 220–39 (*patria podestà*).
4 Civil Code of 1865, Articles 148–58 (on marital separation). On Italian divorce laws, see Mark Seymour, *Debating Divorce in Italy: Marriage and the Making of Modern Italians, 1860–1974* (New York: Palgrave Macmillan, 2006).
5 Maria Laetitia Riccio, "Donna (Diritto privato e pubblico)," in *Nuovo Digesto Italiano* (Turin: UTET, 1938), 5: 213. The most progressive preunification code in terms of gender was that of Austria, which allowed elite women in Lombardy and the Veneto to exercise local, administrative suffrage.
6 The restrictions on civil testimony were abrogated by Legge 9 dicembre 1877, n. 4176. For a discussion of its passage, see Giovanni Castellari, *Della condizione giuridica della donna secondo il codice italiano* (Turin: Vincenzo Bona, 1877), 176–80.
7 Criminal Code of 1889, Article 354.
8 Criminal Code of 1889, Article 369 (infanticide) and Article 385 (abortion).
9 This exact wording was contained in both Articles 369 and 385. On honor crimes from the male perspective, see Steven C. Hughes, *Politics of the Sword: Dueling, Honor, and Masculinity in Modern Italy* (Columbus: Ohio State University Press, 2007).
10 Criminal Code of 1889, Article 21.
11 Criminal Code of 1889, Article 23.
12 Enrico Pessina, *Il nuovo Codice Penale Italiano con brevi note dilucidative* (Milan: Hoepli, 1890), 70.

13 Marina Graziosi, "Infirmitas sexus: La donna nell'immaginario penalistico," *Democrazia e diritto*, no. 2 (1993):106–7.
14 Prison Regulation of 1862, Articles 84–93 and Articles 99–102.
15 Ibid., Article 192.
16 Ordinance of 1891, Articles 148–60.
17 Ibid., Article 148.
18 Ibid., Article 202f. This was one of several (Arts. 201, 202, 203, 205, and 557) that applied both to male guards and nuns.
19 On the history of Rome, see Italo Insolera, *Roma moderna. Un secolo di storia urbanistica, 1870–1970* (Turin: Einaudi, 1993); Bartoccini, *Roma nell'Ottocento. Il tramonto della "città santa". La nascita di una capitale*; and Vittorio Vidotto, *Roma contemporanea* (Rome-Bari: Laterza, 2001).
20 Roma, Direzione Comunale di Statistica, *Rapporto complementare sul censimento di Roma* (Rome: Salviucci, 1872), Allegato 8. The figure for 1871 comes from the first census of Rome conducted after unification. According to the census of 1911, Rome numbered 542,123, an increase of 122 percent.
21 Angiolina Arrù, "Il prezzo della cittadinanza. Strategie di integrazione nella Roma pontificia," *Quaderni storici* 91 (1996): 160.
22 Roma, Direzione Comunale di Statistica, *Rapporto preliminare sul censimento di Roma* (Rome: Salviucci, 1872), 6. The original fourteen districts of Rome were Monti, Trevi, Colonna, Campomarzio, Ponte, Parione, Regola, S. Eustaschio, Pigna, Campitelli, S. Angelo, Trastevere, Ripa, and Borgo.
23 *Rapporto complementare sul censimento di Roma*: 12.
24 Morichini, *Degli istituti di carità per la sussistenza e l'educazione dei poveri e dei prigionieri in Roma*, 543–65. On Trastevere as a neighborhood of institutions of enclosure, see Chiara Lucrezio Monticelli, "Trastevere come spazio della reclusione tra XVIII e XIX secolo: Il carcere femminile di San Michele a Ripa," in *Trastevere: Un analisi di lungo periodo*, ed. Letizia Ermini Pani and Carlo Travaglini (Rome: Società Romana di Storia Patria alla Biblioteca Vallicelliana, 2010).
25 Gabriella Zarri, "Fra costrizione e devozione: aspetti dello sviluppo dei monasteri femminili tra Quattrocento e Cinquecento," in *La Chiesa e il potere politico dal Medioevo all'età contemporanea*, ed. G. Chittolini and Giovanni Miccoli, (Turin: Einaudi, 1986), 399–424.
26 Marina Caffiero, "Femminile/popolare: La femminilizzazione religiosa nel Settecento tra nuove congregazioni e nuove devozioni," *Dimensioni e problemi della ricerca storica*, no. 2 (1994):236–7. For an overview of changes in female religious orders in the modern period, see Giancarlo Rocca, *Donne religiose. Contributo a una storia della condizione femminile in Italia nei secoli XIX–XX* (Rome: Paoline, 1992).
27 ACS, M. Int., DGC., AA (1896–1905), b. 78, f. 1-A.
28 See the list of "Convenzioni colle Suore di Carità" in M. Int., DGC., AA (1896–1905), b. 78, fasc. 1-A.
29 Bruna Amendola and Laura Indrio, eds., *Villa Altieri sull'Esquilino a Roma* (Rome: Bonsignori, 2009), 33–50. Roman villas traditionally were divided into an urban part (*pars urbana*), for the palace and manicured gardens, and a rustic part (*pars rustica*) for orchards, vines, and fields.
30 Although the exact dates of construction are subject to debate, etchings of Villa Altieri appeared by 1780; Nolli's famous map of 1748 is the first to confirm the existence of a villa on the extensive holdings of the Altieri family near Santa Croce.

31 When elevated to Cardinal, Camillo Massimo Altieri, the future pope, moved the family residence to Piazza Gesù and initiated the construction of the large and imposing Palazzo Altieri. The architect, Giovanni Antonio de Rossi, was subsequently hired by his nephew to design the rural villa. See http://www.060608.it/en/cultura-e-svago/beni-culturali/beni-architettonici-e-storici/palazzo-altieri.html, accessed October 22, 2015.
32 Amendola and Indrio, *Villa Altieri sull'Esquilino a Roma*, 43–7.
33 The first railway station in Rome at Termini, named after the nearby springs or *terme*, was initiated by Pope Pius IX in 1867 and finished by the Italian state in 1874. The original structure was torn down and replaced in the 1930s by Mussolini.
34 Paolo Bardi, *Roma piemontese (1870–1876)* (Roma: Bardi Editore, 1970), 173.
35 http://www.catholic.com/encyclopedia/frederic-francois-xavier-ghislain-de-merode, accessed March 5, 2016. On De Mérode, see also his entry in the Enciclopedia Treccani (http://www.treccani.it/enciclopedia/frederic-francois-xavier-de-merode_%28Dizionario-Biografico%29/), accessed March 5, 2016.
36 Amendola and Indrio, *Villa Altieri sull'Esquilino a Roma*, 57.
37 For maps of each floor, as well as the new guardhouse, see ibid., 56.
38 See ASR, Casa di detenzione alle Terme Diocleziane (1817–91), b. 160 for correspondence about Domenico Brasan, a male guard at Villa Altieri.
39 The early prisoner dossiers from Diocletian's Baths were simply slipped into new folders marked "Villa Altieri," showing the continuity in religious management.
40 Stat. Carc. (1870–95). Unless otherwise noted, all government statistics refer to total numbers recorded by Italian authorities on December 31 of each year.
41 Of the women in the earlier sample (1871–76), 63 percent had committed property crimes and 26 percent violent crimes; in the later sample (1889–92), the situation was reversed with 35 percent convicted of property crimes and 49 percent of violent crime. ASR, Casa Penale Femminile di Villa Altieri, b. 203, 253, 254, 255.
42 ASR, Villa Altieri, b. 203, f. 170.
43 Ibid., b. 203, f. 45.
44 Ibid., f. 196 and 197.
45 Ibid., f. 26.
46 See ibid., f. 149 for the case of Domenica Olivieri, who was arrested for defrauding Pietro Frattali di Collebaccaro by claiming that she would make him rich "through direct communication between herself and the spirit world."
47 Ibid., f. 172.
48 Ibid.
49 Ibid., f. 159.
50 For a case of abortion where the penalty was decreased "for reasons of honor," see ibid., f. 150.
51 Ibid., f. 40. Her original sentence of fifteen years was reduced by two-thirds.
52 Ibid., f. 160.
53 See also ibid., f. 188 for another case of violence committed "in a fit of rage" by Rosalia Pezzutti.
54 For conviction of brigandage, see ibid, f. 18 (Angiola Giorgi) and f. 38 (Teresa Costanzi).
55 The percent residing in rural areas was 60 percent in the 1870s and 79 percent in the 1890s.
56 ASR, Villa Altieri, b. 203.

57 65 percent of the early group were married or widowed, a rate that increased to 72 percent in the later group.
58 In the early group, two-thirds of married women and over half the widows had children.
59 ASR, Villa Altieri, b. 203, f. 149 (Olivieri) and 40 (Noce); for other examples, see f. 32 (Fortunata Prosperi); f 29 (Teresa Costanzi); and f. 23 (Giuseppa Neri).
60 These include Campania, Calabria, Basilicata, Molise, Puglia, and Abruzzo.
61 During the early 1880s, the number of inmates sometimes exceeded the official limit but only by a few extra women.
62 Stat. Carc.
63 For example, see the dossiers of Filomena Gallo (Matricola # 183), Margherita De Felici (# 173), Olimpia Marinelli (#157) in ASR, Casa penale Femminile di Villa Altieri, b. 203.
64 Statistics on education and prison libraries for individual prisons are available only for the 1870s and the early 1880s. Stat. Carc.
65 ASR; in the early group, 57 percent were destitute and 41 percent poor; in the second group, destitution had grown to 91 percent.
66 ASR, 1870s and 1890s. In the latter group, 19 percent declared themselves to be housewives but this category often overlapped with agricultural workers.
67 Stat. Carc.
68 ASR, Terme Diocleziane, Amministrazione delle carceri di Roma (1853–71), b. 78 and 137.
69 *RDC*, 21 (1891): 31 (Atti parl).
70 Ibid., 126.
71 No disciplinary council seems to have been organized at Villa Altieri despite its requirement by the Ordinance of 1891. See Stat. Carc. (1897), 188 and 191, where all punishments for 1894–5 are attributed directly to the prison director.
72 ASR, Villa Altieri, b. 203, f. 40 (Noce); f. 38 (De Barrè); and f. 31 (Benigni).
73 This pattern of relatively light sentences for women shows continuity with the Papal States; in 1834, only 6 out of 107 women in San Michele had been sentenced to more than three years. See Archivio del Vicariato, Atti della Segretaria del Vicariato [San Michele], Palchetto 26, Plico 41, f. 13.
74 ASR, Villa Altieri, b. 203, f. 160 (Bocci) and f. 9 (Napoleoni).
75 On an average, 36 percent completed their sentences but this rate varied widely since in certain years, amnesties effectively emptied prisons of inmates nearing the end of their sentences (Stat. Carc.). During the years immediately following unification, Italian justice officials frequently complained about incomplete records inherited from their papal predecessors, which complicated the calculation of release times. See ASR, Villa Altieri, b. 203, f. 40 (Noce), f. 17 (Di Cosimo), f. 7 (Periponi), and f. 4 (Zaccari).
76 Only during the first few years after the establishment of Villa Altieri were women released without any funds; thus their plight seems to have improved slightly with unification.
77 *RDC*, 22 (1897): 15–16 (Boll. Uff.).
78 Morichini, *Degli istituti di carità per la sussistenza e l'educazione dei poveri e dei prigionieri in Roma*, 692–3.
79 Grantaliano, "Le Carceri Nuove (1658–1883)," 41.
80 Morichini, *Degli istituti di carità per la sussistenza e l'educazione dei poveri e dei prigionieri in Roma*.

81 On the Buon Pastore and other conservatories of Rome, see Angela Groppi, *I conservatori della virtù: Donne recluse nella Roma dei Papi* (Rome-Bari: Laterza, 1994). The penal functions of the Buon Pastore are discussed in Chapter 6.
82 Cardinal Giacomo Rospigliosi and the aristocratic Borghese family offered financial support for the building of the first convent. The Sisters of the Visitation had been founded by S. Giovanna Maria Francesca Fremiot di Chantal.
83 The Serve di Maria were dedicated to the tradition the Florentine saint, Giuliana Falconieri (1270–1341). In official state documents, the building was designated the Monastero della S. Maria Addolorata.
84 ACS, M. Lav, Segretariato generale, Roma capitale, b. 15, f. 13. Quote is from the expropriation law for Rome (DR 26 genn. 1873) that drew on the earlier Legge 25 giugno 1865, n. 2359 for the rest of the kingdom.
85 A list of the Roman monasteries and convents liable to appropriation (approved by the Civil Court of Rome on May 8, 1873) as well as a description of their lands and buildings can be found in ACS, M. Lav., Seg. Gen., Roma capitale, b. 15, f. 13.
86 ACS, M. Lav., Seg. Gen., Roma Capitale, b. 59, f. 29.
87 Ibid. The property was bordered by Via delle Mantellate on the north, Vicolo Lante on the west, Vicolo di San Francesco di Sales on the south, and the Monastery of Regina Coeli on the east.
88 Ibid.
89 Ibid. The inventory includes several maps of the property, which show a variety of outbuildings in addition to the monastery and its church. The church is sometimes designated as Santa Maria della Visitazione after the earlier order of Salesian nuns.
90 Ibid.
91 Ibid.
92 ACS, M. Int., DGFC, Corporazioni religiose (1855–1929), b. 82, posizione 179. At state expense, the Mantellate nuns were moved first to Via S. Agata dei Goti and later, after their number had fallen to six, to share the Monastery of the Paolotte.
93 ACS, M. Int., DGC., AA (1896–1905), b. 78, f. 56-A (contract of 1895); f. 1-A (contract of 1872).
94 The phrase is from the 1872 (Art. 4).
95 Stat. Carc.
96 About 10 percent of all convicts in the Mantellate received sentences of more than two years.
97 In 1914, the Mantellate had 13 dormitories to house 100 inmates and 20 individual cells. Stat. Carc. (1914), 330–1.
98 According to personnel forms, some of which are missing, at least twelve nuns retired while twenty-one were hired at the Mantellate between 1890 and 1900. ACS, M.Int., DGC, AA. (1896–1905), b. 78, f. 56-A.
99 ACS, M. Int., DGC., AA. (1896–1905), b. 365, f. 55.
100 ACS, M. GG, DGIP, AA. (1906–25), b. 465, f. 55.
101 Ibid.
102 ACS, M. Int., DGC, AA (1896–1905), b. 153, f. 56D.
103 Ibid., b. 207, f. 55a.
104 Ibid., b. 365, f. 55.
105 ACS, M. GG, DGIP, AA (1906–25), b. 157, f. 55.
106 ACS, M. Int., DGC, AA (1896–1905), b. 365, f. 55.
107 Ibid.

108 For a coffee-table book extolling fascist penal policy, see Dino Grande, *Bonifica umana*, 2 vols. (Rome: Mantellate, 1941).
109 Isa Mari, *Roma, Via delle Mantellate* (Rome: Corso, 1953), 8–9 (floor plans). I want to thank Dottoressa Assunta Borzacchiello of the Department of Penitentiary Administration for lending me her copy of this rare book.
110 For the original lyrics by Giorgio Strehler and Fiorenzo Carpi, and the slightly modified versions sung by Vanoni and later Gabriella Ferri, see http://lyrics.wikia.com/wiki/Ornella_Vanoni:Le_Mantellate (accessed March 16, 2016).
111 The bell was originally cast in 1835 for the New Prison and later transferred to the Mantellate.
112 Bellazzi, *Prigioni e prigionieri nel Regno d'Italia*, 23.
113 For the number of penitentiaries, see Stat. Carc. (1862–1914). After the closing of the Ambrogiana, a second women's penitentiary was opened in Florence (Santa Verdiana) in 1884. The three remaining women's penitentiaries on the eve of World War I were located in Venice, Perugia, and Trani.
114 On the closing of the Messina penitentiary, see Italy, CD, *Disegni*, Legis. 23:1 (1909–13), v. 2, N. 25A, 265 bis A, and 26 ter A, p. 7. On the closing of penitentiaries at Florence and Turin, because of insufficient inmates, see *RDC*, 37 (1912): 213 (Doria).
115 *RDC*, 35 (1910): 263–4. This new structure, planned for Turin, was motivated not by the abysmal conditions of female inmates but instead the desire to clean up the city for the fiftieth anniversary of Italian unification.
116 Somm. Stat. (1958), 102.
117 Stat. Carc.
118 Somm. Stat. (1958); Ann. Stat.
119 Ann. Stat.
120 Ministero dell'Interno (Piemonte), *Relazione del Consiglio Generale delle Carceri al Minstero dell'Interno sullo stato e sulle condizioni delle carceri giudiziarie* (Turin: G. Favale e Compagnia, 1852), 181.
121 Ibid., 44.
122 This principle was also incorporated into the Regolamento pel Corpo delle guardie carcerarie, n. 1511 (27 luglio 1873), Article 2: "Internal duties in women's prisons will be carried out by persons of their own sex."
123 Stat. Carc.
124 Stat. Carc.
125 Exact comparisons are difficult because the categorization of regions changed in 1881. For penitentiaries, Southerners comprised over 55 percent of all female inmates in 1871 and exactly 69 percent in 1914.
126 Stat. Carc.
127 Stat. Carc.
128 Stat. Carc.
129 On the large network of foundling homes in nineteenth-century Italy, see David Kertzer, *Sacrificed for Honor: Italian Infant Abandonment and the Politics of Reproductive Control* (Boston: Beacon, 1993).
130 Stat. Carc. (1871).
131 Stat. Carc.
132 Stat. Carc.
133 Stat. Carc.
134 Stat. Carc. The number of separate sleeping cells increased significantly for a short period at the turn of the twentieth century. However, the large majority of female

penitentiary inmates always lived in large dormitories, as did those in local jails. On the prevalence of dormitories, see also. See also *RDC*, 2 (1872): 391–2.
135 M. GG, DGIP, AA (1906–25), b. 482, f. 21. See also *RDC*, 3 (1873): 501 (Atti parl.).
136 *RDC*, 2 (1872): 390 and *RDC*, 17 (1887): 255 (Atti parl.).
137 Stat. Carc.
138 Stat. Carc.
139 Stat. Carc. Beginning in 1902, official statistics did not break down the size of libraries by gender.
140 Stat. Carc.
141 Ann. Stat., 1903 (1905–7), 392. For a detailed report on women's work in the penitentiaries of Perugia and Trani, see Italy, Direzione delle Carceri e dei Riformatori, "Il lavoro negli stabilimenti carcerari e nei RR riformatori" (Roma, Tipografia Mantellate, 1923), 393–404 and 458–62.
142 In 1871, Italian female prisoners earned 31 *centesimi* daily comparted to 83–85 *centesimi* for their French counterparts. See *RDC*, 3 (1872): 496–7 (Atti parl.).
143 Stat. Carc.
144 Ordinance of 1891, Article 320.
145 Ibid., Article 317.
146 The number of visits for those in reclusion increased to four per year after the first stage of confinement. See Ordinance of 1891, Article 305.
147 For the rules on personal visits to inmates, see ibid., Articles 302–15.
148 Ibid., Article 311.
149 In 1883, Deputy Pierantoni described his recent visit to the Women's Penitentiary in Perugia, during which many inmates asked him to write to their hometown mayors, often in the South, for news of their children. See *RDC*, 13 (1883): 287 (Atti parl.)
150 Stat. Carc.
151 Congrès Pen. (1885), 608–11.
152 Stat. Carc.
153 Ordinance of 1891, Articles 304 (visits) and 317 (correspondence).
154 Ibid., Article 314.
155 Ibid., Article 321.
156 Ibid., Articles 382, 387, 387, and 389.
157 Stat. Carc. (1870–88 with gaps).
158 Stat. Carc. Comparison of 1863–83 (average 5.53 percent) with 1896–1914 (average 3.76 percent).
159 Stat. Carc. Average for 1896–1901 was 3.1 percent; for 1902–14, 10.3 percent.
160 For a useful overview of modern Italian women's history, see Perry Willson, *Women in Twentieth-Century Italy* (Houndmills, Basingstoke: Palgrave Macmillan, 2010).
161 Claudia Frattini, *Il primo congresso delle donne italiane, Roma, 1908: Opinione pubblica e femminismo* (Rome: Biblink, 2008).
162 On "practical feminism" in Italy, see the pioneering article by Annarita, "La filantropia come politica. Esperienze dell'emancipazionismo italiano nel Novecento," in *Ragnatele di rapporti. Patronage e reti di relazione nella storia delle donne*, ed. Lucia Ferrante (Turin: Ronsenberg & Sellier, 1988). Feminist organizational activity is analyzed in FiorenzaTaricone, *L'Associazionismo femminile in Italia dall'Unità al fascismo* (Milan: Unicopli, 1996).
163 *RDC*, 7 (1877): 371–2 (Carpenter); *RDC*, 17 (1887): 372–9 (Concezione Arenal).
164 *Actes du congrès penitentiaire de Rome, Novembre 1885*, 3 (pt. 2): 411–13.

165 For the life and work of Regina Terruzzi, see Federica Falchi, *L'itinerario politico di Regina Terruzzi: Dal mazzinianesimo al fascismo* (Milan: Franco Angeli, 2008).
166 The father of her son, the Sicilian physician Gargitano, refused to marry her or support the child. See ibid., 46–7.
167 Regina Terruzzi, *Una visita alle recluse* (Naples: Tipografia "monsignor Perrelli", 1906), 25.
168 Ibid., 16.
169 Ibid., 11.
170 Ibid., 26.
171 Ibid., 26.
172 Adriana Tartarini Masellis, "Zina Centa Tartarini (Rossana), 1866–1948" in "Schede delle donne presentate al convegno 150 anni," www.consiglio.regione.lazio.it (accessed July 4, 2016).
173 Rossana, "Case penali per donne," *Nuova Antologia* 62 (1912): 658–70. For her more extended analysis, see *Sotto la ferula: Dolore, povertà, degenerazione muliebre* (Turin: Fratelli Bocca, 1911).
174 The play, "Casa di pena," was first performed in 1908 and published in 1909. See *RDC*, 34 (1909): 272.
175 Rossana, "Case penali per donne," 663–4.
176 Ibid., 662.
177 Ibid., 664.
178 Ibid., 667.
179 On the life and political activities of Maria Rygier, see Barbara Montesi, *Un'"anarchica monarchica": Vita di Maria Rygier (1885–1953)* (Naples: Edizioni Scientifiche Italiane, 2013). Rygier later moved to the right, becoming an interventionist during World War I and later a monarchist. After World War II, she joined the moderate Liberal Party.
180 Maria Rygier, "Il monachismo nelle carceri femminili: La Casa penale di Torino," *Il Grido del Popolo*, n. 245 (April 10, 1909): 1.
181 Ibid.
182 Ibid.
183 Ibid.
184 Ibid.
185 Ibid.
186 See Daniela Rossini, *Donne e propaganda internazionale: Percorsi femminili tra Italia e Stati Uniti nell'età della Grande Guerra* (Milan: Franco Angeli, 2015), 170–92, for an excellent discussion of Ronconi's feminism and establishment of the *Opera di Vita Morale*.
187 "Il voto alle donne. Dal Camera dei Comuni a Piazza Fiametta," in AARP, Fondo Ronconi, busta 5, fasc. 2, doc. #31.
188 Sofia Bisi Albini, "La festa delle culle nel carcere," *La Tribuna*, 22-1-1910 located in AARP, Fondo Ronconi, busta 5, fasc. 2, doc. #52.
189 Diego Pasquali, "Lina Pennesi e l'assistenza femminile alle donne carcerate a Roma durante il fascismo" (Tesi di laurea, Università degli Studi Roma Tre, 2011–12), 55.
190 "Certificato di Prof. Alessandro Regnoli 28-1-12." This description, as well as articles from *La Tribuna* and *Il Messaggero* about the lecture, can be found in AARP, Fondo Ronconi, b. 5, f. 2.
191 "Dagli Atti del Congresso Internazionale Femminile, Roma 16–23 maggio 1914," located in AARP, Fondo Ronconi, b. 2, fasc. 3.

192 Albini, "La feste delle culle."
193 Dagli Atti del Congresso Internazionale Femminile," AARP, Fondo Ronconi, b. 2, f. 3.
194 ACS, MGG, DGIP, AA. (1906–25), b. 190, f. 63.
195 *RDC*, 34 (1909): 8 (Doria).
196 *RDC*, 34 (1909): 272.
197 *RDC*, 40 (1915): 161–2 (Boll. Uff.).
198 "Lettera a G. Ronconi dal direttore delle Carceri Giudiziarie," 5-1-2012, AARP, b. 1, f. 7.
199 Certificato di Prof. Alessandro Regnoli, 28-1-2012, AARP, b. 5, f. 2.
200 Lettera a G. Ronconi dal directtore generale delle carceri e riformatori, 20-10-1920, AARP, b. 1, f. 7.
201 ACS, M GG, DGIP, AA (1906–25), b. 190, f. 46.
202 ACS, MGG, DGIP, AA (1906–25), b. 190, f. 67.
203 Ibid.
204 M GG, DGIP, AA. (1906–25), b. 109, f. 67.
205 Ibid.
206 Ibid.
207 ACS, M GG, DGIP, AA (1906–25) b. 427, f. 63.
208 ACS, M Int., DGC, AA (1896–1905) b. 78, f. 68A.
209 ACS, M GG, DGIP, Atti ammin. (1906–25), b. 109, f. 67.
210 *RDC*, 35 (1910): 77. For related reports at the 1908 congress, see Consiglio Nazionale delle Donne Italiane, *Atti del 1 Congresso nazionale delle donne italiane (Rome, 24–30 aprile 1908)* (Rome: Società Editrice Laziale, 1912), 258–63 (Berta Turin, "La tratta delle bianche") and 284–9 (Guglielmina Ronconi, "La protezione della giovinetta").
211 *RDC*, 35 (1910): 77.
212 *RDC*, 38 (1913): 258–60 (Ferriani).
213 Rossini, *Donne e propaganda internazionale*, 120.

5 Men: From Chains to the Penitentiary

1 Decreto 7 marzo 1878 (Regolamento disciplinare per i condannati che scontano la pena dei lavori forzati).
2 Decreto 7 marzo 1878, Article 3.
3 Ibid., Articles 76 and 77.
4 *RDC*, 27 (1902): 329 (Ronchetti).
5 RD 6 gennaio 1887, n. 4318, Article 3.
6 *RDC*, 21 (1891): 610 (Beltrani Scalia).
7 *RDC*, 10 (1880): 187, 188 (Beltrani Scalia).
8 Ibid., 188.
9 Steven C. Hughes, "The Theory and Practice of Ozio in Italian Policing: Bologna and Beyond," *Criminal Justice History* 7 (1986): 89–103.
10 *RDC*, 6 (1876): 85 (Atti parl.).
11 For examples of executive support, see *RDC*, 5 (1875): 97–8 (Atti parl.).
12 *RDC*, 8 (1878): 293 (Atti parl.). For a similar argument, see the report of Deputy Giuseppe Mussi (*RDC*, 9 (1897): 59 (Atti parl.)).
13 *RDC*, 26 (1901): 30 (Atti parl.).

14 For the text of the proposed law, see *RDC*, 26 (1901): 36–7 (Atti parl.).
15 Legge 26 giugno 1904, n. 283 sul lavoro dei condannati all'aperto. Under certain conditions, agricultural colonies could now admit convicts sentenced to reclusion, detention, and arrest.
16 *RDC*, 28 (1903): 29 (Atti parl.).
17 Direzione Generale delle Carceri e dei Riformatori, Ministero dell'Interno, *La colonizzazione interna nelle sue applicazioni col mezzo delle Colonie penali agricole* (Rome: Mantellate, 1912), 216.
18 Alfredo Gambardella, "Nascita ed evoluzione delle colonie penali agricole durante il Regno D'Italia," *Rassegna penitenziaria e criminologica*, no. 1 (2008): 39.
19 Atti parl., CD, Discussione sul bilancio del Ministero dell'Interno, 8 aprile 1905, 239–41 (Lucchini).
20 Ibid., 239.
21 Gambardella, "Nascita ed evoluzione delle colonie penali agricole durante il Regno D'Italia," 48.
22 *RDC*, 31 (1906): 161 (Gianturco). For this multipart analysis of Italy's prison system, see *RDC*, 31 (1906): 36–70, 104–12, and 156–62.
23 *RDC*, 31 (1908): 451 and 36 (1911): 265 (Doria).
24 Criminal Code of 1889, Articles 12 and 13. For reclusion, the first stage constituted a proportion of the overall duration of the sentence.
25 Ordinance of 1891, Article 247. For the rules on silence, see the Criminal Code of 1889 (Arts. 12 and 13) and the Ordinance of 1891 (Art. 247).
26 Inmates sentenced to reclusion received two-fifths and those in detention, one-half (Ordinance of 1891, Art. 287).
27 Manfredi Porena, *Roma Capitale nel decennio della sua adolescenza (1880–1890)* (Rome: Edizioni di Storia e Letteratura, 1957), 30–1. Born in 1873, Porena describes the changing nature of Rome in the 1880s, a period that he dubs "the adolescence of *Roma capitale*" (4).
28 Emma Perodi is cited in Bardi, *Roma piemontese (1870–1876)*, 346. On De Mérode, see Bartoccini, *Roma nell'Ottocento. Il tramonto della "città santa". La nascita di una capitale*, 115.
29 Atti del Consiglio Comunale di Roma (1870–1) 1: 96–102.
30 ACS, M. Lav., Seg. Gen., Opere governative ed edilizie per Roma, b. 154, f. 419.
31 Ibid.
32 Domenico Orano, *Come vive il popolo a Roma: Saggio demografico sul quartiere Testaccio* (Pescara: Ettore Croce-Casa Editrice Abruzzese, 1912), 51.
33 Because of an absence of a municipal population register, Orano collected the statistics by knocking on the doors of over two thousand families. As a member of a philanthropic committee, he founded a number of social welfare institutions in Testaccio including a school, recreational club for youth, and a center for distributing food to mothers and children. See ibid., XIII, XVI.
34 Ibid., XI.
35 Ibid., 469.
36 Ibid., 228.
37 Ibid., 517.
38 Daniela Rossini, "Esperienze di assistenza femminile nei quartieri popolari romani in età giolittiana: Guglielmina Ronconi a San Lorenzo," in *Roma in transizione: Ceti popolari, lavoro, territorio nella prima età giolittiana*, ed. Paolo Carusi (Rome: Viella,

2006), 105. This paragraph relies on Rossini's description of San Lorenzo, which has been little studied for the period before World War I.
39 Maria Rosa Protasi, *Emigrazione ed immigrazione nella storia del Lazio dall'Ottocento ai giorni nostri* (Viterbo: Sette Città, 2012), 91–2.
40 Most notably, Elizabeth Wharton titled one of her greatest short stories "Roman Fever." On travelers' anxiety about malaria, see Christopher Hoolihan, "Health and Travel in Nineteenth-Century Rome," *Journal of the History of Medicine and Allied Sciences* 44 (1989): 479–82.
41 Field, *Rome*, 1: 5.
42 Mario Belardinelli, "Società romana, classe politica e problemi del territorio all'inizio del Novecento," in *Roma in transizione: Ceti popolari, lavoro, territorio nella prima età giolittiana*, ed. Paolo Carusi (Rome: Viella, 2006), 33–7. The so-called Bacelli Law of 1904 was strengthened in 1907 but on the eve of World War I, two-thirds of the Agro remained in the possession of large landholders. See Lidia Moretti, "L'Agro romano tra persistenza di questioni secolari e presupposti per nuovi processi di strutturazione dello spazio," in *La capitale della nazione: Roma e la sua provincia nella crisi del sistema liberale*, ed. Paolo Carusi (Rome: Viella, 2011), 85.
43 For an excellent account of the pioneering role of Celli and other members of the "Roman School" of malariology, see Frank M. Snowden, *The Conquest of Malaria: Italy, 1900–1962* (New Haven: Yale University Press, 2006), 27–52.
44 Moretti, "L'Agro romano tra persistenza di questioni secolari e presupposti per nuovi processi di strutturazione dello spazio," 82.
45 On labor agitation in and around Rome, see Paola Salvatori, "Associazionismo e lotte operaie," in *Roma Capitale*, ed. Vittorio Vidotto (Rome-Bari: Laterza, 2002), 250–7 and Belardinelli, "Società romana, classe politica e problemi del territorio all'inizio del Novecento," 32–5.
46 On Rome's monuments during the liberal period, see Vittorio Vidotto, "Political Public Space in Rome from 1870 to 2011," in *Perspectives on Public Space in Rome, from Antiquity to the Present Day*, ed. Gregory Smith and Jan Gadeyne (Burlington, VT: Ashgate, 2013); Terry Kirk, "The Political Topography of Modern Rome, 1870–1936: Via XX Settembre to Via dell'Impero," in *Rome: Continuing Encounters between Past and Present*, ed. Dorigen Caldwell and Lesley Caldwell (Burlington VT: Ashgate, 2011); and Francesco Bartolini, *Rivali d'Italia: Roma e Milano dal Settecento a oggi* (Rome-Bari: Laterza, 2006).
47 Attilio Zuccagni-Orlando, *Roma e l'Agro Romano: Illustrazioni storico-economiche* (Florence: Alessandro Caselli Editore, 1870), 75.
48 Luciano De Licio, *L'area di Termini a Roma: Progetti e trasformazioni* (Roma: Officina Edizioni, 1995), 17.
49 An inscription to this effect is still visible over the door on Via delle Terme di Diocleziano.
50 Monica Calzolari, "La Casa di detenzione alle Terme diocleziane di Roma (1831–1891)," in *Carceri, carcerieri, carcerati. Dall'antico regime all'Ottocento*, ed. Livio Antonielli (Soveria Mannelli: Rubbettino, 2006), 49–50. This useful article focuses on the history of the prison at Diocletian's Baths before unification.
51 Atti del Consiglio Comunale di Roma (1872–73) (Rome: Salviucci, 1873) 3: 628.
52 Ibid.
53 Porena, *Roma Capitale nel decennio della sua adolescenza (1880–1890)*, 31.
54 *RDC*, 9 (1879): 161 (Atti parl.)
55 *RDC*, 6 (1876): 428 (Pavolini).

56 Atti del Consiglio Comunale di Roma (1872–73) 3: 628.
57 Ibid.
58 Ibid.
59 Ibid., 629.
60 The number of male inmates generally ranged between 450 and 500, even exceeding 500 during the early 1880s (Stat. Carc; Ann. Stat.; Stat. Dec.; and Prosp. Stat.).
61 Alessandro Casali, *Rendiconto statistico delle malattie chirurgiche curate durante il quinquennio 1880–84 nella Casa di pena alle Terme dioclezionane in Roma* (Rome: Prasca Luigi (Tip. alle Terme dioclaziane), 1886), 5. Scrofula is a type of tuberculosis, the major symptom of which is swollen lymph glands on the neck.
62 For a description of these two groups of workers during the papal years of Diocletian's Baths, see Morichini, *Degli istituti di carità per la sussistenza e l'educazione dei poveri e dei prigionieri in Roma*, 702–3.
63 For correspondence from the Director of the Prison at Diocletian's Baths, Martino Garrone, about the production of guards' uniforms, see ACS, M. Int., DGC, AA (1896–1905), b. 183.
64 Calzolari, "La Casa di detenzione alle Terme diocleziane di Roma (1831–1891)," 62.
65 For a list of prisoners at Diocletian's Baths who were pardoned by the Pope during the last year of his secular rule, see ASR, Casa di detenzione, Terme Diocleziane, b. 135. Most of the prisoners had only a few months left to serve on their sentences.
66 Atti del Consiglio Comunale di Roma (1872–3) 3: 628.
67 *RDC*, 29 (1904): 234–7 (Atti parl.).
68 *RDC*, 26 (1901): 158 (Atti parl.).
69 Ibid., 401 (Beltrani Scalia). Indeed, the state took up the problem of the Agro Romano immediately after the annexation of Rome, nominating a commission of study with RD 20 ottobre 1870.
70 *RDC*, 26 (1901): 160 (Atti parl.). Beltrani Scalia's arguments changed little over the decades; see *RDC*, 10 (1880): 177–211 (Beltrani Scalia) and his multipart article, "Il Bonificamento dell'Agro Romano," published over the course of 1901 in vol. 26 of the *RDC*.
71 *RDC*, 26 (1901): 405 (Beltrani Scalia).
72 Ibid., 408.
73 On the Tre Fontane, see Monica Calzolari and Mario Da Passano, "Il lavoro dei condannati all'aperto: L'esperimento della colonia delle Tre Fontane (1880–95)," in *Le colonie penali nell'Europa dell'Ottocento*, ed. Mario Da Passano (Rome: Carrocci, 2004), 49–78.
74 Zuccagni-Orlando, *Roma e l'Agro Romano*, 135. Field counseled tourists that the "very ordinary churches" were not worth seeing (Field, *Rome*, 98).
75 *RDC*, 12 (1882): 75. Franchino's dismissal of the value of drainage was not shared by most parliamentary experts on the problem of the Agro Romano. In 1884, a special commission sent by the Minister of Agriculture, Industry and Trade to the environs of Rome found "no evidence that planting trees, in and of itself, diminishes malaria in the surrounding area"; instead, the land had to be drained. See *RDC*, 14 (1884): 230.
76 Ibid., 79.
77 Ibid., 81.
78 Pietro Nocito, "Una excursione alla colonia penale delle Tre Fontane," *Nuova Antologia* (1882): 272.
79 Ibid., 275.
80 Ibid., 272.

81 Ibid., 290.
82 *RDC*, 13 (1883): 373 (Atti parl.).
83 Ibid., 42.
84 Ibid., 45.
85 *RDC*, 10 (1880): 398, 400 (Carpi).
86 Ibid., 389. The italics are in the original.
87 Ibid., 389-90.
88 Ibid., 402.
89 Ibid., 402, 404.
90 *RDC*, 13 (1883): 46 (Atti parl.)
91 Ibid., 59.
92 *Actes du congrès penitentiaire de Rome, Novembre 1885*, 2 (pt. 1): 177-8. According to the report of Adolphe De Foresta, both the Hygiene Congress of 1880 (Turin) and the Ninth Medical Congress (Geneva) passed resolutions commending Tre Fontane.
93 For an example of an archival document for the Tre Fontane, in which the word "bagno" has been crossed out and replaced by "penal agricultural colony," see M. Int., DGC., AA (1896–1905), b. 49.
94 *RDC*, 10 (1880): 187 (Beltrani Scalia). Not only does Nocito express the same opinion but, according to Calzolari and Da Passano, both Lucchini and Lombroso, the leaders of the classical and positivist schools respectively, agreed ("Il lavoro dei condannati all'aperto," 159).
95 Nocito, "Una excursione alla colonia penale delle Tre Fontane," 271.
96 Ibid., 286.
97 The exact specifications for these huts (*campannone*), as well as for other buildings planned for the hard labor camp at Tre Fontane, can be found in *RDC*, 11 (1881): 360-7 (Bucci).
98 Calzolari and Da Passano, "Il lavoro dei condannati all'aperto: L'esperimento della colonia delle Tre Fontane (1880–95)," 160. An exact list of the rations for inmates of the Tre Fontane, which included wine but not meat, can be found in ACS, M. Int., DGC, AA (1896–1905), b. 49, f 56-A. Inmates and guards with malaria enjoyed the luxury of white bread, rather than the usual brown bread distribtued to the *bagn*i, because it was easier to digest.
99 Ferri is quoted in ibid. 181. Beltrani Scalia's arguments can be found in his seven-part series, "Il Bonificamento dell'Agro Romano con la mano d'opera dei condannati," published in the *RDC* in 1901. The last installment includes an appendix by G. Cusmano with building plans for houses (*casa colonica*) that could be built for prisoners working in the Agro Romano and then converted to residences for free labor.
100 Atti del Consiglio Comunale di Roma (1872–3) 3: 629.
101 Ibid., 629.
102 Ibid., 631.
103 Atti del Consiglio Communale di Roma (1877, pt. 2) (Rome: Salviucci, 1877) 11: 1031.
104 Vidotto, *Roma contemporanea*, 65.
105 A map of the original monastery can be found in ACS, M. Lav., Seg. Gen., Roma Capitale, b. 123.
106 Quoted in Adinolfi, *Storia di Regina Coeli e delle carceri romane*, 46.
107 ACS, M. Lav, Seg gen., Roma capital, b. 15, f. 13.

108 Ibid., b. 13, f. 7. For a more detailed description of the church, see the notarial report by Constantino Bobbio in Ibid., b. 123, f. 7.
109 Ibid., b. 59, f. 29.
110 CDA, DPLIC, v. 310, AC69, p. 713. The New Prison could hold five hundred prisoners, San Michele three hundred, and Regina Coeli two hundred.
111 CDA, DPLIC, v. 310 AC69, pp. 721, 728–30.
112 Atti del Consiglio Comunale di Roma (1885, pt. 2) (Rome: L Cecchini, 1885) 31: 350.
113 CDA., DPLIC, v. 427 (1886), 7.
114 CDA, DPLIC, v. 427 (1886), 252–3.
115 *RDC*, 14 (1886): 280 (Atti parl.). The work was initiated by Filippo Bucci, chief engineer in the Division of Prisons. See *RDC*, 11 (1881): 232 (Boll. Uff.).
116 *Actes du congrès penitentiaire de Rome, Novembre 1885*, 3 (pt. 2): 557.
117 *RDC*, 20 (1890): 57 (Boll. Uff.).
118 For detailed maps of each floor, see Antonietta Navarra, *La edilizia carceraria dagli inizi al Novecento* (Naples: Libreria scientifica editrice, 1967), 119–28.
119 *RDC*, 14 (1884): 278 (Atti parl.).
120 *RDC*, 19 (1889): 586.
121 Stat. Carc. (1884–1914).
122 Stat. Carc. In 1902, 21 percent were convicts and in 1903, 26 percent.
123 The "penal section" of Regina Coeli became an autonomous institution, with its own warden, in 1908, although its location remained the same. *RDC*, 33 (1908): 465 (Boll. Uff.).
124 Stat. Carc. (1908–14).
125 For 1886, see Prosp. Stat., 28–9; for 1914, see Stat. Carc., 292–3.
126 ACS, MGG, DGIP (1906–25), b. 87, f. 55. Administrators at Regina Coeli were awarded special bonuses in 1910 for successfully taking over the complicated task of printing the *Leggi e Decreti* from the private publisher, Ditta Ripamonte.
127 For example, the Stat. Dec. lists the printer as the "Bagno Penale."
128 *Actes du congrès penitentiaire de Rome, Novembre 1885*, 3 (pt. 2): 558.
129 Alberto Caracciolo, "Continuità della struttura economica di Roma prima e dopo il 1870," *Nuova rivista storica* 2 (1954): 332.
130 Ibid., 196 (Atti parl.). Maffi was a member of the Radical Party and the first working-class member of parliament.
131 Free workers oversaw the composition, pagination, and correction of each publication. *RDC*, 22 (1897): 258 (Doria). On the small numbers of convicts employed by the prison system, see *RDC*, 13 (1883): 118 (Atti parl); *RDC*, 13 (1883): 300 (Atti parl.).
132 *RDC*, 13 (1883): 215 (Atti parl.); *RDC*, 26 (1901): 298–9.
133 The number of Roman typographers was 2,617 in 1901 rising to 4,610 in 1911 in contrast to construction workers, whose numbers increased from 13,028 in 1901 to 19,400 in 1911. See Salvatori, "Associazionismo e lotte operaie," 251–2. On typographers' strikes, see Belardinelli, "Società romana, classe politica e problemi del territorio all'inizio del Novecento," 21–2.
134 RD n. 1510, 27 luglio 1873 Regolamento per la istituzione di scuole per le Guardie carcerarie.
135 Marinelli, *Memoriale sull'ordinamento del Personale di Custodia degli Stabilimenti Carcerari e dei Riformatorii Governativi del Regno*, 17.
136 *RDC*, 35 (1910): 283 (Doria).

137 M. Int., DGC, AA (1896–1905), b. 153, f. 56F.
138 Ibid.
139 Ibid. For a similar complaint, to which Doria admits that "it is easy to see and talk with inmates" from the nearby streets and Janiculum Hill, see b. 65, f. 56.
140 For the words of the song, see *Enciclopedia di Roma dalle origini all'anno Duemila.* (Milan: Franco Maria Ricci, 1999), 757. In Roman dialect, the prison is popularly known as "er Coeli."
141 M. GG, DGIP, Studi per la riforma penitentiaria. (1897–1930), b. 1, f. 3.
142 *Actes du congrès penitentiaire de Rome, Novembre 1885*, v. 3, pt. 1 (Cardosa).
143 The number of *bagni* rose from twenty-two in 1868 to a high of forty in 1886 and dropped slightly before 1891. Some of the *bagni* were technically sub-camps, like Tre Fontane that drew its forced laborers from Civitavecchia. Stat. Carc.
144 Stat. Carc., 1862–1914. These totals included penitentiaries, agricultural colonies, and criminal insane asylums.
145 Somm. Stat., 1958.
146 Stat. Carc.
147 Stat. Carc.
148 Stat. Carc.
149 Stat. Carc
150 Stat. Carc.
151 Stat. Carc.
152 Stat. Carc.
153 Stat. Carc.
154 Stat. Carc
155 Stat. Carc. (1871–82).The remaining working inmates were employed in domestic upkeep of the prison or in "various" types of work that were not categorized.
156 Stat. Carc.
157 Stat. Carc.
158 Stat. Carc.
159 Stat. Carc., 1866–80 and 1914.
160 Stat. Carc.
161 Stat. Carc. Those under thirty composed 48 percent in 1871 and 41 percent in 1914.
162 Stat. Carc.
163 Stat. Carc.; from 1901 to 1914, men received on the average thirteen letters per year and sent eight.
164 Stat. Carc.; only 6 percent of all male inmates received visits from 1909 to 1914.
165 Stat. Carc.; between 1901 and 1914, men received on the average 25 lire; only 19 percent sent home money (averaging 21 lire).
166 AV, Atti della Segretaria del Vicariato, Palchetto 26, Plico 179, f. 3.
167 ACS, M. Int., DGC., AA (1896–1905) b. 350, f55A.
168 Ibid.
169 *RDC*, 2 (1872): 186-7 (Boll. Uff.); 3 (1873): 5, 41 (Boll. Uff.); and 4 (1874): 178–88 (Boll. Uff.).
170 *RDC*, 2 (1872): 518 (Cardon).
171 Stat. Carc.
172 Stat. Carc.
173 Stat. Carc.

174 *RDC*, 9 (1879): 629 (Beltrani Scalia); ACS, M. Int., DGC, AA (1896–1905), b. 183, and *RDC*, 26 (1901): 321.
175 *RDC*, 22 (1897): 1–4 (Boll Uff.).
176 ACS, M GG, DGIP, AA (1906–1925), b. 47, f. 1.
177 Giulianelli, *L'industria carceraria in Italia: Lavoro e produzione nelle prigioni da Giolitti a Mussolini*, 102, 105.
178 Stat. Carc. (1913), 143.
179 Ibid.
180 Giulianelli, *L'industria carceraria in Italia: Lavoro e produzione nelle prigioni da Giolitti a Mussolini*, 70–1.
181 Murder rates declined from 1.9/10,000 population in 1880 to 0.8 in 1914. See Somm. Stat. (1958), 90–1.
182 Stat. Carc.
183 Stat. Carc. As an effect of the Zanardelli Code, the percent of male inmates interned for violent crime jumped from 40 percent in 1888 to 55 percent in 1891.
184 Stat. Carc. (1913), 143.
185 Edmondo About, *Roma contemporanea* (Milan: Francesco Colombo, 1861), 97.
186 Daniele Boschi, "Homicide and Knife Fighting in Rome, 1845–1914," in *Men and Violence*, ed. Pieter Spierenburg (Columbus: Ohio State University Press, 1998). For a similar portrait of violence in nineteenth-century Greece, see Thomas W. Gallant, "Honor, Masculinity, and Ritual Knife Fighting in Nineteenth-Century Greece," *American Historical Review* 105, no. 2 (2000).
187 Stat. Carc.
188 Hughes, *Politics of the Sword*.
189 Stat. Carc.
190 Stat. Carc.
191 Stat. Carc.
192 Stat. Carc.
193 Mario Da Passano, "Il 'delitto di Regina Coeli,'" *Diritto@Storia*, no. 4 (2005) [http://www.dirittoestoria.it/4/in-Memoriam/Mario-Da-Passano-e-la-storia-del-diritto-moderno/Da-Passano-Delitto-Regina-Coeli.htm, accessed September 9, 2017].
194 *RDC*, 29 (1904): 177–8.
195 Ada Lonni, "Stampa e problema carcerario nell'età giolittiana," *Rivista di Storia Contemporanea*, no. 2 (1976): 591–2.
196 *RDC*, 33 (1908): 65 (Doria).
197 *RDC*, 34 (1909): 224 (Lorenzo Ellero).
198 *RDC*, 33 (1908): 37–8 (Doria).
199 Ibid., 69.
200 *RDC*, 33 (1908): 68 (Lombroso).
201 Ibid., 113 (Sergi).
202 Ibid., 140–1 (Rossana).
203 Ibid., 230 (Polidori).
204 Ibid., 249 (Mirabella).
205 Ibid., 245 (Mirabella).
206 Ibid., 167 (Saporito).
207 Ibid., 175 (Perrando).
208 Ibid., 111 (Stoppato).
209 Ibid., 478.
210 Ibid., 33 (1908): 143 (Rossana).

6 Juvenile Reformatories between State and Charity

1. On the symbolic connotations of Pinocchio, see Carl Ipsen, *Italy in the Age of Pinocchio: Children and Danger in the Liberal Era* (New York: Palgrave Macmillan, 2006); and Suzanne Stewart-Steinberg, *The Pinocchio Effect: On Making Italians, 1860–1920* (Chicago, IL: University of Chicago Press, 2007).
2. Antonio Guarnieri-Ventimiglia, *La delinquenza e la correzione dei minorenni* (Rome: Nazionale, 1906), 11.
3. On San Michele, see Chapter 1.
4. Beltrani Scalia, *Sul governo e sulla riforma delle carceri in Italia: Saggio storico e teorico*: 259–60; Thorsten Sellin, "Filippo Franci. A Precursor of Modern Penology," *Journal of Criminal Law and Criminology* 17 (1926):105–12; and Domenico Izzo, "Da Filippo Franci alla riforma Doria (1667–1907)," *Rassegna di studi penitenziari* 4, no. 3 (1956): 292–6.
5. On child musicians, see Ipsen, *Italy in the Age of Pinocchio*, 54–9.
6. On criminal anthropological views of childhood, see Gibson, *Born to Crime*, 181–7.
7. Nicolo Pinsero, "Sulla punizione dei delinquenti minorenni," *Scuola positiva* 3, no. 23–24 (1893): 1062.
8. On agricultural colonies for youth, see Jeroen J. H. Dekker, *The Will to Change the Child: Re-Education Homes for Children at Risk in Nineteenth Century Western Europe* (Frankfurt am Main: Peter Lang, 2001); and Marie-Sylvie Dupont-Bouchat and Éric Pierre, eds., *Enfance et justice au XIXe siècle: Essais d'histoire comparée de la protection de l'enfance, 1820–1914* (Paris: Presses Universitaires de France, 2001).
9. See Civil Code of 1865 for *patria podestà* (Arts. 220–39), marriage (Art. 55), and "emancipation" (Arts. 311, 323).
10. Civil Code of 1865, Article 222.
11. Public Security Law of 1865, Articles 72, 103, and 107.
12. Public Security Law of 1889, Articles 113–16.
13. Criminal Code of 1859, Articles 87–91.
14. Criminal Code of 1889, Articles 53–6. If found to have acted with *discernimento*, youth between nine and twelve were among those who received reduced sentences.
15. *RDC*, 30 (1905): 151. During 1904, 6,508 of the 12,340 persons given probation were children under eighteen years old.
16. Legge 26 giugno 1904, n. 267, Article 7. Only those under fourteen were prohibited from adult jails.
17. Regulation on the Houses of Custody, Articles 45–49.
18. RD 17 novembre 1876 and RD 29 novembre 1877.
19. Article 2, RD 17 novembre 1876.
20. RD 19 novembre 1876, n. 3512 (serie 2) reprinted in *RDC*, 6 (1867): 105–8.
21. Ugo Conti, "Case di Custodia," in *Il digesto italiano: Enciclopedia metodica e alfabetica di legislazione, dottrina e giurisprudenza*, ed. Luigi Lucchini (Turin: Unione Tip.-Editrice Torinese, 1884–93), vol. 6, part 2 (1891), 222–4.
22. Ordinance of 1891, Article 4.
23. Ibid., Article 487.
24. Ibid.
25. Ibid.
26. Ibid., Article 128.
27. Legge 3 Luglio 1904, n. 318.

28 RD 24 marzo 1907, n. 122, Article 24.
29 RD 10 novembre 1905, n. 572.
30 RD 14 luglio 1907, n. 606, Article 1.
31 Ibid., Article 165.
32 Ibid.
33 Ibid., Article 167.
34 *RDC*, 6 (1876): 297-8 (Lombroso).
35 Ibid., 298. For a similar argument, see Angelo Bargoni, "I piccoli corrigendi," *Archivio di Antropologia criminale, psichiatria e medicina legale* 3 (1882): 245-62.
36 *RDC*, 6 (1876): 298-9 (Lombroso).
37 Ann. Stat.
38 *RDC*, 35 (1910): 254 (Doria).
39 Ann. Stat.
40 *RDC*, 13 (1883): 83 (Barzilai).
41 Ibid.
42 Ibid., 95.
43 Ibid., 91, 92.
44 Vanna Nuti, *Discoli e derelitti: L'infanzia povera dopo l'Unità* (Florence: La Nuova Italia, 1992), 119.
45 *RDC*, 6 (1879): 439 (Beltrani Scalia).
46 *RDC*, 35 (1910): 248 (Doria).
47 Ibid., 248.
48 *RDC*, 39 (1914): 203 (Girardi).
49 *RDC*, 33 (1908): 21 (Girardi).
50 Domenico Izzo, "Il trattamento dei minorenni delinquenti dalla circolare Orlando al progetto Ferri (1908-1921)," *Rassegna di studi penitenziari* 8, no. 2 (1957): 145-6.
51 *RDC*, 30 (1905): 415-23.
52 Ibid., 421.
53 Barbara Montesi, *Questo figlio a chi lo do? Minori, famiglie, istituzioni (1865-1914)* (Milan: Franco Angeli, 2007), 41.
54 Ibid.
55 Ibid., 49, 51.
56 Maura Piccialuti Caprioli, "Il patrimonio del povero. L'inchiesta sulle opere pie del 1861," *Quaderni storici* 45 (1980): 935.
57 Stefano Lepre, *Le difficoltà dell'assistenza: Le opere pie in Italia fra '800 e '900* (Rome: Bulzoni, 1988), 10.
58 Giovanna Farrell-Vinay, *Povertà e politica nell'Ottocento: Le opere pie nello Stato liberale* (Turin: Scriptorium, 1997), 179-82.
59 Stefano Sepe, "Amministrazione e mediazione degli interessi: il controllo sugli istituti di pubblica assistenza e beneficenza," in *L'amministrazione nella storia moderna*, ed. ISAP (Milan: Giuffrè, 1985), 2: 1709.
60 Ibid., 2: 1710.
61 For a cautiously optimistic evaluation of the Giolitti law, see Carlo Shanzer, "La nuova legge sulla beneficenza pubblica," *Nuova Antologia* 123 (1906): 270-81.
62 Vidotto, *Roma contemporanea*, 300. For a similar estimate, see Bartoccini, *Roma nell'Ottocento. Il tramonto della "città santa". La nascita di una capitale*, 2: 745.
63 Maura Piccialuti Caprioli, "Lo stato liberale e la beneficenza pubblica: A proposito delle opere pie romane dopo il 1870," in *Istituzioni e borghesie locali nell'Italia liberale*, ed. Mariapia Bigaran (Milan: Franco Angeli, 1986), 178.

64 Morichini, *Degli istituti di carità per la sussistenza e l'educazione dei poveri e dei prigionieri in Roma*, 543.
65 See Groppi, *I conservatori della virtù: Donne recluse nella Roma dei Papi*, 19, for a list of the conservatories of papal Rome. On conservatories in other cities, see Laura Guidi, *L'onore in pericolo: Carità e reclusione femminile nell'ottocento napoletano* (Naples: Liguori, 1991); Sherrill Cohen, *The Evolution of Women's Asylums since 1500* (New York: Oxford University Press, 1992); and Lucia Valenzi, *Poveri, ospizi e potere a Napoli (XVIII-XIX sec.)* (Milan: Franco Angeli, 1995). Valenzi counts fifty-one conservatories in Naples in 1861, demonstrating their large numbers in major cities (15).
66 Groppi, *I conservatori della virtù: Donne recluse nella Roma dei Papi*, 19; and Piccialuti Caprioli, "Lo stato liberale e la beneficenza pubblica: A proposito delle opere pie romane dopo il 1870," 185.
67 Groppi, *I conservatori della virtù: Donne recluse nella Roma dei Papi*, 32–3.
68 Ibid., 28.
69 Morichini, *Degli istituti di carità per la sussistenza e l'educazione dei poveri e dei prigionieri in Roma*, 726. See also Monachino, *La carità cristiana in Roma*, 257–8; and Luigi Grifi, *Breve ragguaglio delle opere pie di carità e beneficenza, ospizi e luoghi d'istruzione della città di Roma* (Rome: Tipografia della Rev. Cam. Apostolica, 1862), 24–5.
70 M. Int., DGC, AA (1896–1905), b. 40.
71 *Dizionario degli istituti di perfezione* (Rome: Edizioni Paoline, 1980), 6: 368–9.
72 Angela Groppi, "Le monastère du Bon Pasteur à Rome (1838–1870)," in *Les exclus en Europe, 1830–1930*, ed. André Gueslin and Dominique Kalifa (Paris: Les Éditions de l'Atelier, 1999), 175.
73 Morichini, *Degli istituti di carità per la sussistenza e l'educazione dei poveri e dei prigionieri in Roma*, 730–1.
74 AV, Atti della Segretaria del Vicariato, [Prisons-misc], Palchetto 26, Plico 179, f. 3.
75 Atti del Consiglio comunale di Roma (1870–1) 1: 1125.
76 ACS, GG, DGIP, AA (1906–25), b. 177, f. 55.
77 Atti del Consiglio Comunale di Roma (1875–6, pt. 2) 8: 135. There is evidence of conflict between the city council and the central state, which initially wanted to confiscate the entire monastery under the Law of 1865. See M. Int., DGFC, Corporazioni religiose (1855–1929) (b. 82), Posizione 179.
78 ACS, M. Int., DGC., AA (1901–5), b. 192, f. 55.
79 In 1893, the state employed four nuns in the Buon Pastore jail. See ACS, M. Int., DGC, AA (1896–1905), b. 40, f. D.
80 ACS, M. Int., DGC, AA (1901–5), b. 192, f. 55.
81 Ibid.
82 Ibid.
83 ACS, M. Int., DGC, AA (1896–1905), b. 65, f. 56-D.
84 Ibid., b. 180, f. AR.
85 ACS, M. GG, DGIP, AA (1906–25), b. 177, f. 55.
86 Ibid.
87 Stat. Carc., Ann. Stat., Stat. Rif.
88 Stat. Carc., Stat. Rif.
89 Stat. Rif.
90 ACS, M. GG, DGIP, AA (1906–25), b. 177, f. 55.
91 Stat. Rif. (1904–14).

92 Ibid.
93 Stat. Carc., Stat. Rif.
94 Ann. Stat., Stat. Rif.
95 From 1910 to 1911, the number of rewards jumped from 365 to 1892. See Stat. Rif. (1910), 142–5 and (1911), 154–7.
96 Stat. Rif (1904–14).
97 M. Int., DGC, *Relazione del Direttore Generale e degli Ispettori delle Carceri per gli anni 1878–1883* (Rome: Mantellate, 1884), 452.
98 ACS, M. Int., DGC, AA (1896–1905), b. 40, f. D.
99 Ibid.
100 Ibid. Italics in the original.
101 ACS, M. Int., DGC, b. 84, f. 56A.
102 For generally positive reports in 1908–10, see ACS, M. GG, DGIP, AA (1906–25), b. 177, f. 55.
103 Ibid.
104 Ibid.
105 http://www.casainternazionaledelledonne.org/index.php/it/chi-siamo/who-what-we-are (accessed June 4, 2018). At the time of writing, the mayor of Rome, Virginia Raggi of the Five-Star party, has threatened to close the center.
106 On the annex to the New Prison, see Tafuri, "Le 'Carceri Nuove' e la casa di correzione per i minorenni," 368–9.
107 Claudia Ferreri, "Il complesso di S. Balbina a Roma: L'insediamento ecclesiastico e le trasformazioni urbane," *Alma Roma* 37, no. 1 (1996): 58.
108 Stat. Dec. (1870–79), 156.
109 Atti del Consiglio Comunale di Roma (1870–71) 1: 1130.
110 Daniela Basti, "L'ospizio di S. Michele a Ripa dopo la Breccia di Porta Pia," *Archivio della società romana di storia patria* 93 (1970): 177.
111 On the conversion of the charity section of San Michele into an *opera pia*, see Atti del Consiglio Comunale di Roma (1870–71) 1: 1128–31.
112 Giorgio Rossi, "Giovani e formazione al lavoro: l'istruzione professionale e tecnica a Roma nel periodo giolittiano," in *Roma in transizione: Ceti popolari, lavoro, territorio nella prima età giolittiana*, ed. Paolo Carusi (Rome: Viella, 2006), 142.
113 ACS, M. Int., DGC, AA (1896–1900), b. 176, f. 56/A.
114 In 1902, Giolitti signed a decree directing the prison administration to establish a women's jail at San Michele but it was never implemented. See *RDC*, v. 27 (1902): 89 (Boll. Uff.). The government had earlier contemplated using it as a museum of criminal anthropology and a school to train police in anthropometry and other methods of criminal identification. See ACS, DGC, AA (1896–1905), b. 40, f. B. The final decree reestablishing the boys' reformatory was issued on April 4, 1903.
115 M. Lav., Seg. Gen., Roma Capitale, b. 38, f. 75a.
116 For correspondence about hiring teachers, see ACS, M GG, DGIP, AA (1906–25), b. 100, f. 55; about the chaplain, see ACS, M. Int., DGC, Arch Gen., AA (1901–5), b. 350, f. 55a and M GG, DGIP, AA (1906–25), b. 98, f. 55.
117 Tutors were forbidden from punishing the boys and instead reported bad behavior to the proctors. See Article 96 of RD 22 dicembre 1904, n. 716.
118 See the tables appended to RD 24 marzo 1907, n. 227 (for reformatory staff) and RD 24 marzo 1907, n. 150 (for prison guards).
119 See ACS, M GG, DGIP (1906–25), b. 109, f. 55, for the quote; punishment of the staff was confirmed in b. 155, f. 55L.

120 Stat. Rif., 1904–14.
121 ASR, Altavista, Register 226.
122 ACS, M GG, DGIP, AA (1906–25), b. 115, f. 55L.
123 Stat. Rif., 1904–14.
124 ACS, M. Int., DGC, AA (1896–1905), b. 286, f. 24.
125 ASR, Altavista, Reg. 226. This water-damaged register contains the original handwritten tables on most of the statistics, cited in the next few paragraphs, which were then forwarded to the central ministry.
126 ACS, M. Int., DGC, AA (1896–1905), b. 351, f. 55.
127 ACS, M GG, DGIP, AA (1906–25), b. 100, f. 55.
128 ACS, M. Int., DGC, AA (1896–1905), b. 351, f. 55.
129 Stat. Rif., 1904–14. For an example of the reports by San Michele of the results of each exam, by teacher, see ACS, M GG, DGIP, AA (1906–25), b. 115, f. 55.
130 ASR, Altavista, Reg. 226.
131 ACS, M GG, DGIP, AA (1906–25), b. 87, f. 55; ASR, Altavista, Reg. 226.
132 Ibid., 322, f. 1.
133 Ibid., b. 35, f. 18.
134 Stat. Rif. (1904–14); rarely a very young boy would be exempted from work.
135 ASR, Altavista, Reg. 224.
136 Stat. Rif., 1904–14. The rate for 1904 was much higher but this may be an anomaly explained by the unsettled nature of the first year of operation.
137 *RDC*, 32 (1907): 216.
138 Stat. Rif. (1904–14).
139 See, for example, ACS, M GG, DGIP (1906–25), b. 109, f. 55.
140 ACS, M. Int., DGC, AA (1896–1905), b. 365, f. 55.
141 ACS, M. GG, DGIP, AA (1906–25), b. 109, f. 55.
142 *RDC*, 35 (1910): 60–1.
143 ASC, M GG, DGIP, AA (1906–25), b. 87, f. 55 (for the prefect); b. 109, f. 55 (for Doria).
144 *RDC*, 31 (1906): 236 (Montessori).
145 Ibid., 304. For more on Montessori's admiration for criminal anthropology, see "L'antropologia ne' suoi rapporti con le scienze mediche, giuridiche e pedagogiche," *RDC*, 31 (1906): 369–411.
146 *RDC*, 37 (1912): 159 (Boll. Uff.).
147 *RDC*, 37 (1912): 409.
148 *RDC*, 37 (1912): 22.
149 M GG, DGIP, AA (1906–25), b. 239, f. 2.
150 ASR, Altavista, Reg. 226.
151 http://www.davinotti.com/index.php?option=com_content&task=view&id=204.
152 Ann. Stat. These numbers are for those present on December 31 of each year.
153 Prosp. Stat., Ann. Stat., Stat Rif.
154 Ann. Stat. From 1871 to 1914, boys composed on the average two-thirds of the juvenile population.
155 Ann. Stat.
156 Stat. Carc. (1902–3), 126.
157 In 1913, 198 juveniles were serving their sentences in the adult penitentiary system. See Stat. Carc. (1913), 582.
158 For example, see Stat. Rif. (1914), 45.
159 Ibid.

160 For the categorization of reformatories in 1914, see ibid., 4.
161 Ibid., 47.
162 Ibid., 49.
163 Stat. Carc., Ann. Stat., Stat. Rif.
164 The Regolamento per i riformatori governativi, 14 luglio 1907, n. 606, ran to 299 articles compared to the 7 short sections of the 1877 law.
165 Regolamento per riformatori (1907), Article 65.
166 Ibid., Article 65.
167 Ibid., Article 66.
168 Ibid., Article 80.
169 Stat. Carc., Ann, Stat., Stat. Rif.
170 Regolamento per riformatori (1907), Article 136.
171 Stat. Carc., Stat. Rif.
172 Montesi, *Questo figlio a chi lo do? Minori, famiglie, istituzioni (1865–1914)*,182–3.
173 Stat. Rif. (1908), 61.
174 *RDC*, 28 (1903): 103.
175 Stat. Rif. (1904–14).
176 Stat. Rif. (1914), 38.
177 M. Int., DGC., Circolare, 7 novembre 1907, n. 74065-25-18, reprinted in *RDC*, 32 (1907): 809–13. On the craze for gymnastics in Italy, see Stewart-Steinberg, *The Pinocchio Effect: On Making Italians, 1860–1920*, Chapter 4.
178 ACS, M GG, DGIP, AA (1906–25), b. 35, f. 18.
179 Stat. Carc.(1901–3); Stat. Rif.(1904–14).
180 Regolamento per riformatori (1907), Article 95.
181 Stat. Carc. (1899–1900), CCLXI-CCLCII.
182 *RDC*, 34 (1909): 35.
183 Ann. Stat. (1881), 540–41.
184 Stat. Carc. (1901), CCLXIV.
185 Stat. Rif. (1914), 34.
186 Stat. Carc.
187 *RDC*, 39 (1914): 444.
188 For example, see the correspondence between national administrators and the directors of the reformatories in Turin and Forli in ACS, M GG, DGIP, AA (1906–25), b. 33, f. 9.
189 Stat. Rif. (1910–14).
190 *RDC*, 39 (1914): 446.
191 Stat. Carc., Stat. Rif.
192 For the circular instituting "bonus excursions" of several weeks for boys in state reformatories, see *RDC*, 32 (1897): 277–81.
193 Guglielmo Curli and Alessandro Bianchi, *Le nostre carceri e i nostri riformatori* (Milan: Enrico Rechiedei, 1902), 245.
194 *RDC*, 27 (1902): 318 (Curli and Bianchi).
195 Curli and Bianchi, *Le nostre carceri e i nostri riformatori*, 248.
196 Ibid., 260.
197 Stat. Carc., Stat. Rif.
198 Stat. Carc., Stat. Rif.
199 See Circolare, 25 agosto 1901, n. 9810 (Ministero della Guerra) reprinted in *RDC*, 25 (1901): 257 (Boll. Uff.).
200 *RDC*, 13 (1883): 191–2 (Atti parl).

201　Ibid., 29 (1904): 79.
202　Ibid., 35 (1910): 325.
203　For problems in the Perugia reformatory, see ACS, M GG, DGIP, AA (1906–25), b. 190, 6-20-25-A.
204　Atti Parl, CD, Disc, Legis 23:1 (1909–13), 1761–2.
205　Ibid., 1761.
206　Ibid., 1763. The italics are in the original.
207　Ibid.
208　Ibid., 1760.
209　*RDC*, 34 (1909): 291 (Bernabò-Silorata).
210　Ibid., 35 (1910): 19 (D'Alessandro).
211　Ibid., 37 (1912): 22 (Nello).
212　For articles and lectures by Rossana, see *RCD*, 34 (1911): 274–6, 321–7, 397–9.
213　Rossana, *Sotto la ferula: Dolore, povertà, degenerazione muliebre*: 4.
214　Ibid., 27.
215　Ibid., 160.
216　Ibid., 28.
217　Montesi, *Questo figlio a chi lo do? Minori, famiglie, istituzioni (1865–1914)*: 145.
218　*RDC*, 34 (1909): 498. For Doria's plans for a lay reformatory for girls, see *RDC*, 34 (1909): 51–2; 35 (1910): 317; and 36 (1911): 230 (Doria).
219　*RDC*, 39 (1914): 210 (Girardi).
220　For a list of the circulars, see *RDC*, 37 (1912): 379–80 (Doria). Crispi confirmed his support of *patronati* to a parliamentary commission in 1889. See also CD, Arch., DPLIC, v. 494, AC 78, p. 573.
221　*RDC*, 37 (1912): 379–80 (Doria).
222　For details, see ACS, M GG, DGIP, Studi per la riforma (1897–1930), b. 3, f. 7.
223　Atti del Consiglio Communale di Roma (1873–4) 4: 677.
224　AV, Atti della Segretaria del Vicariato, Palchetto 65, Plico 123 [f.] 3. On the widespread practice of providing dowries for poor girls, see Groppi, *I conservatori della virtù: Donne recluse nella Roma dei Papi*: 176–8.
225　*RDC*, 8 (1878): 119–28.
226　For yearly reports on the Sacra Famiglia, see ACS, M. Int., DGC, AA (1896–1906), b. 84, f. 56A.
227　M. Int., DGC, AA (1896–1905), b. 84, f. 56-A.
228　Ibid., b. 367, f. 1. S. Margherita transformed itself into an old-age home.
229　For a partial but impressive list of child-saving organizations, see Ipsen, *Italy in the Age of Pinocchio: Children and Danger in the Liberal Era*: 176–8.
230　For date of founding, see *RDC*, 38 (1913): 40, although other sources give a later date.
231　Patronato dei minorenni condannati condizionalmente di Roma, *Discorso della presidente onoraria e fondatrice Lucy C. Bartlett* (Rome: Officine Tipografiche Italiane, 1909). On Bartlett, see Barbara Montesi, "Emancipazionismo femminile e legislazione a favore dell'infanzia traviata. L'opera di Lucy Bartlett in Italia," *Storia e problemi contemporanei*, no. 24 (1999):153–74.
232　Patronato dei minorenni condannati condizionalmente di Roma, *Relazione morale e finanziaria per l'Anno 1911* (Roma: Officine Tipografiche Italiane, 1912), 17. According to this report, the *patronato* had about seventy members.
233　*RDC*, 34 (1909): 156–60 (Calabrese).

234 ACS, M. GG, DGIP, Studi per la riforma, 1897/1940, b. 3, f. 7. This report by Girardi, Doria's successor as director general, describes *patronati* throughout Italy.
235 *RDC*, 35 (1910): 339–40.
236 For the statute of Beltrani Scalia's charity for the children of inmates, see *RDC*, 23 (1898): 43–9.
237 Annarita Buttafuoco, *Le Mariuccine: Storia di un'istituzione laica l'Asilo Mariuccia* (Milan: Franco Angeli, 1985), 49.
238 Carlo Scotti, ed. *Guida pratica della beneficenza a Roma* (Rome: Società Anonima Poligrafica Italiana, 1927), 32–3.
239 Congresso Nazionale Femminile, *Patronati per le liberate dal carcere: Relazione di Rossana* (Rome: Tipografia dell'Unione Editrice, 1917). For statistics showing the comparatively few women released to patronati, see *RDC*, 38 (1913): 42.
240 Congresso Nazionale Femminile, *Patronati per le liberate dal carcere*, 14.
241 Bellazzi, *Prigioni e prigionieri nel Regno d'Italia*: 38.
242 Stat. Carc. (1913), 500–1.
243 Laura Guidi, "La storia dell'infanzia in Italia: Studi recenti, zone oscure, questioni aperte," *Studi Storici* 22, no. 2 (1999): 848.

7 Prisons on the Margins: Police Camps and Criminal Insane Asylums

1 Stephan Steiner, "'An Austrian Cayenne': Convict Labour and Deportation in the Habsburg Empire of the Early Modern Period," in *Global Convict Labour*, ed. Christian De Vito and Alex Lichtenstein (Leiden: Brill, 2015), 126–43.
2 Daniela Fozzi, "Una 'specialità italiana': Le colonie coatte nel Regno d'Italia," in *Le colonie penali nell'Europa dell'Ottocento*, ed. Mario Da Passano (Rome: Carocci, 2004).
3 *RDC*, 88–9 (Atti parl.).
4 *RDC*, 4 (1874): 68. (Beltrani Scalia).
5 *RDC*, 10 (1880): 85, 83 (De Foresta).
6 G. Emilio Cerruti, *Della deportazione come base fondamentale delle riforme carcerarie e della colonizzazione italiana. Lettera al Cavaliere Tancredi Canonico* (Turin: Gius. Civelli, 1872), 13–8.
7 Ibid., 27.
8 Ibid.
9 *RDC*, 6 (1876): 169 (Pessina).
10 *RDC*, 9 (1879): 355 (Beltrani Scalia). Beltrani Scalia's campaign against deportation began earlier; see for example "La deportazione," in *RDC*, 4 (1874): 61–88.
11 For example, the issue of deportation was revived by Rocco De Zerbi in his book "L'inchiesta sulla colonia Eritrea e la deportazione" (see *RDC*, 21 (1891): 161) and Armando Rosa in his series of articles in the *RDC* entitled "Deportazione e colonizzazione penale," which invited Doria's criticism. See *RDC*, 40 (1915): 367–80, 395–408, 424–32, 451–6, 465–83 (Rosa) and 483 (Doria).
12 Testo unico della Legge di Pubblica Sicurezza, n. 6144, 30 giugno 1889, Article 104. On the shifting categories of individuals subject to *domicilio coatto*, see, in addition to Fozzi and Jensen, Ernesto De Cristofaro, ed. *Il domicilio*

coatto: Ordine pubblico e politiche di sicurezza in Italia dall'Unità alla Repubblica (Acireale-Rome: Bonanno, 2015).

13 Lorenzo Benadusi, "Il domicilio coatto contro oziosi, vagabondi e omosessuali," in *Il domicilio coatto: Ordine pubblico e politiche di sicurezza in Italia dall'Unità alla Repubblica*, ed. Ernesto De Cristofaro (Acireale-Rome: Bonanno, 2015), 199–206.

14 For the moral panic spread by the press about the dangers posed by transvestites and other forms of "deviant" sexual identity, see Laura Schettini, *Il gioco delle parti. Travestimenti e paure sociali tra Otto e Novecento* (Florence: Lo Monnier, 2011).

15 Before unification, external exile had been frequently used against liberal opponents; the Papal States, for example, deported political prisoners to South America, Australia, and the United States. See Elio Lodolini, "Deportazione negli Stati Uniti d'America di detenuti politici dello Stato Pontificio (1854–1858)," *Rassegna Storica del Risorgimento* (2001), 323–54.

16 For fascinating examples, see Francesco Benigno, *La mala setta: Alle origini di mafia e camorra* (Turin: Einaudi, 2015).

17 On the use of *domicilio coatto* by police during the 1890s, see Richard Bach Jensen, *Liberty and Order: The Theory and Practice of Italian Public Security Policy, 1848 to the Crisis of the 1890s* (New York: Garland, 1991).

18 The quote, from Ferri, is cited in Camilla Poesio, "La questione criminale e il domicilio coatto nel giudizio dei socialisti," in *Il domicilio coatto: Ordine pubblio e politiche di sicurezza in Italia dall'Unità alla Repubblica*, ed. Ernesto De Cristofaro (Acireale-Rome: Bonanno, 2015). 108.

19 Poerio, *A scuola di dissenso*, 95, 99–100.

20 Ann. Stat., Stat. Carc.

21 Cesare Lombroso, *Sull'incremento del delitto in Italia* (Turin: Bocca, 1879), 64.

22 Ibid., 65.

23 AAC, 10 (1889): 21 (Ferri).

24 Ibid., 26.

25 Ibid., 21.

26 For more on her investigation, see Fiorenza Tarozzi, "Il sistema penitenziario e il domicilio coatto nell'analisi di Jessie White Mario," in *Il domicilio coatto: Ordine pubblico e politiche di sicurezza in Italia dall'Unità alla Repubblica*, ed. Ernesto De Cristofaro (Acireale-Rome: Bonanno, 2015), 169–89.

27 Jessie White Mario, "Il sistema penitenziario e il domicilio coatto in Italia," Parte 1, *Nuova Antologia* 148 (July–Aug., 1896): 19.

28 Ibid.

29 Each prisoner in the penal colonies received the tiny amount of 50 *centesimi* each day for food.

30 White Mario was writing only three years after the brutal repression of protests by the Sicilian *fasci*.

31 White Mario, "Il sistema penitenziario e il domicilio coatto in Italia," Parte II, *Nuova Antologia* 149 (Sept.–Oct., 1896): 320.

32 ACS, DGPS, Pol. Giud. (1913–15), b. 68.

33 Ibid.

34 Ibid.

35 RDC, 9 (1879): 446 (Beltrani Scalia).

36 Ibid.

37 Italy, CD, *Disegni*, Legis. 23:1 (1909–13), v. 12, n. 599, 5.

38 Ibid., 4.

39 Ibid.
40 Ibid., 6.
41 Ann. Stat.
42 Stat. Carc.
43 Stat. Carc.
44 Stat. Carc.
45 Ettore Croce, *Domicilio coatto* (Casalvelino Scalo: Galzerano Editore, 2000), 19.
46 Jensen, "Italy's Peculiar Institution," 101.
47 For a detailed reconstruction of this Assad debacle, see Marco Lenci, "Deportati in Eritrea: Il "Caso" Assab," in *Il domicilio coatto: Ordine pubblico e politiche di sicurezza in Italia dall'Unità alla Repubblica*, ed. Ernesto De Cristofaro (Acireale-Rome: Bonanno, 2015), 207–24.
48 Quoted in ibid., 214.
49 Francesca Di Pasquale, "The 'other' at home: Deportation and Transportation of Libyans to Italy during the colonial era (1911–1943)," *International Journal of Social History* 63 (2018), 213.
50 ACS, M GG, DGIP, AA (1924–5), b. 974.
51 Ibid.
52 Ibid. The article, titled "Lon Ferri ad Aversa con gli studenti della Scuola d'applicazione giuridica-criminale," was published in the prominent Neapolitan newspaper *Roma*. For another positive evaluation of Aversa from the same period, see Luigi Rusticucci, *Nelle galere. Studio di clinica criminale con descrizione dei penitenziari e dei manicomi criminali d'Italia* (Naples: Società Editrice Partenopea, 1925) and *Visitando le case di pena. Ergastoli-reclusori, manicomi criminali e domicilii coatti* (Campobasso: Cav. Uff. Gov. Colitti e Figlio di Raffaele, 1918).
53 *Codice Penale per gli Stati di S. M. il Re di Sardegna* (Rome: Regia Tipografia, 1882), Article 94.
54 Quoted in Marco Nicola Miletti, "La follia nel processo. Alienisti e procedura penale nell'Italia postunitaria," *Acta Histriae* 15 (2007): 323.
55 *Il Nuovo Codice Penale Italiano*, ed. Enrico Pessina (Milan: Hoepli, 1890), 86 (Art. 46).
56 Quoted in Miletti, "La follia nel processo. Alienisti e procedura penale nell'Italia postunitaria," 324.
57 Vincenzo Manzini, *Trattato di Diritto Penale Italiano* (Turin: UTET, 1981), vol 2, 116.
58 *Il Nuovo Codice Penale*, ed. Pessina, 93 (Art. 51).
59 Ibid., 93–4.
60 For example, see Arrigo Tamassia, "Il nuovo codice penale italiano: Appunti di Medicina forense," *Rivista sperimentale di freniatria e medicina legale delle alienazioni mentali* 16 (1890): 11–12.
61 Article 95 of the Piedmontese code and Article 64 in the Tuscan code.
62 Quoted in Valeria P. Babini, "La responsabilità nelle malattie mentali," in *Tra sapere e potere: La psichiatria italiana nella seconda metà dell'Ottocento*, ed. Valeria P. Babini et al. (Bologna: Il Mulino, 1982), 140.
63 Miletti, "La follia nel processo," 322.
64 Renzo Villa, "Perizie psichiatriche e formazione degli stereotipi dei devianti: Note per una ricerca," in *Follia, psichiatria e società: Istituzioni manicomiali, scienza psichiatrica e classi sociali nell'Italia moderna e contemporanea*, ed. Alberto De Bernardi (Milan: Franco Angeli, 1982), 385. Villa estimates that several thousand *perizie* were published during the last two decades of the nineteenth century (394); most journals

of legal medicine, psychiatry, and criminology featured frequent reprints of expert testimony.

65 From Cesare Lombroso, *La perizia psichiatrico-legale coi metodi per eseguirla e la casuistica penale classificata antropologicamente* (Torino: Fratelli Bocca, 1905) cited in Miletti, "La follia nel processo," 335.

66 For the full narrative of the trial, see the micro-history by Patrizia Guarnieri, *A Case of Child Murder: Law and Science in Nineteenth-Century Tuscany* (Cambridge: Polity, 1993).

67 On public opinion and the courtroom, see Floriana Colao, Luigi Lacchè, and Claudia Storti, eds., *Processo penale e opinione pubblica in Italia tra Otto e Novecento* (Bologna: Il Mulino, 2008).

68 Lombroso, *Criminal Man*, 48.

69 Ibid., 213.

70 Ibid., 263–4.

71 On this early periodical, see Germana Agnetti and Angelo Barbato, "L'"Appendice Psichiatrica" di Milano nel processo di nascita della psichiatria italiana," in *Follia, psichiatria e società: Istituzioni manicomiali, scienza psichiatrica e classi sociali nell'Italia moderna e contemporanea*, ed. Alberto De Bernardi (Milan: Franco Angeli, 1982). It was enfolded into the *Experimental Journal of Frenology* in 1891.

72 Lombroso mentioned criminal insane asylums in his treatise on forensic medicine, *La medicina legale delle alienazioni mentali studiata col metodo sperimentale* (Padua: Prosperini, 1865); he gave them a more systematic treatment in "Sull'istituzione dei manicomi criminali in Italia," *Rendiconti del Reale Istituto Lombardo di Scienze, Lettere e Arti*, 1872. There has been little research into the history of Italian insane asylums. For three useful articles, see Renzo Villa, "Pazzi e criminali: Strutture istituzionali e pratica psichiatrica nei manicomi criminali italiani (1876–1915)," *Movimento operaio e socialista* 3, no. 4 (1980): 363–93; Valeria P. Babini, "Alcune osservazioni su una terapia ottocentesca: I manicomi criminali," *Curare e ideologia del curare in psichiatria*, ed. Luciano Del Pistoia and Franco Bellato (Lucca: M. Pacini Fazzi, 1981); and Pierpaolo Martucci and Rita Corsa, "Scienza e diritto in lotta: Per il controllo sociale. Origini del manicomio criminale nella psichiatria positivista del tardo Ottocento," *Studi sulla Questione Criminale* 1, no. 3 (2006).

73 Lombroso, *Criminal Man*, 146.

74 Ibid., 147.

75 Ibid., 148.

76 Annamaria Tagliavini, "Aspects of the history of psychiatry in Italy in the second half of the nineteenth century," in *The Anatomy of Madness, vol 2: Institutions and Society*, ed. W. F. Bynum, Roy Porter, and Michael Shepherd (Cambridge: Cambridge University Press, 1985), 10. The number of private asylums increased even more dramatically, from five in 1866 to nineteen in 1898 to thirty in 1918.

77 There were exceptions, such as the asylum in Girifalco, which experimented with new practices. See Oscar Greco, *I demoni del mezzogiorno: Follia, pregiudizio e marginalità nel manicomio di Girifalco (1881–1921)* (Soveria Mannelli: Rubbettino, 2018).

78 Articles 172 and 174 of the Legge comunale e provinciale, 20 marzo 1865, n. 2248 held the provincial governments financially responsible for the upkeep of asylums and the care of the mentally ill poor.

79 Legge 14 febbraio 1904, n. 36 also allowed for admission of non-dangerous individuals if the asylum had empty beds. The procedures were spelled out more clearly in the Regolamento 16 agosto 1909, n. 615, which implemented the 1904 law.

80 Although Italy's rate of violent crime was high among European nations, it tended to fall after unification in contradiction to the hysterical warnings of positivist criminologists. See Gibson, *Born to Crime*, 12–13.
81 *RDC*, 3 (1873): 47 (Tamburini).
82 Ibid., 48.
83 Ibid.
84 Reference was also sometimes made to a fourth group, those categorized as "semi-insane" who had received a reduced sentence for mental imbalance. For debates about the legal responsibility of this group, see Babini, "Alcune osservazioni su una terapia ottocentesca: I manicomi criminali," 176–81.
85 *RDC*, 13 (1881): 401–10 (Tamburini).
86 A. Tamassia, "Il Nuovo Codice Penale Italiano," 13. Article 46 of the criminal code allowed judges to maintain in custody defendants whom they considered dangerous but had been acquitted under the insanity defense. Later legislation specified that they must be sent to civil asylums.
87 Reggio Decreto 1 febbraio 1891, n. 260, Articles 469–80. In this law, the term "judicial insane asylum" was used, possibly to mollify classical jurists who insisted that the courts, rather than the prison administration, control the process of admission and release. Parts of this decree were modified by the Law on Mental Hospitals of 1904.
88 Legge 14 febbraio 1904, n. 36.
89 Villa, "Pazzi e criminali," 370.
90 Babini, "La responsabilità nelle malattie mentali," 194–5.
91 Stat. Carc. (1909–14).
92 See for example, the correspondence between the civil asylum of S. Maria della Pietà in Rome and the prison administration in ACS, M. Int., DGC, AA (1896–1905), b. 209, f. 55. Requests for payment regarded not only suspects under observation but also a prison guard who had been treated for two months. For an excellent history of S. Maria della Pietà, and of Italian psychiatry more generally, see Vinzia Fiorino, *Matti, indemoniate e vagabondi: Dinamiche di internamento manicomiale tra Otto e Novecento* (Venice: Marsilio, 2002).
93 See ACS, M GG, DGIP, AA (1906–25), b. 25, f. 55.
94 Originally an annex of the civil asylum at Aversa, the section for lunatics was redesignated a full-fledged criminal insane asylum in 1890.
95 Stat. Carc. (1902–14). The fact that no punishments are registered for most years after 1905 may reflect the desire of the prison administration to present the criminal insane asylums as hospitals rather than prisons.
96 Renzo Villa interprets the close correlation between official capacity and the actual numbers of inmates as proof that admittance and release depended more on administrative needs than the health of inmates. See Villa, "Pazzi e criminali," 378.
97 *RDC*, 18 (1888): 3–27 (Algeri).
98 Stat. Carc.(1883–1914).
99 Stat. Carc.(1894–5, 1904–7).
100 Stat. Carc. (1909–14).
101 Stat. Carc. (1904–13).
102 Stat. Carc. (1904–14).
103 Stat. Carc. (1901–14).
104 Stat Carc. (1908–14).
105 Stat. Carc. (1894–5, 1904–7).
106 ACS, M. Int., DGC, AA (1896–1905), b. 373, f 29.

107 *RDC*, 35 (1910): 165 (Tamburini and Martello).
108 Ibid.
109 *RDC*, 38 (1913): 363, 361 (Saporito).
110 *RDC*, 35 (1910): 166 (Tamburini and Martello).
111 Ibid., 172.
112 *RDC*, 37 (1912): 233–41 (Tamburini).
113 Criminal Code of 1930, Article 88.
114 Ibid., Articles 202, 203, and 222.
115 For example, see *Enciclopedia del diritto* (Milan: A. Giuffrè, 1973), 27: 653.
116 On the women's section of Aversa, see Laura Schettini, "La misura del pericolo. Donne recluse nel manicomio giudiziario di Aversa (1931–50)'," *Dimensioni e problemi della ricerca storica*, no. 2 (2004): 295–318.
117 Paolo Francesco Peloso, *La guerra dentro: La psichiatria italiana tra fascismo e resistenza (1922–1945)* (Verona: Ombra Corte, 2008), 34. The rate of hospitalization for mental diseases increased from 1.5 to 2.12 per 1,000 inhabitants during this period.
118 Taken from the title of Grande, *Bonifica umana*.
119 Alberto Manacorda, *Il manicomio giudiziario: Cultura psichiatrica e scienza giuridica nella storia di un'istituzione totale* (Bari: De Donato, 1982).
120 Ibid., 114.
121 The "Basaglia Law" is the popular label for the Legge 13 maggio 1978, n.180, which was the result of a long and passionate campaign by the psychiatrist and asylum director Franco Basaglia.

8 Laboratories of Criminal Anthropology

1 *RDC*, 8 (1878): 169 (Andronico).
2 Ibid.
3 Ibid., 174.
4 Guido Neppi Modona, "Quali detenuti per quali reati nel carcere dell'Italia liberale," in *Cesare Lombroso Cento Anni Dopo*, ed. Silvano Montaldo and Paolo Tappero (Turin: UTET, 2009), 83.
5 Gina Lombroso-Ferrero, *Cesare Lombroso: Storia della vita e delle opere narrata dalla figlia* (Turin: Bocca, 1915), 247–8.
6 For the *RDC*'s laudatory obituary of Lombroso, see 34 (1909): 345–7.
7 *RDC*, 9 (1879): 49 (Beltrani Scalia's introduction to Garofalo's review).
8 *RDC*, 2 (1872): 143–8 (Golgi and Lombroso). On Verzeni and Agnoletti, see *RDC*, 3 (1873): 193–213; on Cavaglia see 8 (1878): 208–16.
9 *RDC*, 17 (1887): 434–52; 8 (1888): 145–62; and 20 (1890): 73–199 (Sergi).
10 For example, see Ferri reviewing Garofalo in *RDC*, 10 (1880): 160–6 and Garofalo reviewing Ferri in *RDC*, 11 (1881): 52–4.
11 *RDC*, 20 (1890): 698–701.
12 For example, see *RDC*, 5 (1875): 483–92 (Tamburini); 4 (1874): 381–402, 485–506; 18 (1888): 21–77; 19 (1889): 149–51 (Virgilio).
13 *RDC*, 26 (1901): 244; 31 (1906): 102–3.
14 *RDC*, 3 (1873): 50, 51 (Rosi).
15 *RDC*, 15 (1885):136 (Tamburini).

16 Ibid.,140 (Benelli).
17 *RDC*, 16 (1886): 5 (Beltrani Scalia); *RDC*, 27 (1902): 156 (Doria).
18 See *RDC*, 16 (1886): 264 (Marro) for an excerpt from Antonio Marro, *I caratteri dei delinquenti: Studio antropologico-sociologico* (Turin: Bocca, 1887).
19 *RDC*, 17 (1887): 42 (Virgilio).
20 *RDC*, 12 (1882): 137–48 (Veratti); 18 (1888): 71–7 (Penta); and 28 (1903): 23–4 (Parisetti).
21 *RDC*, 19 (1889): 90–103 and 499–511 (Salsotto).
22 Ordinance of 1891, Article 202.
23 *RDC*, 35 (1910): 422–3.
24 *RDC*, 11 (1881): 220 (Lucchini).
25 Ibid., 337 (Ferri). For one of his visits covered by a newspaper, *La Tribuna*, see *RDC*, 17 (1887): 415–19.
26 ACS, M GG, DGIP, AA (1906–25), b. 33, f. 9 and b. 20, f. 25. Doria granted a request from an inmate in Sulmona but denied another from Alessandria.
27 ACS, M. Int., DGC., AA (1896–1905), b. 256, f. 24.
28 ACS, M GG, DGIP, AA (1906–25), b. 33, f. 9.
29 For example, see *RDC*, 6 (1876): 275–83 (Zonca) and 9 (1879): 304–12 (Salini).
30 Lombroso listed over thirty-five discrete studies as the data for Edition 4 of *Criminal Man*. See Lombroso, *Criminal Man*, 234.
31 David Horn, *Social Bodies: Science, Reproduction and Italian Modernity* (Princeton: Princeton University Press, 1994), 82.
32 *RDC*, 31 (1906): 76 (Boll. Uff.).
33 ACS, M. Int., DGC, AA (1896–1905), b. 286, f. 24.
34 Ibid., b. 286, f. 24.
35 *Atti del Secondo Congresso Nazionale della Società di Patronato per Minorenni e Carcerati* (Turin: O.P.E.S., 1912), 7.
36 *RDC*, 28 (1903): 4–11 (Binda) with a positive review by Doria in *RDC*, 27 (1902): 440.
37 *RCD*, 28 (1903): 194 (Perusini). Italics in the original.
38 ACS, M GG, DGIP, AA (1906–25), b. 49, 24.
39 Ibid., b. 20, f. 25.
40 Circular 27 aprile 1882, reprinted in *RDC*, 12 (1882): 103–6 (Boll. Uff.).
41 Circular 28 marzo 1883, reprinted in *RDC*, 13 (1883): 49 (Boll. Uff.).
42 Circular 27 gennaio 1898, reprinted in *RCD*, 23 (1898): 85 (Boll. Uff.).
43 Circular 4 maggio 1910, reprinted in *RDC*, 35 (1910): 170 (Boll. Uff.). For more on the adoption of fingerprinting by the Italian state, see Gibson, *Born to Crime*, 144–9.
44 *RDC*, 28 (1903): 423 (Gasti).
45 *RDC*, 33 (1908): 472–6; 35 (1910): 20–30; 35 (1910): 442–7; and 36 (1911): 80–2.
46 *RDC*, 29 (1904): 117 (Ottolenghi).
47 *RDC*, 30 (1905): 177–8 (Ottolenghi).
48 ASC, M. Int., Scuola Superiore di Polizia, b. 17, f. 262.
49 For examples of Lombroso's interviews, see Lombroso, *Criminal Man*, 153–7.
50 On the importance place of narrative in Lombroso's work, see Mary Gibson, "Science and Narrative in Italian Criminology, 1880–1920," ed. Amy Gilman Srebnick and René Lévy, *Crime and Culture: An Historical Perspective* (Aldershot: Ashgate, 2005).
51 Lombroso-Ferrero, *Cesare Lombroso*, 355.
52 On the museum, see Silvano Montaldo, "The Lombroso Museum from its origins to the present day," in *The Cesare Lombroso Handbook*, ed. Paul Knepper and

P. J. Ystehede (London: Routledge, 2013), 98–112 and Silvano Montaldo, ed., *Il Museo di Antropologia criminale dell'Università di Torino* (Turin: Silvana, 2015).

53 A small number of writings also came from a women's jail but the large majority were from male prisoners.
54 Cesare Lombroso, *Palimsesti del carcere: Raccolta unicamente destinata agli uomini di scienza* (Turin: Bocca, 1888), 6.
55 Pierpaolo Leschiutta, *Palimsesti del carcere: Cesare Lombroso e le scritture proibite* (Naples: Liguori, 1996), 4–5.
56 Lombroso, *Palimsesti del carcere*, 10, 14, 25. The following statistics come from handwritten tables reproduced between pp. 272 and 273.
57 Ibid., 256.
58 Ibid., 7.
59 Ibid., 279.
60 Ibid., 278.
61 The Criminal Anthropology Museum of Cesare Lombroso (University of Turin), Brocca #177. The Lombroso Museum features a splendid 3D video of this entire collection of prison ceramics; examples can be seen on the excellent website http://museolombroso.unito.it.
62 Luca Spanu, "Gli orci in terracotta. La parola ai detenuti," in *Il Museo di Antropologia criminale Cesare Lombroso dell'Università di Torino*, ed. Silvano Montaldo (Turin: Silvana, 2015), 136.
63 Assunta Borzacchiello, ed. *The Criminology Museum* (Rome: Department of Prison Adminstration, 2003), 5.
64 *RDC*, 38 (1913): 170 (Polidori). Now located in the annex to the New Prison on Via Gonfalone, the Criminological Museum is open to the public and has an interesting website at http://www.museocriminologico.it.
65 Lombroso, *Criminal Man*, 344.
66 Cesare Lombroso, *L'uomo bianco e l'uomo di colore: Letture sull'origine e le varietà delle razze umane* (Padua: F. Sacchetto, 1871).
67 *RDC*, 40 (1915): 163 (Mirabella).
68 Ibid., 161 (M. Carrara).

Bibliography

AAVV, ed. *Le prigioni più rinomate d'Italia*. Florence: A spese degli editori, 1859.
About, Edmondo. *Roma contemporanea*. Milan: Francesco Colombo, 1861.
Actes du congrès penitentiaire de Rome, Novembre 1885, 4 vols. Rome: Mantellate, 1887–9.
Adams, Bruce, E. *The Politics of Punishment: Prison Reform in Russia, 1863–1917*. DeKalb: Northern Illinois University Press, 1996.
Adinolfi, Giuseppe. *Storia di Regina Coeli e delle carceri romane*. Roma: Bonsignori, 1998.
Agnetti, Germana, and Angelo Barbato. "L'"Appendice Psichiatrica" di Milano nel processo di nascita della psichiatria italiana." In *Follia, psichiatria e società: Istituzioni manicomiali, scienza psichiatrica e classi sociali nell'Italia moderna e contemporanea*, edited by Alberto De Bernardi, pp. 350–68. Milan: Franco Angeli, 1982.
Aguirre, Carlos. *The Criminals of Lima and Their Worlds: The Prison Experience, 1850–1935*. Durham, NC: Duke University Press, 2005.
Amendola, Bruna, and Laura Indrio, eds. *Villa Altieri sull'Esquilino a Roma*. Rome: Bonsignori, 2009.
Anderson, Clare, ed. *A Global History of Convicts and Penal Colonies*. London: Bloomsbury, 2018.
Andreucci Lenza, Maria Ludovica, ed. *Roma: Cento Anni (1871–1971)*. Florence: La Nuova Italia, 1971.
Adinolfi, Giuseppe. *Storia di Regina Coeli e delle carceri romane*. Rome: Bonsignori, 1998.
Arrù, Angiolina. "Il prezzo della cittadinanza. Strategie di integrazione nella Roma pontificia." *Quaderni storici* 91 (1996): 157–71.
Atti del Consiglio Communale di Roma, vols. 1–35. Roma: Salviucci/Bencini, 1870–85.
Atti del Secondo Congresso Nazionale della Società di Patronato per Minorenni e Carcerati. Turin: O.P.E.S., 1912.
Babini, Valeria P. "Alcune osservazioni su una terapia ottocentesca: I manicomi criminali." In *Curare e ideologia del curare in psichiatria*, edited by Luciano Del Pistoia and Franco Bellato. Lucca: M. Pacini Fazzi, 1981.
Babini, Valeria P. "La responsabilità nelle malattie mentali." In *Tra sapere e potere: La psichiatria italiana nella seconda metà dell'Ottocento*, edited by Valeria P. Babini et al., pp. 135–98. Bologna: Il Mulino, 1982.
Badinter, Robert. *La prison républicaine (1871–1914)*. Paris: Fayard, 1992.
Banti, Alberto M. *La nazione del Risorgimento. Parentela, santità e onore alle origini dell'Italia unita*. Turin: Einaudi, 2000.
Bardi, Paolo. *Roma piemontese (1870–1876)*. Roma: Bardi Editore, 1970.
Bargoni, Angelo. "I piccoli corrigendi." *Archivio di Antropologia criminale, psichiatria e medicina legale* 3 (1882): 245–62.
Bartoccini, Fiorella. *Roma nell'Ottocento. Il tramonto della "città santa". La nascita di una capitale*, 2 vols. Bologna: Cappelli, 1985.
Bartolini, Francesco. *Rivali d'Italia: Roma e Milano dal Settecento a oggi*. Rome-Bari: Laterza, 2006.

Basti, Daniela. "L'ospizio di S. Michele a Ripa dopo la Breccia di Porta Pia." *Archivio della società romana di storia patria* 93 (1970): 175–82.
Beccaria, Cesare. *On Crimes and Punishments.* Indianapolis, IN: Hackett, 1986 [1764].
Belardinelli, Mario. "Società romana, classe politica e problemi del territorio all'inizio del Novecento." In *Roma in transizione: Ceti popolari, lavoro, territorio nella prima età giolittiana*, edited by Paolo Carusi, pp. 17–41. Rome: Viella, 2006.
Bellazzi, Federico. *Prigioni e prigionieri nel Regno d'Italia.* Florence: G. Barbèra, 1866.
Beltrani Scalia, Martino. *Lettera al Sig. Cav. Federigo Bellazzi sul libro Prigioni e prigioneri.* Florence: Tipografia delle Murate, 1867.
Beltrani Scalia, Martino. *Sul governo e sulla riforma delle carceri in Italia: Saggio storico e teorico.* Turin: G. Favale, 1868.
Benadusi, Lorenzo. "Il domicilio coatto contro oziosi, vagabondi e omosessuali." In *Il domicilio coatto: Ordine pubblico e politiche di sicurezza in Italia dall'Unità alla Repubblica*, edited by Ernesto De Cristofaro, pp. 191–206. Acireale-Rome: Bonanno, 2015.
Benedetti, Roberto. "Tribunali e giustizia a Roma nel Settecento attraverso la fonte delle liste di traduzione alla galera (1749–1759)." *Roma Moderna e Contemporanea* 12, no. 3 (September–December 2004): 507–38.
Benigno, Francesco. *La mala setta: Alle origini di mafia e camorra.* Turin: Einaudi, 2015.
Berlinguer, Giovanni, and Floriana Colao, eds. *La "Leopoldina" nel diritto e nella giustizia in Toscana.* Milan: Giuffrè, 1989.
Bernault, Florence, ed. *A History of Prison and Confinement in Africa.* Portsmouth, NH: Heinemann, 2003.
Bertolotti, A. "Le prigioni di Roma nei secoli XVI, XVII e XVIII." *Rivista di Discipline Carcerarie* 20 (1890): 533–49, 645–66.
Bonacchi, Gabriella. *Legge e peccato. Anime, corpi, giustizia alla corte dei papi.* Rome-Bari: Laterza, 1995.
Borzacchiello, Assunta, ed. *The Criminology Museum.* Rome: Department of Prison Adminstration, 2003.
Borzacchiello, Assunta. "Modi e luoghi della giustizia a Roma al tempo di Beatrice Cenci." Paper presented at the Mostra sul quattrocentenario della morte di Beatrice Cenci, Fondazione Basso, Rome, 1999.
Boschi, Daniele. "Homicide and Knife Fighting in Rome, 1845–1914." In *Men and Violence*, edited by Pieter Spierenburg, pp. 128–58. Columbus: Ohio State University Press, 1998.
Botsman, Daniel V. *Punishment and Power in the Making of Modern Japan.* Princeton, NJ: Princeton University Press, 2005.
Braunfels, Wolfgang. *Urban Design in Western Europe: Regime and Architecture, 900–1900.* Chicago, IL: University of Chicago Press, 1988.
Brice, Catherine. *Storia di Roma e dei romani da Napoleone ai nostri giorni.* Roma: Viella, 2009.
Buttafuoco, Annarita. "La filantropia come politica. Esperienze dell'emancipazionismo italiano nel Novecento." In *Ragnatele di rapporti. Patronage e reti di relazione nella storia delle donne*, edited by Lucia Ferrante. Turin: Rosenberg & Sellier, 1988.
Buttafuoco, Annarita. *Le Mariuccine: Storia di un'istituzione laica l'Asilo Mariuccia.* Milan: Franco Angeli, 1985.
Caffiero, Marina. "Femminile/popolare: La femminilizzazione religiosa nel Settecento tra nuove congregazioni e nuove devozioni." *Dimensioni e problemi della ricerca storica*, no. 2 (1994): 235–45.

Caimari, Lila. "Whose Criminals Are These? Church, state, and Patronatos and the Rehabilitation of Female Convicts (Buenos Aires, 1890–1940)." *The Americas* 54, no. 2 (October 1997): 185–208.

Cajani, Luigi. "Pena di morte e tortura a Roma nel Settecento." In *Criminalità e società in età moderna*, edited by Luigi Berlinguer and Floriana Colao. Milan: Giuffrè, 1991.

Cajani, Luigi. "Sorvegliare e redimere: La Casa di Correzione di S. Michele a Ripa di Roma (secoli XVIII e XIX)." In *Criminalità, giustizia penale e ordine pubblico nell'Europa moderna*, edited by Luigi Cajani. Milan: Unicopli, 1997.

Calzolari, Monica. "La Casa di detenzione alle Terme diocleziane di Roma (1831–1891)." In *Carceri, carcerieri, carcerati. Dall'antico regime all'Ottocento*, edited by Livio Antonielli, pp. 49–78. Soveria Mannelli: Rubbettino, 2006.

Calzolari, Monica, and Mario Da Passano. "Il lavoro dei condannati all'aperto: L'esperimento della colonia delle Tre Fontane (1880–95)." In *Le colonie penali nell'Europa dell'Ottocento*, edited by Mario Da Passano, pp. 129–87. Rome: Carrocci, 2004.

Canosa, Romano, and Isabella Colonnello. *Storia del carcere in Italia dalla fine del'500 all'unità*. Roma: Sapere, 2000 [1984].

Capelli, Anna. *La Buona Compagnia. Utopia e realtà carceraria nell'Italia del Risorgimento*. Milan: Franco Angeli, 1988.

Caracciolo, Alberto. "Continuità della struttura economica di Roma prima e dopo il 1870." *Nuova rivista storica* 38 (1954): 182–207; 693–710.

Cardosa, G. "Statistiques des prisons de l'Italie." In *Actes du congrès penitentiaire de Rome*, vol. 3, pt. 1 (Novembre 1885), pp. 471–637. Rome: Mantellate, 1888.

Carpi, Leone. "Prigioni di Stato Borboniche/Prigioni di Stato Austriache." In *Il Risorgimento Italiano: Biografie storico-politiche d'illustri italiani contemporanei*, edited by Leone Carpi, vol. 3, pp. 531–47. Milan: Antica Casa Editrice/Dottor Francesco Vallardi, 1884.

Carrafiello, Susan B. *"The Tombs of the Living": Prisons and Prison Reform in Liberal Italy*. New York: Peter Lang, 1998.

Casali, Alessandro. *Rendiconto statistico delle malattie chirurgiche curate durante il quinquennio 1880–84 nella Casa di pena alle Terme diocleziane in Roma*. Rome: Prasca Luigi (Tip. alle Terme diocleziane), 1886.

Castellari, Giovanni. *Della condizione giuridica della donna secondo il codice italiano*. Turin: Vincenzo Bona, 1877.

Castromediano, Sigismondo. *Carceri e galere politiche: Memorie del Duca Sigismondo Castromediano*, 2 vols. Lecce: Editrice Salentina, 1895.

Catalanetto, Pina. "Il carcere patogeno: Malattie e repressione nella Palermo di primo Ottocento." In *Malattie, terapie, e istituzioni sanitarie in Sicilia*, edited by Calogero Valenti, pp. 215–31. Palermo: Centro italiano di storia sanitaria e ospitaliera, 1985.

Cerruti, G. Emilio. *Della deportazione come base fondamentale delle riforme carcerarie e della colonizzazione italiana. Lettera al Cavaliere Tancredi Canonico*. Turin: Gius. Civelli, 1872.

Chiarotti, Laura. "La popolazione del carcere nuovo nella seconda metà del XVII secolo." *Archivio della Società Romana di Storia Patria* 115 (1992): 147–79.

Ciucci, Giorgio, ed. *Roma moderna*. Rome-Bari: Laterza, 2002.

Cohen, Sherrill. *The Evolution of Women's Asylums since 1500*. New York: Oxford University Press, 1992.

Colao, Floriana, Luigi Lacchè, and Claudia Storti, eds. *Processo penale e opinione pubblica in Italia tra Otto e Novecento*. Bologna: Il Mulino, 2008.

Consiglio Nazionale delle Donne Italiane. *Atti del 1 Congresso nazionale delle donne italiane (Rome, 24–30 aprile 1908)*. Rome: Società Editrice Laziale, 1912.

Croce, Ettore. *A domicilio coatto. Appunti di un relegato politico*. Casalvelino Scalo: Galzerano, 2000 [1899].

Curli, Guglielmo, and Alessandro Bianchi. *Le nostre carceri e i nostri riformatori*. Milan: Enrico Rechiedei, 1902.

D'Errico, Rita. "La navigazione sul Tevere a valle di Roma dall'Unità al secondo dopoguerra." *Roma moderna e contemporanea* 12 (2004): 61–96.

Da Passano, Mario. "Il 'delitto di Regina Coeli.'" *Diritto@Storia*, no. 4 (2005), available at http://www.dirittoestoria.it/4/in-Memoriam/Mario-Da-Passano-e-la-storia-del-diritto-moderno/Da-Passano-Delitto-Regina-Coeli.htm.

Davis, John. *Conflict and Control: Law and Order in Nineteenth-Century Italy*. Atlantic Highlands, NJ: Humanities Press, 1988.

De Cristofaro, Ernesto, ed. *Il domicilio coatto: Ordine pubblico e politiche di sicurezza in Italia dall'Unità alla Repubblica*. Acireale-Rome: Bonanno, 2015.

De Jaco, Aldo. *Antistoria di Roma Capitale: Cronaca inedita dell'Unità d'Italia*. Rome: Riuniti, 1970.

De Licio, Luciano. *L'area di Termini a Roma: Progetti e trasformazioni*. Roma: Officina Edizioni, 1995.

De Paolis, Carlo. "Galere, ciurme e forzati nella Civitavecchia pontificia." *Lazio ieri e oggi* 16 (1980): 54–6.

De Renzis, Francesco. "L'Esposizione e il Congresso Penitenziario." *Nuova Antologia* 84 (1885): 421–45.

de Strobel, Gabriella. "La concezione penitenziaria nel pensiero e nell'opera di Martino Beltrani Scalia." University of Bologna, 1981–82.

De Vito, Christian. *Camosci e girachiavi: Storia del carcere in Italia*. Bari/Roma: Laterza, 2009.

De Vito, Christian, and Alex Lichtenstein, eds. *Global Convict Labor*. Leiden: Brill, 2015.

Dekker, Jeroen J. H. *The Will to Change the Child: Re-Education Homes for Children at Risk in Nineteenth Century Western Europe*. Frankfurt am Main: Peter Lang, 2001.

Di Mattia Spirito, Silvana. "Nazionalità e condizione sociale dei condannati a morte assistiti dall'arciconfraternità di S. Giovanni Decollato di Roma (1497–1527)." In *Popolazione e società a Roma dal medioevo all'età contemporanea*, edited by Eugenio Sonnino, 597–613. Rome: Il "calamo", 1998.

Di Pasquale, Francesca. "The 'Other' at Home: Deportation and Transportation of Libyans to Italy during the Colonial Era (1911–1943)." *International Journal of Social History* 63 (2018): 211–31.

Di Sivo, Michele. "Il popolo e il suo giudice. Studi sui documenti del Tribunale Criminale del Senatore di Roma (1593–1599)." In *Popolazione e società a Roma dal medioevo all'età contemporanea*, edited by Eugenio Sonnino, pp. 615–40. Rome: Il "calamo", 1998.

Di Sivo, Michele. "Sulle carceri dei tribunali penali a Roma: Campidoglio e Tor Di Nona." In *Carceri, carcerieri, carcerati. Dall'antico regime all'Ottocento*, edited by Livio Antonielli, pp. 9–22. Soveria Mannelli: Rubbettino, 2006.

Di Sivo, Michele. "Il tribunale criminale capitolino nei secoli XVI–XVII: note da un lavoro in corso." *Roma moderna e contemporanea* 3 (1995): 201–16.

Didi, Roberto. *Correggere e non punire. Medicina e carcere nel Risorgimento: Carlo Morelli e il laboratorio di Volterra*. Manduria: Piero Lacaita, 2006.

Dikötter, Frank. *Crime, Punishment and the Prison in Modern China*. New York: Columbia University Press, 2002.

Dizionario degli istituti di perfezione. 10 vols. Rome: Edizioni Paoline, 1980.
Duggan, Christopher. *Francesco Crispi: 1818–1901: From Nation to Nationalism.* Oxford: Oxford University Press, 2002.
Dupont-Bouchat, Marie-Sylvie, and Éric Pierre, eds. *Enfance et justice au XIXe siècle: Essais d'histoire comparée de la protection de l'enfance, 1820–1914.* Paris: Presses Universitaires de France, 2001.
Ebner, Michael R. *Ordinary Violence in Mussolini's Italy.* Cambridge: Cambridge University Press, 2006.
Enciclopedia del diritto. 52 vols. Milan: A. Giuffrè, 1973.
Enciclopedia di Roma dalle origini all'anno Duemila. Milan: Franco Maria Ricci, 1999.
Falchi, Federica. *L'itinerario politico di Regina Terruzzi: Dal mazzinianesimo al fascismo.* Milan: Franco Angeli, 2008.
Farrell-Vinay, Giovanna. *Povertà e politica nell'Ottocento: Le opere pie nello Stato liberale.* Turin: Scriptorium, 1997.
Ferreri, Claudia. "Il complesso di S. Balbina a Roma: L'insediamento ecclesiastico e le trasformazioni urbane." *Alma Roma* 37, no. 1 (January–April 1996): 27–66.
Field, Walter Taylor. *Rome*, 2 vols. Boston, MA: L. C. Page, 1904.
Fiorino, Vinzia. *Matti, indemoniate e vagabondi: Dinamiche di internamento manicomiale tra Otto e Novecento.* Venice: Marsilio, 2002.
Fornili, Carlo Cirillo. *Delinquenti e carcerati a Roma alla metà del '600: Opera dei Papi nella riforma carceraria.* Roma: Editrice Pontificia Università Gregoriana, 1991.
Fosi, Irene. "Il Governo della Giustizia." In *Roma moderna*, edited by Giorgio Ciucci, pp. 115–42. Rome-Bari: Laterza, 2002.
Foucault, Michel. *Discipline and Punish: The Birth of the Prison.* New York: Vintage, 1977.
Fozzi, Daniela. "Una 'specialità italiana': Le colonie coatte nel Regno d'Italia." In *Le colonie penali nell'Europa dell'Ottocento*, edited by Mario Da Passano, 215–304. Rome: Carocci, 2004.
Frattini, Claudia. *Il primo congresso delle donne italiane, Roma, 1908: Opinione pubblica e femminismo.* Rome: Biblink, 2008.
Frigessi, Delia. *Cesare Lombroso.* Turin: Einaudi, 2003.
Gallant, Thomas W. "Honor, Masculinity, and Ritual Knife Fighting in Nineteenth-Century Greece." *American Historical Review* 105, no. 2 (April 2000): 359–82.
Gambardella, Alfredo. "Nascita ed evoluzione delle colonie penali agricole durante il Regno D'Italia." *Rassegna Penitenziaria e Criminologica*, no. 1 (2008): 25–69.
Garfinkel, Paul. *Criminal Law in Liberal and Fascist Italy.* Cambridge: Cambridge University Press, 2016.
Garin, Eugenio. "Il positivismo italiano alla fine del secolo XIX fra metodo e concezione del mondo." *Giornale critico della filosofia italiana* Serie 5, 1 (January–December 1980): 1–27.
Gatto, Ludovico. "Le carceri nell'antichità." *Roma ieri, oggi, domani* 7, no. 72 (1994): 60–4.
Geltner, Guy. "A Cell of Their Own: The Incarceration of Women in Late Medieval Italy," *Signs* 39 (2013): 27–51.
Geltner, Guy. "*Detrusio*, Penal Cloistering in the Middle Ages." *Revue Bénédictine* 118 (2008): 89–108.
Geltner, Guy. *The Medieval Prison: A Social History.* Princeton, NJ: Princeton University Press, 2008.

Ghidoli, Marta. "La pena detentiva e i suoi spazi architettonici. La Casa di correzione nel sistema carcerario milanese di metà Settecento." *Rivista online di ricerca storica, letteratura e arte*, no. 13 (2010): 1–5.

Ghisalberti, Carlo. *La codificazione del diritto in Italia, 1848–1948.* Rome-Bari: Laterza, 1994.

Gibson, Mary. "Biology or Environment? Race and Southern "Deviancy" in the Writings of Italian Criminologists, 1880–1920." In *Italy's "Southern Question": Orientalism in One Country*, edited by Jane Schneider, pp. 99–115. New York: Berg, 1998.

Gibson, Mary. *Born to Crime: Cesare Lombroso and the Origins of Biological Criminology*. Westport, CT: Praeger, 2002.

Gibson, Mary. "Cesare Lombroso, Prison Science, and Penal Politics." In *The Lombroso Handbook*, edited by Paul Knepper and P. J. Ystehede, pp. 30–46. New York: Routledge, 2012.

Gibson, Mary. "Global Perspectives on the Birth of the Prison." *American Historical Review* 116, no. 4 (2011): 1040–63.

Gibson, Mary. *Prostitution and the State in Italy, 1860–1915.* New Brunswick: Rutgers University Press, 1986.

Gibson, Mary. "Science and Narrative in Italian Criminology, 1880–1920." In *Crime and Culture: An Historical Perspective*, edited by Amy Gilman Srebnick and René Lévy. Aldershot: Ashgate, 2005.

Giordano, Felice. *Cenni sulle condizioni fisico-economiche di Roma e suo territorio*. Florence: Stabilimento di Giuseppe Civelli, 1871.

Giulianelli, Roberto. *L'industria carceraria in Italia: Lavoro e produzione nelle prigioni da Giolitti a Mussolini*. Milan: Franco Angeli, 2008.

Gladstone, William E. *Two Letters to the Earl of Aberdeen on the State Prosecutions of the Neapolitan Government*. New York: J. S. Nichols, 1851.

Goffman, Erving. *Asylums: Essays on the Social Situation of Mental Patients and Other Inmates*. New York: Doubleday, 1961.

Grande, Dino. *Bonifica umana*, 2 vols. Rome: Mantellate, 1941.

Grantaliano, Elvira. "Le Carceri Nuove (1658–1883)." In *Carceri, carcerieri, carcerati. Dall'antico regime all'Ottocento*, edited by Livio Antonielli, pp. 23–47. Soveria Mannelli: Rubbettino, 2006.

Graziosi, Marina. "Infirmitas sexus: La donna nell'immaginario penalistico." *Democrazia e diritto*, no. 2 (1993): 99–143.

Greco, Oscar. *I demoni del mezzogiorno: Follia, pregiudizio e marginalità nel manicomio di Girifalco (1881–1921)*. Soveria Mannelli: Rubbettino, 2018.

Griffiths, Paul. *Lost Londons: Change, Crime, and Control in the Capital City, 1550–1660*. Cambridge: Cambridge University Press, 2008.

Grifi, Luigi. *Breve ragguaglio delle opere pie di carità e beneficenza, ospizi e luoghi d'istruzione della città di Roma*. Rome: Tipografia della Rev. Cam. Apostolica, 1862.

Groppi, Angela. *I conservatori della virtù: Donne recluse nella Roma dei Papi*. Rome-Bari: Laterza, 1994.

Groppi, Angela. "Le monastère du Bon Pasteur à Rome (1838–1870)." In *Les exclus en Europe, 1830–1930*, edited by André Gueslin and Dominique Kalifa, pp. 170–9. Paris: Les Éditions de l'Atelier, 1999.

Groppi, Angela. "Roman Alms and Poor Relief in the Seventeenth Century." In *Rome-Amsterdam: Two Growing Cities in Seventeenth-Century Europe*, edited by P. van Kessel and E. Schutte, pp. 180–91. Amsterdam: Amsterdam University Press, 1997.

Groppi, Angela. *Il welfare prima del welfare: Assistenza alla vecchiaia e solidarietà tra generazioni a Roma in età moderna.* Rome: Viella, 2010.
Guarnieri, Patrizia. *A Case of Child Murder: Law and Science in Nineteenth-Century Tuscany.* Cambridge: Polity, 1993.
Guarnieri-Ventimiglia, Antonio. *La delinquenza e la correzione dei minorenni.* Rome: Nazionale, 1906.
Guidi, Laura. *L'onore in pericolo: Carità e reclusione femminile nell'ottocento napoletano.* Naples: Liguori, 1991.
Guidi, Laura. "La storia dell'infanzia in Italia: Studi recenti, zone oscure, questioni aperte." *Studi Storici* 22, no. 2 (October–December 1999): 847–74.
Hawthorne, Nathaniel. *Passages from the French and Italian Note-Books.* Boston, MA and New York: Houghton, Mifflin, 1892.
Head, George. *Rome: A Tour of Many Days.* London: Longman, Brown, Green and Longmans, 1849.
Heullant-Donat, Isabelle, Julie Claustre, Élisabeth Lusset, and Falk Bretschneider, eds. *Enfermements III. Le genre enfermé: Hommes e femmes en milieux clos (xiiie-xxe siècle).* Paris: La Sorbonne, 2017.
Hibbert, Christopher. *Rome: The Biography of a City.* New York: Viking, 1985.
Hoolihan, Christopher. "Health and Travel in Nineteenth-Century Rome." *Journal of the History of Medicine and Allied Sciences* 44 (1989): 462–85.
Horn, David. *Social Bodies: Science, Reproduction and Italian Modernity.* Princeton, NJ: Princeton University Press, 1994.
Hughes, Steven C. *Crime, Disorder and the Risorgimento: The Politics of Policing in Bologna.* New York: Cambridge University Press, 1994.
Hughes, Steven C. *Politics of the Sword: Dueling, Honor, and Masculinity in Modern Italy.* Columbus: Ohio State University Press, 2007.
Hughes, Steven C. "The Theory and Practice of Ozio in Italian Policing: Bologna and Beyond." *Criminal Justice History* 7 (1986): pp. 89–103.
Ignatieff, Michael. *A Just Measure of Pain: The Penitentiary in the Industrial Revolution, 1750–1850.* New York: Columbia University Press, 1978.
Ignatieff, Michael. "State, Civil Society, and Total Institutions: A Critique of Recent Social Histories of Punishment." In *Social Control and the State*, edited by Stanley Cohen and Andrew Scull, pp. 75–105. New York: St. Martin's Press, 1983.
Innes, Joanna. "Prisons for the Poor: English Bridewells, 1555–1800." In *Labour, Law and Crime: An Historical Perspective*, edited by Francis Snyder and Douglas Hay, pp. 42–122. London: Blackwell, 1987.
Insolera, Italo. *Roma moderna. Un secolo di storia urbanistica, 1870–1970.* Turin: Einaudi, 1993.
Ipsen, Carl. *Italy in the Age of Pinocchio: Children and Danger in the Liberal Era.* New York: Palgrave Macmillan, 2006.
Italy, Direzione Generale delle Carceri e dei Riformatori, "Il lavoro negli stabilimenti carcerari e nei RR riformatori." Roma, Tipografia Mantellati, 1923.
Italy, Direzione Generale della Statistica. *Annuario Statistico Italiano.* Roma: Elzeviriana/G. Bertero, 1878–1914 (irregular).
Italy, Direzione Generale delle Carceri. *Statistica decennale delle carceri (1870-1879).* Civitavecchia: Tip. Bagno Penale, 1880.

Italy, Direzione Generale delle Carceri. *Prospetti statistici per il periodo 1 luglio 1884-30 giugno 1886*. Rome: Eredi Botta, 1886.

Italy, Direzione Generale delle Carceri e dei Riformatori. *Statistica dei Riformatori*. Rome: Mantellate, 1904-14.

Italy, Direzione Generale delle Carceri. *Statistica delle Carceri*. Rome: Favale/Arturo/Mantellate, 1862-82, 1894-1914 (irregular).

Italy, Istituto Centrale della Statistica. *Sommario di statistiche storiche italiane, 1861-1955*. Rome: Istituto Poligrafico dello Stato, 1958.

Izzo, Domenico. "Da Filippo Franci alla riforma Doria (1667-1907)." *Rassegna di studi penitenziari* 4, no. 3 (May-June 1956): 289-332.

Izzo, Domenico. "Il trattamento dei minorenni delinquenti dalla circolare Orlando al progetto Ferri (1908-1921)." *Rassegna di studi penitenziari* 8, no. 2 (March-April 1957): 146-94.

Jensen, Richard Bach. "Italy's Peculiar Institution: Internal Police Exile, 1861-1914." In *Essays in European History*, edited by June K. Burton, pp. 99-114. Lanham, MD: University Press of America, 1989.

Jensen, Richard Bach. *Liberty and Order: The Theory and Practice of Italian Public Security Policy, 1848 to the Crisis of the 1890s*. New York: Garland, 1991.

Johnston, Norman. *Forms of Constraint: A History of Prison Architecture*. Urbana: University of Illinois, 2000.

Kertzer, David. *Sacrificed for Honor: Italian Infant Abandonment and the Politics of Reproductive Control*. Boston, MA: Beacon, 1993.

Kirk, Terry. "The Political Topography of Modern Rome, 1870-1936: Via XX Settembre to Via dell'Impero." In *Rome: Continuing Encounters between Past and Present*, edited by Dorigen Caldwell and Lesley Caldwell, pp. 101-28. Burlington, VT: Ashgate, 2011.

Klopp, Charles. *Sentences: The Memoirs and Letters of Italian Political Prisoners from Benvenuto Cellini to Aldo Moro*. Toronto: University of Toronto Press, 1999.

Lacchè, Luigi. *La giustizia per i galantuomini: Ordine e libertà nell'Italia liberale. Il dibattito sul carcere preventivo (1865-1913)*. Milan: A. Giuffrè Editore, 1990.

Lenci, Marco. "Deportati in Eritrea: Il "Caso" Assab." In *Il domicilio coatto: Ordine pubblico e politiche di sicurezza in Italia dall'Unità alla Repubblica*, edited by Ernesto De Cristofaro, pp. 207-24. Acireale-Rome: Bonanno, 2015.

Lepre, Stefano. *Le difficoltà dell'assistenza: Le opere pie in Italia fra '800 e '900*. Rome: Bulzoni, 1988.

Leschiutta, Pierpaolo. *Palimsesti del carcere: Cesare Lombroso e le scritture proibite*. Naples: Liguori, 1996.

Lodolini, Elio. "Deportazione negli Stati Uniti d'America di detenuti politici dello Stato Pontificio (1854-1858)." *Rassegna Storica del Risorgimento* (July-September 2001): 323-54.

Lombroso-Ferrero, Gina. *Cesare Lombroso: Storia della vita e delle opere narrata dalla figlia*. Turin: Bocca, 1915.

Lombroso, Cesare. *Criminal Man*. Translated by Mary Gibson and Nicole Hahn Rafter. Durham NC: Duke University Press, 2006.

Lombroso, Cesare. *Palimsesti del carcere: Raccolta unicamente destinata agli uomini di scienza*. Turin: Bocca, 1888.

Lombroso, Cesare. *Sull'incremento del delitto in Italia*. Turin: Bocca, 1879.

Lombroso, Cesare. *L'uomo bianco e l'uomo di colore: Letture sull'origine e le varietà delle razze umane*. Padua: F. Sacchetto, 1871.

Lombroso, Cesare, and Guglielmo Ferrero. *Criminal Woman, the Prostitute, and the Normal Woman*. Translated by Nicole Hahn Rafter and Mary Gibson. Durham, NC: Duke University Press, 2004.

Lonni, Ada. "Stampa e problema carcerario nell'età giolittiana." *Rivista di Storia Contemporanea* 5, no. 4 (1976): 581–607.

Lucchini, Luigi, ed. *Il digesto italiano: Enciclopedia metodica e alfabetica di legislazione, dottrina e giurisprudenza*. 24 vols. Turin: Unione Tip.-Editrice Torinese, 1884–1926.

Lucrezio Monticelli, Chiara. "Donne dietro le sbarre. Il carcere femminile nella Roma dei secoli XVIII e XIX." Tesi di laurea, Università di Rome-La Sapienza, 2002–3.

Lucrezia Monticelli, Chiara. "La nascita del carcere femminile a Roma tra XVIII e XIX secolo." *Studi Storici* 48 (2007): 447–76.

Lucrezia Monticelli, Chiara. "Trastevere come spazio della reclusione tra XVIII e XIX secolo: Il carcere femminile di San Michele a Ripa." In *Trastevere: Un analisi di lungo periodo*, edited by Letizia Ermini Pani and Carlo Travaglini, pp. 397–418. Rome: Società Romana di Storia Patria alla Biblioteca Vallicelliana.

Maestro, Marcello. *Cesare Beccaria and the Origins of Penal Reform*. Philadelphia: Temple University Press, 1973.

Manacorda, Alberto. *Il manicomio giudiziario: Cultura psichiatrica e scienza giuridica nella storia di un'istituzione totale*. Bari: De Donato, 1982.

Manzini, Vincenzo. *Trattato di Diritto Penale Italiano*. 5th ed., 11 vols. Turin: UTET, 1981 [1908].

Mari, Isa. *Roma, Via delle Mantellate*. Rome: Corso, 1953.

Marinelli, Andrea. *Memoriale sull'ordinamento del Personale di Custodia degli Stabilimenti Carcerari e dei Riformatorii Governativi del Regno*, 2nd ed. Catania: Giuseppe Russo, 1899.

Marro, Antonio. *I caratteri dei delinquenti: Studio antropologico-sociologico*. Turin: Bocca, 1887.

Martucci, Pierpaolo, and Rita Corsa. "Scienza e diritto in lotta: Per il controllo sociale. Origini del manicomio criminale nella psichiatria positivista del tardo Ottocento." *Studi sulla Questione Criminale* 1, no. 3 (2006): 73–89.

McConville, Sean. "The Victorian Prison: England, 1865–1965." In *The Oxford History of the Prison: The Practice of Punishment in Western Society*, edited by Norval Morris and David J. Rothman, pp. 117–50. New York: Oxford University Press, 1998.

Melis, Guido. *Storia dell' amministrazione italiana: 1861–1993*. Bologna: Il Mulino, 1996.

Melossi, Dario, and Massimo Pavarini. *The Prison and the Factory: Origins of the Penitentiary System*. New York: Macmillan, 1981 [1977].

Meniconi, Antonella. *Storia della magistratura italiana*. Bologna: Il Mulino, 2012.

Migliori, Franco, ed. *Testimonianze di vita romana dell'800*, vol. 3. Florence: La Nuova Italia, 1969.

Miletti, Marco Nicola. "La follia nel processo. Alienisti e procedura penale nell'Italia postunitaria." *Acta Histriae* 15, no. i (2007): 321–46.

Ministero dell'Interno, Direzione Generale delle Carceri e dei Riformatori. *La colonizzazione interna nelle sue applicazioni col mezzo delle Colonie penali agricole*. Rome: Mantellate, 1912.

Ministero dell'Interno, Direzione Generale delle Carceri. *Relazione del Direttore generale e degli ispettori delle carceri per gli anni 1878–83*. Rome: Mantellate, 1884.

Monachino, Vincenzo, ed. *La carità cristiana in Roma*. Bologna: Cappelli, 1968.

Montaldo, Silvano, ed. *Il Museo di Antropologia criminale dell'Università di Torino*. Turin: Silvana, 2015.

Montaldo, Silvano. "The Lombroso Museum from Its Origins to the Present Day." In *The Cesare Lombroso Handbook*, edited by Paul Knepper and P. J. Ystehede, pp. 98–112. London: Routledge, 2013.

Montesi, Barbara. "Emancipazionismo femminile e legislazione a favore dell'infanzia traviata. L'opera di Lucy Bartlett in Italia." *Storia e problemi contemporanei*, no. 24 (1999): 153–74.

Montesi, Barbara. *Questo figlio a chi lo do? Minori, famiglie, istituzioni (1865–1914)*. Milan: Franco Angeli, 2007.

Montesi, Barbara. *Un'"anarchica monarchica": Vita di Maria Rygier (1885–1953)*. Naples: Edizioni Scientifiche Italiane, 2013.

Moretti, Lidia. "L'Agro romano tra persistenza di questioni secolari e presupposti per nuovi processi di strutturazione dello spazio." In *La capitale della nazione: Roma e la sua provincia nella crisi del sistema liberale*, edited by Paolo Carusi. Rome: Viella, 2011.

Morichini, Carlo-Luigi. *Degli istituti di carità per la sussistenza e l'educazione dei poveri e dei prigionieri in Roma*. Rome: Edizione Novissima, 1870.

Morris, Norval, and David J. Rothman, eds. *The Oxford History of the Prison: The Practice of Punishment in Western Society*. New York: Oxford University Press, 1998.

Navarra, Antonietta. *La edilizia carceraria dagli inizi al Novecento*. Naples: Libreria scientifica editrice, 1967.

Neppi Modona, Guido. "Carcere e società civile." In *Storia D'Italia*, vol. 5, pt. 2, pp. 1905–98. Turin: Einaudi, 1973.

Neppi Modona, Guido. "Quali detenuti per quali reati nel carcere dell'Italia liberale." In *Cesare Lombroso Cento Anni Dopo*, edited by Silvano Montaldo and Paolo Tappero, pp. 83–97. Turin: UTET, 2009.

Nocito, Pietro. "Una excursione alla colonia penale delle Tre Fontane." *Nuova Antologia* 35 (1882): 264–91.

Nuti, Vanna. *Discoli e derelitti: L'infanzia povera dopo l'Unità*. Florence: La Nuova Italia, 1992.

Nuvolone, Pietro. "Giuseppe Zanardelli e il codice penale del 1889." In *Giuseppe Zanardellli*, edited by Roberto Chiarini, pp. 163–82. Milan: Franco Angeli, 1985.

O'Brien, Patricia. *The Promise of Punishment: Prisons in Nineteenth-Century France*. Princeton, NJ: Princeton University Press, 1982.

Orano, Domenico. *Come vive il popolo a Roma: Saggio demografico sul quartiere Testaccio*. Pescara: Ettore Croce-Casa Editrice Abruzzese, 1912.

Ormanni, Enrica. "L'estensione a Roma dell'ordinamento giudiziario italiano." In *Studi in occasione del Centennario*, vol. 1, pp. 73–125. Milan: A. Giuffrè, 1970.

Palazzo, Donato. "A proposito di 'Riforma delle prigioni' nella prima metà del secolo scorso." *Rassegna di Studi Penitenziari* 20 (1970): 677–703.

Parente, Antonio. "Architettura ed archeologia carceraria: Santo Stefano di Ventotene ed il "Panopticon"." *Rassegna Penitenziaria e Criminologica* 3, no. 1 (January–December 1999): 43–137.

Parente, Antonio. "Il tribunale della visita." *Rassegna Penitenziaria e Criminologica* 1, no. 1–2 (January–August 1997): 111–40.

Pasquali, Diego. "Lina Pennesi e l'assistenza femminile alle donne carcerate a Roma durante il fascismo." Tesi di laurea, Università degli Studi Roma Tre, 2011–12.

Patriarca, Silvana. *Italian Vices: Nation and Character from the Risorgimento to the Republic*. Cambridge: Cambridge University Press, 2010.

Paya, Jean-Baptiste. *Les Cachots du Pape*, 2nd ed. Paris: Achille Faure, 1865.

Pellico, Silvio. *Le mie prigioni*. Milan: RCS Libri, 1984 [1832].

Peloso, Paolo Francesco. *La guerra dentro: La psichiatria italiana tra fascismo e resistenza (1922–1945)*. Verona: Ombra Corte, 2008.
Peri, Carlo. *Notizie sulla riforma delle prigioni in Toscana*, 2nd ed. Florence: Tipi della Stamperia nel Carcere delle Murate, 1850.
Pessina, Enrico. *Il nuovo Codice Penale Italiano con brevi note dilucidative*. Milan: Hoepli, 1890.
Petitti di Roreto, Carlo Ilarione. *Saggio sul buon governo della mendicità, degli istituti di beneficenza e delle carceri*, 2 vols. Turin: Giuseppe Bocca, 1837.
Piccialuti Caprioli, Maura. "Il patrimonio del povero. L'inchiesta sulle opere pie del 1861." *Quaderni storici* 45 (1980): 918–40.
Piccialuti Caprioli, Maura. "Lo stato liberale e la beneficenza pubblica: A proposito delle opere pie romane dopo il 1870." In *Istituzioni e borghesie locali nell'Italia liberale*, edited by Mariapia Bigaran, pp. 176–92. Milan: Franco Angeli, 1986.
Piemonte, Ministero dell'Interno. *Relazione del Consiglio Generale delle Carceri al Ministero dell'Interno sullo stato e sulle condizioni delle carceri giudiziarie*. Turin: G. Favale e Compagnia, 1852.
Pike, Ruth. *Penal Servitude in Early Modern Spain*. Madison: University of Wisconsin Press, 1983.
Pinsero, Nicolo. "Sulla punizione dei delinquenti minorenni." *Scuola positiva* 3, no. 23–4 (1893): 1060–70.
Pires Marques, Tiago. *Crime and the Fascist State, 1850–1940*. London: Pickering & Chatto, 2013.
Pittaluga, Arturo. "Galeotti agli scavi di Ostia Antica." *Lazio ieri e oggi* 11, no. 1 (January 1975): 171–4.
Platt, Anthony. *The Child Savers: The Invention of Delinquency*. Chicago, IL: University of Chicago Press, 1977.
Poerio, Ilaria. *A scuola di dissenso: Storie di resistenza al confino di polizia (1926–43)*. Rome: Carocci, 2016.
Poesio, Camilla. "La questione criminale e il domicilio coatto nel giudizio dei socialisti." In *Il domicilio coatto: Ordine pubblio e politiche di sicurezza in Italia dall'Unità alla Repubblica*, edited by Ernesto De Cristofaro, pp. 103–21. Acireale-Rome: Bonanno, 2015.
Porena, Manfredi. *Roma Capitale nel decennio della sua adolescenza (1880–1890)*. Rome: Edizioni di Storia e Letteratura, 1957.
Protasi, Maria Rosa. *Emigrazione ed immigrazione nella storia del Lazio dall'Ottocento ai giorni nostri*. Viterbo: Sette Città, 2012.
Querci-Seriacopi, Epaminonda. *Il passato, il presente e l'avvenire dell'Amministrazione delle carceri in Italia (Memorie storico-critico-aneddotiche)*. Rome: Tipografia delle Mantellate, 1925.
Rafter, Nicole Hahn. *Partial Justice: Women in State Prisons, 1800–1935*. Boston, MA: Northeastern University Press, 1985.
Ravaglioli, Armando. *Roma la Capitale, immagini di cento anni*, 2 vols. Rome: Edizioni del Banco di Roma, 1970–1.
Riccio, Maria Laetitia. "Donna (Diritto privato e pubblico)." In *Nuovo Digesto Italiano*, edited by Mariano d'Amelio and Antonio Azara, vol. 5, pp. 210–17. Turin: UTET, 1938.
Rizzo, Domenico. *Gli spazi della morale: Buon costume ed ordine delle famiglie in Italia in èta liberale*. Rome: Biblink, 2004.

Rocca, Giancarlo. *Donne religiose. Contributo a una storia della condizione femminile in Italia nei secoli XIX-XX*. Rome: Paoline, 1992.

Roma, Direzione Comunale di Statistica. *Rapporto complementare sul censimento di Roma*. Rome: Salviucci, 1872.

Roma, Direzione Comunale di Statistica. *Rapporto preliminare sul censimento di Roma*. Rome: Salviucci, 1872.

Rossana. "Case penali per donne." *Nuova Antologia* 62 (November–December 1912): 659–70.

Rossana. *Sotto la ferula: Dolore, povertà, degenerazione muliebre*. Turin: Fratelli Bocca, 1911.

Rossi, Giorgio. "Giovani e formazione al lavoro: l'istruzione professionale e tecnica a Roma nel periodo giolittiano." In *Roma in transizione: Ceti popolari, lavoro, territorio nella prima età giolittiana*, edited by Paolo Carusi. Rome: Viella, 2006.

Rossini, Daniela. *Donne e propaganda internazionale: Percorsi femminili tra Italia e Stati Uniti nell'età della Grande Guerra*. Milan: Franco Angeli, 2015.

Rossini, Daniela. "Esperienze di assistenza femminile nei quartieri popolari romani in età giolittiana: Guglielmina Ronconi a San Lorenzo." In *Roma in transizione: Ceti popolari, lavoro, territorio nella prima età giolittiana*, edited by Paolo Carusi, pp. 103–27. Rome: Viella, 2006.

Rothman, David J. *Conscience and Convenience: The Asylum and Its Alternatives in Progressive America*. Boston, MA: Little, Brown, 1980.

Rothman, David J. *The Discovery of the Asylum: Social Order and Disorder in the New Republic*. Boston: Little, Brown, 1971.

Rotman, Edgardo. "The Failure of Reform: United States, 1865–1965." In *The Oxford History of the Prison: The Practice of Punishment in Western Society*, edited by Norval Morris and David J. Rothman, pp. 151–77. New York: Oxford University Press, 1998.

Rusticucci, Luigi. *Nelle galere. Studio di clinica criminale con descrizione dei penitenziari e dei manicomi criminali d'Italia*. Naples: Società Editrice Partenopea, 1925.

Salvatori, Paola. "Associazionismo e lotte operaie." In *Roma Capitale*, edited by Vittorio Vidotto, pp. 240–58. Rome-Bari: Laterza, 2002.

Sbriccoli, Mario. "La penalistica civile: Teorie e ideologie del diritto penale nell'Italia unita." In *Stato e cultura giuridica in Italia dall'unità alla repubblica*, edited by Aldo Schiavone, pp. 147–232. Rome-Bari: Laterza, 1990.

Schettini, Laura. *Il gioco delle parti. Travestimenti e paure sociali tra Otto e Novecento*. Florence: Lo Monnier, 2011.

Schettini, Laura. "La misura del pericolo. Donne recluse nel manicomio giudiziario di Aversa (1931–50)."" *Dimensioni e problemi della ricerca storica*, no. 2 (2004): 295–318.

Scotti, Carlo. *Guida pratica della beneficenza a Roma*, edited by Congregazione di Carità di Roma. Rome: Società Anonima Poligrafica Italiana, 1927.

Sellin, Thorsten. "Filippo Franci. A Precursor of Modern Penology." *Journal of Criminal Law and Criminology* 17 (1926): 104–12.

Sellin, Thorsten. "The House of Correction for Boys in the Hospice of San Michael in Rome." *Journal of Criminal Law and Criminology* 20, no. 4 (1930): 533–53.

Sepe, Stefano. "Amministrazione e mediazione degli interessi: il controllo sugli istituti di pubblica assistenza e beneficenza." In *L'amministrazione nella storia moderna*, edited by ISAP, pp. 1701–90. Milan: Giuffrè, 1985.

Seymour, Mark. *Debating Divorce in Italy: Marriage and the Making of Modern Italians, 1860–1974*. New York: Palgrave Macmillan, 2006.

Shanzer, Carlo. "La nuova legge sulla beneficenza pubblica." *Nuova Antologia* 123 (May 16, 1906): 270–81.
Sirovich, G. M. "Correzionale del San Michele e istanze di reclusione a Roma (XVIII–XIX secolo)." *Ses* 50 (1990): 827–45.
Sisinni, Francesco, ed. *Il San Michele a Ripa Grande*. Rome: Istituto Poligrafico e Zecca delle Stato/Editalia, 1991.
Snowden, Frank M. *The Conquest of Malaria: Italy, 1900–1962*. New Haven, CT: Yale University Press, 2006.
Spanu, Luca. "Gli orci in terracotta. La parola ai detenuti." In *Il Museo di Antropologia criminale Cesare Lombroso dell'Università di Torino*, edited by Silvano Montaldo, pp. 135–44. Turin: Silvana, 2015.
Spierenburg, Pieter. *The Prison Experience: Disciplinary Institutions and Their Inmates in Early Modern Europe*. New Brunswick, NJ: Rutgers University Press, 1991.
Steiner, Stephan. "'An Austrian Cayenne': Convict Labour and Deportation in the Habsburg Empire of the Early Modern Period." In *Global Convict Labour*, edited by Christian De Vito and Alex Lichtenstein, pp. 126–43. Leiden: Brill, 2015.
Stewart-Steinberg, Suzanne. *The Pinocchio Effect: On Making Italians, 1860–1920*. Chicago, IL: University of Chicago Press, 2007.
Stronati, Monica. *Il governo della 'grazia': Giustizia sovrana e ordine giuridico nell'esperienza italiana (1848–1913)*. Milan: Giuffrè, 2009.
Tafuri, Manfredo. "Le 'Carceri Nuove' e la casa di correzione per i minorenni." In *Via Giulia: una utopia urbanistica del 500*, edited by Luigi Salerno, Luigi Spezzaferro, and Manfredo Tafuri, pp. 358–69. Rome: Aristide Staderini, 1973.
Tagliavini, Annamaria. "Aspects of the History of Psychiatry in Italy in the Second Half of the Nineteenth Century." In *The Anatomy of Madness, vol 2: Institutions and Society*, edited by W. F. Bynum, Roy Porter, and Michael Shepherd. Cambridge: Cambridge University Press, 1985.
Tamassia, Arrigo. "Il nuovo codice penale italiano: Appunti di Medicina forense." *Rivista sperimentale di freniatria e medicina legale delle alienazioni mentali* 16 (1890): 1–27.
Taricone, Fiorenza. *L'Associazionismo femminile in Italia dall'Unità al fascismo*. Milan: Unicopli, 1996.
Tarozzi, Fiorenza. "I giorni e le notti dalle lunghe ore nel Carcere di San Giovanni in Monte nell'Ottocento." In *Criminalità e controllo sociale a Bologna nell'Ottocento*, edited by Giovanni Greco, pp. 51–65. Bologna: Pàtron, 1998.
Tarozzi, Fiorenza. "Il sistema penitenziario e il domicilio coatto nell'analisi di Jessie White Mario." In *Il domicilio coatto: Ordine pubblico e politiche di sicurezza in Italia dall'Unità alla Repubblica*, edited by Ernesto De Cristofaro, pp. 169–89. Acireale-Rome: Bonanno, 2015.
Terpstra, Nicholas. "Confraternal Prison Charity and Political Consolidation in Sixteenth-Century Bologna." *Journal of Modern History* 66 (1994): 217–48.
Terruzzi, Regina. *Una visita alle recluse*. Naples: Tipografia "monsignor Perrelli", 1906.
Tessitore, Giovanni. *Carcere e fascistizzazione. Analisi di un modello totalizzante*. Milan: Franco Angeli, 2005.
Tessitore, Giovanni. *Cesare Beccaria: l'uomo e il mito*. Milan: Franco Angeli, 2008.
Tessitore, Giovanni. *L'utopia penitenziale borbonica. Dalle pene corporali a quelle detentive*. Milan: Franco Angeli, 2002.
Tosatti, Giovanna. "Il Ministero dell'Interno." In *L'amministrazione centrale dall'unità alla Repubblica. Le strutture e i dirigenti*, edited by Guido Melis. Bologna: Il Mulino, 1992.

Trombetta, Simona. "Public vices, private remedies in nineteenth-century Italy: Giulia Falletti di Barolo Colbert and Le Forzate." *Journal of Modern Italian Studies* 7, no. 1 (2002): 56–73.
Trombetta, Simona. *Punizione e carità. Carceri femminili nell'Italia dell'Ottocento.* Bologna: Il Mulino, 2004.
Valenzi, Lucia. *Poveri, ospizi e potere a Napoli (XVIII-XIX sec.).* Milan: Franco Angeli, 1995.
Vidotto, Vittorio. "Political Public Space in Rome from 1870 to 2011." In *Perspectives on Public Space in Rome, from Antiquity to the Present Day*, edited by Gregory Smith and Jan Gadeyne, pp. 251–74. Burlington, VT: Ashgate, 2013.
Vidotto, Vittorio. *Roma contemporanea.* Rome-Bari: Laterza, 2001.
Villa, Renzo. *Il deviante e i suoi segni: Lombroso e la nascita dell'antropologia criminale.* Milan: Franco Angeli, 1985.
Villa, Renzo. "Pazzi e criminali: Strutture istituzionali e pratica psichiatrica nei manicomi criminali italiani (1876–1915)." *Movimento operaio e socialista* 3, no. 4 (October–December 1980): 369–93.
Villa, Renzo. "Perizie psichiatriche e formazione degli stereotipi dei devianti: Note per una ricerca." In *Follia, psichiatria e società: Istituzioni manicomiali, scienza psichiatrica e classi sociali nell'Italia moderna e contemporanea*, edited by Alberto De Bernardi, pp. 384–401. Milan: Franco Angeli, 1982.
White Mario, Jessie. "Il sistema penitenziario e il domicilio coatto in Italia." *Nuova Antologia* 148, pt. 1 (1896): 16–35; 149, pt. 2 (1896): 313–35; 152, pt. 3 (1897): 680–707; 154, pt. 4 (1897): 503–19; 155, pt. 5 (1897): 121–42.
Whitman, James Q. *Harsh Justice: Criminal Punishment and the Widening Divide between America and Europe.* New York: Oxford University Press, 2005.
Whitman, James Q. "The Transition to Modernity." In *The Oxford Handbook of Criminal Law*, edited by Markus D. Dubber and Tatjana Hörnle, pp. 84–110. Oxford: Oxford University Press, 2014.
Willson, Perry. *Women in Twentieth-Century Italy.* Basingstoke: Palgrave Macmillan, 2010.
Zárate Campos, Maria Soledad. "Vicious Women, Virtuous Women: The Female Delinquent and the Santiago de Chile Correctional House, 1860–1900." In *The Birth of the Penitentiary in Latin America: Essays on Criminology, Prison Reform, and Social Control, 1830–1940*, edited by Ricardo D. Salvatore and Carlos Aguirre, pp. 44–77. Austin: University of Texas Press, 1996.
Zarri, Gabriella. "Fra costrizione e devozione: aspetti dello sviluppo dei monasteri femminili tra Quattrocento e Cinquecento." In *La Chiesa e il potere politico dal Medioevo all'età contemporanea*, edited by G. Chittolini and Giovanni Miccoli, pp. 359–429. Turin: Einaudi, 1986.
Zedner, Lucia. *Women, Crime, and Custody in Victorian England.* Oxford: Oxford University Press, 1991.
Zinoman, Peter. *The Colonial Bastille: A History of Imprisonment in Vietnam, 1862–1940.* Berkeley: University of California Press, 2001.
Zuccagni-Orlando, Attilio. *Roma e l'Agro Romano: Illustrazioni storico-economiche.* Florence: Alessandro Caselli Editore, 1870.

Index

administration of prisons and jails
  and administrative staff 62
  Alberini family, and prison
    management by 22
  background and social status of staff 63–64
  Confraternity of San Girolamo della
    Carità, and control of prisons 21
  Division of Prisons, and responsibility
    for 60–61
  female institutions, and administration
    of 115–16
  female prison guardians 64, 93, 115
  nuns, and role of 62–63, 93, 97, 100,
    103–04, 115–16, 121–22, 128
  prison guards 63–64
  Regulation of 1862 61
  remit and reform of
    (post-unification) 61
  Rome, and arrangements in 61
  staff, numbers of and pay
    (post-unification) 90
  wardens, and role of 61–62
Alberini family 22
Albini, Sofia Bisi 126
Andronico, Carmelo (Dr.) 161
  Messina women's penitentiary and study
    of inmates 225
Arrivabene, Antonio 57–58
'Auburn' penal model 8, 10, 36
  Piedmont, Kingdom of, and
    implementation of 38
  post-unification 57
Austrian Hapsburgs 41

Babini, Valeria 216
bagni (hard labor camps) 89
  abolition of 9
  activities at 153–54
  conditions at 132–33, 153
  demographic of inmate population, and
    regional differences 153

  legchains and shackles, and use of
    131, 132–33
  men held in (1868–85) 152, *153*
  post-unification reform of 58–59
Barolo, Giulia 122–23
Bartlett, Lucy 194
Bartoccini, Fiorella 16
Barzilai, Salvatore 169
Beccaria, Cesare 3, 8–9, 32
Bellazzi, Federico 58
  *Prisons and Prisoners in the Kingdom of
    Italy* 55
Beltrani Scalia, Martino 69, 70
  *On the Administration and Reform of
    Italian Prisons* 77–78
  'agricultural colonies,' and support
    for 133–34
  Agro Romano, reclamation of and
    support for 142–43
  background of 70
  convict labor, use of in civil projects and
    support for 143–44, 145–46
  criminal insane asylums, support
    for 217
  criminal insanity, and view of treatment
    for 75–76, 210
  deportation, view of 200, 203
  educational reformatories, and support
    for 168–69
  *On the Governance and Reform of
    Prisons in Italy* 72
  International Penitentiary Commission,
    role in 72–73, 75
  'Irish penal model,' and support
    for 77–78
  Journal of Prison Sciences (RDC)
    69, 71–72
  paternal correction system, and
    view of 170
  Penitentiary Reform in Italy 78
  positivist views of 72

Prison Ordinance (1891), drafted
    by 70
  and prison reform 47, 70
Benadusi, Lorenzo 201
Bernabò-Silorata, Gino 188, 191
Binda, Cosimo 230
birri (papal police) 22, 23
Borgo prison (Rome) 22–23
'born criminals' 3, 94, 213, 235
  character of 160–61
  concept of 69
  and treatment of 132
Boschi, Daniele 158
Boschi, Giuseppe 61, 158
Braunfels, Wolfgang 27
bridewells 6
Buon Pastore reformatory 173–78
  categories of inmates 176
  civil oversight of 174–75
  education and training, and lack
    of 176–78
  inspections of 178
  as International Women's Center 178
  jail, designated as 175
  location of 174
  opera pia status 174
  public funding received by 176
  Sisters of the Good Shepherd, and
    administration of 174
  as a women's refuge 173
Buttafuoco, Annarita 195

Capelli, Anna 7, 37
Capitoline prison (Rome) 22
Cardon, Felice 155–56
Carpi, Leone 42, 43, 146
  convict labor, and view of use 145
Casanova, Giacomo 1
Castel Sant'Angelo prison (Rome) 22,
    139, 239
  prisoners held at 23
Castromediano, Sigismondo (Duke) 42–43
Catholic Church
  and Christian charity 19–20, 171
  'convent prisons' 3, 8, 10, 15–16, 46–47
  Corneto prison for Roman clergy 19
  discipline and punishment,
    traditions of 3
  feminist movement within 122

  monastic model of punishment 8
  nuns, and administrative role in prisons
    62–63, 93, 97, 100, 103–04, 115–16,
    121–22, 128
Cattaneo, Carlo 37
Cavour, Camillo 49
  'Philadelphia' penal model, and
    advocate for 38
Cerruti, Emilio 199
*Characteristics of Criminals: An
    Anthropological-Sociological Study,
    The*, (Marro, Antonio) 228
Charitable House of Refuge (Florence) 163
charity *see also* philanthropy
  charitable support for children, and
    history of 170–71
  Charity for Youth on Probation 194
  and the Church 19–20, 46–47, 171
  confraternities 20–21, 193
  and laws governing 171–72
  opere pie (pious works) 171, 172
  prisoner aid societies 79, 192–96
  Refuge of Santa Margherita 194
  Refuge of the Holy Family 193–94
  secularization of, and problems with
    172, 194–95
Chiesa, Eugenio 190
children
  and adult institutions, separation
    from 168
  boys' reformatories (1871–95) 184
  and categories of juvenile inmates 165–
    66, 167, 168
  Charitable House of Refuge
    (Florence) 163
  charitable support for children, and
    history of 170–71
  and child labor 164
  child protection, and development
    of 166–67
  conservatories, and protection for
    girls 172–73
  criminal anthropology, and studies on
    229–30, 236
  criminal laws relating to 165–70
  discernimento (understanding of right
    and wrong), and age of 166
  education and educational reformatories
    167, 168, 180–81, 187–88

girls' reformatories (1871–95)
juvenile courts 164–65
juvenile institutions, and reform of 10, 54, 87–88, 163, 167–68
legislation for prisons, relating to 165–70
and monastic model of punishment 8
numbers of prison inmates, and fluctuations in 89
paternal correction system 169–71, 184
Pisanelli Civil Code (1865), and laws relating to 165–66
positivism, and approach to youth discipline 163, 164
prisoner aid societies, and support for 79
probation and suspended sentences for 166–67
San Michele, boys' prison at 15, 29–30, 163
state reformatories, and reforms to 10, 54, 164–65
Zanardelli Code, and approaches to 166
Civitavecchia (forced labor camp) 18, 33, 146, 151
Clement XI, Pope
prison reform, and support for 29
San Michele convent prison (Rome), new wing opened by 28
Clement XII, Pope 30
colonial punishment 7
and transportation 7
Committee for Prison Inspection 21
prison visitations 21
Scanaroli, Gianbattista, secretary of and work for 26
Conforti, Raffaele 58
confraternities
charitable activities of 20–21
Pietà dei Carcerati 20–21
San Giovanni Decollato 20, 193
San Girolamo della Carità 20–21, 23, 193, 194
Confraternity of San Giovanni Decollato 193
death penalty, and support for prisoners 20
Confraternity of San Girolamo della Carità 20–21, 193, 194
administrative control of prisons 21
Tor di Nona prison, administration of 23

Congress of Criminal Anthropology (1885) 73
Conti, Ugo 93–94
'convent prisons' 10, 11, 21 *see also* San Michele convent prison (Rome)
establishment of 3
for women and children, and rehabilitation of 8, 46–47
court systems *see also* criminal law
Capitoline Court 17
early modern period 17
Papal States, and unification of criminal code (1832) 17
systemization of (19th C.), and attempt at 33
'Cradle Project' 126–27
criminal anthropology
children, and study of 229–30, 236
collection of prisoner artifacts, and study of 232–35, *234*
and criminal classifications 231, 235–36
and criminal culture 232
inmates, studies on and measurement tools 228–31, *230*
interviews with inmates as research tool 232
Journal of Prison Sciences (RDC), support for field of research 227
and nature of criminality 3, 69, 157
photography, and use of in research 231
and prison research 11, 228–31
race, and study of 236–37
study, and development of 10, 225, 227–28
women, and study of 236
criminal insane asylums 197–98, 209–10 *see also* criminal insanity
annual deaths in (1900–1914) *220*
Aversa (Naples) 209–10, 217, 219–21, 223
'Basaglia Law' (1978) 223
creation of 10, 75–76
criticisms of 221–22
establishment of 217
fascism, and impact on 222–23
gender disparity in 198
health of inmates 219
legislation for 215–17
Montelupo Fiorentino 217–18, *218*, 223

numbers of inmates (1881–1901) 217
positivist views of 210
practical conditions of 217–21
Reggio Emilia 217, 218
social profiles and ages of
inmates 218–19
therapies developed at 223
work carried out by inmates 219
criminal insanity
asylums, and creation of 10,
75–76, 197–98
insanity pleas 210–13
management and treatment of 161
positivism, and approach to 75
subgroups and categories of 213,
215–16
criminal law 48–51 *see also* legislation for
prisons
children, and laws relating to 165–70
Code of Criminal Procedure 50, 51, 212
Criminal Code of 1832 18, 20, 33
death penalty and forced labor 50
and gender disparity 99
and insanity plea 210–13
Piedmont's Criminal Code (Sardinian-Italian Code), 1859 48, 49, 132
Rocco Criminal Code (1930) 222, 223
Statuto of the Kingdom of Piedmont
(1848), and implementation of 48
Tuscany's Criminal Code (1786)
34–35, 39, 48
Zanardelli Code 76, 77, 82, 98, 132, 134
Criminal Man (Lombroso, Cesare) 3, 69,
72, 78, 213
criminal violence 157–58
Criminological Museum (Rome) 235
Crispi, Francesco 68, 171, 193, 240
social reform, and support for 68
Croce, Ettore 206

D'Angelo, Giacomo 86, 159
Davis, John 45
De Foresta, Adophe 74
transportation, and support for 199
De Mérode, Frédéric-François-Xavier
105–06, 179
property and land ownership in
Rome 136
De Negri, Carlo 85

De Renzis, Francesco 74
De Vito, Christian 7
Diocletian's Baths prison (Rome) 32, 33,
136, 139–42
categories of inmates 141
closure of 140–41
prisoner turnover 142
site of, and history 139–40
Villa Altieri women's penitentiary,
transfers to 106
Di Pasquale, Francesca 208
Di Sivo, Michele, 24
Disciplinary Regulation for the Houses of
Punishment (1830) 33
Division of Prisons, and prison
administration 60
domicilio coatto (internal exile) *see also*
penal colonies; police camps
ammonizione (legal warning), and
violation of conditions of 200–01,
202
'colonies of confinement' 204
conditions of 201–02
confino 200, 204
criticism of 202–03
Finocchiaro-Aprile-Pelloux proposal
(1899) 203
Gianturco Plan (1900) 203
grounds for 201
homosexuality, as grounds for 201
indeterminate sentencing 204
Pica Law (1863), and
formalization of 200
political crimes, as grounds for and
changing definitions of 201
positivist views of 202
Doria, Alessandro 69–70, 80–81, 93, 240
background of 80
D'Angelo, Giacomo, death in custody
and verdict on 159
juvenile institutions, and reform of
87–88, 168
legchains and shackles, and
abolition of 86
male penitentiaries, reform of 85–86
policies of 81
reform of prisons for women, and
reaction to 127
retirement of 88

survey on prison discipline, and responses to 159–61
Dungeons of the Pope, The (Paya, Jean-Baptiste) 43–44

education in prisons 85, 87
　in female institutions 108
　and juvenile reformatories 167, 180–81, 187–88
　and lack of 108–09, 118
　male penitentiaries 131, *152*, 155–57
　state reformatories and juvenile offenders 10, 27, 88, 94
Enlightenment era 8–9
　papal prisons, and treatment of prisoners 31–32
　prison reform, and impact of 8–9, 34–39
　punishment, and view of 3, 5

Falletti di Barolo, Giulia 38
fascism
　criminal insane asylums, and impact on 222–23
　reform of prisons, and impact on 88
fatti di maggio (demonstation, 1898) 1
feminist movement 122
　female suffrage in Italy 126
　and reform of prisons for women 123–29
Ferri, Enrico 69, 72, 82, 86
　'agricultural colonies,' and support for 135
　Aversa (Naples) criminal insane asylum, visit to 209–10
　prison visitations 229
Forzate, Le (female jail) 38
Fosi, Irene 17
Fossa, Pietro Antonio 83
Foucault, Michel
　Discipline and Punish: The Birth of the Prison 2
　prison reform, and view of 5
'Foundation for Moral Life' 126
foundling homes and orphanages 8, 15, 19, 20, 117, 171, 172
Fozzi, Daniela 198
Franci, Filippo 163
Fuga, Ferninando 30
funding for prisons (post-unification) 58

Gambardella, Alfredo 134
Garibaldi, Giuseppe 45
Garin, Eugenio 3
Garofalo, Raffaele 69, 72
Geltner, Guy 7, 16, 19
gender *see also* women
　criminal insane asylums, and gender disparity 198
　criminal law, and punishment disparity 99
　disparities in treatment and punishment 10–11, 46, 173
　and prison reform 4, 6, 46
General Division of Prisons and Reformatories 168
Giolitti, Giovanni 80, 240
　'agricultural colonies,' and support for 134
　reform of prisons, and support for 86
Giulianelli, Roberto 7
Gladstone, William, 'Letters' 43
Gramsci, Antonio
　Letters From Prison 1–2
　Risorgimento (1861), and view of 47
Grandi, Carlo 213
Grantaliano, Elvira 32
Graziosi, Marina 99
Gregory XIV, Pope, Criminal Code (1832), issued by 33
Groppi, Angela 19, 172
Guidi, Laura 196

hard labor 50, 59 *see also bagni* (hard labor camps)
　abolition of 131
　and corporal punishment 59
　Criminal Code (1786), Tuscany 34–35
　'forzati' 18
　'galera' 18
　galley slavery, and use of male convicts 17–18
　legchains and shackles, and use of 131
　Montesarchio camp 43
　Montesfusco camp 43
　'public works' 18
　reform of 56, 57, 58–59
Horn, David 229
How the Roman People Live (Orano, Domenico) 137

Howard, John 26
  New Prison (Rome), view of 27
Hughes, Steven 45

Ignatieff, Michael 4
  prison reform, and view of 5
Innocent X, Pope 27
Innocent XII, Pope 28
Inquisition's Court 23
International Penitentiary Commission
  Beltrani Scalia, Martino, role in 72–73, 75
  Congresses organized by 73
International Penitentiary Congress (Rome, 1885) 73–75
Ipsen, Carl 194
'Irish penal model' 77–78
Italian School of Positivist Criminology 69
Italian Socialist Party (PSI) 134, 159
  establishment of 68
  feminist movement 122

Jensen, Richard Bach 55, 206
Journal of Prison Sciences (RDC) 71–72, 81, 227
  criminal insanity, and view of treatment for 75
  foundation of 69
  survey on prison discipline, and responses to 159–60
juvenile institutions *see also* children
  ages of inmates 187
  Buon Pastore reformatory 173–78
  classification of inmates, and arrangements for 186
  education in 187–88
  female reformatories 189–91, *192*
  gender equality and disparities 188–89
  letters to and visits from family members 187
  national approach to reformatories 184–92
  paternal correction system 169–71, 184
  private institutions, and issues with 190
  and reform of 10, 54, 87–88, 163, 167–68, 190
  reformatories 173, *177*
  religious correction in female penitentiaries 190–91
  revolts in reformatories (1890s-early 1900s) 189–90
  rituals of admission 186–87
  rule breaches, and punishments for 189
  secularization of female reformatories 191–92
  sentences for inmates, and lengths of 190
  social profiles and regional variations of inmates 186

Klopp, Charles 41
Kuliscioff, Anna 1

Labriola, Teresa 128–29
Lacava, Pietro 58
Lacchè, Luigi 50, 51
League for the Protection of Women's Rights 123
legislation for prisons *see also* criminal law
  children, and laws relating to 165–70
  Piedmont model, and changes to (post-unification) 56
  post-unification 47–48
  and pre-unification reforms 37–38
  Prison Ordinance (1891) 68–69, 76–80
  and prison reform 48–49
  special commission to investigate (post-unification) 56–57
Lenci, Marco 208
Leopold, Pieter (of Tuscany)
  Criminal Code (1786), issued by 34–35
  penal reform, and criminal code (1789) 9
Lepre, Stefano 171
Leschiutta, Pierpaolo 232
Lombroso, Cesare 241
  collection of prisoner artifacts 232–35, *234*
  criminal insanity, and advocate of prison reform 10, 210, 212, 214
  Criminal Man 3, 69, 72, 78, 213
  Criminal Woman 3
  criminological research conducted by 227, 232
  On the Increase in Crime 202
  'Irish penal model,' and view of 78, 135
  Italian School of Positivist Criminology, and founding of 4, 69

juvenile institutions, reform and view of 168–69
moral insanity, view of 213
Palimpsests 232–33
parole and probation, and support for 82
penal colonies, view of 200
penitentiaries, and view of 78
psychiatric training 213
race, and study of 236–37
Lombroso, Gina 227, 232
Luzzatti, Luigi 203–204

Maconochie, Alexander 77
Maietti, Raffaele 194–95
Majno Bronzini, Ersilio 125, 195
male penitentiaries 152–57
 conditions at 155
 education and training 131, *152*, 155–57
 men held in (1868–85) 152, *153*
 number of, and inmate totals (1863–1902) 152
 religious instruction in 155
 social profiles and regional variations 154–55, *154*
 work in, and use of convicts 157
Mamertine prison (Tulliano) (Rome) 239
 see also Capitoline prison
Mantellate womens' jail (Rome) 97, 98, 110–14
 arrangements at 112–13
 former convent at 111
 New Prison, former home of 110
 opening of, and difficulties with 111–12
 Ronconi, Guglielmina, visit to 126
Mantuan prison (Mainolda) 41–42
Marchese di Rudini, Antonio Starabba 55, 90, 208
Marinelli, Andrea 93
Mariuccia Home (Milan) 195
Marro, Antonio, *Characteristics of Criminals: An Anthropological-Sociological Study, The* 72, 73, 228
Mazza, Gina 195
 reform of prisons for women, and support for 126
Mazza, Pilade 87
Melis, Guido 70
Melossi, Dario 34
Messina women's penitentiary 161, 225

Mettray, Frédéric-Auguste Demetz 164
Mirabella, Emanuele 237
Modesta, Maria di Santa 175
Modona, Guido Neppi 226
 'Prison and Civil Society, The' 7
Montesi, Barbara 170, 187
Montesi, Barbara 170, 187
San Michele convent prison (Rome), and view of 183
Montini, Erminia 192
Morichini, Carlo-Luigi (Cardinal) 27, 110, 172, 174

Napoleonic Criminal Code (1810) 31, 35
Neppi Modona, Guido 7, 61, 242
New Prison (Rome) 19, 25–28, 102–03, 110
 architecture and layout of 27
 building and location of 25–26
 Confraternity of San Girolamo della Carità, administrative control of 21
 pre-unification period 32
 religious segregation in 27–28
 survey of (19th C.) 27
Nicotera, Giovanni 87, 193
Nocito, Pietro 144
numbers of prison inmates
 1871–1914, 88–89, *89*
 boys reformatories (1871–95) 184
 children, and fluctuations in 89
 criminal insane asylums (1881–1901) 217
 girls reformatories (1871–95) 184
 men (1863–1902) 152
 men held in *bagni* and penitentiaries (1868–85) 152, *153*
 parole and probation, and effect on 89
 penal colonies 204
 in public and private reformatories (1871–1914) 184–86, *185*
 women, and ratios with men 89, 115, *116*
Nuova Antologia (periodical) 74, 124
 'An Excursion' (Nocito, Pietro) 144

'occasional criminals' 3, 94
 concept of 69
On Crimes and Punishments (Beccaria, Cesare) 3, 8–9, 32

On the Administration and Reform of Italian Prisons (Beltrani Scalia, Martino) 77–78
On the Governance and Reform of Prisons in Italy (Beltrani Scalia, Martino) 72
Orano, Domenico, *How the Roman People Live* 137
Ordinance on Prison and Reformatories (1891) 68–69, 76–80, 135
　basis of, and new approaches to reform 77
　children, protection of and articles relating to 167–68
　female institutions, and articles relating to 100
　merit system, and introduction of 78
　oversight councils 78–79
　penalties and punishments for rule-breaking 80, 120–21
　prison reform, and impact of 9–10, 11
　sections of 76, 80
　visiting committees of 79
Ottolenghi, Salvatore 81, 225–26
　classification of criminals, and study of 226
　photography and fingerprinting, and use of in research 231–32

Palermo, Ucciardone prison 39
Panattoni, Carlo Italo 60
papal prisons
　pre-unification 31–34
　reputation of 43–44
　treatment of prisoners (Enlightenment period) 31–32
Papal States
　anti-papal cartoons 46
　Criminal Code (1832), issued by Gregory XIV 33
　Index of Forbidden Books 32
　papal repression and punishment 33–34
　prisons, and reputation of 43–44
　secular sovereignty, and challenge to 45, 101
　secularization of justice, and threat to 32
　and unification of criminal code (1832) 32
pardon and amnesty 33, 82, 83, 84, 85, 95, 109, 121, 123, 142, 144, 219, 236

Parente, Antonio 35
parole and probation 81–85
　critics of 83–84
　introduction of 81–82
　juvenile offenders 166–67
　numbers of prison inmates, and effect on 89
　terms of 83–84, 85
　women prisoners 121
Parpaglia, Salvatore 58
patronati (prisoner aid societies) 79, 192–96 *see also* charity
　Charity for Youth on Probation 194
　Refuge of Santa Margherita 194
　Refuge of the Holy Family 193–94
　remit of 195
Pavarini, Massimo 34
Paya, Jean-Baptiste, *Dungeons of the Pope, The* (1865) 43–44
Pellico, Silvio 1
　My Prisons (1832) 41–42
penal colonies 55, 238 *see also domicilio coatto* (internal exile)
　age of exiles 205
　'agricultural colonies' 74, 133–35
　and convict labor 60
　education and training, and lack of 205–06
　length of sentences 205, *205*
　life in 204–07, *207*
　numbers exiled (1876–1914) 204–05
　political prisoners 206
　rule breaches, and punishments for 206
Penitentiary Reform in Italy (Beltrani Scalia, Martino) 78
'Pennsylvania' system 8, 36
　'Philadelphia' penal model 10, 37, 38, 47, 50, 57, 77
　post-unification 56–57
Peri, Carlo (of Tuscany)
　Notes on Prison Reform in Tuscany 36
　prison reform, and advocate for 35
Perusini, Gaetano 230
Peruzzi, Ubaldino 57
Pessina, Enrico 49, 73
　parole, view of 83
　transportation, and view of 199–200
　Zanardelli Code, commentary on 99, 211

Petitti di Roreto, Carlo Ilarione (of
   Piedmont)
   *Essay on the Good Governance of
   Almshouses, Institutions of Charity
   and Prisons, An* (1837) 36
   prison reform, and advocate for 35, 37
philanthropy 19–20 *see also* charity
   and philanthropic institutions
   20–21, 171
Piedmont, Kingdom of
   'Auburn' penal model, and
   implementation of 38
   Petitti di Roreto, Carlo Ilarione,
   inspector of institutions of charity and
   punishment for 36
   Piedmont's Criminal Code (Sardinian-
   Italian Code), 1859 48, 49, 56, 211
   and prison reform 37–38
   Statuto of the Kingdom of Piedmont
   (1848), and implementation of 48
Pierantoni, Augusto 73
Pinsero, Nicolo 164
Piranesi, Giovanni Battista, 'An Imaginary
   Prison,' 1, *2*
Pisanelli Civil Code (1865) 98–99, 132
   children, and laws relating to 165–66
Pius IX, Pope, and loss of papal
   sovereignty 44
Platt, Anthony 87
Poët, Lydia 74–75
police camps 197–98
   deportation, and debates relating to
   198–200
   domicilio coatto (internal exile) 198, 200
   Eritrea, establishment of and life
   in 207–08
   Libya, deportation from 208–09
political prisoners 4
   and accounts of prison life 41–44
   Pellico, Silvio, and prison memoir
   of 41–42
   penal colonies, and exile to 206
   post-unification 51
   Risorgimento, and supporters of 9
   and written testimony of 1–2
positivism 94
   and approach to prison reform 10,
   67, 226
   Beltrani Scalia, Martino, support for 72

criminal insane asylums, view of 210
criminal insanity, and approach to 75
definition of 3
domicilio coatto (internal exile),
   view of 202
Italian School of Positivist
   Criminology 4
in Italy, post-unification 3–4, 67, 68
and power of positivists 235–38
psychiatry, and approach to 214
youth discipline, and approach to
   163, 164
Positivist School, The (journal) 164, 170
Prison and the Factory, The (Melossi,
   D. and Pavarini, M.) 7
prison buildings
   improvements to (post-unification)
   90–91, 94
   new buildings 94
   and physical state of (at
   unification) 55–56
   as symbols of modernity 6–7
prison guards *see also* administration of
   prisons
   1871–1914, staffing numbers and pay 90
   background and social status of 63, 64
   female guardians 64
   post-unification 54
   role of (post-unification) 63–64
   school for 151–152
   terms of employment 91–93
prison types
   'agricultural colonies' 74, 133–35
   'convent prisons' 3, 8, 10, 11, 21, 46–47,
   103, 163
   criminal insane asylums 10, 75–76
   institutions of enclosure, protection and
   reformation 20
   juvenile institutions 10, 54,
   87–88, 163–64
   long and short term institutions
   52, 58, 77
   penal colonies 55, 200–07
   pre-unification 52–56
   'prison workhouses' 6
   'proto-prisons' 7, 15, 46
   women's prisons 20, 102–04, 122–29
'proto-prisons' 7, 15, 46 *see also* San
   Michele convent prison (Rome)

Catholic stage of 8
and penal reform 6
psychiatry *see also* criminal insanity
  and civil asylums 214, 217
  development of as a discipline 213–14
  Italian Society of Phrenology 214, 216
  positivism, and approach to 214
Public Security Law (1889) 166
punishment
  and age 4
  and changes in approach to 2–3, 4
  corporal, and abolition of 3, 4, 6, 35, 59, 76
  death penalty 20, 50
  and deaths in custody 159
  detrusio (penal cloistering) 19
  early modern period 17
  and ecclesiastical justice 18–19
  education and training, and lack of 108–09, 118
  Enlightenment view of 3
  executions 17
  female punishment, and theories for 6, 114–21
  forced labor 50
  galley slavery, and use of male convicts 17–18
  and gender 4, 10–11, 46
  global networks of 2
  incarceration, as a mode of 15, 16, 18–19, 163
  jail terms, and reasons for release 52, 53
  legchains and shackles 42–43, 86, 131, 132–33
  letters to and visits from family members 119–120
  long-term convicts, and treatment of 58
  male penitentiaries 152–57
  merit system 78
  monastic model of 8, 29, 46
  paternal correction system 169–71, 184
  'penal substitutes' 82
  pre-trial and preventative detention 52, 58, 89
  and prison work 59–60
  and rehabilitation 5
  rule breaches, and punishments for 80, 120–21, 158–59
  and social class 50–51
  straitjackets, and use of 80, 86, 159
  and types of crimes 49–50
  work in prisons 6, 28, 143–46, 149, *119,* 157
  Zanardelli Code, and approaches to 76

Querci-Seriacopi, Epaminonda 80, 86, 90

Raffaele, Antonio 211
  Practical Guide to Expert Testimony 212
Rassgna Settimanale (newspaper) 145–46
Rebibbia prison (Rome) 114
reform of prisons
  corporal punishment, and approaches to 3, 4, 6, 86
  Enlightenment thought, and impact on 8–9, 34–39
  fascism, and impact on 88
  female institutions, and lack of 100, 122–29
  'first wave' 4, 7, 9, 16, 34, 65
  international discourse on 37
  Italian Peninsula (Enlightenment era) 34–39
  juvenile institutions 87–88
  legislation, and impact on 48–49
  male penitentiaries 85–86, 131–32
  masculization of 46–48
  Ordinance of 1891, and impact on 9–10
  parliamentary response to (post-unification) 56–60
  Piedmont, Kingdom of, and implementation of 38
  political changes (post-unification), and impact of 67–68
  positivism, and approach to reform 67
  post-unification 47–48, 51
  pre-unification 16
  revisionist view of 5–7
  Risorgimento, and impact on 3, 9, 47–48
  scientific approaches 67
  'second wave' 4, 9, 65
Reformatory Aristide Gabelli 183
Refuge at Santa Maria (Rome) 173
Regina Coeli prison (Rome) 113, 147–52, 225–26, 239
  building and location of 147–50
  categories of inmates 150

convict labor, and use of 149, 150–51
D'Angelo, Giacomo, and death in
   custody 86, 159
design and arrangement of 150
printshop at, and convict labor 150–51
school for prison guards 151
religion *see also* Catholic Church
ecclesiastical punishments and
   repentance 7–8
penal reform, and influence of 5
Ricasoli, Bettino 56
Ricchi, Giuseppe 179–80, 181, 182–83
Ripa jail (Rome) 31
Risorgimento (1861)
political changes (post-unification), and
   impact of 67–68
and post-unification prison
   reform 47–48
and pre-unity penal institutions 9, 41
and prison reform 3, 9, 51
punishment, and new approaches to 45
and release of political prisoners 51
and wars of independence 44–45
Roma: Via delle Mantellate (Mari, Isa) 114
Romagnosi, Gian Domenico 48–49
Roman prisons 11–12, 22–25
administration of 61
Alberini family, and management of
   prisons 22
Buon Pastore reformatory 173–78
Capitoline prison 22
Castel Sant'Angelo prison 22, 23,
   139, 239
characteristics of 24
charity and punishment, and penal
   reform 25
convict labor, and conflict with
   industrial workers 11
Criminal Code (1832), and impact on 33
Diocletian's Baths prison 32, 33,
   106, 139–42
female institutions 20, 102–04
locations of 23–24, *26*
male penitentiaries 139–52
Mamertine prison (Tulliano) 22, 239
Mantellate womens' jail 97, 98, 110–14
mixed cells, gender and types of
   offence 24
municipal jails 22

New Prison 21, 25–28, 32, 102–03
pre-unification 31–32
and public appearances of inmates 24
Rebibbia prison 114
Regina Coeli prison 113, 147–152,
   225–26, 239
religious segregation in 27
Ripa jail 31
San Michele convent prison 11, 28–31,
   29, 46, 103, 139, 178–84, 239, 241
Savelli prison 22, 23
and social divisions in 25
statistics and data from 12
Tor di Nona prison 21, 22, 23
torture of inmates 24, 28
Tre Fontane penal institution
   142–47, *143*
Via Giulia 22
Villa Altieri women's penitentiary 97, 98,
   104–10, *105*
Rome *see also* Roman prisons
Agro Romano, and reclamation
   of malarial lands 137–38,
   142–43, 146–47
'breach of the Porta Pia' 44, 45
Church and state, and conflict with 11
immigration and population growth
   (late 19th C.) 101–02
judicial systems and ecclesiastical
   administration, conflict with (early
   modern period) 16–17
liberal era, and impact on 136–39
malaria, and problems with
   137–38, 145–46
new buildings and development in (late
   19th C. – early 20th C.) 102
'penal zone' (Trastevere) 12, 136–37, 148
railway, and introduction of 140
San Lorenzo 137
secular sovereignty, and introduction of
   45, 101
Testaccio 137
Tobacco Factory 136–37
Trastevere, and 'penal zone' at 12,
   136–37, 148
Via Nazionale 102, 136
Ronchetti, Mario 84
Ronconi, Guglielmina 126–27, 129, 137,
   181, 195

'Cradle Project' 126–27
'Foundation for Moral Life' 126
Mantellate womens' jail (Rome),
   visit to 126
Rosi, Leopoldo 227
Rossana *see* Tartarini, Zina Centa
   (Marchesa)
Rothman, David 5
Rygier, Maria 125–26, 129
   'Monasticism in Women's Prisons: The
   Penal Institution of Turin (*Il Grido del
   Popolo*) 125

San Caterina della Rosa de' Funari (Rome)
   172, 173
San Michele convent prison (Rome) 8, 11,
   15, 28–31, *29*, 46, 103, 139, 178–84,
   239, 241
   administrative arrangements at 180
   architecture and layout of 29
   boys' prison at 15, 29–30, 163, 179
   Clement XI, Pope, and new wing
      opened by 28
   education and instruction at 180–82
   establishment and purpose of 28
   as house of correction 29–30, 179–80
   location of 30
   modern uses of 184
   monastic model of punishment 29
   opera pia status 179
   as a penal and charitable institution
      171, 179
   physical education and exercise 181, *182*
   reputation of 183
   rule breaches, and punishments for 181
   women's prison at 15, 30
   workshops at and economic output of
      28, 181
Santa Balbina reformatory 173, 179, 194
Santo Stefano panopticon prison 9, 35
Savelli family 23
Savelli prison (Rome) 22, 23
Scanaroli, Gianbattista 26, 27
Sergi, Giuseppe 72, 227
Settembrini, Luigi 42
Sisters of Providence 104, 106
   Villa Altieri women's penitentiary
      (Rome), administrators at 109
Sisters of the Good Shepherd 110, 114
   Buon Pastore reformatory 174–78

Mantellate women's jail (Rome),
   administration of 112
social reform (late 19th century) 68
Speciale, Martino 58–59
Spielberg prison (Brno) 41–42
Spierenburg, Pieter 6
Stoppato, Alessandro 88

Tamburini, Augusto 227
   criminal insane asylums, view of 215,
      216–17, 221
   criminal insanity, and view of
      treatment for 75
Tartarini, Zina Centa (Marchesa)
   123–24, 195
   female institutions, visits to and
      reports on 127
   *Subject to the Rod: Pain, Poverty, and
   Female Degeneration* 191
Terruzzi, Regina 123
Tiber, River 12, 15, 22–24, 25, 30–31,
   101, 103, 137, 139, 148, 174, 178, 179,
   239
Tocci, Guglielmo 57
Tommasi-Crudeli, Corrado 145
Tor di Nona prison (Rome) 22
   administration of 23
   Confraternity of San Girolamo della
      Carità, administrative control
      of 21, 23
Tosatti, Giovanna 61
Tre Fontane penal institution
   (Rome) 142–47
   closure of 146
   convict labor, and use of 143–46
   living conditions at 146–47
   malaria, and problems with 145–46
   monastery at site of *143*, 144
   penal experiment at 142
   Tommasi-Crudeli, Corrado,
      criticism of 145
Trombetta, Simona 7, 38
Turati, Filippo 1
Turin, International Exposition (1911) 183
Tuscany
   Criminal Code (1786) 34–35, 39, 48
   'Philadelphia' penal model, and
      implementation of 38–39
   Volterra long-term prison, and
      conditions at 38–39

Ucciardone prison (Palermo) 39
unification of Italy (1861) *see*
    Risorgimento (1861)
uniforms
    for inmates 79
    of prison guards *91*

Vaini, Giovanni Minghelli 57
Via Giulia prison (Rome) 22
Vidotto, Vittorio 148
Villa Altieri women's penitentiary (Rome) 97, 98, 104–10, *105*
    admission registers (1889–95) 106
    categories of crimes and convictions 107
    closure of 110
    Diocletian's Baths prison, transfers from 106
    education and training, and lack of 108–09
    inmate dossiers (1871–76) 106
    location of 104
    and prison conversion 106
    prison work for women 109
    as residential building, and design of 104–06
    residential patterns of prisoners 108
    sentences, and lengths of 109–10
    Sisters of Providence, administrators at 109
    transfers of inmates to 106–07
Visit to Women Inmates, A (Terruzzi, Regina) 123
Volpicella, Filippo (of Naples) 36
    'Instructions for Prisons' 39
    On Prisons and the Improvement of their Organization 37
Volterra long-term prison (Tuscany) 38–39

White Mario, Jesse 90
    domicilio coatto (internal exile), view of 202–03
Whitman, James 8, 49
women
    'convent prisons' 3, 8, 10, 11, 21
    criminal anthropology, and studies on 236
    criminal insane asylums, and gender disparity 198
    female institutions 20, 102–04
    female prison guardians 64, 93
    female punishment, and theories for 6, 114–21
    feminist movement 122
    Forzate, Le (female jail) 38
    'honor' crimes, and sentences for 107
    and monastic model of punishment 8, 46, 103
    numbers of prison inmates, and ratio with men 89, 115, *116*
    nuns, and administrative role in prisons 62–63, 93, 97, 100, 103–04, 115–16, 121–22, 128
    offenses committed by 115–16
    parole and probation for women prisoners 121
    Pisanelli Code (1865), and rights of 98–99
    post-unification period, and treatment of prisoners 54
    pre-unification period, and treatment of prisoners 32–33
    prison types and jail terms for 54
    punishments of men, and disparity with 10–11, 46, 99
    reform measures, compared with male institutions 4, 6, 46, 97, 190
    religious correction in female penitentiaries 6, 97, 190–91
    San Michele convent prison (Rome), women's section at 15, 30
    secularization of female reformatories 191–92
    sentences for prisoners, and lengths of 119–20, 121
    social profile and family status of prisoners 116–17, *117*
work in prisons
    and conflict with industry 11, 150–51
    convict labor, and civil projects 143–46, 149
    disciplinary value of 59–60
    female institutions 123, 125
    male penitentiaries 157
    objects made by inmates, and exhibitions of 74
    'prison workhouses' 6
    prison workshops, and economic returns of 28, 157
World War I, pre-war penal system 88–89

Zanardelli Code 76, 132
   'agricultural colonies,' inclusion in 134
   children, and approach to child
      protection 166
   corporal punishment, approach to 76
   gender equality and disparities 98
   insanity as a defense 211
   long and short term institutions, and
      introduction of 77
   parole measures 82
Zanardi, Anna Grassetti 44

www.ingramcontent.com/pod-product-compliance
Lightning Source LLC
Chambersburg PA
CBHW070014010526
44117CB00011B/1558